Case Preparation

Authors

Christopher Allen, Barrister, former Senior Lecturer, ICSL

Paul Banks, Head of Library Services, The City Law School

Susan Blake, Barrister, Associate Dean, The City Law School

Nigel Duncan, Principal Lecturer, The City Law School

Nina Ellin, Barrister, Lecturer, The City Law School

Guy Holborn, Librarian, Lincoln's Inn

Peter Hungerford-Welch, Barrister, Associate Dean, The City Law School

Christiaan Moll, Barrister, Middle Temple

Stuart Sime, Barrister, BVC Course Director, The City Law School

Hester Swift, Foreign and International Law Librarian, Institute of Advanced Legal Studies

Margot Taylor, Solicitor, Principal Lecturer, The City Law School

Contributors

James Behrens, Barrister, Middle Temple

Ann Halpern, former Reader, ICSL

Caroline Hutton, Barrister, Middle Temple

Adrian Keane, Barrister, Dean, The City Law School

Robert McPeake, Barrister, Principal Lecturer, The City Law School

Editor

Nigel Duncan, Principal Lecturer, The City Law School

Series Editor

Julie Browne, Barrister, Senior Lecturer, The City Law School

Case Preparation

The City Law School, City University, London

OXFORD
UNIVERSITY PRESS

OXFORD

UNIVERSITY PRESS

Great Clarendon Street, Oxford ox2 6DP

Oxford University Press is a department of the University of Oxford.
It furthers the University's objective of excellence in research, scholarship, and education by
publishing worldwide in

Oxford New York

Auckland Cape Town Dar es Salaam Hong Kong Karachi
Kuala Lumpur Madrid Melbourne Mexico City Nairobi
New Delhi Shanghai Taipei Toronto

With offices in

Argentina Austria Brazil Chile Czech Republic France Greece
Guatemala Hungary Italy Japan Poland Portugal Singapore
South Korea Switzerland Thailand Turkey Ukraine Vietnam

Oxford is a registered trademark of Oxford University Press
in the UK and in certain other countries

Published in the United States by Oxford University Press Inc., New York

British Library Cataloguing in Publication Data
Data available

Typeset by Laserwords Private Limited, Chennai, India
Printed in Great Britain on acid-free paper by
Ashford Colour Press Ltd, Gosport, Hampshire

ISBN 978-0-19-955354-9

10 9 8 7 6 5 4 3 2 1

FOREWORD

I am delighted to write this Foreword to the manuals which are written by practitioners and staff of the Inns of Court School of Law (ICSL [now The City Law School]).

The manuals are designed primarily to support training on the Bar Vocational Course (BVC). They now cover a wide range, embracing both the compulsory and the optional subjects of the BVC. They provide an outstanding resource for all those concerned to teach and acquire legal skills wherever the BVC is taught.

The manuals for the compulsory subjects are updated and revised annually. The manuals for the optional subjects are revised every two years. To complement the Series, the publishers will maintain a website for the manuals which will be used to keep them up-to-date throughout the academic year.

The manuals, continually updated, exemplify the practical and professional approach that is central to the BVC. I congratulate the staff of The City Law School who have produced them to an excellent standard, and Oxford University Press for its commitment in securing their publication. As my predecessor the Hon. Mr Justice Gross so aptly said in a previous Foreword, the manuals are an important ingredient in the constant drive to raise standards in the public interest.

The Hon. Mr Justice Etherton
Chairman of the Advisory Board of the Institute of Law
City University, London
May 2008

PREFACE

This manual explains and demonstrates, in the context of the work of a barrister, the underlying skills of legal research and fact management which will ensure that a case has been thoroughly prepared so that every relevant consideration has been taken into account before the client is given any advice, any document is drafted, or any case presented in court. Its purpose is to assist those who read it to develop effective techniques which, it is hoped, will ensure that the advice they give is sound and the arguments they put forward are convincing.

The development of professional legal skills training with its emphasis on the ability to perform lawyers' tasks has underlined the need to develop case preparation skills to a high standard. If a relevant law or fact is not identified, or if there is only a superficial assessment of the strength of evidence, the advice given is unlikely to be sound, and the argument presented in negotiation or before a tribunal is unlikely to succeed.

The experience of those studying and teaching on the Bar Vocational Course has identified the need to provide clear guidance on how to carry out legal research efficiently and to identify, analyse, and present relevant facts to ensure the best outcome for the client. The methods and techniques adopted in this manual are the outcome of our experience over many years and our discussions with the many practitioners and academics who have kindly contributed to the debate about how best to develop effective case preparation skills.

The advice given in this manual is not intended to be prescriptive. The aim is to provide practical advice and to demonstrate through the inclusion of worked examples how particular techniques can be applied to the preparation of a case. It is hoped that this will provide a framework which will assist each individual to develop his or her own intellectual skills in order to carry out the task of preparation competently and professionally.

Students will find that they will have opportunities to apply these techniques throughout the Bar Vocational Course. Some of the case papers will be used in specific classes. In particular, the sections assisting you with legal research and fact management processes will be invaluable when you are working with sets of papers for the skills exercises and should be particularly useful in preparing for assessment and later when you enter practice.

Acknowledgments

Grateful acknowledgment is made to the publishers of copyright material which appears in this book.

Crown copyright is reproduced under Class License Number C2006010631 with the permission of the Controller of HMSO and HM Land Registry.

Screenshots reproduced by kind permission of Jordan Publishing Ltd, LexisNexis® Butterworths and Thomson Publishing Services.

OUTLINE CONTENTS

DETAILED CONTENTS

Preparation: a forensic skill

The image of successful barristers suggests that their success depends on the ability to think on their feet, to use words persuasively, to mesmerise by their fluency, and to impress by their very presence and charisma those whom they address. Certainly those skills help. However, the real basis for their confidence is effective preparation for the task they are undertaking so that they know the facts of the case thoroughly and, having considered the potential relevance of all the facts to their legal context, can respond effectively to any point made, and, having thought through and planned their argument beforehand, they can deliver it clearly and address in a convincing way all the relevant questions which must be decided.

The work of a barrister (more fully dealt with in **Chapters 9** and **10** below), although more varied than many realise, is focused on answering one question. If the case came before a court, how likely is it that the client would win? The only way that this question can be answered is for the barrister to address the underlying question, which is: how can the case be presented so that evidence can be put before the court which will prove on the facts that the client is legally entitled to a finding in his or her favour? This is why case preparation is a forensic skill.

In order to answer this underlying question, the barrister will need to look closely at the facts of the case to see what the client's problem is and what the client hopes to achieve from any legal claim. The barrister will then need to research the law to see whether there is a legal principle which will give the client a right to the outcome being sought. The facts of the case will then need to be analysed to determine whether they can be presented in such a way that all the component parts of the legal principle can be shown to be fulfilled. The barrister will also need to consider whether there are witnesses who can be called to give evidence which, if believed, will prove the facts on which the argument is based and which, it is hoped, will persuade the court of the client's entitlement to a finding in his or her favour.

This analytical process can be demonstrated in graphical form as in **Table 1.1**.

Table 1.1 **Initial analysis of a case**

Legal framework	Facts in support	Evidence
Insert below each element of the crime, cause of action, and/or defences	Insert below in relation to each legal element, facts which establish that element	Insert below in relation to each fact the evidence which proves that fact

By identifying every element of the legal principle which is relied on and the facts and evidence which support it, the barrister can test whether there is sufficient available evidence of the facts to establish the legal basis of the case. Even then the preparatory work will not be completed, for the barrister, before being able to advise on the likely success of a case, will have to consider all the arguments about fact and law which the other side might raise, and whether and how they can be countered. Only then will the barrister be able to answer, with any hope of that answer being justified, the question of whether the client will win, or be able with confidence to present the case convincingly to the court.

The aim of this manual is to explain and demonstrate some methods of legal research and fact management which, in the context of the work of a barrister, will assist in developing effective case preparation skills.

Chapters 2 to **8** show how legal research can be made more efficient by increasing familiarity with the basic sources of information and by outlining some of the main techniques of research.

Chapters 9 and **10** provide an overview of the stages of first a civil and then a criminal case. The Bar is predominantly a referral profession and a barrister may be consulted at various stages of a case; it is therefore always important that any preparation is focused on the particular instructions that have been received. As particular aspects of the case may require different emphasis at different stages, it is always important to tailor one's preparation to the stage that the case has reached.

Chapter 11 describes the intellectual processes and the analytical skills which are required for effective fact management. The acronym C.A.P. (Context, Analysis, Presentation) has been adopted to summarise the process by which the preparation of a case progresses from an initial understanding of the legal and factual context of a case to a detailed analysis of the issues and the evidence and finally to the construction of a persuasive and pertinent argument which can be presented to whatever audience is appropriate, be it the client or a tribunal.

The chapter also illustrates some of the possible techniques which can be used to ensure that the C.A.P. process is carried out rigorously and may help you to develop your own analytical skills. One technique has already been displayed above at **Table 1.1**. Once that table has been completed in relation to any set of facts it should provide both an overview and a detailed analysis of the interrelation of the law, facts, and evidence, issue by issue. This should make it possible not only to assess the likelihood of success in establishing your client's case but also to carry out your specific instructions more precisely.

For instance, if your advice is sought, whether in a conference or as a written opinion, the completion of **Table 1.1** should make obvious whether there is a prima facie case so that a preliminary assessment of potential success or advice on further steps necessary can be given. If the instructions are to draft a statement of claim, the centre column will have identified the material facts which should be included. Moreover, the inability to complete the table fully will, of itself, identify what further information may be needed.

If a similar analysis is also done of the case for the other side, this should assist—once the strength of all the available evidence has been considered—in providing the basis for planning any negotiation or piece of advocacy and in answering the basic questions: how likely is it that the client will win? How can the case be presented most effectively?

Chapters 12, 13, and **14** explain and demonstrate the practical application of the C.A.P. approach by showing how, in relation to a civil and a criminal case, the process and some of the techniques discussed in **Chapter 11** can be applied to the preparation of realistic sets of papers. The papers for the civil case, *Lowe v Mainwaring*, and the accompanying preparatory notes showing the C.A.P. approach in action are contained in **Chapter 13.** The papers for the criminal case, *R v Costas Georgiou*, and its accompanying notes are contained in **Chapter 14.**

Chapters 13 and **14** demonstrate with examples how fact management techniques can be applied by following through a civil and a criminal case and showing the detailed approach to preparation at each stage.

The remainder of the manual sets out particular aspects of fact management, such as dealing with figures (**Chapter 15**) and using information technology (**Chapter 16**), before providing a set of papers for self-assessment which can be used to put into practice some of the methods of preparation demonstrated in the manual (**Chapter 17**). Finally, the **Appendices** provide assistance with sources for legal research, medical terminology, analysis of evidence, and further reading.

2

Introduction to practical legal research

If you think that the highest function of the barrister is in court-room advocacy, think again. Barristers are 'learned' counsel. They have earned their traditional title, not by their in-court resourcefulness but by being the specialists of the legal profession, lawyers whom other lawyers consult. Barristers are sought for their knowledge and understanding of the law and their resourcefulness in applying it to the legal problem presented by their client.

The ability to provide counsel's opinion is based on effective legal research and is the first requisite of the barrister—first, because it comes long before advocacy or even the drafting of statements of the case. There is of course a close connection between all of these functions; the opinion given is one which the barrister knows he or she must be prepared to deliver in court. It must be well founded on thorough research, to which the advocacy skills of the barrister can then be applied. It is in their ability to find the law and their facility to adapt and apply it to their client's cause that the most able barristers can be recognised.

2.1 What is 'practical' legal research?

Practical legal research is not the same as academic legal research practised at law schools and universities. Students absorb essential legal knowledge and principles presented in textbooks and by their university tutors. They may have the opportunity to research specific areas of law in essays or dissertations, but the research required for academic purposes allows for the pursuit of interesting legal principles and points of law while articles and cases are quoted in support of broad legal arguments.

Practical legal research is 'applied' research and a much more focused discipline. The practising lawyer seeks the law he or she needs in order to answer very specific legal questions posed by a particular problem on which the client seeks advice. The barrister conducts legal research to meet the clients' needs and so must be able to:

- identify the legal issues involved in a legal problem presented by a client;
- research those issues comprehensively while remaining focused on the problem itself;
- identify the primary sources (i.e., case law and legislation) on which an answer would depend;
- identify legal aspects which might pose problems for the client—and which act in favour of the case for the other side;

- formulate an accurate answer and a reliable opinion for the client; and
- research quickly, thoroughly, and effectively.

In some respects, this last point is the most important for the practising barrister. Research must be comprehensive and accurate—going to court poorly prepared and getting the law wrong can amount to negligence—but it must also be quick ('time is money').

2.2 The importance of legal research

We have already seen that barristers are legal experts, sought by clients for their knowledge and expertise. No lawyer, however skilful, experienced or clever, can know the answer to every legal problem—but through effective legal research, they should be able to find a solution. The dangers of conducting poor legal research are amply demonstrated in the case of *Copeland v Smith & Goodwin* [2000] 1 WLR 1371, where three advocates took a case to the Court of Appeal only to find at the hearing that the Court of Appeal had decided exactly the same point of law several months previously. Counsel for the appellants had not researched their case law thoroughly enough and ' . . . such failure had resulted in significant costs being expended on an appeal. It was essential that advocates should take steps necessary to keep abreast of all relevant reported cases.'

Similarly, specialist counsel in a divorce case came in for stinging criticism from Judge Horowitz QC in *Martin Dye v Martin Dye* [2006] 1 WLR 3448. Counsel challenged a division of marital assets by referring to statutory regulations that had been revoked four years previously. In addition to failing to update the legislation and direct the District Judge to the correct regulations, they had also failed to consult the relevant paragraphs of *Rayden & Jackson* (the leading practitioner's text on family law) where it was pointed out in the judgment that there is set out a 'clear and complete statement of the required practice'. The cost of two wasted hearings was put at half a million pounds. Counsel have a duty to direct the judge to the correct law—they can only do so if they do their research properly and get the law right themselves.

Legal research skills are also important in their own right, to you as an individual and to your career. They are skills that will be utilised in whichever area of law you eventually practice. You may learn employment law as a student but never use it in a commercial law practice or for a career as a criminal barrister—but the ability to conduct legal research will be of fundamental importance in all areas of law, throughout your career. On a personal level, learning and practising your legal research skills will:

- widen your knowledge of the law;
- teach you to analyse legal issues;
- encourage you to think laterally, coherently, and independently;
- increase your ability to be accurate and concise; and
- teach you essential information management skills.

Indeed, many employers in the legal world regard the ability to conduct efficient legal research and present it concisely and coherently as the most important skill a newly qualified lawyer should possess. The Bar Standards Board in conjunction with chambers and pupil supervisors, take the view that the ability to conduct legal research is an essential skill for pupil barristers. Consequently, all vocational law courses are required to be taught practical legal research on a course of study in its own right with a formal graded assessment of students' abilities.

2.3 Practical legal research and the pupil barrister

The skills needed for systematic legal research can be taught in law schools—and this manual presents a scheme for learning those skills—but it is no replacement for the experience of doing the research for yourself. If you ask any barrister how he or she learnt to research law, the chances are that they will say they learnt it 'on the job', by 'trial and error' or by 'jumping in at the deep end'. Many will say that they have never actually 'learned' to do it at all.

To some extent, these comments reflect the informal network of assistance and support that has long been provided to new pupils by their pupil supervisors, fellow pupils, and barrister colleagues. New barristers also have access to the structured internal resources offered by the chambers themselves:

- access to printed legal resources (journals, case reports, court forms);
- subscriptions to legal databases;
- information management databases with notes of legal research; and
- professional support for legal research—through updating services or sometimes, a dedicated staff member.

The successful barrister will use both informal networks and structured access to a chambers' own resources, assistance, and advice to assist him or her in researching the law—but these are not replacements for sound legal research skills acquired through experience of researching the law using both printed and electronic sources.

Researching the law for your pupil supervisor on behalf of a client is likely to be one of the first tasks that you, as a new pupil barrister will be given. On entering pupillage, it is difficult to make a significant contribution to chambers until you have acquired some experience, but legal research is one function that a new pupil can perform largely unsupervised. This means that chambers are generally attracted by the prospect of having an effective and reliable legal researcher to research the law for them. Earning a reputation as a good legal researcher is an attractive prospect for yourself and a good incentive for chambers—or, indeed, for any legal employer—to take on a new employee.

But what is actually required of a new pupil barrister researching the law?

Chambers expect pupils to be able to research a client's legal problem and to present a precise, accurate, and succinct summary of their findings which could be used to advise a client. A pupil supervisor would expect the pupil to have written a thorough record of how they've done the research, the sources they have consulted, and the issues they have addressed. The 'research note' allows the research to be checked, followed, and updated at a later date and is an essential part of the information management process in chambers.

A pupil barrister is expected to carry out such a task from day one. A pupil's familiarity with practitioner's texts and the way legal knowledge (statute law, case law, etc.) is organised in the law library and on electronic databases—how they cite the law, classify it, and cross-refer—is simply assumed and is regarded as part of the task. Research methods, techniques, how to analyse the issues, and write the formal research note are not skills that are taught in chambers and again it is assumed that the new pupil barrister already has these skills to some degree.

2.4 Legal research as a process

Successful legal research in chambers in preparation for a case is a process involving three essentials:

- Analysis—a succinct analysis of the law that is focused on the client's legal problem.
- Resources—knowing what resources are available, how to use them, and using them effectively.
- Method—a research method that is comprehensive yet time-efficient.

These elements are interdependent: no amount of careful analysis will make up for a failure to identify key resources, while knowing your resources but failing to use them systematically will not produce a clear analysis of the issues.

The chapters that follow address each of these elements.

Chapter 3 considers the essential ingredients of successful legal research. It will look at planning your legal research, analysing issues, identifying keywords, and applying problem-solving techniques; and it goes on to outline some key techniques for researching the law comprehensively, yet quickly and effectively.

Chapters 4 and **5** will consider more closely the wealth of resources that are available to the legal researcher—printed resources and online legal databases—and how they might be used effectively. Where to start and which to choose. How the law library is organised and the resources you will find there.

Chapters 6 and **7** deal with specific aspects of practical legal research which cause difficulty—the interpretation of words and phrases, interpreting legislative ambiguity, and the reading and interpretation of cases.

Chapter 8 provides a useful summary of those chapters that have gone before with a thorough worked-through example of a legal research problem.

Legal research methods and techniques

Practical legal research is an intellectual exercise that requires much more than a simple overview of the legal resources available to the practitioner. To prepare for a case, a barrister is expected to analyse the issues involved and, using a research method that is comprehensive and time-efficient, come up with solutions and answers that are tightly focused on the client's legal problems. When faced with a multitude of resources, a sequence of problems to resolve and no clear starting point, this can seem a daunting and time-consuming task rather than a rewarding aspect of the barrister's work. In fact, even when carrying out the research itself, there can be practical problems to face and challenging issues to overcome. It can, for example, be difficult to:

- identify all the relevant legal issues with any certainty;
- access the resources that you need, when you need them;
- know where to start, particularly if the legal problem is itself unclear;
- know if the information you have found is relevant, reliable and up to date;
- keep focused on the client's problem; and
- know when to stop researching, even if you find nothing.

Indeed, there is a need to be realistic about what legal research can actually achieve. Where facts are important to a case rather than the law itself, legal research is of limited use and analysis of those facts is far more important. Legal research can assist with finding and communicating principles of law to the client and determining how they have been applied and interpreted in the courts but however thorough the research, it does not guarantee certainty; many cases come to court simply because the law is unclear.

Furthermore, there is no single 'correct' way to research the law; instinct and experience—making mistakes, misclassifying the law and following 'false leads'—all play a part. Fortunately, however, there are methods and techniques that can be employed to improve your analytical skills and to develop your legal research abilities. The need to think about legal research strategically, to plan beforehand, to adopt an approach that is appropriate to the particular purpose, to research systematically and to utilise your findings in a way that is meaningful to the client and the court, are all fundamental to your success as a legal researcher and a pupil barrister.

3.1 Planning legal research

Planning your legal research plays an important part in ensuring that you stay focused on the key problems, legal issues, and remedies that could lead to an answer to the client's legal problem. It can also help to find the elusive 'starting point'. Extensive 'background' reading, making notes, and collating photocopies are very unlikely to help and will only serve to confuse. In order to plan research effectively, we need to identify the essential steps in practical legal research that we might follow. A typical method might look something like this:

- assemble the facts and identify those that are most relevant;
- analyse the legal issues involved and identify the legal questions that need answering;
- research the legal issues;
- analyse and synthesise the facts and the law; and
- come to preliminary conclusions that can be used to prepare a research note.

In formulating a plan for legal research, the researcher might take each of these stages and consider the following:

- the resources that will be needed (secondary and primary; printed and online);
- the steps to be taken – can the research be divided into more manageable tasks?
- the findings that need to be recorded; and
- the time it will take—how 'big' is the task? A few quick-reference searches or a time-consuming project?

Thinking about these issues helps to identify what needs to be done and when. It also allows the researcher to plan more systematically; it follows that the research itself is likely be more systematic too. Most legal issues involve legislation, case law, and rules of procedure and these can usefully be researched separately. Sometimes a legal question is very focused and so planning is much easier; for example, a trawl through case law to find likely damages for a personal injury claim. At other times, legal issues are unclear or more numerous and therefore require more research and analysis. It is important to assess this at the initial stages of research so that you can give yourself sufficient time, both to find the information you need and to analyse your findings. Legal research nearly always takes longer than you think it will.

3.2 Analysing the problem

Preparing a plan and a schedule for legal research is difficult without first having looked at the facts of the case and analysed the issues. Legal problems arrive in chambers in the form of papers outlining factual situations—letters, contracts or statements from individuals. Translating the 'facts' that they contain into legal issues is one of the most difficult aspects of legal research but it is also central to the barrister's role. A man slips, falls, and is seriously injured on a building site—those are the facts, but what are the legal issues?

3.2.1 Factual analysis

Assembling the facts and analysing them carefully will help you to identify:

- the 'material' facts—those that are important and those that can be omitted;
- connections between the facts; and
- possible areas of law and legal issues to research.

Read the papers carefully and ask yourself:

- What is the case about?
- Which facts are relevant?
- What does the client want?
- What am I being asked to do?

In our example of a man falling at a building site and being seriously injured, we may learn from the facts that he was an employee working on scaffolding and was seen to be talking on a mobile phone just before he fell. These would be material facts. The fact that he had just had lunch is immaterial to his fall (unless he was seen to have drunk alcohol with his lunch).

Having read the papers before you and analysed the facts, you may find it helpful to write a succinct summary of the circumstances. An accurate precis of the information will help you to understand the client's situation. A summary should be concise and focused on the material facts. It is not an investigation of the facts themselves (which would, in any case, be impossible for the barrister to carry out). Avoid elaborating on the original facts but do take into account the client's wishes or needs, as well as facts that are unfavourable to your client (you will need to provide defences for those facts). Analysing and summarising the facts will help with the next stage—identifying the legal issues.

3.2.2 Legal analysis

By taking the facts of the case and analysing them more closely we can begin to identify legal problems or questions that need researching. Legal analysis is a preliminary identification of the legal issues involved in a case. It differs from factual analysis in that the researcher begins to apply his or her knowledge of legal principles to the facts in order to identify:

- key areas of law relevant to the facts;
- possible legal issues in the case; and
- specific points of law.

One way of building up a useful set of issues to research is to ask 'who, how, what, where, when, and why' type questions of your facts and the client's situation and intentions. Questions you might ask yourself include:

- What essential areas of law are important to this case?
- What legal issues emerge from the material facts?
- How do these issues impinge on the facts of the case . . . and vice versa?
- What does the client want as a solution to their legal problem?
- How could they achieve their objectives and what are the alternatives?
- What facts might impede this outcome and how might they be overcome?
- What causes of action are available?
- Who is liable?

Not all of these questions will be relevant all of the time. In our example, health and safety legislation and the employer's duty of care towards employees are legal issues which will need researching. Who is liable here? Is it the employer or is there a contributory element to the fall on the part of the victim? In asking all these questions, be as specific as possible; this will make your research more focused, and the application of the law to your client's case more relevant.

Having analysed the facts, you should be able to draw up a list of questions, issues, and problems that it would appear (from the facts before you) that the court would need to determine. The questions should address the legal aspects of your client's case and the alternative outcomes. The questions posed should be capable of being answered through legal research; you do not have the option of investigating the facts themselves. Note, also, that the legal issues you identify are not the same as the client's original question or problem (which would be resolved by the court); they are simply those matters that need researching before you can even start to form an opinion on the answer to the client's original problem.

3.3 Researching the issues

Once you have sketched out a plan of research, analysed the client's problem and produced a list of legal issues, think about approaching the sources and starting to research. But which issue would you research first and how?

Now that you have identified the legal questions that you need to answer, it would be useful to list them in order of importance and to research them in that order. Having done some research on the principal issues, you might find that some minor aspects of the legal problem prove irrelevant or perhaps do not need researching at the early stages when you are merely determining the strength of a case. At this point it is also useful to categorise the issues, identify the sources you might approach, and the keywords you might use to search that source (whether it be a database or the contents or index to a practitioner text).

3.3.1 Categorising legal issues

For each legal issue:

- Establish if it is a civil or criminal matter.
- Identify the principal area of law—this will become your subject heading (e.g., contract, tort, family law, offences against the person).
- Decide which aspects of the issue are substantive or procedural in nature.

Categorising the issues in this way will help to identify the principal areas of law you need to research (e.g., contract, tort, family law), which will assist in your selection of a secondary source as your starting point. It will also help produce a few broad terms which then become subject headings in your research (e.g., negligence). These terms may be too broad to be of use in an index to a practitioner text but they can be used to search the table of contents. (See **3.3.3.**)

3.3.2 Identifying keywords

Legal issues are researched using electronic databases or the contents or an index to a book. Selecting the 'best' keywords to access these resources will determine how successful your research will be. Formulating legal issues will itself lead you to keywords, while finding relevant keywords during your research will help you to think about legal issues. Choose keywords that describe the legal issues most accurately, avoiding general terms (that would give too many references) and indeed, terms that are too specific (which might be hidden away in a printed index under a broader term). Which words define the problem you are researching? These might be:

- words offered to you by your analysis of the legal issue itself;
- alternatives to those words (i.e. synonyms); and
- concepts behind those words.

EXERCISE 1   SIMPLE KEYWORD PROBLEMS

Example 1

A Bar students' magazine wants to run a competition. Readers are asked to guess the number of Bar exam candidates this year who pass in all subjects. Entry is free. Only one entry is allowed per reader, who must be a BVC student. If no one gets exactly the right figure, the prize (a copy of the new edition of *Civil Court Practice*) will go to the one who made the closest guess. You are asked to advise the magazine on whether there are any restrictions or regulations applicable.

Analysis

Can there be any legal objection to this? What area of law would it be? It doesn't look like wagering or betting. No money is involved. It's not a lottery with tickets. Indeed, some skill is involved. Freedom of the press? Competition law? Prize law? (Surely they mean something quite different?) But maybe 'competition' or 'prize' could be worth trying as keywords.

1. Must London taxis have meters?
2. Is endorsement of a driving licence obligatory for the offence of driving without insurance?
3. The author of a fraudulent misrepresentation thought that the representation was irrelevant or unimportant. Is this defence likely to succeed?
4. Is it true that barristers enjoy immunity from suit for alleged negligence in the conduct of civil proceedings when acting as advocates?
5. Does a witness who deliberately fabricates evidence in legal proceedings have immunity from suit in negligence in relation given to the evidence given in court?
6. In what circumstances may a coroner hold an inquest on a Sunday?
7. Are there any age limits applicable to the appointment of bishops?
8. Are the winnings of a successful gambler or the earnings of a prostitute subject to income tax?

Think laterally about how the problem might be described; those who write practitioner texts and database content do not necessarily describe concepts in the same way. To make the best use of these resources, you may need to browse the contents of a text, look up several keywords in an index or combine keywords when searching a database. In determining the keywords or phrases you might use, bear in mind:

- broader and narrower terms. Words may appear in a printed index as a subdivision of a broader heading rather than a term itself. (e.g., dismissal, unfair);
- alternative, interchangeable terms (e.g., drunkenness, intoxication; drugs, narcotics; pharmaceuticals, prescription drugs);
- terms dependent on context (e.g., forfeiture—of a lease or of the proceeds of crime?);
- concealed keywords. The relevant statute may contain a very precise word that we would tend to broaden or paraphrase in everyday language. See **Exercise 2;** and

- changes to the meanings of words. New words in legal parlance ('Part 20 claims'; the law relating to 'terrorism') and old ('employment law' was once known as 'labour law'). The 'labelling' of terms and their organisation within texts and on databases also varies (though less so) between publishers.

In thinking about concepts you might also consider terms that relate to types of activity, actions, remedies, etc.:

Type of activity	Accident, slip, trip
Causes of action	Tort, negligence, contributory negligence
Remedies	Damages, conviction
Parties / Subjects / Relationships	Employer, employee, third parties
Things	Victims, hazards

Printed tables of contents and indexes are excellent resources in themselves for finding keywords, arranged as they are in a hierarchical form of broad concepts to narrow, more specific terms. The index to *Halsbury's Laws of England and Wales* is perhaps the most useful, its encyclopaedic nature meaning that it offers a wide range of keywords, including cross-references to alternative terms, 'preferred' terms, broader concepts and a separate index of definitions of particular words and phrases. (See **4.4**.)

Choosing keywords to search on a legal database, however, is more problematic and subject to a greater degree of error. An awareness of alternative terms is particularly important, while terms such as 'duty of care' are simply too broad and will produce far too many results to be of any use; knowing how to combine terms and search correctly is crucial. Keywords should be specific enough to yield a manageable quantity of information but not so specific as to find no results at all. Electronic search techniques are dealt with in greater detail at **Chapter 5**.

Finally, look at your list of legal issues and identify at least one keyword for each issue you need to research. Now we can begin to identify the sources you might use and start the research itself.

EXERCISE 2   KEYWORDS AND LEGAL ISSUES

Example 2

Rita, employed by a large company, says that she was frequently bullied or ridiculed by fellow employees, that she became ill as a result, and had to give up her job. She now wants to sue her employers. They say that she gave no reason for leaving other than ill health; that she never complained about her treatment; and that since any such alleged misconduct was never brought to their notice, they cannot be liable.

Analysis

There would no doubt be a conflict here on the facts. However, the legal issue is whether the employers could in principle be vicariously liable; and if so liable, for what? The missing keyword is 'harassment'.

1. Charles's house was badly damaged in a severe gale last night. The upper part is in danger of falling. Charles's surveyor says it must be pulled down and made safe without delay. Workmen are standing by to do the necessary work. But the house is a listed building and no authorisation has been obtained. Can Charles go ahead?
2. Fred Warmington, a travel agent, registered as a domain name 'Warmington.holidays.com'. The borough of Warmington-on-Sea, a well-known holiday resort, wishes to object to this as likely to confuse people looking for holidays there. Fred says he is entitled to use his own name. Advise the borough.

3. The City Council is divided equally between Conservative and Labour members. The mayor, who presides, is a Labour member. Whenever the Council votes on what is a politically loaded matter, the result is a tie. So the mayor, who has already voted with the Labour side, then purports to vote for that side again, changing the balance. The Conservatives wish to challenge his right to do this. Will they succeed?

4. A firm of auctioneers are your clients. Their sale catalogue described a piece of furniture as Georgian. An experienced dealer purchased it at the auction. He says (and they now agree) it is Victorian and that this amounts to a false trade description. The auctioneers point out that their catalogue conditions state that being merely auctioneers, they are not responsible for vendors' statements of authenticity, origin, date, etc., of any article. They also say that, anyway, the purchaser is himself an expert who did not rely on their description. They therefore say that they are not liable for false trade description. Are they right?

3.3.3   Starting to research

You should by now have a list of the legal issues, problems or questions you wish to research and a list of relevant keywords to look up in a printed source or to use as search terms on a legal database. You may also have an idea of the relevant areas of law you need to cover and the case law, legislation or procedure you need to look up. Often you will recognise the legal context (contract, tort, crime, procedure, etc.) even though you may not know the actual answer. If this is the case, then start researching those issues first; accessing the law you are familiar with will lead you to other relevant sources. If it isn't clear what area of law the problem falls into then try classifying the problem; is it more likely to be civil or criminal litigation or health and safety law? Is the answer more likely to be found in legislation than in case law, or does the problem turn on a procedural point?

These questions all help determine which source you choose to use as your starting point for research. There will be a range of resources available to answer any legal question and you may need to use more than one to find what you need. Sources in law are 'primary' (case law and legislation—the law itself) or secondary (expert opinion and commentary on the law). (See **4.1.3.**) These terms refer to their importance in the law rather than the order in which you should refer to them. Unless you are very familiar with the relevant case law or legislation, it is nearly always best to start your research with a secondary source—why start trying to interpret case law or legislation, or to understand how the various legal principles fit together, when an expert has already done it for you?

3.3.3.1   Selecting a secondary source

Use the list of practitioner texts, journals, and law reports arranged by subject in **Appendix 1** to identify a suitable text covering the area of law you need. You may need to use more than one secondary source to feel sure you have a good grasp of the relevant law. Try to use the most appropriate source for the question, only moving onto another if the answer you find is unclear or is not detailed enough. An excellent starting point for almost any area of English law is the comprehensive legal encyclopaedia, *Halsbury's Laws of England and Wales.* (See **4.4.**)

Knowledge of a range of legal resources, and how they work and relate to other sources, is not only useful but is a prerequisite for successful legal research. Take some time to learn how to use a practitioner text, including its table of contents, its index, and its overall layout. (See **4.3.**) Similarly, you should be aware of how legal databases work, their contents, and how they update their material. See **Chapter 5**.

Commentary will help identify other legal issues relevant to your problem and will lead you to the relevant case law and legislation but, however well-regarded the source, secondary sources are not authoritative in court and are no substitute for researching the primary sources of law. When citing authority for a proposition of law, you should refer to statute law and/or case law, not to what is said in a textbook.

3.3.3.2 Locating primary sources

Primary sources are legislation (statutes and statutory instruments) and case law. You would rarely approach the primary sources directly unless the legal problem you face is fairly straightforward and simply involved, for example, finding a definition from a statute, or reading the points of law established in a leading case. Researching legislation is perhaps slightly easier and more finite an activity than researching case law, which can be very time-consuming. Commentaries on (or annotated versions of) statutes and statutory instruments (SIs) very often refer to cases, so providing a means of identifying some of the most important cases that may be relevant. The reverse is also true—reports of cases will cite relevant legislation which again provides a useful 'way in' to researching statute law. (See **4.8** for researching primary sources of law.)

3.4 Following through

Researching a legal problem in secondary sources and finding relevant legislation and case law will start you off in legal research but it is rarely sufficient in itself, though this may not be immediately apparent. Further analysis of the material facts in the light of the information you have found will nearly always reveal legal issues you hadn't originally thought of and which will need investigating, and perhaps new keywords you could use to search the secondary sources and databases. At this point you should return to your list of legal issues and the client's original problem. Here are a few tips and techniques for following through on your research:

Don't rely on your memory. You may have misremembered, or the law may have changed. Even if you think you know an area of law thoroughly and have some knowledge of the specific issue, you should always check your sources and ensure your law is up to date.

No source is comprehensive. You may need to look up the same keywords in several texts to gain both an overview of an area of law and sufficient detail of specific issues. *Halsbury's Laws* provides an excellent starting point for employment law, for example, but a specialist loose-leaf such as *Harvey's* is bound to go into more detail on specific issues. Conversely, the sources will also overlap; don't read through the same material twice unless you are looking for a different perspective on a particular legal issue or point of law.

Use your sources properly. Have you followed *all* the references the index referred to or only some of them? Failing to follow up references in an index or 'hits' on a database, is one of the most common errors in legal research that can lead to crucial information being missed. Random browsing through a text using a table of contents is useful but it must be accompanied by a systematic approach to following up references in the index.

Stay focused on the legal issues, problems, and questions you are trying to answer. Avoid exploring interesting areas of law at the expense of the main issue. Keep referring back to the client's problem and reviewing your progress. Are you answering the question? Are you finding solutions to their problem? Your plan of research may change as new legal issues arise but this should be a matter of positive decision rather than the result of meandering research.

Lateral thinking. Sometimes there is a need to think around a problem and find a different angle on a complex legal issue or to find an alternative source. If you are looking on a case law database for *Re M (a minor)* but found there are twenty cases of that name, you could read the headnotes of them all to find the particular case you need. Or if you know the area of law covered by the case, you could approach a specialist text and use the table of cases, or search a full text database using the case name and a keyword. If something is taking you too long, there is probably a more efficient way of doing it.

Know when to stop. Striking a balance between retrieving too much information and retrieving too little is one of the more difficult aspects of legal research. As practical legal research is a highly focused discipline, researching specific issues in depth is probably more useful than researching more widely (though if it is an unfamiliar area of law then wider research to acquire knowledge of the subject and a 'feel' for the issues, is probably justified). There is, in many cases, no 'right answer', and too much research only serves to confuse and is counter-productive.

Finding nothing. This can be a worrying situation—where despite a lot of research, you can find no relevant commentary on an issue, no legislation, and no case law, and have to face a demanding pupil supervisor with these results. It is worth trying to approach the problem from a different angle but it may simply be that there is no clear answer and no law to find. It is not necessarily a failure, provided you have researched thoroughly and updated your findings correctly. In some circumstances (especially in updating your research), finding nothing is perfectly 'normal'.

3.5 Updating the law

The distinction between the law as originally made and the law as amended and currently in force is fundamental to practical legal research. The law is not static but develops, and from the researcher's point of view we need to see how established law is affected by later legal developments; updating the law is therefore essential. As the law can change so quickly, printed texts obviously become out of date almost as soon as they are published and so most texts have some form of updating. For example, practitioner texts may have a supplement updating the commentary, while legal encyclopaedias have 'noter-up services', so called because the service volume 'notes-up' or updates the main volumes with later developments. (See **4.4.1.**) Similar 'noter-up' services operate for the primary sources of law and these are dealt with in more detail in **Chapter 4.**

Legal databases of case law and legislation are generally more up to date than printed equivalents but the commentary they contain is rarely more recent than the printed version. Most electronic sources started life as a published text and the contents have simply been transferred to a database with no repackaging for the electronic user; this can make them difficult to browse and read online but it also offers no advantage in terms of how up to date the text is. Updating legal sources online is dealt with in more detail in **Chapter 5.**

There are four principal ways in which primary law is amended:

- *Statutes affecting earlier statutes.* Check to see if a statute has come into force, if it is still in force (i.e., has it been repealed?) or if it has been amended. Also, bear in mind the possibility of statutory instruments amending statutes. (See **4.9.2** and **4.10.2.**)

- *Cases affecting earlier case law.* Check to see if a case has been applied, approved, followed, distinguished or overruled. (See **4.11.4**).

- *Cases interpreting statutes.* Check to see if a case has interpreted a statute. (See **4.11.4**).
- *Statutes affecting earlier case law.* The best way of finding out whether the effect of a case has been reversed by statute is to look for the case in a textbook. (See **Table 4.6**)

3.6 Further research techniques

The steps for researching the law outlined above and summarised at **3.6.1** are a well-established method of practical legal research. It is not the only approach, however, and there are several techniques that you can use in conjunction with these essential steps of legal research.

'Funnel' approach: broad to narrow. The importance of starting your research with a broad area of law and a corresponding secondary source should not be underestimated. It is nearly always necessary to access unfamiliar areas of law through the context and meaning provided by a practitioner text, a legal encyclopaedia, a loose-leaf or an article. They provide assistance with finding and interpreting statutes and reported cases. However, the law exists in the primary authorities. Legislation and case law must always be read; it is these that you will use to advise the client and which you will rely on in court, not the secondary sources.

Linear approaches. Use existing knowledge to link to other relevant information. If you know the name of a statute, you can locate an updated version of the Act, any subsidiary legislation and cases referring to the Act. Similarly, if you know the name of a case you will be able to find other related cases and legislation referred to in the case.

Legal definitions. If a specific legal term is relevant to your research then a judicial dictionary will guide you to where the word or phrase is defined within the context of specific statues and cases. As such, they provide invaluable shortcuts to the primary law. See **Chapter 6**.

Researching systematically. Build the techniques and methods described here into your research process. Updating the law, for example, is an essential part of the research process, not an afterthought. It takes little extra time and the updating material itself can be a useful source of information. Similarly, browsing contents tables to find key areas of law, checking all relevant references in the index and following through from practitioner text to case law and legislation are all signs of systematic legal research.

Checklists and flow charts. In planning your legal research you may find it helpful to create a checklist of sources to consult, keywords to use, and steps to follow for each legal issue you have identified. These also serve as brief notes which can be used to prepare a more formal research note. (See **3.8.2**.) If you are a visual learner then use a flow chart instead of a checklist. Also, make good use of the tables within **Chapter 4**; they essentially operate as checklists for the types of information you need to look for within each source you use.

Brainstorming. Writing down everything concerning a legal issue is a useful starting point for thinking about keywords. Empathise with your client and try to think of issues from their point of view—then reverse the process and imagine it from the other side's point of view. This will broaden your thoughts on legal issues and keywords.

Asking questions. This was considered in the context of legal analysis (see **3.2.2**) and can also be usefully employed to think about keywords. In addition to 'who, what, why, how', etc., think about relationships (what caused . . . ? which came first . . . ?), comparisons (what is the opposite . . . ? is this similar to . . . ?), and evidence (what facts are there . . . ? is this possible . . . ?).

Thinking hats. De Bono's 'thinking hats' method explores ways of thinking about issues from different angles—without bias, without emotion, critically, positively, creatively, and finally the 'big picture'. This is particularly useful for thinking through more difficult legal research problems where there is no clear answer.[1]

Visual methods. For analysing issues or communicating ideas such as 'mind mapping' or thinking in terms of processes or 'cycles', these can help break down issues into smaller segments and then connect them and chart the relationships between facts and issues.[2] This can, for example, help to identify cause and effect, or to understand complex contractual relationships.

3.6.1   Practical legal research—a '7-step method'

1. *Plan your legal research.* Identify the 'size' of the research, how long it might take, and where you might find the resources.

2. *Analyse the client's problem.* Summarise the material facts and identify potential legal issues and any questions of law that need to be answered. This will flesh out your initial plan of research.

3. *Categorise the legal issues and identify keywords.* Categorise to find broad subject areas and identify keywords that reflect specific aspects of the problems you need to research.

4. *Research the issues.* Choose as your starting point a secondary source that covers the principal area of law. Follow through all references to your chosen keywords, then to other sources, and finally to primary sources. Establish legal authorities—statutes and case law—for a statement of law.

5. *Update your findings.* Check to ensure the statute has been brought into force, if it has been amended or repealed. Are your selected cases still valid law or have they been overruled or distinguished?

6. *Check back to your client's problem.* Look again at your list of legal issues, the original question, and your client's objectives and check to ensure you have answered all the questions that arise. Have further issues arisen during your research? If so, look for other resources, issues, and update.

7. *Analyse and summarise the law.* Apply the law to the facts of the case before you (see **3.7**). Only then are you ready to advise the client.

3.7   Applying the law to the facts

No amount of research will be of any use to your client if the law you have found is applied incorrectly to the facts before you. Practical legal research is a means to an end, not an end in itself. In order to ensure that your research is focused on finding the relevant legal

---

1   E. De Bono, *Six Thinking Hats* (Penguin, 2000).

2   T. Hutchinson, *Researching and Writing in the Law* (LawBook, 2006).

principles to determine the issues which the court will have to decide, you should keep in mind and check your research regularly against the following:

- the client's problem and their objectives;
- the legal issues that would need to be determined by the court;
- the facts of the case before you;
- the potential persuasive arguments you could use to further your client's cause; and
- the potential persuasive arguments your opponent might use against you.

When you have found the relevant law, you should then:

- carefully reconsider and decide precisely what issues the court will have to determine;
- decide precisely what legal principle(s) you consider may be applied to EACH issue;
- determine whether your opponent is likely to argue either that these legal principles do not apply or that the court should determine differently what the legal principles are;
- apply the precise legal principles to the facts on EACH issue separately;
- be realistic in your application, noting gaps in the evidence and potential conflicts of fact; and
- set out your view on the conclusion the court is likely to reach: (i) on the facts (if possible); and (ii) on the legal issue.

In applying statutory provisions to the facts, you need to consider the precise wording of the provisions and the precise facts of your case. You need to ensure that you know the meaning the court will give to the relevant words:

- Is the word or phrase defined in an interpretation section?
- Is there case law interpreting it?
- Is the case law consistent on this, or are there conflicting judgments?
- Given the meaning of the relevant words, does the provision apply?
- How will the court apply it?
- What conclusion is the court likely to reach in respect of your client's case?

In applying case law to the facts, you need to consider the precise words of the legal principle(s) established by the case(s). If the legal principle is well established, you can rely on an accepted wording of it (for example, as set out in an authoritative practitioner text such as *Chitty on Contract* or *Clerk & Lindsell on Tort*). If the legal principles are not well established, you need to read the judgment(s) which have set them out and to identify the particular part of the judgment on which you will rely, to argue precisely what each legal principle is. You then need to check the facts of the case to determine whether or not your client's problem can be distinguished from those facts. You then need to formulate arguments to support a finding for your client on the issue, and to consider those arguments which your opponent is likely to formulate to persuade the court to find against your client. Then decide the likelihood that the court will be persuaded to find for or against your client on that issue.

It is the application of the law to the facts that forms the basis of the advice you will give to the client. It also informs the development of a persuasive argument and the preparation of a case for court. At this point you may find problems or issues emerge that require further research or clarification:

Inadequate factual information. It may not be possible to advise on some aspects of the client's problem simply because the facts, as presented, are unclear or questions arose during the research that you first need to clarify with the client. The client does not know the law; it is your job to find out the questions that need asking of the client to ensure that the court has all the relevant facts before it. Your opinion should advise the instructing solicitor on the further evidence which is required (for more on this, see the *Opinion Writing* manual).

Insufficient analysis of the problem. Researching the law and applying the law to the facts without having a clear idea of the client's situation can lead to omissions in research, poor application of the law and consequently, bad or negligent advice. Empathise with the client's problem. What would be the best solution for you? Is it achievable within the facts before you or is there a suitable alternative?

Insufficient research. Advising your client on the basis of research using only secondary texts containing commentary and summaries of legislation and case law, is flawed. The author of a practitioner text analyses the law from a perspective that is not necessarily analogous with your client's situation. If you have found relevant law, then you need to know *exactly* what it says—always research the law in the primary sources once you have exhausted the secondary sources.

Ambiguity. You may find that the law is conflicting and it may not be possible to give a clear indication to the client, of the likely outcome of a case. In such a case, it will be up to the court to decide on the legal issues presented to it. However, when it comes to advising the client, you must still give advice on the approach that the court is likely to adopt (for example, expressing a view on how likely it is that the court will follow one line of authority in preference to another, or how the court is likely to construe a provision that has not previously been the subject of judicial interpretation). Ensure you have researched ambiguous case law thoroughly; a conflict in case law may, for example, have been commented on in journal articles or by judges in other cases. In applying the law to the facts, consider whether cases which are less favourable to your client's case might be 'distinguished' (and bear in mind that your opponent may try to distinguish authorities that are favourable to your client's case). If there is no relevant case law at all, then you should base your advice on appropriate general principles and hypothesise how these principles might be applied to your client's situation.

Disregarding the law. It may be tempting to outline a favourable outcome to a client when in fact the law does not support their position, or does so only partially. A false impression of a successful outcome when the application of the law to the facts says otherwise, is both negligent advice and a disservice to a paying client.

3.8 Recording your research

As a pupil barrister, you are very likely to be conducting research for a more senior barrister. Your pupil supervisor will usually ask you to prepare a note of your research that will form the basis of an opinion. Keeping a thorough record of the legal research you have undertaken is crucial when it comes to preparing this formal note of legal research. The research note serves several purposes and may be used:

- as a means for the pupil supervisor to check the research you have carried out and to ensure no legal issues have been missed and all findings have been updated;

- as a formal record of the research undertaken that would stay on a client's file and which might be referred back to, at a later stage in the proceedings;
- to advise a client verbally in a meeting or in writing through an opinion;
- in the preparation of a skeleton argument; and
- in the construction of legal argument where an issue in a case depends on a point of law.

The research note serves a multitude of purposes, each of which requires a different level of detail. Some clients, for example, may be more interested in the advice itself rather than knowing the details of relevant legal sources, while a formal opinion would always contain references to key authorities. The research you carry out must be recorded in sufficient detail as to be able to serve all those purposes; if it omits crucial information, then it could mean repeating some of your research at a later date or, at worst, if an error goes undetected, deficient advice may be given to the client.

3.8.1   Taking notes during your research

The quality of the formal research note you prepare will depend to some extent on how well you have recorded your research as you were carrying it out. Careful note-taking will avoid trips back to the library to consult texts for a second time or further electronic searches to find legislation or case law that you referred to but failed to update. While carrying out research, record your progress so that you are clear as to the research you have completed and that which is still to be done. In researching printed sources you should note:

- the full reference of the sources consulted (and any sources that were unavailable; if you have a note of them, you can always check for them later in your research);
- the part of a book consulted (contents, indexes, tables);
- the keywords used in an index and the references given;
- paragraph numbers and footnotes referred to and the information they contain;
- full references for any legislation and case law referred to;
- any supplements or updating materials consulted; and
- a note of how up to date your findings are.

In using electronic sources, you would in addition need to take note of:

- the database you searched and any limitations in its scope which might require research elsewhere (e.g., case law only back to 1980 on *Lawtel*);
- Specific sources within databases (e.g; Cases on *LexisNexis*, Crime Practice Area on *Westlaw,* or Legal Journals Index on *Lawtel*);
- the search terms (or keywords) you used and the exact search carried out on each database. (It is very easy randomly to try out different searches on a database; but without systematically planning your electronic searches, you will miss relevant information. See **Chapter 5**);
- how you updated the legislation or case law you found; and
- the date you carried out the electronic research (you may need to conduct the same electronic search at a much later stage to bring your research up to date).

Notes should be clear, well-organised and easy to follow, with sufficient detail to prevent the research having to be repeated. You may find it helpful to keep a checklist for each legal issue you research; sources consulted, keywords used, references to follow up, updating information, and so on. A checklist provides a useful format for keeping detailed notes and acts as a visual reminder of the stages in legal research you need to complete. In preparing the formal research note for the pupil supervisor, you may not need to use all the notes you have made but if your notes are thorough, you will find it easier to distinguish the important information that you do need to include.

3.8.2 Preparing a formal research note

Your pupil supervisor will not usually require you to produce a full opinion, but rather the notes or a 'research route' which could form the basis for an opinion. Individual chambers and pupil supervisors will have different requirements and expectations of a formal research note but it would typically consist of:

- A *heading*. The client's name (or case name or subject heading) and reference to the issue under consideration. A pupil supervisor is likely to have several cases underway, so a heading will help to identify quickly the case your research note refers to.

- *A legal answer*. A succinct answer to the client's legal problem(s) outlining the application of the law to the facts of the case. If there is no clear answer, then the most likely solution should be set out with the principal reservations and likely alternatives.

- *The research route*. A clear, concise, and accurate record of how the legal authorities (legislation and case law) referred to in the answer were found and what steps were taken to ensure they were up to date.

The research note you produce should be accurate, comprehensive, and concise. It can be in note form provided the notes are intelligible to another reader. It should be structured in such a way that it is clear and easy to read, using headings and bullet points where necessary, for clarity. It should not be an essay nor should it present your research findings in a partisan or emotive way.

The legal answer should address the legal issues and offer a succinct treatment of the law relevant to the client's problem. It should not assume facts for which there is no basis but it may helpfully identify the need for further information on specific issues. It should include where possible some indication of a course of action that would be most likely to produce a favourable outcome for the client.

The research route serves to support the legal answer by providing details of how you found the relevant authority (usually case law and legislation) and how you updated it. It should:

- contain only reference to statutes, cases, and secondary sources that proved relevant to the answer; citing irrelevant authority only serves to confuse. You may have done some background reading on an unfamiliar area of law but this is irrelevant to the client's legal problem and is therefore not cited in the research route;

- show how the authority cited is relevant by relating it to the facts of the case; this demonstrates your legal reasoning that will be checked by the pupil supervisor. Cite primary authority in preference to secondary. Reference to secondary authority might be justified where the law is ambiguous; practitioner texts should be quoted in preference to academic opinion in student textbooks;

- cite primary authorities correctly so that they can easily be found again, with full titles for legislative enactments (see **4.9**) and full citations (including neutral citations) for cases (see **4.11.7**); identify a specific dictum within a case by reference to the relevant paragraph number (or for older cases, page number) of a law report;

- set out key points from each relevant source, avoiding repetition of the same material from different sources and avoiding moving back and forth between sources. If the problem covers distinct subject areas or is otherwise complex it may be helpful to reorganise the research route so as to deal with the legal issues separately;

- avoid cutting and pasting or otherwise copying verbatim quotations from statutes, case law or secondary sources. You should instead identify the specific parts that are relevant and paraphrase, quoting only short paragraphs or precise words that are crucial. Quoting verbatim lengthens a research note unnecessarily and demonstrates an inability to identify relevant legal issues and principles and apply them to the facts of a case;

- always include updating information; how you checked your sources to ensure the law was up to date and the date when you completed the research; and

- include reference to law that does not support the client's case so that legal argument can be prepared to address the case put forward by the other side.

3.9 In conclusion

This chapter has provided an overview of methods and techniques that will equip you with the essential skills of practical legal research. By now you should have some idea of:

- How to analyse a client's problem, identify the material facts, and recognise legal issues.

- How to categorise legal issues and identify keywords.

- How to select a starting point for your research and where to look for an answer.

- The importance of 'following through' your research to ensure that you have covered all relevant legal issues.

- The need to think laterally and apply different research techniques when you face a 'dead end' in your research.

- The need to ALWAYS to update the law you find.

- How to apply the law to the facts and keep your research tightly focussed on the client's needs.

- How to record your research systematically in preparation for a formal research note.

- How to prepare a clear statement of the law as it applies to the client's problem, for a pupil supervisor.

No amount of careful analysis will make up for a failure to identify key resources and knowing your resources but failing to use them systematically will not produce a clear analysis of the issues. Your analysis and the research method you use are only as good as the resources you have available and how you make use of them. This chapter has mentioned a few key resources available to the researcher. **Chapter 4** deals with these legal resources in more detail—what they are and how to use them to research the law. **Chapter 5** considers legal databases and shows the researcher how to develop search strategies that will utilise these resources more effectively. Some of the specific problems that are often encountered in legal research (researching words and phrases and interpreting a case) are addressed in **Chapters 6** and **7**.

Chapter 8 returns to legal research method in the light of these chapters and offers a worked example of researching a legal problem and producing a research note for the pupil supervisor.

Legal resources for the practitioner

4

4.1 Introduction: using the law library

The law library is an excellent starting point for any legal research you do as a student or a pupil barrister. The 'library' might simply be a collection of practitioner texts and law reports in your own chambers or at court, the resources available online via a subscription service such as *LexisNexis* or the much more substantial holdings of your Inn library. The Inn library in particular, is a major resource that London-based barristers will make use of throughout their career at the Bar but with such extensive holdings, its organisation is complex and it can take some time to find what you need. Before you even start in pupillage, you should become familiar with the materials your nearest law library holds, their layout, and organisation, 'finding aids' and the databases they subscribe to. While the types of legal materials that law libraries hold tend to be very similar, no two libraries are the same in terms of their holdings, arrangement, facilities, and software.

4.1.1 Formats of legal resources: printed or online

The online databases that your chambers or Inn library subscribes to will also vary. Most law schools subscribe to an extensive range of electronic resources which would include all the major legal databases—*Westlaw, LexisNexis, Lawtel*, and *Justis*—as well as more academic resources such as *HEIN online* and *JSTOR*. Larger academic institutions can afford these substantial resources and the subscriptions are obtained at academic discounts that are not available to chambers or commercial law libraries. This means few chambers can afford a full suite of resources and those that can are likely to confine themselves to a case law database, a full text legislative service, and perhaps a suite of online resources for a 'practice area' (such as an employment law service). The Inn libraries will subscribe to rather more but remember that their passwords are not available in chambers, making a trip to the library necessary and your research dependent on the availability of PCs.

At law school, your choice between printed and electronic resources (and most likely that of your tutors) will probably have been governed by personal preference and their easy availability and apparent ease of use. As a pupil barrister, your use of these online resources is likely to be governed by a wider variety of factors:

- the availability of PC facilities at the library and in court;
- technical hazards of passwords and online access at the time you need it;
- the availability of online subscriptions and the particular database content subscribed to;

- your own skills in searching databases—for example, you can't afford to miss cases through poor searching or fail to update legislation; and

- time—if *Current Law* is easily to hand, why log on to update a case?

4.1.2   Availability of legal materials

It is highly unlikely then, that you will have all the resources you need for legal research either literally at your fingertips via an online subscription or easily to hand in your chambers' library. An essential part of legal research is knowing where legal materials are held, planning your use of these resources, and preparing to research. A new pupil barrister will need to be able to:

- identify the resources that will be required before starting the research;

- plan library visits and use of online facilities and passwords;

- know what resources are available and where to find them; and

- know how to use them and deal with issues that arise (or know how to find out or when to ask).

These skills become much more important in chambers when you need to complete your legal research quickly and effectively. This chapter will introduce the key printed resources that are available and provide some guidance on how to use them.

4.1.3   Types of legal materials

The principal resources for practitioners' legal research can be classified into 'primary' and 'secondary' materials. Primary sources are 'the law' itself—legislation and case law precedent that form the raw materials a barrister calls upon to argue his case:

- statutes detail the law as passed by Parliament—either in its original form or as amended by later legislation; and

- law reports provide detailed analysis of individual cases.

Secondary sources cannot be relied upon in court as a statement of 'the law', but they do offer opinion and interpretation of the law:

- legal encyclopaedias such as *Halsbury's Laws*, *Current Law*, etc., are excellent and authoritative tools and a good starting point for legal research;

- practitioner texts and loose-leaf works (or their electronic equivalents) provide more in-depth coverage of the law and it is these texts that form the 'meat' of the practitioners' legal resources;

- journals offer discussion and analysis of the law and serve to inform and keep the barrister up to date—recent case law, legislation coming into force, and legal practice in general, or in specific subject areas; and

- legal dictionaries such as *Stroud's Judicial Dictionary* or *Words and Phrases Legally Defined* combine statutory and case law definitions of words in one reference work—a quick shortcut in legal research.

Most law libraries will take a mixture of these materials, allowing access to all types of material electronically or in print. Smaller collections may offer access to a limited range of secondary sources in hard copy while providing access to primary sources only in electronic format.

4.1.4 Exercises

Familiarity with the printed and online legal resources and the efficiency with which you use them, are skills that are acquired through practice and experience, not just by reading about them. A few exercises are included throughout this chapter to help you practice; doing these will help you tackle the longer research problem set out in **Chapter 8**.

4.2 Secondary sources of law

As secondary sources often contain highly regarded expert opinion and interpretation of the law (and some leading texts are occasionally quoted in court), this makes them a useful starting point for legal research—why start trying to interpret the 'raw data' of legislation and case law when someone more expert has already done the work for you in a practitioner text or in a legal encyclopaedia such as *Halsbury's Laws*? If on starting to research your legal problem, you are sure of the area of law involved and have some knowledge of it, then it makes sense to go straight to a legal encyclopaedia or to the appropriate practitioners' textbook. Commentary from a secondary source can provide:

- an overview of an area of law and contextual information;
- a summary of legal principles;
- definitions of terms;
- commentary on specific points of the law; and
- footnotes leading you to relevant case law and legislation.

4.3 Practitioners' textbooks

Student textbooks such as *Street on Torts* or the popular *Nutshells* series are excellent guides to the law but they are rarely used in legal practice. The *Practical Approach to . . .* series and the more substantial and well-regarded academic textbooks such as *Treital on Contract*, are of more value to practitioners researching the law but they are rarely authoritative enough to cite in court. The most useful texts are the more heavy weight (and expensive) legal tomes written by judges, barristers, and solicitors, for the profession—titles such as *Chitty on Contract*, *Clerk & Lindsell on Torts*, *Archbold's Criminal Pleadings*, and *McGregor on Damages* are used on an almost daily basis in chambers and in court.

Practitioners' texts in law are nearly always known by their author's names and for long-established titles running to many new editions, the original author's name has become part of the title even where the author or editor has changed. Many practitioners' texts run to several volumes (*Stone's Justices' Manual* or *Rayden and Jackson on Divorce and Family Matters*, for example), while others, such as *Kemp & Kemp: Quantum of Damages*, come in a multi-volume, loose-leaf format and are updated with the issue of new sets of pages, several times a year. A complete list of practitioners' textbooks by subject area is at **Appendix 1**. If you know the area of law you wish to consult, then this listing will lead you to the most authoritative texts.

4.3.1 Using a practitioners' textbook

The layout of a practitioners' text differs to that of an ordinary student textbook. Their large size, complex layout, and specialist legal language proves daunting to most lay readers and can make them difficult to navigate even for those more experienced in their use. Spending some time with the text to learn how it works can avoid frustration and hours of wasted research. A few tips and techniques will help to ensure you make more effective use of them:

1. Ensure that you have all the volumes in a multi-volume work—including any supplements (see **4.3.2**); the contents or index may refer you to a volume you don't have to hand.

2. Start by using the general table of contents to find your broad subject headings. Tables of contents are particularly useful when you have broad terms for a less familiar area of law and need some context first before researching more specific issues.

3. Look up your chosen keywords in the index. You are more likely to find references to specific issues through the index than by browsing the table of contents. You could also make use of the tables of statutes and cases which again pinpoint specific issues within a text.

4. Be aware that there may be more than one index. *Halsbury's Laws* boasts three volumes of index, the last of which includes an additional index of legal definitions of words and phrases. *Stone's Justices' Manual* has a separate index to each of its four volumes, while encyclopaedic loose-leaf works often have separate supplementary indexes.

5. References in contents and indexes are to paragraph numbers not pages; paragraph numbers are generally quoted in square brackets [ ] when you are taking notes.

6. Avoid reading large sections of text—the textbooks are laid out in short, titled paragraphs to facilitate browsing to the part you need. You should be able to scan to the most relevant part.

7. Read the footnotes carefully; useful commentary on case law and legislation is referred to here.

8. Follow cross-references and after finding what you need always check back to the index for further references to your keywords.

9. Update your findings *before* moving on to another source (see **4.3.2**)—you'll only forget and have to return to the library to do the research again.

10. Can't find what you need within the leading practitioner text on the subject?

    - Use different keywords, perhaps broader or more specific terms.
    - Try a different angle. If you know a relevant case, look for it in the table of cases; if you know the statute, look for it in the table of statutes.
    - No textbook is comprehensive and it may simply not cover the point you need (or that point may not exist)—try another text with the same keywords.

4.3.2 Updating a practitioners' textbook

Books are out of date as soon as they are printed and most practitioner texts are not published annually. Always use the latest edition of any printed text and check to see if it has itself been updated by another publication. Publishers update their texts using a combination of one or more of the following:

- cumulative supplements: hardback volumes for legal encyclopaedias such as *Halsbury's Laws, Atkin's Court Forms,* etc.; paperback supplements for practitioner works (e.g., first supplement to *McGregor on Damages,* fourth supplement to *Stroud's Judicial Dictionary,* etc);
- loose-leaf noter-ups: loose sheets housed in a separate hardback binder (e.g., *Halsbury's Laws*);
- loose bulletins, inserts or newsletters (e.g., *Wilkinson's Road Traffic Bulletin*); and
- online updates and companion websites using an internet service. A relatively recent means of updating but it may become more common in the future (e.g., *Blackstone's Criminal Practice* companion website).

It is also important to know whether the law within the printed text is up to date. Consider the following:

- new editions and/or supplements: check for a statement 'the law is as stated at . . . [date]' or 'up to date to . . . [date]', usually located at the end of the preface or shortly after the title page;
- loose-leaf noter-up: look at loose-leaf issue numbers and dates printed on each individual page and check the filing record located at the front or rear of the first or last volumes in the set; and
- online updates: look for a statement when you log on to the publisher's web page.

Note that if the commentary within the practitioners' text or its update refers to legislation or case law, you may need to bring those authorities more up to date using an electronic database or another printed source.

4.3.3 Electronic versions of practitioners' texts

Some of the leading legal practitioner works are available online in full text—for example, *Clerk & Lindsell on Torts* on *Westlaw* or *Halsbury's Laws* on *LexisNexis*. These rarely offer many advantages over their printed equivalents, especially for the pupil barrister unfamiliar with the language and layout of the texts. Normally, the electronic publishers have simply transferred the practitioners' text online and only occasionally do they try to provide more sophisticated means for the text to be searched and viewed. In short, if a practitioner's work is available in printed form, then you will generally find this quicker and easier to use than its online equivalent. You should also be aware that not all electronic services are updated as frequently as you might think; just because a text is online does not mean it is any more up to date than its printed equivalent. The merits and pitfalls of using and updating electronic resources are dealt with in more detail in **Chapter 5.**

EXERCISE 3   USING PRACTITIONER TEXTS

Archbold's, Criminal Pleading Evidence or Practice

1. What is the maximum penalty on indictment, in years, for taking indecent photographs of children? How many categories of material are there?
2. What is the maximum sentence on indictment for having a knife in a public place?

Stone's Justices' Manual or Blackstone's Criminal Practice

3. Does the fact that disqualification of a driver would make his disabled wife's life unbearable amount to 'special reasons'?
4. How many points may be endorsed on a driving licence for the offence of driving without insurance?

Clerk & Lindsell on Torts

5. Is a claim against a fast-food restaurant, claiming that it broke its common duty of care under the Occupiers' Liability Act 1957, by serving tea and coffee piping hot, likely to succeed?
6. Is it contributory negligence if a coach passenger injured in an accident failed to wear a seat belt?

Chitty on Contracts

7. Can mistakes in the grammar of a contract be disregarded if the intended sense is clear from the surrounding text? Are there any recent cases on this subject?

Kemp & Kemp: The Quantum of Damages

8. Find the details of a case of unwanted pregnancy following failed sterilisation. What was the award in this case and for what specific reasons were the damages awarded?

4.4   Legal encyclopaedias

A multi-volume work such as *Halsbury's Laws*, *Halsbury's Statutes* or *Atkins' Court Forms* is often described as a legal encyclopaedia. A full listing of legal encyclopaedias is provided in **Appendix 1**. Here, we are concerned with the leading encyclopaedic secondary source, *Halsbury's Laws*, which serves as an excellent starting point for nearly all areas of legal research.

Halsbury's Laws is the definitive encyclopaedic treatise on the law of England and Wales. The law is arranged by subject across more than fifty volumes. Not only is the encyclopaedia very comprehensive, covering every area of law currently in force, but each subject is also written by a leading expert in the field. Some subjects (such as employment law or crime) are covered in less detail than dedicated practitioner texts but other subjects seldom encountered (such as ecclesiastical law) receive an in-depth treatment that would not be found in a regular textbook. The encyclopaedia as a whole receives monthly updates and is available in full text electronically via the *LexisNexis* service.

Halsbury's Laws is particularly useful for those starting out in legal research simply because it is so comprehensive. Explore one point of law that you need and you will invariably find a reference to another area of law that you hadn't thought of. The index is similarly thorough; look up one keyword in the index and it will guide you to other keywords and concepts you hadn't thought of. The printed index is an excellent companion to lateral thinking and keyword analysis (see **3.3.2**), but be warned that this cannot be replicated on the electronic version of the text. The index is not yet available online and you'll need to rely on your own ability to think of keywords to input.

4.4.1   Using and updating legal encyclopaedias

Most legal encyclopaedias follow a similar format, so learning how to use *Halsbury's Laws* will help you to use the other encyclopaedias more effectively. Updating the work is crucial as individual volumes are published infrequently and are often many years out of date. Yet legal encyclopaedias are amongst the most up-to-date commentaries available to the practitioner by virtue of a system of updating that combines the use of:

- *cumulative supplements:* hardback volumes issued annually, providing cumulative updates to the text of the main volumes (e.g., *Halsbury's Laws*) or paperback supplements (e.g., *Current Law Monthly Digest*); and
- *loose-leaf noter-ups:* loose sheets housed in a separate hardback binder issued monthly (or sometimes quarterly), providing updates to the text of the cumulative supplements.

The electronic versions of printed encyclopaedias have the advantage here, in that updates are either included within the text online (*Atkins' Court Forms*) or just underneath, or linked from, the text of the main paragraph (*Halsbury's Laws*). Note, however, that the online text is no more up to date than its printed equivalent; if you are updating using the printed *Halsbury's Laws*, there is no need to go online to view the electronic version for updates.

4.4.1.1 How to use *Halsbury's Laws*

Halsbury's Laws is an authoritative and comprehensive statement of the law of England and Wales, annotated with references to legislation, case law, judicial interpretation, and other works. Quick and easy to use, *Halsbury's Laws* offers convenient access to expert commentary on any area of law. It is available online via *LexisNexis*.

Volume	Arrangement	Frequency
1–52	The law is divided into subject areas defined by a *title*. Titles appear on the spine and the volumes are arranged alphabetically by title.	Irregular
53	Consolidated Tables . . . legislation, practice directions & European materials	Annual
54	Consolidated Table of Cases	Annual
55–57	Consolidated Index. An index of *words & phrases* appears to rear of vol. 57	Annual
	Cumulative Supplement Parts 1 and 2 – updates the law in volumes 1–52.	Annual
Current Service	Vol. 1 – *Noter-up* service notes developments in the law since publication of the Cumulative Supplement. Vol. 2 – *Halsbury's Laws Monthly Review*, a monthly digest of recent legal developments.	Monthly

4.4.1.1.1 *How do I use* Halsbury's Laws?

- Choose keywords that define the problem you wish to research and look them up in the **Consolidated Index.** All references lead you to a volume number (in bold) and a paragraph number.
- Occasionally using the indexes may lead you to an incorrect paragraph number because the main volume has been reissued since the **Index** or **Tables** were published. Where this occurs, check the reissued volume's own index or list of contents for the correct paragraph number.

4.4.1.1.2 *How do I update* Halsbury's Laws?

- Note down the volume number and paragraph number you are updating. Look them up in the hardback **Cumulative Supplement** and then in the loose-leaf **Noter-Up**. Volume numbers appear across the top of the page, page numbers down the side. Always check both cumulative supplement and noter-up, as there may be changes in both: one does not supersede the other.
- You might also check the index to the *Monthly Reviews* (to the rear of the **Current Service** binder) for summaries of relevant cases or legislation. The references lead you to the paragraph of the relevant monthly review.

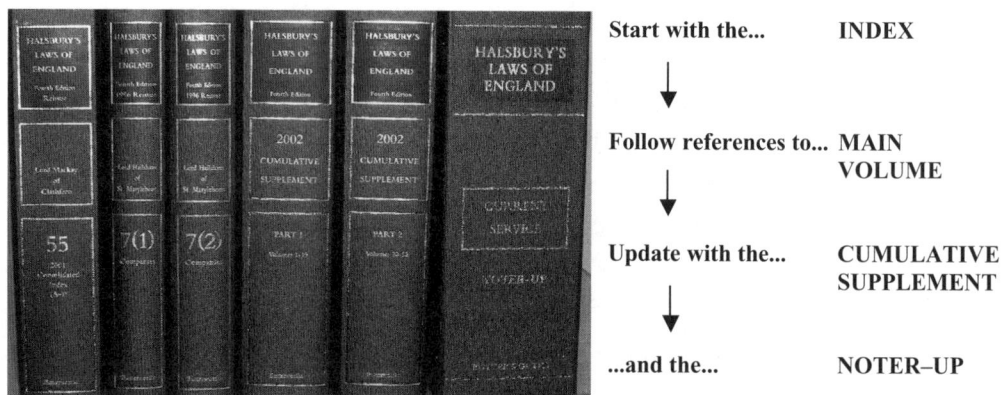

Figure 4.1 Correct sequence for using *Halsbury's Laws*.

4.5 Legal journals

Legal journals offer discussion and analysis of the law and keep the practising lawyer up to date with developments in the legal world. The three legal weeklies, *New Law Journal*, *Solicitors' Journal*, and *Law Gazette*, for example, serve to inform the practising lawyer of recent case law, legislation coming into force, and legal news and practice in general. Long-established titles such as *Modern Law Review* or *Law Quarterly Review* offer more academic in-depth analysis of the law. More specialist titles (*Criminal Law Review*) offer substantial analytical articles or come as newsletters (*Corporate Law Update; Company Law Newsletter*), covering particular practice areas or aspects of the law. Some newsletters (*Archbold News, Kemp News*) 'update' practitioner texts of the same title; bulletins in loose-leaf texts serve a similar purpose.

A barrister would very rarely quote articles from legal journals in court but would consult articles that provided in-depth analysis of the law. For legal research purposes, you may have recourse to journal articles for:

- background information for an unusual area of law or legal issue;
- opinion and discussion of new and unreported cases and forthcoming legislation;
- ideas to develop an argument in a case;
- current awareness—to keep up to date with the law; and
- to update specific practitioner texts (*Kemp News*) or areas of law (*Corporate Briefing*).

4.5.1 Finding legal journal articles

There are well over 400 legal journal titles and finding references to articles that are relevant and then finding a library that takes the specific journal (or otherwise getting hold of a copyright-cleared copy) can be difficult, time-consuming, and expensive—in terms of practical legal research, it may not be worth the pursuit. That said, a quick search on a legal journal's database can be very enlightening, revealing articles discussing very recent cases perhaps on the legal issue you're interested in, and alerting you to new legislation; it all serves as useful background information.

4.5.1.1   To find references to articles by subject

- *Lawtel's Articles Index* indexes articles from around fifty leading UK law journals from 1998, providing a short summary of the article with links to relevant case law and legislation.

- *Legal Journals Index* started in 1986 and is a much more comprehensive referencing service. Extensively indexed with abstracts of articles from over 400 UK, Irish, and European journals, it's available via the *Current Legal Information* (*CLI Online*) database and *Westlaw*. (See **Chapter 5**.)

- *Index to Legal Periodicals* is less comprehensive for UK articles but has a more international scope with articles from leading journals in English-speaking jurisdictions. Useful for more historical legal research as it started indexing legal journal articles back in the 1920s.

4.5.1.2   To find references to very recent articles on a particular area of law

- *Halsbury's Laws* Noter-up: the Articles Index lists articles by subject area. Updated monthly and provides a cumulative list. Quick and easy to check what's new in a practice area.

- *Current Law Monthly Digest*: again, a cumulative list of recent articles appearing in leading UK legal journals, published monthly.

- Update services on electronic databases such as *Lawtel* and *Westlaw* alert you by email to recent articles published in a specific area of law.

4.5.1.3   To find the full text of an article for which you now have the reference

- approach your Inn library—they have good journal holdings and are very likely to have it;

- search a full text database such as *Westlaw* or *LexisNexis*. Both services hold the full text of many journals—though often retrospective coverage is poor. They offer the additional facility of being able to search for very specific items (company names, for example) throughout the entire journal rather than just the title of the article;

- contact your database provider—chambers subscribing to *Lawtel* or *Legal Journals Index* can often obtain copies of articles electronically or by fax through their subscription; and

- make use of a document delivery service such as the *DocDel* service from *Sweet & Maxwell*, or those provided by the *Institute of Advanced Legal Studies* or *The Law Society* (for solicitors).

4.5.1.4   To find leading journals on a particular area of law

- key journals in specific practice areas are listed under subject headings in **Appendix 1**.

EXERCISE 4   LEGAL JOURNALS

1.   Find a journal article which discusses a case in which the court was asked to consider the scope of the exemption the driver of a police car has when driving dangerously at high speed.

2. Find an article in 1988 about pupillage in chambers being more like unpaid labour than education.
3. Find the most recent article you can on: (a) Romalpa clauses; (b) lawyer–client confidentiality; and (c) the reform of the Bar Vocational Course.

4.6 Judicial dictionaries

Legal definitions (i.e., the meanings of words in statutes and statutory instruments and how they have been interpreted in case law) form a significant element of legal research. Legal dictionaries such as *Stroud's Judicial Dictionary* or *Words and Phrases Legally Defined* combine statutory and case law definitions of words in one reference work which forms a quick short cut in legal research. Researching words and phrases is studied in greater detail at **Chapter 6**.

4.7 Forms and precedents

Court forms and precedents of contracts, etc., are generally required for very specific procedural purposes. The two leading encyclopaedic sources are *Atkin's Court Forms* and the *Encyclopaedia of Forms and Precedents*. Both sets run to more then forty volumes apiece, with indices and form-finding aids to provide easy access by keyword and a loose-leaf updating service. The commentary that accompanies both forms and precedents is itself an unrivalled source of procedural law. Both are available online via *LexisNexis*.

Many court forms are also available on the HM Court Service website (see **5.4.3**) and precedents can be found in the appendices of practitioner texts or in dedicated loose-leaf texts such as *Butterworths Civil Court Precedents*. You should, however, be aware that they will need updating.

4.8 Primary sources of law

Secondary sources provide commentary and expert legal opinion but are only a route to the primary sources. Having exhausted the secondary sources, the researcher should have a list of primary sources to peruse—legislative enactments to analyse and interpret and cases to read and update. Occasionally, a researcher may approach the primary sources directly but to do so without a confident knowledge of the area of law would be to run the risk of missing essential statutes, statutory instruments or cases.

While secondary sources are generally easier to approach in their printed form, the opposite is the case for primary sources. Databases are more suited to finding legislative data and case law quickly and easily, and provided the researcher updates the material he or she finds carefully, it is also usually slightly more up to date than equivalent printed sources.

4.9 Primary legislation: Public General Acts ('statutes')

Confusingly, legislation in the UK also uses the terms, 'primary' and 'secondary'. Primary legislation denotes Acts (or 'statutes') passed by Parliament while secondary legislation is delegated—legislation made by government departments, agencies, local authorities, and other public bodies on behalf of Parliament and by the explicit authority of a specific Act.

Within these two general types there are other forms of enactment. Primary legislation includes Public General Acts, Local Acts, Personal Acts, Private Acts, and Church Measures, while secondary legislation includes Statutory Instruments, rules, and by-laws. Usually, the legal researcher will only be concerned with Public General Acts and Statutory Instruments; encounters with the other types are somewhat rarer and will not be dealt with here. **Table 4.1** introduces the principal resources available in the law library to the researcher tracing statutes and statutory instruments.

4.9.1 Finding statutes

In researching statute law, a barrister would need to distinguish between:

- The 'original' version of a statute—the form of wording used when the statute was passed by Parliament and received Royal Assent. It is this 'Queen Printers' version of an Act of Parliament which the barrister would need to cite and quote from in court.

- The 'amended' (or 'consolidated') version of a statute—the wording of a statute after the text from subsequent amendments, revocations, and repeals has been included. The consolidated version of a statute is far more useful than the original version, to a barrister who needs to say what the law is, at the time s/he drafts an opinion or takes a case to court.

- 'Annotated' statutes—the original and/or amended version of a statute with additional commentary by legal editors on, for example, the legislative background to an Act, references to cases or regulations, and guidance on the interpretation of individual sections of the statute. This form of statute is of particular use to the barrister interpreting a statute and exploring the meaning of particular words and phrases. See **Chapter 6** for more details regarding researching words and phrases.

Modern statutes are denoted by a short title and calendar year (e.g., the Theft Act 1968) and a 'chapter' number (e.g., 1968 c 60). The short title and/or chapter number are key to finding the full text of a statute. This form of citation is used in tables of contents within practitioner texts, in alphabetical and chronological listings of statutes within collections such as *Halsbury's Statutes* and *Current Law Statutes* and in online sources of legislation such as *Westlaw* and *LexisNexis*. If you're not sure of the short title, calendar year or chapter number, then you will need to approach the legislation by subject. While this can be done through most of the printed and electronic resources listed in this chapter, it may be quicker and easier to return to the practitioner texts or a legal encyclopaedia such as *Halsbury's Laws* to find more specific references to the legislation you might need, or indeed to find the legislation itself. For example, *Harvey's on Industrial Relations and Employment Law* provides ready access to most of the relevant employment statutes.

Table 4.1 Resources for finding legislation

Legislative service	Description and notes on use . . .
Current Law Statutes, Sweet & Maxwell. Includes: – *Statutes Annotated* – *Legislation Citator* – *Current Law Service*	Printed reference work with the full text of all statutes from 1947 in their original form, including repealed statutes. Extensive annotations and detailed notes to assist with interpretation. Allows for more detailed historical legislative research. Accompanied by tables of legislative amendments in the form of a *Statute Citator 1947*– and an *SI Citator 1993*– ; updated by *Current Law Statutes* loose-leaf service.
Halsbury's Statutes of England and Wales, 4th edn. LexisNexis.	Printed reference work for finding all statutes as amended and currently in force in England and Wales. Statutes are annotated with brief notes and details of commencement, repeals, amendments, etc. Updated by reissued volumes, cumulative supplement, and loose-leaf service. Separate *Statutes Citator* and *Is it in Force?*
Halsbury's Statutory Instruments. LexisNexis.	Printed reference work for finding all statutory instruments from 1951, currently in force in England and Wales. Editors select SIs for fuller treatment providing summaries of some and the full text of only a very few. Fully annotated. Updated by monthly loose-leaf *Noter-up* service.
Justis UK Statutes *Justis UK SIs*	Online subscription service or CD-ROM database containing the original, full text version of all statutes from 1235 with notes of repeals. Statutory instruments from 1671 on a separate database.
Lawtel UK	Online subscription service containing the original full text version of statutes (1984–) and SIs (1988–) with a linked *Statutory Status* table of legislative amendments and an *Index of Amended Legislation*.
LexisNexis, Legislation	Online subscription service containing amended versions of all statutes (1236–) and SIs (1950–) currently in force throughout the UK. Includes some annotations from *Halsbury's Statutes*.
Office for Public Sector Information (OPSI) <http://www.opsi.gov.uk/legislation>	Free website service. Acts from 1988 in original and revised form; revised texts taken from *UK Statute Law Database*. Selected earlier Acts from 1837–1988.
Practitioner texts	Legislation is often reproduced in full text in: – practitioner texts (*Family Court Practice*) – loose-leaf works (*Palmers' Company Law*) – handbooks (*Paterson's Licensing Acts*)
UK Statute Law Database <http://www.statutelaw.gov.uk>	Free website service. "The official revised edition of the primary legislation of the UK" —statutes from 1267 revised fully to 2001 but with some gaps thereafter; mostly up to date, visible warnings for parts that are not. SIs from 1991 but these are not amended.
Westlaw, Legislation	Online database containing amended versions of all statutes (1267–) and SIs (1948–) currently in force throughout the UK. Use the *Advanced Search* facility to find historical versions of statutes in the form in which they were in force at a particular date.

4.9.2 Updating statutes

The distinction between the law as originally passed and the law as amended and currently in force (including statutes that have not yet been brought into force and those that have been repealed) is fundamental to practical legal research. It poses three distinct questions:

- Has the statute come into force?
- Is the statute still in force?
- Was the statute in force at a particular point in time?

These questions can most easily be answered by searching a legislative database. Essentially, we are looking for details of commencement, repeal, and other amendments by subsequent legislation. *Westlaw* and *LexisNexis* provide consolidated, full-text versions of all UK legislation currently in force (including prospective commencements and repeals). Search for the statute by its short title and you will obtain the full text of the statute, as amended by later legislation (details of the amending statutes are provided) and including notes on dates of commencement and, if it is no longer in force, the date of its repeal. These notes are contained within the text of individual sections of the statute, however, so it would be a laborious process to check several sections and a table of legislative amendments such as that provided on *Lawtel*, might prove more useful.

A quick reference, printed source for this type of query is the *Is it in Force?* volume of *Halsbury's Statutes*, updated with an *Is it in Force?* section within the loose-leaf *Noter-up*. If there is no commencement information then it would be wise to check online. If you are using printed sources to update, you also need to check the citation of any statute that is repealing the Act under consideration—the repealing statute may not have been brought into force or may itself have been repealed.

4.9.3 How to use *Halsbury's Statutes*

Halsbury's Statutes contains an up-to-date version of the amended text of every statute currently in force in England and Wales. Each statute is annotated with amending and subordinate legislation, commentary, judicial interpretation, relevant leading case law, and other useful cross-references. As such, it is a leading source for tracing and interpreting legislation; there is no equivalent online source for the annotations.

4.9.3.1 How do I use *Halsbury's Statutes*?

- All references lead you to a volume number (in bold) and a page number in that volume. Where (S) is indicated after a bold volume number this refers to the **Current Statutes Service** binder.

To find a statute when you know . . .	Use the volume entitled . . .	Look up the . . .
. . . the title	Consolidated index	Alphabetical list of statutes
. . . the subject area	Consolidated index	Volume index (i.e., list of titles, to the front)
		OR use the word index
. . . its chapter no.	Consolidated index	Chronological list of statutes
. . . its very recent	Current Statutes Service Binder A	Contents section:
		Alphabetical, chronological, and subject lists

Table 4.2 **How to research a statute**

Looking for . . .	Electronic services	Printed resources
The full text of a statute . . .		
The **original** version of a full text statute as enacted by Parliament	*Justis UK Statutes* *Lawtel* *OPSI* *UK Statute Law Database*	Queen Printers copy bound in: *Law Reports Statutes* *Public General Acts* *Statutes at Large* *Statutes of the Realm*
An **amended** version of a full text statute currently in force	*LexisNexis Legislation* *UK Statute Law Database* *Westlaw Legislation*	*Halsbury's Statutes* *Current Law Statutes Annotated*
Annotated statutes	Very limited annotations on: *LexisNexis Legislation* *UK Statute Law Database* *Westlaw Legislation*	*Halsbury's Statutes* *Current Law Statutes Annotated*
Alphabetical or chronological index to the statutes	Most online services provide the facility to browse an alphabetical or chronological list of statutes.	*Chronological Index to the Statutes 1235–1990* *Current Law Statutes Service* *Halsbury's Statutes*
Subject index to the statutes	All online services can be searched by keyword. See **Chapter 5** for further details.	*Chronological Index to the Statutes 1235–1990* *Halsbury's Statutes*
Repealed statutes in full text, possibly as amended by later enactments up to a particular date, but no longer in force	*Justis UK Statutes* *UK Statute Law Database* *Westlaw Legislation—use* Advanced Search for historical versions of statutes.	*Current Law Statutes Annotated* *Halsbury's Statutes—*use old editions for earlier statutes. *Law Reports Statutes* *Public General Acts* *Statutes at Large* *Statutes of the Realm*
A very **recent statute**	*LexisNexis Legislation* *OPSI* *UK Statute Law Database* *Westlaw Legislation*	*Current Law Monthly Digest* *Current Law Service* *Halsbury's Statutes Current Service* volumes A–D + *Noter-up*
Updating information . . .		
Commencement dates for statutes and sections of statutes including **forthcoming** dates – *Is the statute in force?* – *Has the statute come into force?*	*LexisNexis Legislation* *UK Statute Law Database* *Westlaw Legislation*	*Current Law Monthly Digest* *Current Law Statutes Citator* *Halsbury's Laws Noter-up* *Halsbury's Statutes—Is it in Force? + Noter-up*
Tables of amendments within an alphabetical or chronological **index** to statutes	*UK Statute Law Database* *Lawtel—Statutory Status* table	*Chronological Index to the Statutes 1235–1990* *Current Law Legislation Citator* *Halsbury's Statutes Citator*
Cases under a section of a statute	*Lawtel* *LexisNexis Legislation* *Westlaw Legislation*	*Current Law Statutes Citator* *Halsbury's Statutes*

- If the statute is not listed, the title or date of the statute may be incorrect, the statute may have been repealed or not yet brought into force. *Halsbury's Statutes* only contains legislation currently in force. Check its status in *Halsbury's Statutes Citator* or *Is it in Force?*

4.9.3.2   How do I update *Halsbury's Statutes*?

- Note down the volume number and page reference of the statute you are updating. Look them up in the hardback **Cumulative Supplement** and then in the loose-leaf **Noter-up**. Volume numbers appear across the top of the page, page numbers down the side. Always check both supplement and noter-up, as there may be changes in both: one does not supersede the other.

- In both the **Cumulative Supplement** and the **Noter-up**, the update for a particular volume in the **Current Statutes Service** will follow the update for the main volume of the same name (e.g., the update to *Volume 12 (S) Criminal Law* immediately follows the update to *Volume 12 (1997 reissue)*.

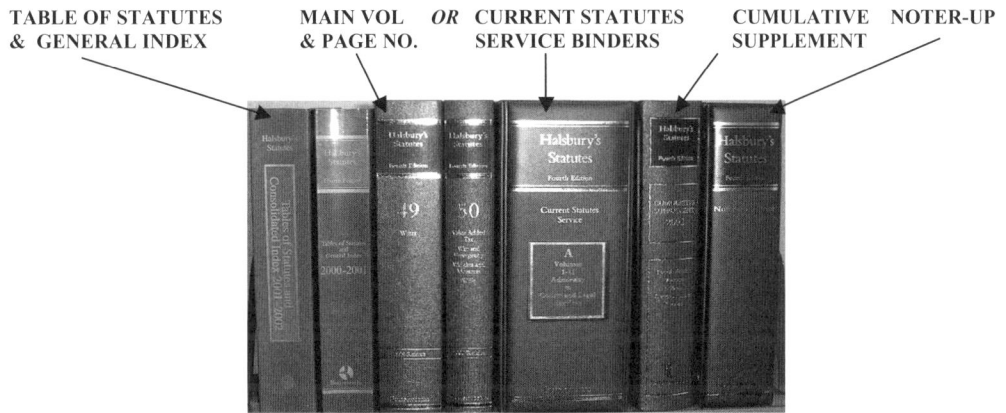

TABLE OF STATUTES   MAIN VOL   *OR* CURRENT STATUTES   CUMULATIVE   NOTER-UP
& GENERAL INDEX   & PAGE NO.   SERVICE BINDERS   SUPPLEMENT

Figure 4.2   Corrrect sequence for using *Halsbury's Statutes*.

4.9.4   How to use *Current Law Statutes*

Current Law is a comprehensive legal information service covering all case and statutory developments from 1947 to date.

Volume	Arrangement . . .
Current Law Legislation Citator: Statute Citator	Notes up statutes dating back to 1235. Amendments, cases, and subordinate legislation under an Act are listed from 1947. Arranged chronologically in chapter order and are published in the following sequence of volumes: 1947–1971; 1972–1988; 1989–1995; 1995–1999; 2000–2001; 2002–2004
*Current Law Statutes Annotated	Each bound volume incorporates the Public General Acts for the year in chronological order and by chapter and with annotations and commentary. This part of the service is published annually.
Current Law Statutes: Service Files	Volumes 1 and 2 update changes to the Public Acts since publication of the last bound volume and are updated monthly.

* Current Law Statutes since 1994.

Table 4.3 explains how to use Current Law Statutes.

Table 4.3 **How to use Current Law Statutes**

To find . . .	Use the . . .
A statute where the name and date of the statute are known . . .	**Current Law Statutes** volume for the year; then update using the **Current Law Legislation Citator** for each subsequent year; then check the **Current Law Statutes Service file** for any recent changes.
Amendments to sections of a statute or the date an Act came into force . . .	**Current Law Legislation Citator** for the year of the Act and for each subsequent year then update with the relevant section of the **Current Law Statutes Service file**.
Commencement orders and statutory instruments . . .	
Cases brought under a section of an Act . . .	**Current Law Legislation Citator** for the year of the Act and for each subsequent year then update the case using the cumulative table of cases in the most recent **Current Law Monthly Digest**.

EXERCISE 5   STATUTES

1. What are the short titles of the following statutes?
    (a)   21 Geo 3 c 49
    (b)   1997 c 55
2. What is the heading to Part VIII of the Law of Property Act 1925?
3. Are the following statutes currently in force?
    (a)   Employment of Children Act 1973
    (b)   Sale of Offices Act 1551
    (c)   Family Law Act 1996
4. Is s.1 of the Perjury Act 1911 still in force? Name 2 cases brought under this section. Does this Act extend to Scotland?
5. Find the text of s.34A and 34B of the Enterprise Act 2002 and update them to find notes of amendments, repeals, etc.
6. What is the punishment prescribed by the Piracy Act 1837, s.2 as amended?

4.10 Secondary legislation: Statutory Instruments

Statutory Instruments (SIs) account for the bulk of secondary legislation in the UK. Over 3,000 SIs are issued by government departments, agencies, and public bodies each year on behalf of Parliament and under the explicit authority of a specific Act of Parliament. SIs serve numerous functions and come in various forms, the most common of which are:

- rules and regulations regarding the technical detail of how a statute operates;
- commencement orders bringing statutes (or individual sections of statutes) into force; and
- regulations bringing European legislative enactments into force.

Of these, rules and regulations are of most use to the practitioner and SIs of this type feature in nearly all areas of law, employment law, landlord and tenant and financial regulation, to name a few. While a statute provides a broad framework outlining what the law should be, an SI provides the technical detail of how that law will operate. Thus, *The Civil Procedures Rules* SI 1998/3132 or *The Management of Health and Safety Regulations* SI 1999/3242 provide rules, regulations, and procedures that must be followed and statutory duties that need to be met.

The importance of SIs should not be overlooked. Relevant SIs should be referred to in advice to a client and may need to be quoted in court. The precise wording of a regulation is often important to a case (for example, for an alleged breach of employment regulations) and unlike statutes, SIs can be challenged as ultra vires, where it is alleged that an SI has outlined the law to an extent or in a form that was not originally intended by the parent Act.

4.10.1   Finding Statutory Instruments

Like statutes, SIs are denoted by a short title, a calendar year, and a unique series number (e.g., *Criminal and Defence Service (Very High Cost Cases) Regulations* 2008/40). Often only the year and the number of the SI are quoted (e.g., SI 2007/3201) but this citation should be sufficient to find the SI in either a printed or an electronic source. On *Westlaw* and *LexisNexis*, the citation can simply be entered into the relevant fields on the search screen. With *Halsbury's Statutory Instruments*, make use of the indices found in the looseleaf volume which will refer you to the SI within a bound volume. Further details on finding SIs are provided in **4.10.2**.

4.10.2   Updating Statutory Instruments

While statutes are only occasionally repealed, SIs are frequently revoked and replaced, or amended. Updating them is crucial to practical legal research and the questions posed regarding statute law (see **4.9.2**)) are just as pertinent for SIs. Again, electronic databases provide the easiest way of accessing the most up-to-date, full-text version of an SI. Search for a citation and you will obtain the full text of the SI, as amended by later SIs and including notes on the date when it came into force and, if it is no longer in force, the date of its revocation. *Justis UK* SIs and *Lawtel* are particularly adept at producing tables of SIs that have been amended or revoked by a subsequent SI. Using *Halsbury's Statutory Instruments,* update using the *Noter-up* section in service volume 1.

EXERCISE 6   STATUTORY INSTRUMENTS

1. What is the correct title and citation of an SI relating to maternity and parental leave issued in 1996?
2. The Football Spectators (Seating) Order affects certain football grounds. To which grounds has it been applied and what requirements does it impose?
3. The Terrorism Act 2000 lists 'proscribed organisations'. When was 'Jundallah' added to the list and how? (i.e., by which statute or statutory instrument).
4 How many statutory instruments were issued in 1996?
5. What is the date of the earliest piece of subordinate legislation that is still in force?
6. When you have contact lenses fitted, to what after-sales service are you legally entitled?
7. Beryl is deaf and has a hearing dog. She gets into a taxi at a rank but when Mick, the driver, sees the dog he refuses to take her. He says he is allergic to dogs and points to a notice inside the cab which he says allows him to refuse. Beryl says he is discriminating against her and will report him. Who is right?
8. Percy applied for a pupillage. His interview with the chambers committee seemed to go well. However, afterwards the clerk in private conversation with Percy let slip that the head of chambers, who is gay, said he 'liked the look of' Clarence, a rival applicant. Clarence, who is gay, got the pupillage. Percy is aggrieved. Has the law anything to say to assist him?

Table 4.4 **How to research a Statutory Instrument**

Looking for . . .	Electronic services	Printed resources
An SI . . . in full text or summary form		
An SI by its **title** or its series number . . . . . .within an **alphabetical** or **chronological** (i.e., numerical) **index** to the SIs	Most online services provide the facility to browse an alphabetical or chronological list of statutes; full text is mostly in original form	*Halsbury's SIs*—vol. 1
An **amended** version of a full text SI currently in force	*LexisNexis Legislation* *Westlaw Legislation*	*Halsbury's SIs*—an edited few are as amended and in full text; others have annotations of amendments
Annotated SIs	Very limited annotations on: *LexisNexis Legislation* *Westlaw Legislation*	Halsbury's SIs—a few are annotated Practitioner text by subject area
Repealed SIs	*Justis UK SIs* OPSI *UK Statute Law Database* *Westlaw Legislation*—use Advanced Search	*Halsbury's SI Citator*
A very **recent SI**	*LexisNexis Legislation* OPSI *UK Statute Law Database* *Westlaw Legislation*	*Current Law Monthly Digest* *Halsbury's Sis,* vol. 1 + Monthly Index to rear of Service volume
A **Subject Index** to the SIs	Inadvisable to search for SIs by subject but all online services can be searched by keyword	Practitioner text by subject area *Halsbury's SIs*—Consolidated Index
An SI **known by a different title** (e.g., Civil Procedures Rules, Insolvency Rules)	Available on most online databases but may be difficult to find	Practitioner text by subject area–likely to include annotations and amendments
Updating information . . .		
Tables of amendments within an alphabetical or chronological **index** to SIs	*Lawtel—Statutory Status table*	*Current Law SI Citator* + Service file update *Halsbury's SI Citator* + Noter-up
To see if Regulations (i.e., SIs) have been **made under a statute** . . .	Look for annotations under a specific section of a statute on: *Lawtel—Statutory Status* table *LexisNexis Legislation* *Westlaw Legislation* *UK Statute Law Database*	*Current Law Monthly Digest Current Law Statutes Citator* + Service file update *Halsbury's Laws Noter-up* *Halsbury's Statutes—Is it in Force?* + *Noter-up*
Cases brought under an SI or specific **SIs considered in cases**	*Lawtel* *LexisNexis Legislation* *Westlaw Legislation*	*Current Law SI Citator* + Service file update *Halsbury's SI Citator* Practitioner text by subject area

4.11   Case law and law reports

The secondary sources invariably lead the researcher to the relevant case law. References to cases relevant to an area of law or a legal issue are to be found in the footnotes of practitioner texts and legal encyclopaedias such as *Halsbury's Laws,* within annotated statutes or as links within the resources of a legal database. Should these materials not provide references to the case law that you are looking for, then it could be that there is no relevant case law or that no cases have dealt with that particular point of law in sufficient depth for it to be deemed fit to be reported. Only around 5 per cent of cases in the UK are actually reported at all. To merit reporting, a case might:

- modify or introduce a new principle of law;
- settle a doubt as to what the law should be; and
- interpret statute or case law precedent in a new way.

This principle is applied to the *Official Series* of law reports (see **4.11.2**) but is not always followed in the commercial series and in fact many cases 'of interest', but which add nothing new to the law, are frequently reported.

Searching for case law with few leads from the secondary sources, selecting relevant cases from a multitude of law reports, reading and interpreting the case, and determining which cases to cite in court can prove very time-consuming. Case law research should not be undertaken lightly. While legislative research is reasonably finite, the corpus of material available for case law means that researching case law is far less so. Before starting your search for relevant cases, plan your research strategically and determine:

- Do you need to search for cases at all? Many cases are determined by their facts, not by precedent.
- Are there any issues which case law might help with? Reported cases deal with points of law and there is no need to quote only loosely comparable cases.
- How much research and more detailed reading of case law are justified by the issue you need to resolve? A case used simply to advise a client, by providing examples of other cases similar in fact or to illustrate a point of law or the current approach of the courts, probably does not warrant extensive research. Cases (or 'authorities') chosen to be quoted in court and to assist the judge, however, should be chosen with great care. (See **4.11.6**.)

4.11.1   Legal citations and abbreviations

4.11.1.1   Printed law reports series

Having found a reference to relevant case law, the abbreviations used to describe the law report series must be deciphered. For unknown abbreviations, refer to the following:

- *Cardiff Index of Legal Abbreviations:* <http://www.legalabbrevs.cardiff.ac.uk>
- Raistrick, *Index to Legal Citations and Abbreviations*
- *Current Law Case Citator*
- *Halsbury's Laws*—Volume 1
- *The Digest*—annual supplement volumes.

Both square and round brackets are used when citing the year of publication and these should be written correctly when citing a case:

- where the year is given in square brackets thus [2001] 1 WLR 270, it is part of the reference and the year operates as a volume number;

- where a date appears in round brackets, it is useful information as to the actual year of the publication, but non-essential because the publishers have given each volume its own number in sequence in the set. For example, (1985) 80 Cr App R 117. This volume-number method is now mainly used for journals.

4.11.1.2 Online subscription services

Many case reports now appear on legal databases well before they appear in the pages of any of the standard series of reports. The use of these electronic sources in court has been officially approved but it calls for a system of 'neutral' citation, not only because citation by series, volume, and page number no longer applies but also because citations have to be uniform and recognisable, whichever medium or provider or publisher has been used for a particular report. So each judgment when transcribed is given a unique case number, with paragraph numbers instead of page numbers. See *Practice Note* [2001] 1 All ER 293, and *Practice Direction* [2002] 1 WLR 346.

The following citations are used:

- UKHL   House of Lords
- UKPC   Judicial Committee of the Privy Council
- EWCA Civ   Court of Appeal Civil Division
- EWCA Crim   Court of Appeal Criminal Division
- EWHC Admin   High Court Administrative Court
- EWHC   High Court

For example, *White v White* [2001] EWCA Civ 955 [1] indicates case number 955 in the Court of Appeal, first paragraph; *Lewisham LBC v Hall* [2002] EWHC Admin 960 [22] is case 960 in the Administrative Court, QBD, at paragraph 22.

4.11.1.3 Practice Directions

Practice Directions (also known as Practice Notes or Practice Statements) are not case reports but they are reported as such in law reports. As their title suggest, they give essential guidance on practice demanded by the court that must be followed. Numerous and often difficult to find, they are also subject to change and can be overruled or partially amended (for example, the 2001 Practice Direction mentioned here has been amended in part).

4.11.2 Law reports

Today, an extensive range of law reports are available to the practitioner:

1. *The Law Reports* (known as the *Official Series*) from 1865, are preferred as the 'senior' series of law reports checked by judges before publication and usually including a summary of counsels' argument, in addition to head notes, facts, and the judgment itself. Today, they comprise just four series (*Appeal Cases, Chancery, Queens Bench* and *Family*) out of the original set and are accompanied by cumulative ten-year and latest-year 'Pink and Red' indices. The entire series is available online in full text via *Justis, LexisNexis*, and *Westlaw*. (For a full list of titles in *The Law Reports*, see **Appendix 1**.)

2. *Weekly Law Reports* are the 'junior' official series, published since 1953, within a month or so of a case having been decided. The entire series is available online in full text via *Justis*, *LexisNexis*, and *Westlaw*.

3. *All England Law Reports* from 1936 are a well-established commercial series and regarded as comparable in all respects to the *Weekly Law Reports*. Available online in full text via *LexisNexis*.

4. Specialist series of subject-based law reports have proliferated in recent years. Some, such as *Lloyds Law Reports* are very well-established and authoritative series; others, such as *Road Traffic Reports* are a little younger but very highly regarded. More recent creations such as *European Human Rights Reports* or *Business Law Reports* appear when specific issues become of more concern in the legal world; some survive, some don't. Many of these are available online via their respective publishers' legal databases. Thus, *Westlaw* makes its own *Road Traffic Reports* available but the researcher will need to subscribe to *LexisNexis* for access to the *Times Law Reports*. Law reports are listed by subject in **Appendix 1**.

5. Legal journals very often carry law reports either as brief summaries (*New Law Journal, Solicitors Journal*) or in more detailed reports that don't appear elsewhere (*Estates Gazette*). This is particularly useful as a source for very recent case law. The full text of many journals, including the law reports, are available online either free (*Law Gazette*) or via a fee-based legal database (*New Law Journal*) on the same basis as law reports.

6. Newspaper law reports are the most current form of law report and appear a few days after the case. The *Times Law Reports* are perhaps the most well-regarded series and the newspaper has been publishing law reports since 1884. Available online as part of *The Times* newspaper via *LexisNexis*.

7. Older reports are still valuable for legal research and are surprisingly well used:

   • *Nominate reports*. Until *The Law Reports* were established in 1865, law reporting was left to individual judges and barristers whose names came to be applied to published collections of cases spanning 350 years of law reporting. Recognised by their names and initials, these individual volumes are still available in older law libraries.

   • *English Reports (ER)*. In 1865, the nominate reports were collected into 176 volumes and reprinted as the *English Reports* with a two-volume index at the end of the sequence. This lists cases by name, citing the original reporters' name and the volume and page number. Available electronically via *Justis* and HEIN online.

   • *Continuous Series*. Several journals in the nineteenth century included regular law reports and these were bound into volumes of cases: *Law Journal Reports (LJ), Law Times Reports (LT),* and *Times Law Reports (TLR)*.

   • *Year Books*. The oldest anonymous law reports from 1235 to 1535. Summarised at <http://www.bu.edu/law/seipp>

4.11.3 Finding case law

In researching case law for practical legal research, the barrister is likely to be looking for cases:

• in the same area of law;

• with similar facts and circumstances;

- covering one or more specific points of law;
- issues arising out a point of law; and
- analysis and reasoning to assist in developing an argument.

In doing so, he or she is likely to need:

- A summary of the case. By reading a brief abstract of the case first, it is possible to assess how relevant it is to your research. For this reason, always read the 'head notes' to a reported case first; they give a concise account of the legal issues, what was 'held' and any statements on the law.
- A detailed law report for a closer analysis of the legal issues and argument.
- The judicial history of the case, to see where a case has been cited in later cases (see **4.11.4**).

The legal researcher is best served by legal databases for all three aspects. *Westlaw*, for example, provides a summary of the case with links to the full text law report and the judicial history and subsequent citation. *LexisNexis* performs a similar function, though you need to restrict your search to 'head notes' to obtain a summary. *Lawtel* specialises in providing detailed abstracts so it is a particularly useful compromise where the full text of a report is not required.

This, however, does not render the printed sources obsolete. They are particularly useful for quick reference work, especially where you know the parties to the case and need to quickly find an abstract of a case and update it (while waiting in court, for example). Online databases are not always available (again, whilst in court) and there are problems with searching for case law electronically with keywords that are too broad, which can result in having too many cases to trawl through or too few that are actually relevant.

4.11.3.1   Search strategies for researching case law

As a pupil barrister, you may be asked to find all the case law in a particular subject area or more specifically, involving a particular point of law. Practical legal research where time is pressing, requires a systematic approach to researching case law. A few techniques:

1. Start with secondary sources to find references to relevant case law; it is easier to find a case when you know the parties and an approximate date. Following these and updating them will help identify possible legal issues, as well as leading to the other relevant cases.

2. If you need cases defining specific words and phrases then start with a judicial dictionary which will outline all the cases where a particular definition has been considered in court.

3. Select your keywords carefully before searching a case law database, otherwise you are very likely to retrieve too many cases; this is a common problem with searching online services. See **3.3.2** for assistance with identifying keywords and **5.5** for search strategies using legal databases.

4. If you have specific legislation in mind, then search for cases under the relevant section of a statute or an SI, using a citator (see **4.11.4**).

5. Search more than one resource and know the contents of each resource. If your chambers only have a subscription to *LexisNexis*, a search will identify the leading cases on a particular legal issue but it will not be a comprehensive search. *Current Law* is the most comprehensive citator of case law since 1947 in the UK and this is only available on *Westlaw*.

Table 4.5 Resources for finding case law

Case law service	Description and notes on use . . . . . .
BAILII <http://www.bailii.org>	Free website service from the *British and Irish Legal Information Institute* offering access to transcripts of cases from the High Court and Court of Appeal, from 1996.
Casetrack <http://www.casetrack.com>	Online subscription service providing full-text transcripts of judgments from 1996.
Court Service <http://www.courtservice.gov.uk>	Free website service. Database of selected High Court judgments, links to tribunals (many with their own judgments); full text of Practice Directions.
Current Law Cases, Sweet & Maxwell. Includes: – *Current Law Year Books* – *Current Law Monthly Digest*	Printed reference work includes annual printed *Year Book* volumes containing brief digests of UK cases since 1947, taken from over 70 UK law report series. Accompanied by *Case Citators*, listing cases in alphabetical order with notes of where a case has been digested in the *Year Books*, where reported in law reports and where it has been cited in later cases. Updated by cumulative table within latest issue of *Current Law Monthly Digest*. Particularly useful for quick reference work. Available online via *Westlaw Cases*.
Current Legal Information—Cases (CLI Online)	Online subscription service providing abstracts of cases from 1986 onwards. Owned by Sweet & Maxwell and coverage is approximately the same as Lawtel UK.
The Digest.	Printed reference work for finding case British, European, and Commonwealth
LexisNexis.	Selected cases are available online via *LexisNexis Cases*.
JustCite *Justis English Reports, The Law Reports, Times Law Reports*, etc.	Online subscription service or CD-ROM. Separate databases offering access to individual series of law reports (see **4.11.2**). The JUSTCITE service is particularly useful as a searchable archive of cases which notes where they have been reported.
Lawtel UK	Online subscription service providing abstracts of cases from 1980, many with links to full text transcripts. Comprehensive coverage of decisions from HL, CA, PC, and High Court. *Lawtel PI* offers personal injury cases.
LexisNexis, Cases	Online subscription service containing most of the text of *The Digest* and wide coverage of UK, EU case law with links to the full text law reports of earlier and subsequent cases where available. The series of law reports it connects to are largely limited to those published by LexisNexis Butterworths.
Westlaw, Cases	Online subscription service containing the full text of *Current Law Cases*. Wide coverage of UK case law and includes brief digests of UK cases since 1947 with links to the full text law reports of earlier and subsequent cases where available. The series of law reports it connects to are largely limited to those published by Sweet & Maxwell.

Table 4.6 **How to research a Case**

Looking for . . .	Electronic services	Printed resources
A citation for a case where you know the name and/or the year. . .		
Cases **from 1980**	*CLI Online* *Lawtel UK* *LexisNexis Cases* *Westlaw Cases*	*Current Law Case Citator*—use citator for relevant year, or earliest citator if year unknown *The Digest*—Index
A very **old case, pre-1947**	*LexisNexis Cases*	*Current Law Case Citator* 1947– *The Digest*—Table of cases volumes for cases pre-1947
A very **recent case** within the last year	*BAILII* *Lawtel UK* *LexisNexis Cases* *Westlaw Cases*	*Current Law Monthly Digest*—most recent monthly issue *Halsbury's Laws Monthly Review*
Alphabetical or **chronological** table of cases	Most online services provide the facility to browse achronological or alphabetical table of cases	*Current Law Case Citator* *The Digest*—Index Practitioner text by subject area
Subject index to the cases	All online services can be searched by keyword. See **Chapter 5** for further details.	*Halsbury's Laws* *Current Law Year Book* *The Digest*
The full text digest, report, or transcript of a case . . .		
A **digest** or an **abstract** of a case	*CLI Online* *Lawtel UK Cases* *LexisNexis Cases* *Westlaw Cases*	*Current Law Cases* *The Digest*
The **full text law report** of a case	*Justis* (by title) *LexisNexis Cases* *Westlaw Cases*	*Law Reports (Official Series)* *Weekly Law Reports* *All England Law Reports* Individual series, etc.
An **unreported** case or a **transcript** of a case	*BAILII* (1996–) *Casetrack* *CLI Online* *Lawtel UK Cases* (1993–) *LexisNexis Cases* (1980–)	HL, PC, CA (Civ) 1950– CA (Crim) 1989– Other courts—various years *Current Law Year Books* 1973–89 (summaries only)
Updating information . . .		
The **judicial history** of a case	*Lawtel UK Cases* *LexisNexis Cases* *Westlaw Cases*	*Current Law Case Citator* + most recent *Monthly Digest* *The Digest* + Cumulative vol. + Quarterly Supplement
Discussion of a recent case in a journal article or **commentary** on leading cases	*Lawtel UK's Articles Index* *Legal Journals Index*	*Current Law Monthly Digest* *Halsbury's Laws Noter-up*—Articles Index Practitioner text by subject area
Cases brought **under a legislative enactment** (statute or SI)	*Lawtel* *LexisNexis Legislation* *Westlaw Legislation*	*Current Law Legislation Citator* *Halsbury's Statutes*
Cases overruled or otherwise **amended by statutes**	Look for articles or commentary discussing the case (see Discussion . . . above)	*Current Law Statutes Annotated*

4.11.4 Updating case law

A case may have been overruled or indeed had its authority strengthened by a subsequent 'affirming' case at a higher court. This means you need take note of the 'judicial history' of a case—to see where a case has been cited in later cases—to ensure it is still 'good law'. A list of 'meanings' you will find online is given in **Table 4.7** below. **Table 4.6** shows you how to research and update a case. However, there is one aspect of updating which is more difficult to ascertain—where statutes affect case law.

A well-established body of case law may have been overturned by recent legislation either deliberately so, or as an incidental side-effect. Neither legal databases nor their printed equivalents (*Current Law Cases, The Digest*) indicate where this has occurred. There may eventually be an annotation in *Current Law Statutes Annotated*. In the meantime, if you have a suspicion that case law may have been overturned by a statute, search for a journal article on the subject or the particular case (see **4.5**), or if the case is referred to in a practitioner text, check for a supplement to the text or search for a more recent text on the same subject that might mention the case or relevant statute.

Table 4.7 **Case law annotations**

Applied	The principle of law described in the annotated case has been applied to a new set of circumstances in the annotating case.
Approved	The earlier case has been deemed good law by the later case in a higher court.
Considered	The earlier case has been given careful consideration in the later case but gives no remarks on the quality of the case.
Digested	The case is summarised in a short digest at the reference provided. In Current Law this gives the Year Book and paragraph no., e.g. 05/634 = *Current Law Year Book* 2005, [634]
Distinguished	The earlier case is not necessarily doubted but an essential difference in facts or in law is highlighted between it and the later case.
Doubted	The court in the later case has found the earlier case to be inaccurate in some way, but has not gone to the length of stating that the case is wrong.
Followed	The same principles of law have been applied in both cases (though there may be a difference in facts or circumstances between the cases)
Overruled	The later case in a higher court has ruled that the judgment in the earlier case was wrong.

4.11.5 How to use *Current Law Cases*

Current Law is a comprehensive legal information service covering all case and statutory developments from 1947 to date.

Volume	Arrangement . . .
Current Law Case Citator	This part of the service consists of a number of index volumes listing both UK and Scottish cases in alphabetical order. They are published in the following sequence of volumes: 1947–1976, 1977–1997, 1998–2001, 2002–2004, 2005–
Current Law Year Book	The Year Books date back to 1947 and contain brief details of all cases cited. They are published annually.
Current Law Monthly Digest	This is a paperback volume of the service which updates the case citator index with cases reported in the current year. It contains a subject index in alphabetical order and cumulative table of cases.

Table 4.8 **How to use** *Current Law Cases*

To find . . .	Use the . . .
The full name of a case, a digest of the case and where it has been reported	Case Citator covering the year of the case if known, or the earliest Citator if unknown. This directs you to a digest of the case in the relevant Year Book.
The judicial history of a case . . .	Case Citator covering the year of the case if known, or the earliest Citator if unknown. This provides details of later cases that have considered, applied, distinguished, etc. the earlier case.
	Update using each subsequent Case Citator, in chronological order, following references to the Year Book for a digest of any relevant cases.
	Complete the updating process using the cumulative table of cases in the most recent Monthly Digest.
Cases on a specific subject . . .	Year Books which lists contents by paragraph number under subject headings alphabetically. Some entries include summaries or *Digests* of a case as well as references to articles.
A recent case, including Scottish cases	Latest Monthly Digest's cumulative table of cases which includes a Scottish Cases Citator

4.11.6 Selecting cases: the importance of precedent

Having found a body of case law which seems relevant, you will need to read the law reports and interpret the cases. Only a detailed analysis of the case will enable you to identify the arguments that you will put forward on behalf of your client. Reading and interpreting a case is dealt with in more detail in **Chapter 7**. Here we are concerned with the preceding stage: identifying and selecting the cases you might use and cite in court. There are several aspects to consider:

- Determine if the case is meritous. As noted at **4.11**, just because a case has been reported does not mean it adds anything new to the law—this is a matter for you to interpret through your reading of a case.

- Note which court made the decision. A Court of Appeal decision carries more weight than that of a county court. A decision in the county court is in any case of little relevance, even if the point of law is similar to that which you need. The rules on the application of precedent also vary from court to court, which means there may be different practices, depending on whether a court is operating in a supervisory or an appellate capacity. (See *Halsbury's Laws*, vol. 26 [573]—judgments and orders section).

- Obtain the fullest report available. It is not always clear from the law report exactly what the court decides—the *ratio decidendi*. Brief reports rarely carry sufficient detail of the judgment or analysis of the full reasoning and there may be incidental arguments that are of use. Reliance on a short report instead of obtaining a fuller report is a poor use of case law.

- Determine if the case will be of use in court. A case may be of assistance to the judge if there is a clear legal issue to be considered and if the case itself can show the judge how similar facts have been dealt with or a point of law been interpreted, in another court.

- Cite the case correctly within rules prescribed by the court and with the correct legal abbreviation (see **4.11.1**).

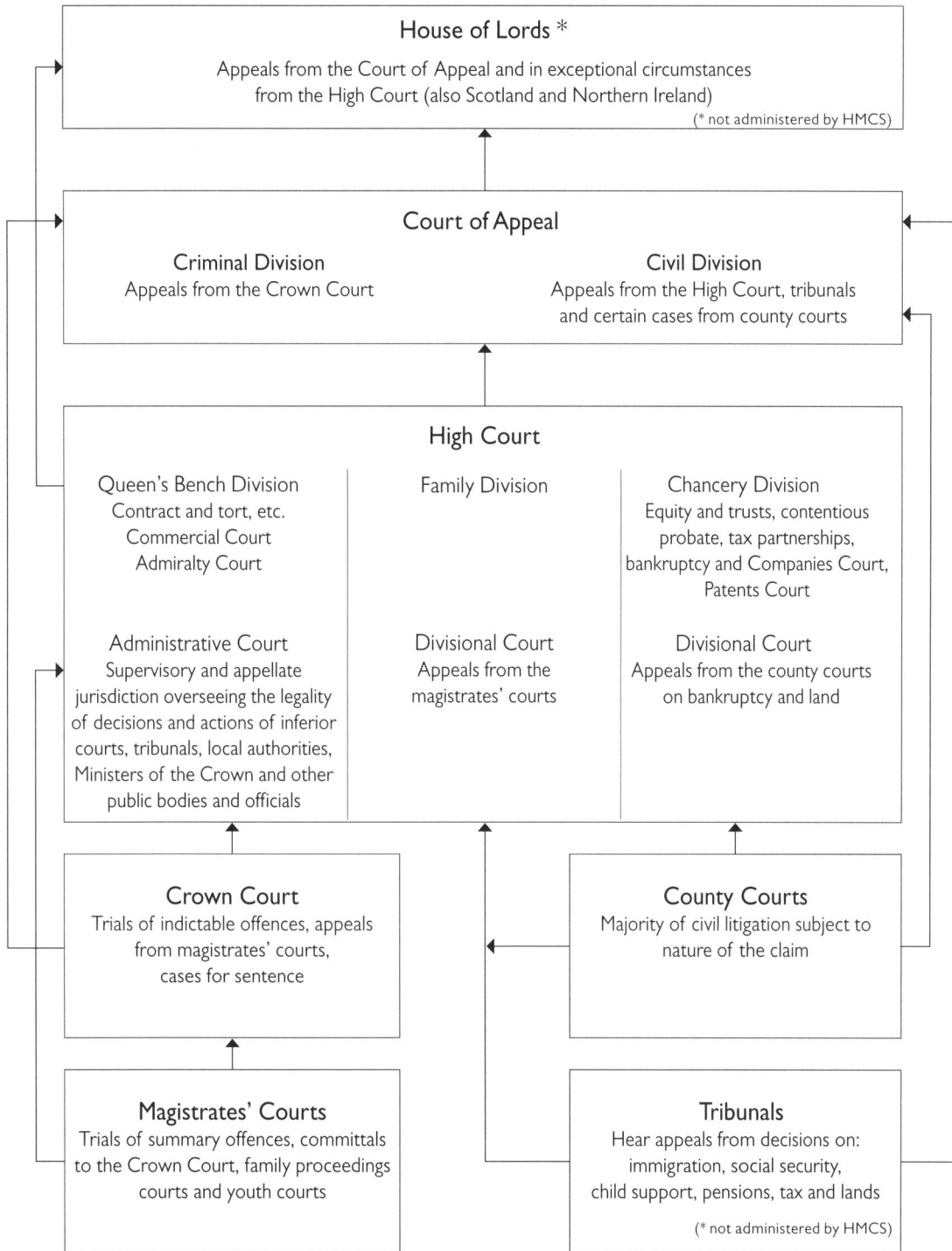

Figure 4.3   Court Structure of HM Courts Service (HMCS). *Reproduced from <http://www.hmcourts-service.gov.uk> with the kind permission of Her Majesty's Court Service.*

4.11.7   Citation of cases in court

The growth in commercial law reporting and the much more extensive use of legal databases over the last decade led to a proliferation in the citation of legal authorities in court. This practice is now actively discouraged by the courts, and rules regarding the use of legal authorities in civil courts were laid out by the Court of Appeal in the *Practice Direction (Citation of Authorities)* (2001) 1 WLR 1001. Lawyers are directed to:

- cite a case only if it clearly establishes a new principle of law, extends the law or if its use can otherwise be justified;
- state the proposition of law that each case portrays;
- justify citing more than one authority for a given proposition of law; and
- justify the citation of any authority from outside England, the European Court of Justice or the European Court of Human Rights.

If a case is to be quoted in court then the most authoritative series of law reports must be cited and there is a strict hierarchy of authority. Again, the correct procedure has been laid out by the Court of Appeal in *Practice Direction (Court of Appeal: Citation of Authority)* [1995] 1 WLR 1096. Cases must be cited from law reports in the following order:

- *The Law Reports* (Official Series) are preferred as the 'senior' series of law reports checked by judges before publication but notoriously slow to be published.
- *Weekly Law Reports* are the 'junior' official series.
- *All England Law Reports* are regarded as comparable in all respects to the *Weekly Law Reports*.

"if a case is reported in the official Law Reports . . . that report should be cited. If a case is not (or not yet) reported in the official Law Reports, but is reported in the Weekly Law Reports or the All England Law Reports, that report should be cited. If a case is not cited in any of these series of reports, a report in any of the authoritative specialist series of reports may be cited. It is always helpful if alternative references are given . . . "

Practice Direction (CA: Citation of Authority) 22 June 1995. [1995] 1 WLR 1096.

Where a case to be cited in court has not appeared in any of these series of law reports, then the lawyer may cite authoritative specialist series of subject-based law reports such as *Lloyds Law Reports*, *Road Traffic Reports* or more recent creations such as *European Human Rights Reports*. Very occasionally, where an unreported case is to be cited (in so far as it may be citable), the 1995 practice direction stipulated that the only acceptable version is the official transcript (available next day via *Lawtel* or the *Casetrack* service). In principle, every unreported case has the same value as a reported case but it is assumed that every judgment of any importance has been or will be reported and so the restrictions on citation outlined in the 1995 practice direction have particular force with regard to unreported cases.

EXERCISE 7   CASE LAW

1. What do the following abbreviations stand for:
   a)   L.T.O.S.
   b)   L.J.C.C.R.
   c)   S.J.L.B.
   d)   E.R.
   e)   R.T.R.
   Which of these law reports (if any) are in your nearest law library?

2. Where can I find a report of the case *Sachdeva v Sandhu?*
3. *Pepper v Hart* [1993] AC 593 is out of the library. Find an alternative citation.
4. Find the case cited as *Inglis v Mansfield*; identify the court which heard the case.
5. Find a summary of the case *Ashburner v Macquire* (1786).
6. Find a case where a local authority was held liable in damages for the conduct of its environmental officer.
7. Find the most recent cases in the library on:
    a) a bank paying a cheque after the death of the drawer;
    b) the attitude of courts to TV crews accompanying police operations; and
    c) whether the prosecution are obliged to reveal their witnesses' previous convictions to the defence.

4.12 European Union legal documents

European Union law forms a substantial part of the law of the UK. This is reflected by its prominence in law school syllabuses. Knowing how to look up an EU directive or trace a case heard by the European Court of Justice is therefore a key skill for the practitioner.

The larger firms of solicitors and some chambers hold a range of EU materials and Middle Temple Library has an extensive collection. There are also European Documentation Centres (EDCs) throughout the UK and the rest of the EU which receive all EU official publications; to find your nearest EDC, see the European Information Network website at <www.europe.org.uk/info>.

The EU produces types of law corresponding broadly to the categories of UK domestic law: primary legislation, secondary legislation, and case law.

4.13 EU legislation

4.13.1 Primary legislation

The European Union's primary legislation consists of the three founding treaties, which created the European Economic, Coal and Steel and Atomic Energy Communities in the 1950s, and subsequent treaties concerning the structure and functions of what is now the EU. The two key treaties are:

*   *Treaty Establishing the European Community,* 1957, often known as the *Treaty of Rome* or *EC Treaty*. One of the founding treaties, it was originally called the *Treaty Establishing the European Economic Community*.

*   *Treaty on European Union,* 1992, often known as the *Maastricht Treaty* or *EU Treaty*.

The remaining primary legislation includes: the *Single European Act* (1986), the *Treaty of Amsterdam* (1997), the *Treaty of Nice* (2001), and the *Treaty of Lisbon* (2007, not yet in force). The *Treaty of Lisbon* replaces the ill-fated *Treaty Establishing a Constitution for Europe*. Beware that the articles of the *EC Treaty* were renumbered by the *Treaty of Amsterdam*. There is a table of the old and new numbers in an annex to the latter.

Primary legislation appears in the *Official Journal of the European Communities* (now called the *Official Journal of the European Union*) (see **4.13.3**). The most recent consolidation of the EC and EU treaties can be found in *Official Journal* C 321E, 29/12/06. The EU

Publications Office also publishes most of the treaties as monographs. There is a convenient collection of EU primary legislation—both original and amended versions—on the EUR-Lex website (see **4.17**). Although the treaties are also on subscription databases such as *Westlaw, Justis Celex*, and *LexisNexis*, they are not presented in such a user-friendly format as on EUR-Lex. It should be pointed out that the EU does not officially regard electronic texts as authentic (see **4.13.5**).

The treaties may be found in UK publications, such as Sweet & Maxwell's *Encyclopaedia of European Union Law*. See **Appendix 1**.

4.13.2   Secondary legislation

EU secondary legislation consists of regulations, directives, decisions, recommendations, and opinions (recommendations and opinions, however, are not binding, despite being classed as legislation). The legal basis of these types of legislative instrument is Article 249 of the EC Treaty.

Regulations, directives, and decisions are cited by their year and running number, for example:

- Council Regulation (EC) No 44/2001 of 22 December 2000 on jurisdiction and the recognition and enforcement of judgments in civil and commercial matters.

- Directive 2003/88/EC of the European Parliament and of the Council of 4 November 2003 concerning certain aspects of the organisation of working time.

- 2001/145/EC: Commission Decision of 21 February 2001 concerning certain protection measures with regard to foot-and-mouth disease in the United Kingdom.

4.13.3   The *Official Journal*

Legislation is published in the *Official Journal of the European Union*, the EU's official gazette. Before February 2003, it was called the *Official Journal of the European Communities*. It is divided into two main series, 'L' and 'C', cited as OJ L and OJ C. The OJ C has an electronic-only sub-series, the OJ C E, which is found on the EUR-Lex website (see **4.17**) and in other electronic sources.

The OJ L contains all secondary legislation. Primary legislation, on the other hand, is mostly found in the OJ C, although the *Single European Act* and the new Member States' accession treaties are in the OJ L. Until 2002, proposals for legislation appeared in the OJ C, but from 2003 onwards they have only been published in the COM DOCS series (see **4.13.8**), which is available on EUR-Lex (see above). Most of the OJ C is taken up by non-legislative documents, such as case summaries and Commission notices.

Table 4.9 **Key contents of the *Official Journal***

L series	C series
Secondary legislation	Most primary legislation
Some primary legislation (*Single European Act*, accession treaties)	Proposals for legislation (until 2002; now only found on EUR-Lex)
	Case summaries and court notices
	Notices from the European Commission
	European Parliament minutes
	Common positions of the Council of the EU

4.13.4   Finding secondary legislation

The quickest way to find a particular instrument is to use the EUR-Lex website—or a subscription database such as *Westlaw*, *Justis Celex*, *LexisNexis* or *Lawtel EU*. However, strictly speaking, the EU does not regard electronic versions of legislation as authentic (see **4.13.5**).

EUR-Lex and the subscription databases can be searched by keyword or instrument number. They will give the full text of the instrument, plus its OJ reference; you could then use the OJ reference to find the authentic printed text, if required. EUR-Lex also provides a browsable subject index of current legislation, the *Directory of Legislation in Force*, although this can be difficult to use.

There is no overall printed index to the *Official Journal*, only monthly and annual ones, which are not cumulative.

4.13.5   Electronic sources of EU legislation

The EU provides a free legal database on the EUR-Lex website <http://eur-lex.europa. eu/en/index.htm>, as mentioned above. This includes all EU primary and secondary legislation, whether in force or not; the *Official Journal* from 1998 onwards; and COM DOCS from 1999 onwards. EU legislation can also be found on subscription databases, such as *LexisNexis*, *Lawtel EU*, *Westlaw*, and *Justis Celex*.

It should be reiterated, however, that the EU does not, strictly speaking, regard electronic versions of legal documents as authentic: see 'Important legal notice' on the EUR-Lex home page.

Table 4.10 **How to research EU legislation**

Looking for . . .	Electronic services	Printed resources
Primary legislation, original text	EUR-Lex website (Treaties collection) *Westlaw EU* *JUSTIS Celex* *LexisNexis* *Lawtel EU*	*Official Journal of the European Communities / European Union* (get citation from EUR-Lex); does not include the founding treaties UK command papers, *Miscellaneous* series (founding treaties)
Primary legislation as amended	EUR-Lex website (Treaties collection)	*Consolidated versions of the Treaty on European Union and of the Treaty establishing the European Communities* (Office for Official Publications of the European Communities, 2006)
Secondary legislation, original text, in force or not (with lists of amendments)	EUR-Lex website (use Simple Search; see Bibliographic Notice for amendments) *Westlaw* (click on References for amendments) *Justis Celex* (for amendments, click on Outline and scroll down) *LexisNexis* (list of amendments towards top of each document)	*Official Journal of the European Communities / European Union*
Secondary legislation, consolidated amended text	EUR-Lex website (use Simple Search to find original text, then see Bibliographic Notice for links to consolidated versions)	Encyclopaedias and textbooks, such as *Gore-Browne on EU Company Law* and *Documents in European Community Environmental Law*

4.13.6   Is it in force?

When you search for EU legislation on a website or database, you will usually be presented with the original, unamended text, accompanied by a list of amendments (if any). On EUR-Lex, you will find this list in the 'Bibliographic Notice' for each instrument, under the heading 'Amended by'. On *Westlaw*, click on References. On *LexisNexis*, the amendments are given towards the top of each document.

Consolidated amended versions of most, but not all, legislation are available on EUR-Lex and *LexisNexis*. However, they are provided for research purposes and are not regarded as official texts. On EUR-Lex, there are links to them from each instrument's Bibliographic Notice and they are also included in the *Directory of Legislation in Force*. On *LexisNexis*, go to the main Legislation screen, then click on International Legislation to access EU legislation; now click on Browse. Consolidated legislation is also found in many commercially-published encyclopaedias and textbooks—see Table 4.10.

4.13.7   Implementation of directives

A directive sets out the result to be achieved and the date by which this must be done, but leaves each Member State to transpose its provisions into national law; this process is known as implementation. In the UK, almost all implementation is done by statutory instrument; only occasionally is an Act of Parliament required (e.g., the Consumer Protection Act 1987, which implemented the Product Liability Directive). At the other extreme, a directive relating to banking practice may need only an internal circular from the Bank of England to the clearing banks. And no implementing legislation is required at all where the government consider that the scope of a directive is already covered by existing UK law.

On EUR-Lex, the 'Bibliographic Notice' for each directive gives details of implementation by all Member States. *Justis Celex* and *Westlaw* give the same information, whereas *Lawtel EU* only covers implementation by the UK. Be warned, however, that these databases have some gaps and are not always up to date. If they say 'No reference available' for a particular country, it is not safe to assume that it has not been implemented there; check several other sources and ask any relevant contacts to make sure.

Printed sources of implementation data include *Current Law*, *European Current Law*, and *Butterworths' EC Legislation Implementator*. The latest monthly part of *Current Law* lists all of the present year's statutory instruments which have implemented directives in the UK. *European Current Law* covers implementation by all Member States. *Butterworths' EC Legislation Implementator* is part of *Halsbury's Statutory Instruments*; it covers UK implementation only.

For a very recent directive, details of UK implementation can often be found on the website of the government department concerned; failing that, contact the department's legal section. If you have the language skills, you could try to search the Internet for other Member States' implementation measures as well. There is even a multi-lingual gateway to the national legislation websites of Member States, N-Lex (see **4.18**), although it is rather difficult to use effectively. N-Lex is in fact best used to find the full text of a foreign implementing instrument once you have got the title and reference from EUR-Lex or elsewhere.

Table 4.11: **How to trace the implementation of EU directives into UK law**

First try . . .

EUR-Lex website <http://eur-lex.europa.eu/en/index.htm>	Search for directive, then go into Bibliographic Notice; click on 'MNE'
or *Westlaw*	Search for directive, then click on National Measures
or *Justis Celex*	Search for the directive and scroll down

If above sources say "No reference available", check elsewhere . . .

Government websites	Use Google Advanced Search to search government web domains, e.g. .gov.uk or .gouv.fr.
European Current Law	Covers all Member States
Current Law	Check latest monthly part; gives UK information only
Butterworths EC legislation implementator	UK implementation information only
Commercial Laws of Europe (Sweet & Maxwell)	The annual volumes have tables of implemented legislation for all Member States (not cumulative)
Newsletters and journals	Search Legal Journals Index (on Westlaw and CLI Online) for articles about implementation of the directive
	Also try printed journals (e.g. EIPR, ECLR), because small news items are not included in Legal Journals Index
N-Lex website <http://eur-lex.europa.eu/n-lex/pays.html?lang=en>	Multi-lingual gateway to national legislation websites of most EU Member States. Can be searched in English, but the results are in the original language.

If all else fails . . .

Contact the relevant Directorates-General of the European Commission—see <http://ec.europa.eu/dgs_en.htm>

4.13.8   EU draft legislation

Generally speaking, the procedure is that the European Commission proposes new secondary legislation and the Council eventually approves it, usually in tandem with the European Parliament. The Commission's proposals are published in the COM Documents (or COM DOCs) series, on the EUR-Lex website. Significant new proposals are reported in the various legal news sources, such the *Legal and Regulatory Developments Index* (LRDI, part of Sweet & Maxwell's *Current Legal Information* database, *CLI Online*). All new COM documents are eventually listed in the printed *Official Journal* C, but the full text is not reproduced there.

When finally adopted, the legislative instrument will appear in the *Official Journal* L. The entire law-making process, from adoption of the original proposal to publication of the legislation in the OJ, can be tracked on the Internet using the Commission's *PreLex* website or the European Parliament's *Legislative Observatory* (see **4.17**).

EXERCISE 8   EU LEGISLATION

1. What is the latest available consolidation of the EC Treaty on the EUR-Lex website?
2. What is the official title of the *Maastricht Treaty*? What is the subject of Title VI of the Treaty?
3. Find Regulation 44/2001 on *Westlaw*, *LexisNexis* or *Justis Celex*. What is the *Official Journal* reference? (Tip: to find EU legislation on Lexis, go to the main Legislation screen and click on the 'International Legislation' link on the right-hand side.)
4. Find Directive 93/104 on the organisation of working time, using an online database. Is it still in force?
5. Has Directive 2001/30 been implemented in Greece?

4.14   EU law reports

4.14.1   The *European Court Reports*

Decisions of the European Court of Justice (ECJ), the Court of First Instance (CFI), and the Civil Service Tribunal at Luxembourg are reported in an official printed series, the purple-covered *European Court Reports* (ECR). Although all cases formerly appeared in the ECR, since mid-2004 less significant cases, such as uncontested infringement proceedings, are omitted (these are, however, available in the recent cases database on the ECJ website). Within the ECR are three series: Court of Justice, Court of First Instance, and Staff Cases.

New volumes of the ECR are slow to appear, but provisional case reports can be found on the ECJ website on the day of the judgment, in the recent cases database (see **4.17**). The ECR itself is on the EUR-Lex website; as with legislation, a legal notice warns that electronic texts are not seen as authentic, but the Help section of EUR-Lex says that the text provided is 'generally speaking' the same as that in the *European Court Reports* (Simple Search Quick Start Guide, p. 8). The same electronic version of the ECR is also found on subscription databases such as *Justis Celex*, *Westlaw*, *LexisNexis*, and *Lawtel EU*.

4.14.2   CMLR

The best-known EU law reports published in the UK are the *Common Market Law Reports* (CMLR). They include relevant cases from UK and other Member States, as well as those of the ECJ. A noteworthy ECJ case will usually appear in the CMLR long before it comes out in the *European Court Reports*.

4.14.3   Finding EU cases

If you do not have a law report citation, you can find a case on EUR-Lex, or one of the above-mentioned subscription databases, using the party names, case number, area of law, year or other criteria. Searching by party name alone can be difficult, since many EU cases have names which are so common as to be meaningless; for example, there are around a hundred cases involving the Commission and the UK.

If you know the number with which the case was originally registered, it will be easy to find on EUR-Lex. These case numbers are prefixed by a C for ECJ cases, a T for the Court of First Instance or an F for the Civil Service Tribunal, for example: *European Parliament*

Researching European Union Law

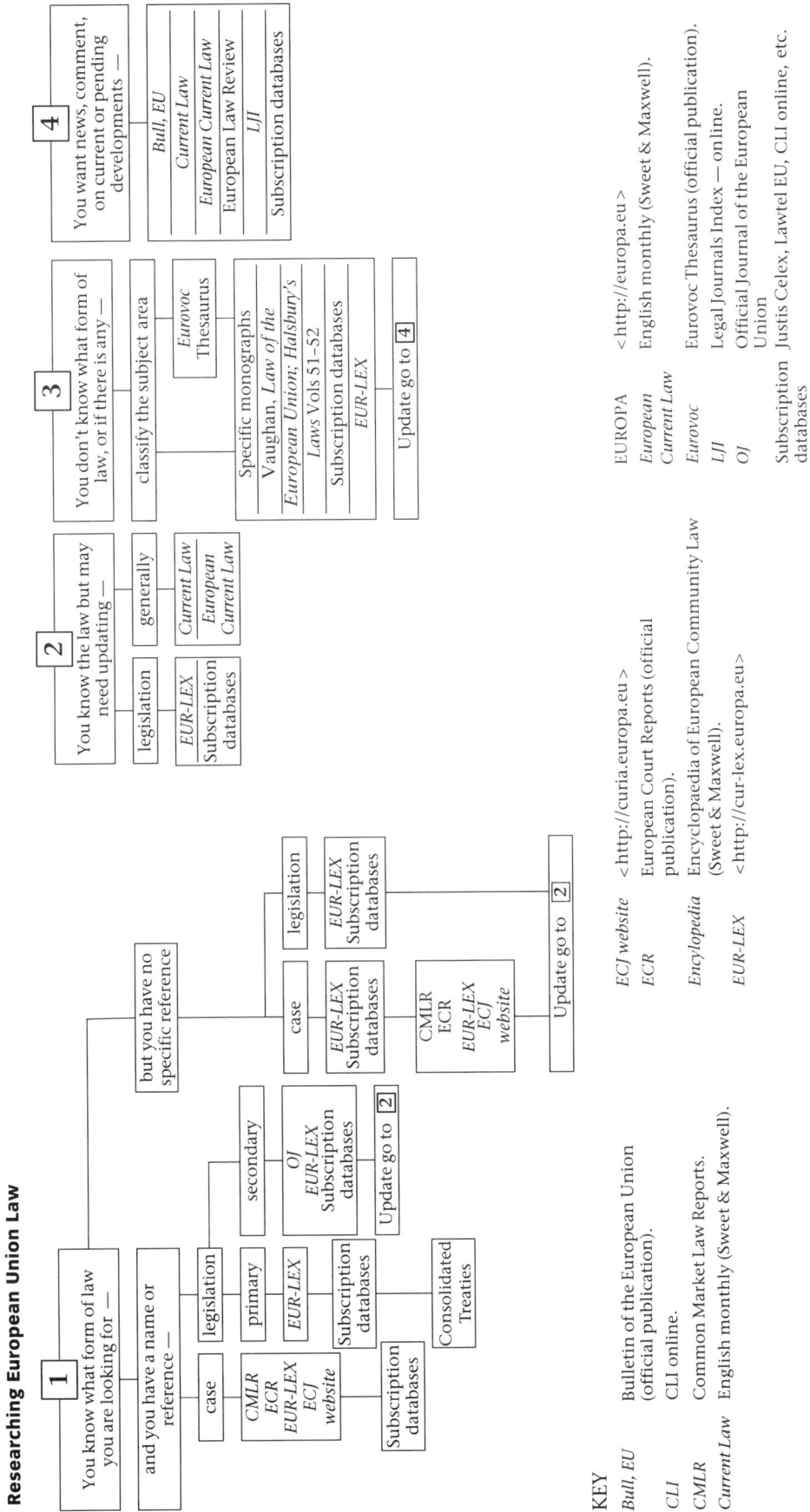

1

You know what form of law you are looking for —

and you have a name or reference —

- case
  - CMLR
    ECR
    EUR-LEX
    ECJ website
  - Subscription databases

- legislation
  - primary
    - EUR-LEX
    - Subscription databases
    - Consolidated Treaties
  - secondary
    - OJ
      EUR-LEX
      Subscription databases
    - Update go to **2**

but you have no specific reference

- case
  - EUR-LEX
    Subscription databases
  - CMLR
    ECR
    EUR-LEX
    ECJ website
- legislation
  - EUR-LEX
    Subscription databases
- Update go to **2**

2

You know the law but may need updating —

- legislation
  - EUR-LEX
    Subscription databases
- generally
  - Current Law
    European Current Law

3

You don't know what form of law, or if there is any —

classify the subject area

- Eurovoc Thesaurus
- Specific monographs
  Vaughan, Law of the European Union; Halsbury's Laws Vols 51–52
- Subscription databases
- EUR-LEX
- Update go to **4**

4

You want news, comment, on current or pending developments —

- Bull, EU
- Current Law
- European Current Law
- European Law Review
- LJI
- Subscription databases

KEY

Bull, EU	Bulletin of the European Union (official publication).
CLI	CLI online.
CMLR	Common Market Law Reports.
Current Law	English monthly (Sweet & Maxwell).
ECJ website	<http://curia.europa.eu >
ECR	European Court Reports (official publication).
Encylopedia	Encyclopaedia of European Community Law (Sweet & Maxwell).
EUR-LEX	<http://cur-lex.europa.eu>
EUROPA	<http://europa.eu >
European Current Law	English monthly (Sweet & Maxwell).
Eurovoc	Eurovoc Thesaurus (official publication).
LJI	Legal Journals Index — online.
OJ	Official Journal of the European Union
Subscription databases	Justis Celex, Lawtel EU, CLI online, etc.

Figure 4.4   Researching European Union Law

v Council of the European Communities, C–65/90. If you do not have the case number, it is usually best to search by a combination of party names, year and/or area of law.

Printed indexes which cover EU cases include the *Current Law Case Citator* and *European Current Law*.

Cases at the European Court of Justice go through two stages: first, the Advocate General will deliver his or her opinion, then, some time later, the judgment is given. The same case number is used for both stages and the opinion appears in the same printed and electronic sources as the judgment. CFI and Civil Service Tribunal cases only have one stage: the judgment.

All registered cases are listed on the ECJ website at (see 4.17). They are arranged in case-number order, but the lists can be searched by party name using Edit-Find. It will say here whether a case has been heard, dropped ('removed from the register') or is still pending. For hearing dates, see the News section of the ECJ website, which provides a schedule up to a few weeks in advance.

EXERCISE 9a   EU CASES

1. What is the *European Court Reports* citation for *Arsenal Football Club plc v Reed*?
2. Use EUR-Lex to find case number C–199/04. Which court heard it?
3. Use *Westlaw* to find the CMLR citation for *Salgoil SpA v Foreign Trade Ministry of Italy*. Now find its ECR citation. (Tip: you will have to use the main Cases screen for the CMLR, then the EU screen for the ECR.)
4. Use the ECJ website to find out whether case T–66/08 is still pending, or whether it has been heard.
5. Use *LexisNexis*, *Westlaw*, or *Justis CELEX* to find ECJ cases concerning working time. (Tip: on Lexis, go to the main Cases screen and click on 'International cases'.)

4.15 EU periodical literature

The various institutions of the EU produce a large number of official periodicals and newsletters. The most general one is the *Bulletin of the European Union*, which provides an overview of EU activities. It is available on the Internet at <http://europa.eu/bulletin/en/welcome.htm>, but there is a time-lag of several months before each issue appears. Print publication of the *Bulletin* ceased in 2006.

Various law publishers have their own general journals, many of which are available online as well as in printed form. They include:

- *Common Market Law Review* (on databases including *Kluwer Law Online* and *Business Source Premier*)
- *European Law Review* (on *Westlaw*).
- *Journal of Common Market Studies* (on *Ingenta Connect* and *Business Source Premier*).
- More specialist titles include the *European Intellectual Property Review* (on *Westlaw*) and *European Industrial Relations Review*.

To find journal articles on a particular topic, use *Legal Journals Index*, which is on *CLI Online* and *Westlaw*. Alternatively, significant articles on EU law are listed each month in the printed series, *Current Law*.

4.16 Current awareness: finding out about new developments

Various publishers offer monthly, weekly or even daily updates on paper and online. News of EU developments can be found on *Lawtel EU*, in the *Legal and Regulatory Developments Index* on *CLI Online* and in the Current Awareness section of *Westlaw*. On the Internet, the EU's press release website provides news on all subjects and *PreLex* or *Legislative Observatory* (mentioned above) can be used to track the legislative process. Independent sites such as *EurActiv* can also be useful (see 4.17).

Current Law has a 'European Union' subject heading, but developments affecting the UK are digested under the appropriate UK law headings. *European Current Law* is valuable, as it covers every country in Europe, not just the EU. For more frequent news in a printed format, a bulletin such as *Europolitics* is worth reading; this is produced twice-weekly in Brussels by the European Information Service, in English, and there is an associated website for subscribers.

4.17 Key EU websites

The principle sources for EU law that are of most use to practising lawyers are all freely available on the internet. Table 4.12 lists some of the most important websites you are likely to need.

Table 4.12

Bulletin of the European Union	Monthly overview of EU activities	<http://europa.eu/bulletin/en/welcome.htm>
ECJ case index	Index with links to full text; gives case status, e.g. pending, removed from the register	<http://curia.europa.eu/en/content/juris/index.htm>
ECJ recent case law database	All cases since 17/06/97	<http://curia.europa.eu/jurisp/cgi-bin/form.pl?lang=en>
EU Press Room	EU press releases	<http://europa.eu/press_room/index_en.htm>
EUR-Lex	EU legislation, cases, Official Journal, COM Docs, etc.	<http://eur-lex.europa.eu/en/index.htm>
EurActiv	Independent EU news website	<http://www.euractiv.com>
European Information Network	Directory of European documentation Centres	<http://www.europe.org.uk/info>
Legislative Observatory	Progress of legislation—European Parliament site	<http://europarl.europa.eu/oeil/index.jsp>
N-Lex	Experimental gateway to national law of EU member states	<http://eur-lex.europa.eu/n-lex/pays.html?lang=en>
PreLex	Progress of legislation—European Commission site	<http://ec.europa.eu/prelex/apcnet.cfm?CL=en>

4.18 Human rights documentation

Since the Human Rights Act 1998 came into force, UK citizens have been able to use domestic courts to enforce the European Convention on Human Rights. However, the European Court of Human Rights (ECHR), the judicial institution of the Council of Europe (CoE), is of course still very active. The human rights lawyer therefore needs to be familiar with both UK and ECHR legal sources.

Many ECHR publications are available on the Internet. Printed materials can be found in major law libraries; Gray's Inn Library has a good human rights collection.

4.19 The European Convention on Human Rights

The 1950 European Convention on Human Rights is properly called the *Convention for the Protection of Human Rights and Fundamental Freedoms*. Officially published as number five in the Council of Europe's *European Treaty Series* (ETS 005), it is also reproduced in UK human rights textbooks. Numerous protocols have amended the Convention and these are also part of the *European Treaty Series*. Both the Convention and its protocols can be found on the Council of Europe (CoE) conventions website (<http://www.conventions. coe.int>). For commentary on the Convention, see *Theory and practice of the European Convention on Human Rights*,[1] and *Jacobs and White: The European Convention on Human Rights*.[2]

4.20 Human rights law reports

4.20.1 Official printed series

The official printed series of European Court of Human Rights cases is *Reports of Judgments and Decisions* (cited as ECHR). Before 1996, cases appeared in *Series A: Judgments and Decisions* (cited as ECHR or Series A). From 1960 to 1987, there was also *Series B: Pleadings, Oral Arguments and Documents* (cited as Series B).

The European Commission of Human Rights, now defunct, published its rulings in *Decisions and Reports* (cited as D.R.) from 1975 to 1998; before then, they appeared in the *Collection of Decisions of the European Commission on Human Rights* (cited as C.D. or Coll. of Dec.).

Resolutions of the Council of Europe's Committee of Ministers in application of the Convention are published in *Collection of Resolutions Adopted by the Committee of Ministers in Application of Articles 32 and 54 of the European Convention for the Protection of Human Rights and Fundamental Freedoms*.

---

1   Pieter van Dijk, et al. (eds.), *Theory and practice of the European Convention on Human Rights* (Intersentia, 2006).

2   Clare Ovey, *Jacobs and White: The European Convention on Human Rights*, 4th edn. (Oxford University Press, 2006).

4.20.2   The HUDOC case database

The CoE's free HUDOC website (see 4.22) aims to provide every ECHR judgment and decision, back to 1959, although there are some gaps. It also includes admissibility decisions and public reports of the European Commission of Human Rights back to 1986 and some of the Commission's older admissibility decisions, plus all the resolutions of the CoE's Committee of Ministers.

Each ECHR case has an application number, consisting of a serial number followed by the year it was lodged: for example, 21413/02. HUDOC can be searched by application number, party names, Convention article number or key words. Note that some documents are only available in French, so it is advisable to select both English and French on the HUDOC search screen.

4.20.3   Other law reports

Selected ECHR cases are published in the *European Human Rights Reports* (EHRR) and UK human rights cases appear in the *Human Rights Law Reports* (HRLR); both series are published by Sweet & Maxwell and are also available on *Westlaw*. The EHRR series is particularly useful as a source of English versions of cases whose original language was French. *Butterworths Human Rights Cases* (BHRC) covers decisions from both national courts and the ECHR. It is on *LexisNexis* as well as being available in print. Further sources are listed in **Appendix 1**.

4.20.4   Finding human rights cases

If you are looking for an ECHR case but do not have a citation, the HUDOC website is the best tool to use (see above). Other case-finding tools include the *Lawtel Human Rights* database, the *Current Law Case Citator* (available in printed form and in *CLI Online* and *Westlaw*).

The printed versions of series such as EHRR have indices. If all else fails, Barbara Mensah's *European Human Rights Case Locator 1960–2000* (Cavendish, 2000) is a useful resource.

Several case digests are also available. These include the six-volume *Digest of Strasbourg Case-Law Relating to the European Convention on Human Rights*, produced by the CoE's Directorate of Human Rights and the Europa Instituut at the University of Utrecht (Carl Heymanns, 1984–85); *A Systematic Guide to the Case-Law of the European Court of Human Rights*, edited by Peter Kempees (Martinus Nijhoff, 1996), which is arranged by Convention Article; and *Human Rights Case Digest*, (Martinus Nijhoff, 1990–). Recent issues of the latter are on the Hein Online database.

Information concerning forthcoming ECHR cases is available on the European Court of Human Rights website (<http://www.echr.coe.int/echr>) under the heading 'Pending Cases'.

EXERCISE 9b   ECHR CASES

1. What does DR stand for in a case citation?
2. Use HUDOC to find *Murray v United Kingdom* (application number 18731/91). Was it ruled that there had been a breach of Article 6–2, or not?
3. Use HUDOC to find cases on Article 12 of the European Convention on Human Rights.
4. Use *Westlaw* to find *Allenet de Ribemont v France (No.2)* (1996) 22 EHRR 582.

4.21   Human rights serials

Official serial publications include the free *Human Rights Information Bulletin*, summarising recent developments; and *Case-Law Information Notes*, consisting of case digests and statistics. The *Bulletin* is on the CoE website and the *Information Notes* on the ECHR website (see **4.22**); a printed edition of the *Bulletin* is also available.

There are various commercially published serials, such as the *European Human Rights Law Review* (Sweet & Maxwell), the *Human Rights Law Review* (Oxford University Press) and the *Human Rights Updater* (LexisNexis).

4.22   Key human rights websites

The principle online sources for researching European human rights law are listed in Table 4.13.

Table 4.13

Council of Europe Conventions	<http://www.conventions.coe.int>
Council of Europe: Human Rights Information Bulletin	<http://www.coe.int/t/e/human_rights/hribe.asp>
European Court of Human Rights	<http://www.echr.coe.int/ECHR>
HUDOC case database	<http://cmiskp.echr.coe.int/tkp197/search.asp?skin=hudoc-en>

5

Using electronic research tools

This chapter offers a practical overview of the main strategies and techniques you will need to employ when researching legal problems using an electronic source. It does not give detailed instructions as to how to use each resource; mastering the mechanics of the databases is best achieved by reading the user guides available online or attending a training session or demonstration given by an experienced user (such as a law librarian).

When searching an electronic legal database you need to be aware of three major issues, all of which are dealt with in greater detail in this chapter:

(a) *Know the precise scope and content of the database you are searching.* The overviews of the major commercial legal databases given in this chapter provide a good starting point. This issue also applies to printed sources, of course, but there is a temptation to assume that 'everything' is available on a database. This is not an assumption one would make with a book, nor is it one that applies to electronic sources.

(b) *Learn how to search the database.* The risk of failing to retrieve material simply because you don't know how to use the database correctly is much greater for the untrained user than it is when you use printed sources. The correct formulation of a search strategy is all-important.

(c) *Update your findings.* It is tempting to assume that information available electronically is always more up to date than any printed equivalent. Often this is the case but not always . . . and updated information is rarely incorporated into the main text on the database straight away. You need to learn how each database updates its material.

5.1 Electronic formats

There are three main methods of accessing electronic databases.

5.1.1 Online 'dial-up' databases

Now regarded as 'old' technology, the traditional online service required the user to dial up to a remote database, incurring an online charge for conducting a search. Internet technology has now made this type of online database largely obsolete, but the 'pay-as-you-go' approach is still attractive to light users of legal databases. While most providers now require an annual subscription, some have continued with the 'pay-as-you-go' option.

5.1.2 Internet

The Internet offers database publishers the ability to combine sophisticated search mechanisms with a technology that allows them to remotely update their databanks on a daily basis. The currency of the information is particularly attractive to those producing and using legal databases. Commercial databases on the Internet are usually made available on subscription under licence, the price charged varies, depending on the number of users, the type of organisation, and how the organisation uses the information retrieved. For example, a large commercial law firm would be charged more than an academic institution.

There are disadvantages to using an Internet-based database, however. It is not always clear what information a database contains or how often it is updated, and the search engines on many databases lack functionality and user-friendliness.

5.1.3 CD-ROMs

CD-ROMs remain a popular alternative to database provision via the Internet. They offer limited storage capacity—they could never hold the *Westlaw* or *Lawtel* databases, for example—but searching is often much quicker and more sophisticated on a CD-ROM than it is on the Internet. Users can search at their leisure as there are no hidden online charges or telephone bills and this makes them more suitable for in-depth legal research. These advantages could well be outweighed by their lack of currency, however—updated disks are generally supplied quarterly, or monthly at best. Providers often get round this by supplying the main database on CD-ROM but then allowing users to access updated material on the Internet (see **5.3.2.2** and **5.3.6.2**).

5.2 Types of electronic database

It is important that the user knows both the contents and type of database he or she is searching. Electronic legal databases fall into three broad categories.

5.2.1 Full text services

The full text of a document is added to the database. *LexisNexis* contains the full text of law reports from *The Official Series*, for example. Full text services offer the user the ability to conduct in-depth research at the desktop, without needing to leave the database to search for another source. In this respect, they offer greater flexibility and the possibility of thorough research. In practice, however, they require good search techniques and a sound knowledge of the database contents. Simply because of the size of these databases, the number of results that are returned tends to be unwieldy, whilst at the same time, the user can never be sure that he or she is not missing some relevant information. The need for refined search strategies and techniques rapidly becomes apparent on a full text retrieval database.

5.2.2 Abstracting and indexing services

In these, law reports, journal articles, legislation, and other documents are summarised by professional indexers and the summaries placed on the database. Keywords identifying concepts are assigned to each abstract and links are provided to related summaries and sometimes to the full text of a document. When the user searches the database, he or she is searching the summaries and keywords rather than the full text of the document itself. This allows for much greater precision in searching, reducing the number of extraneous results. *Current Legal Information* and *Legal Journals Index* (available via *Westlaw* or as separate services) and *Lawtel* are all abstracting and indexing services.

5.2.3 Bibliographic services

Bibliographic services offer publication details only. The *Index to Parliamentary Papers* CD-ROM, for example, is a searchable bibliographical database which can help to locate relevant parliamentary Bills and Bill numbers when carrying out *Pepper v Hart* research (see **6.5**). Some bibliographic databases now offer links to the full text of documents and this greatly increases their value to the researcher even if the full text of the document itself is not searchable. The gateway website, *UK Official Publications on the Internet*, is an example of a searchable bibliographic database that links to the full text of many (though not all) of the documents it indexes.

5.3 Commercial legal databases

The databases listed here are the main competitors in the provision of electronic legal information in the UK. There are other legal database providers and the list does not aim to be comprehensive. All are commercial services usually available on subscription. The scope or contents of each database is highlighted and any problems concerning searching and display are briefly summarised.

5.3.1 Current Legal Information (CLI Online)

5.3.1.1 Scope

This is an abstracting and indexing service. Its excellent coverage of law reports and legal journals makes it an indispensable tool for researching UK case law back to 1947. *CLI Online* includes:

- *Current Law Cases*—includes all abstracts taken from printed digests appearing in *Current Law Year Book* and *Monthly Digest* since it began in 1947. It aims to cover all reported cases and unreported cases sent in by barristers and solicitors. Cases are noted-up with the procedural history and subsequent judicial consideration.

- *Case transcripts*—an index of selected transcripts of judgments from 1999.

- *Legal Journals Index*—title details and brief abstracts of articles taken from many legal journals published in the UK from 1986. It also indexes articles commenting on cases and cases reported in journals and so is itself an excellent source for case law.

5.3.1.2 Search and display

The *CLI Online* databases are available in several formats, including CD-ROM (Folio Views software), Blackwell's *Idealist* software (updated fortnightly by disk), on the Internet through a Sweet & Maxwell website, and via *Westlaw*. Searching and display varies depending on the software used. The careful application of keywords to the digests taken from the printed *Current Law* ensures that searching is precise.

5.3.2 *Justis*

5.3.2.1 Scope

Justis is a suite of full text services focusing on individual resources such as statutes or law reports. The resources are largely for the UK jurisdiction but *Justis* also offer several services covering European law. *Justis* allows for a flexible combination of one-off payments and ongoing subscriptions, depending on the product and type of access (Internet or CD-ROM). *Justis* databases include:

- *The English Reports*.
- *The Law Reports* (Official Series).
- *Law Reports Digest*.
- *Times Law Reports* (from 1990).
- *Parlianet* (index to publications and proceedings in Parliament, from 1979).
- Statutes and Statutory Instruments (full text in their *original* form—statutes from 1235; SIs from 1987. Note that these are taken from the *Statutes at Large* series and are unofficial).
- *Justis EU*, including CELEX (the official database of the European Communities).
- *JustCite*, a legal reference and citation search facility.

5.3.2.2 Search and display

Search Wizards guide you through constructing your searches using step-by-step prompts and drop-down menus. Data has clearly been transferred from CD-ROM onto the Internet and searching 'fields' in this way presents some restrictions in terms of searching and display. *Justis* products are suitable for obtaining an electronic version of a resource (law reports, for example), but they are not an alternative to the other online databases listed here.

5.3.3 Lawtel

5.3.3.1 Scope

An abstracting and indexing service for UK law, owned by Sweet & Maxwell. The strengths of the main *Lawtel UK* database lie in its coverage of unreported cases and the speed with which decisions are placed on the service. The main database, *Lawtel UK*, is supplemented by separate, specialist databases such as *Lawtel Personal Injury, Kemp on Lawtel*, and *Lawtel Civil Procedure*. *Lawtel UK* databases include:

- Case law abstracts from 1980. Comprehensive coverage of decisions from the House of Lords, Court of Appeal, Privy Council, and the High Court, many with links to full text transcripts.
- Legislation. Full text UK legislation in its *original* form. Statutes from 1984, Statutory Instruments from 1987. Tables of commencement, amendments, repeals, etc., but the text itself is not amended.
- Articles Index. Summaries of articles from over fifty legal journals, many of which discuss cases unreported elsewhere.

5.3.3.2 Search and display

Searching is relatively simple and the display of results is intuitive and user-friendly.

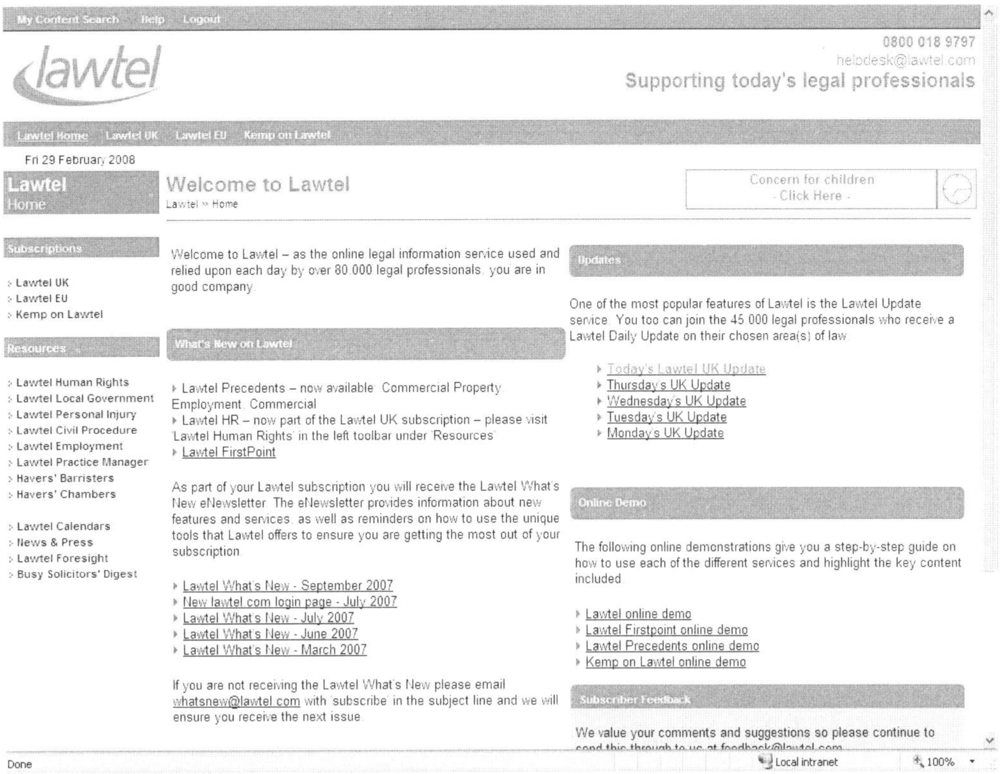

Figure 5.1   *Lawtel* Front Screen 2008. *Reproduced with the kind permission of Sweet & Maxwell.*

5.3.4 *LexisNexis Butterworths*

The *LexisNexis Butterworths* database was launched on the academic market in August 2005, further changes were made in the summer of 2006, when the international and news content of the publishers' 'sister' database, *LexisNexis Professional*, was incorporated.

5.3.4.1 Scope

LexisNexis describe their flagship database as a 'library' of UK law and, indeed, its content is impressive. Extensive case law and legislation databases, both with updating facilities, cover the primary sources for legal research. Many of the publisher's leading publications are available in full text, including loose-leaf works, textbooks, journals, law reports, and legal encyclopaedias such as *Halsbury's Laws* and *Atkins' Court Forms*. These commentaries can be searched independently of each other or as a group. 'Practice Areas' offer subject-based groups of texts that can be searched and browsed. In all, the system boasts over 32,000 sources with a thirty-year archive of some journals and law reports. *LexisNexis* databases include:

- *Case Search*—case summaries with links to full-text law reports. Includes an archive of case law from 1502 taken from *The Digest*.

- *All England*—complete archive from 1936 and recent cases in advance of publication in the printed series.

- *Halsbury's Laws*—full text of the encyclopaedia with cumulative supplement and monthly noter-up.

- *UK Legislation*—full text of legislation in force in England and Wales, as amended by later enactments, with an update facility.

- *Practice Areas*—subject-based services such as Employment, Family, and Property.

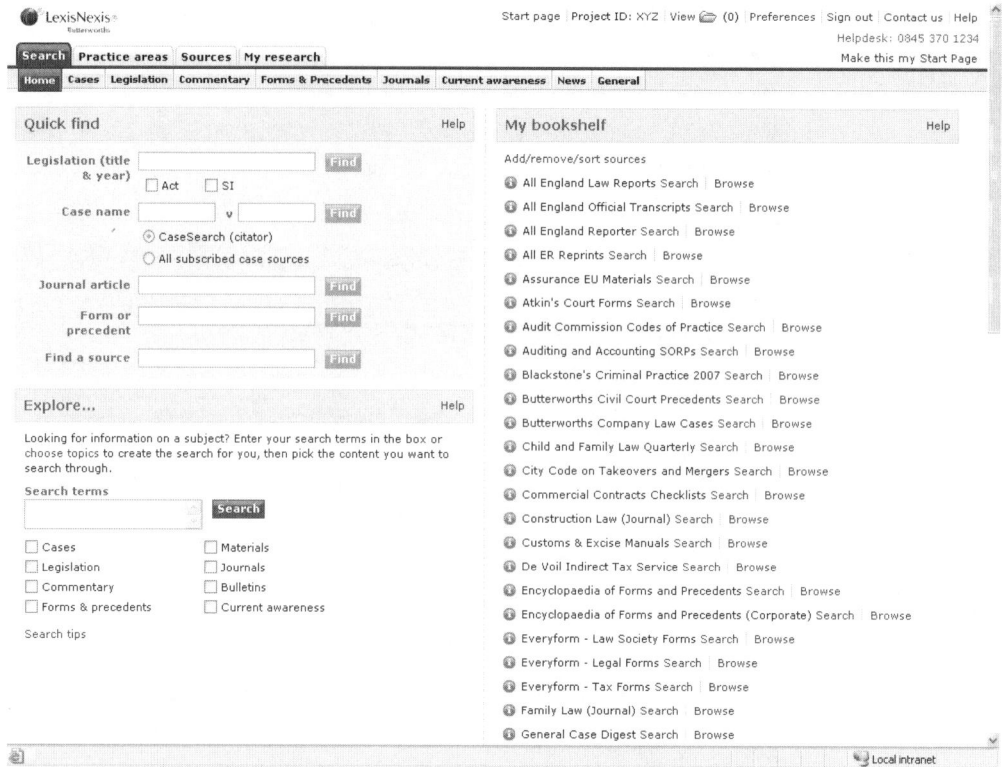

Figure 5.2   *LexisNexis* Front Screen. *Reproduced with the kind permission of LexisNexis.*

5.3.4.2   Search and display

In addition to easy-to-use, content-specific 'forms' for searching, the database has extensive browsing facilities and plays host to traditional search techniques using Boolean (see **5.5.2.4**). Combined with the ability to save favourite searches and customise groups of sources, this means that *LexisNexis* offers sophisticated access to its extensive materials, for the trained user. Most users would need guidance in its use, however, and there is an impressive range of guidance available online (including interactive tutorials, the first of their kind on a legal database and much needed).

The display, however, does not match the databases' searching capability. The opening search screens are cluttered with a plethora of links to different resources and several ways of accessing the same material. This does not make it an easy database for the novice researcher, but those who are more experienced will find the layout reasonably intuitive.

5.3.5   *Westlaw UK*

5.3.5.1   Scope

Formidable and rapidly growing full-text database that has very quickly established a leading market position in the UK to match that of its principal rival, *LexisNexis*.

The full text of many Sweet & Maxwell journals and loose-leaf works are available online. This service is available by subscription or on a 'pay-as-you-go' basis. *Westlaw UK* databases include:

- *Current Legal Information*—databases (see above) with links to the full text of many law reports and journals (though these are mostly limited to Sweet & Maxwell publications).

- *Legislation*—full text statutes and statutory instruments currently in force, as amended.

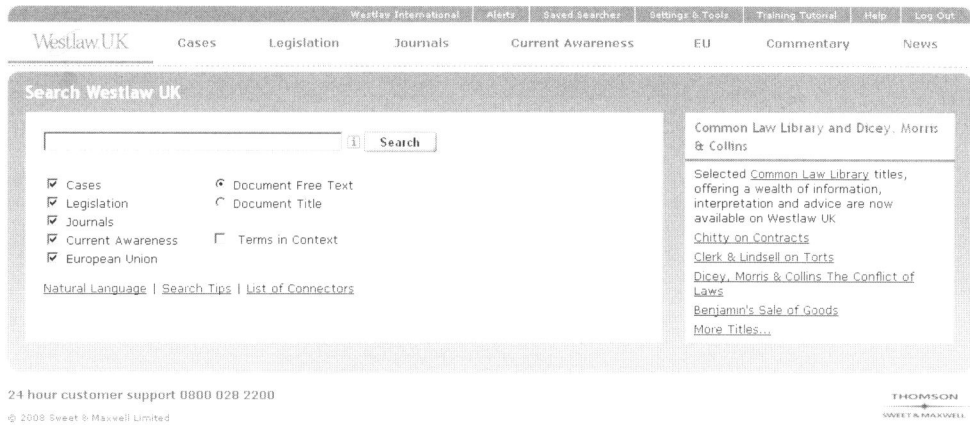

Figure 5.3   *Westlaw UK* Front Screen. *Reproduced with the kind permission of Sweet & Maxwell.*

- *Journals*—full text of around thirty Sweet & Maxwell journals, but retrospective coverage is limited. *Legal Journals Index* on *CLI Online* offers more in terms of journal coverage, despite its lack of full-text content.

5.3.5.2   Search and display

Reasonably user-friendly, the service boasts the full text of many publications within 'commentary' and specialist 'Practice Areas'—and both offer easy access to a suite of resources.

5.3.6   Practitioners' texts, law reports, and journals on the Internet and CD-ROM

5.3.6.1   Scope

Many legal publishers still produce some of their published works electronically either as independent works on the Internet or on CD-ROM. Jordans offers a full suite of family law publications, all its law reports and some specialist EU and employment law databases, as separately packaged services. *Justis* also has a good selection of electronic versions of texts (see **5.3.2**). Many of these are available via CD-ROM. Both Internet and CD-ROM versions are particularly useful for expanding a law collection piecemeal, without the need to buy and store printed copies or to pay an annual subscription for an expensive service such as *LexisNexis* or *Westlaw*. Some of these key services are mentioned in the list of works in **Appendix 1**.

5.3.6.2   Access

Inevitably, the division between resources provided on the Internet and on CD-ROM is blurring. CD-ROMs used to offer faster access with more sophisticated search technologies that allowed data to be manipulated in more ways than was possible at speed on the Internet. This is no longer the case but CD-ROMs still offer the advantage of portable access without the need for an Internet connection, making them popular with those who work on the move.

Many CD-ROMs are supplied free with the printed publications. Others, such as *Kemp & Kemp Personal Injury Practice CD-ROM*, require separate annual subscriptions. Discs are usually supplied on a regular basis (usually monthly or quarterly) to update the work or the user might download updates from an Internet site with a password. Internet-based resources are usually updated more often than the CD-ROM versions.

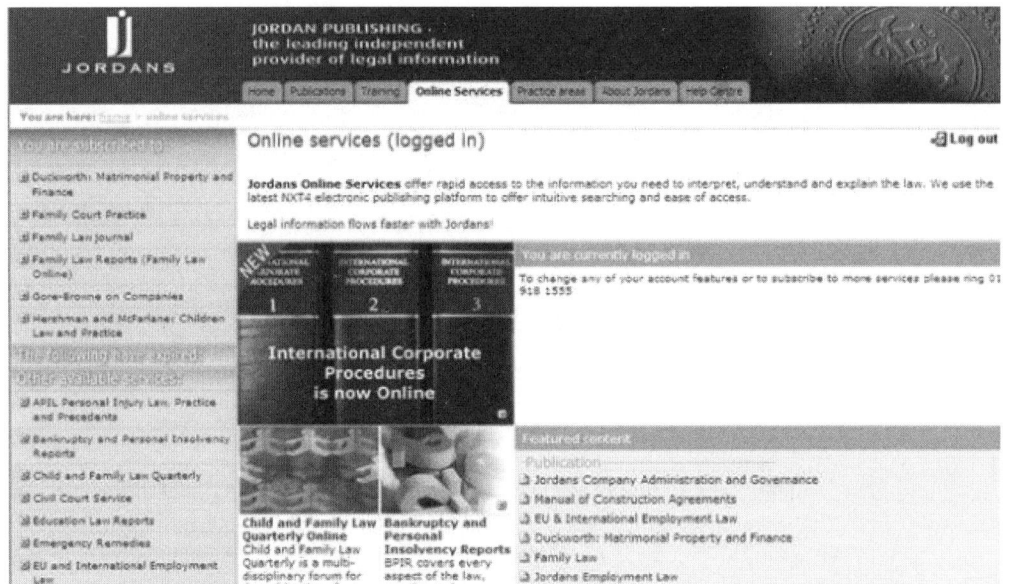

Figure 5.4   Jordans Online Front Screen. *Reproduced with the kind permission of Jordan Publishing Ltd.*

5.3.6.3   Search and display

Online and CD-ROM versions of texts vary considerably in scope and quality. Most allow you to search the texts using forms, and to browse using a 'contents tree'. Jordans products offer 'quick search', 'assisted search', and advanced search facilities, as well as updates such as *Newsline* and *Newswatch*.

The software for CD-ROMs also varies considerably but searching can be faster than the Internet and material can also be downloaded in a format suitable for word processing. Publications such as forms and precedents work well with CD-ROM technology for this reason, as users need to complete forms and precedents before printing them. Many CD-ROMs also offer additional interactive tools such as damages calculators and the ability to save searches, cases, and related data and return to work with them at a later date.

5.4   Free legal information on the Internet

The Internet is a rich source of free legal information, with many websites offering a range of legal databases and documents of great use to practitioners. A few of the most useful websites are listed in the table at **5.4.3**. It is very tempting to see the Internet as *the* source for all legal information. In fact, any websites you find on the Internet should be used with extreme caution, particularly for legal information where currency and accuracy are so important—the quality of a website is crucial when using the Internet for legal research. This makes it necessary to search in a controlled way for the information you need and to evaluate every website you find, in terms of the currency and quality of the information it offers.

5.4.1   Searching the Internet for legal resources

5.4.1.1   Search engines

These are best used when you want to search the Internet for a specific resource. To find the Court Service home page, for example, or to see if there is a transcript of a particular case available for free on the Internet. There are many search engines to choose from but if you need legal resources from the UK, then you should use a UK-based search engine: one of the best is *Google* at <http://www.google.co.uk>.

Other search engines include *AltaVista* at <http://uk.altavista.com>, *alltheweb* at <http://www.alltheweb.com>, and the 'natural language' search engine, *Ask* at <http://www.ask.co.uk>.

5.4.1.2   Directories

These allow you to browse a list of categories and subcategories to narrow down the area of the search until you find what you are looking for. *Yahoo!* at <http://www.yahoo.co.uk> is a good UK-based directory search engine: click Social Science to access listings under Law.

5.4.1.3   Legal gateways

These offer links to good-quality legal resources on the Internet and are of most use when you wish to browse the Internet for authoritative websites. The more general legal gateways, such as Delia Venables's *Portal* (popular in practice as it offers CPD courses) or Inner Temple's *Access to Law*, offer a short description of the linked website, evaluating its contents for the quality and currency of information. City University's *LawBore Pro* offers resources principally for students but the links to recent articles and excellent online tutorials for learning how to research the law may also prove useful.

Other gateways offer links to resources in a particular area of law, such as employment law or company law, often combined with a free current awareness service or newsletter and occasionally an additional database or priced services. Several legal gateways are listed in the table at **5.4.3**.

5.4.2   Evaluating the contents of a website

Once you have found a website offering legal information, you must ascertain how good it is. Currency and accuracy are vital in legal research. When viewing any legal website, ask yourself the following series of questions:

- *WHO* is providing the information and *WHY*? Are they reliable and authoritative?

- *WHEN* was the website, or the database it hosts, last updated? How often is it updated? Does it include all amendments? Is it likely to be there tomorrow?

- *WHERE* is the website published? Which jurisdiction? UK law or US law? England or Scotland?

EXAMPLE

What is the close season for snipe?

If you were to search for the keywords 'close season snipe' on a search engine such as Google, the first few results would look something like this:

Game Preservation (Amendment) Act (Northern Ireland) 2002 <http:www.opsi.gov.uk/legislation>
Shooting Seasons: Rural Sports <http://www.ruralsports.co.uk/shooting-seasons.html>
Naturenet: Shooting, Hunting and Angling Seasons <http://www.naturenet.net/law/seasons.htm>

- *WHO?*—the first link is to an official document, the web address betraying its origin. The OPSI website is a respected source. The third link is a personal website which authoritatively displays close seasons. Is the author up to date with the law?
- *WHEN?*—none of these websites display a date as to when the law (rather than the web page itself) is up to date to! You might deduce some likely dates for the Act and Bill by following the links on the websites but even official websites are notoriously bad at providing dates. Legislation provided on the Internet is in any case in its original format and there is no full text legislation available prior to 1988.
- *WHERE?*—some results on this page relate to Northern Ireland legislation rather than that for England and Wales.

Conducting the search in the example above has supplied us with a date for the close season for snipe—but we must check it on a more authoritative database. Why not use a legal database from the start? If you do use the Internet for legal research, use well-established websites available through legal gateways or use the resource in the same way as you would use an encyclopaedia: to find background information which you would then check with a more authoritative source.

5.4.3   Free legal information on the Internet

Table 5.1 below lists some of the legal materials available for free on the Internet. It is not a comprehensive listing. Web addresses are subject to change but all these websites (and many others) can be found through a legal gateway such as *Delia Venables Portal* or *Intute–Law*.

Table 5.1 **Free legal information on the internet**

LEGAL GATEWAYS	*Gateway sites with links to free legal resources on the Internet*	
British Employment Law	Free area with 4,500 fact cards and locator map of employment lawyers.	<http://www.emplaw.co.uk>
Company Law Club	Excellent gateway to company law. Free on registration. Database of company law topics, links to company-related websites, newsletter, and bulletin board.	<http://www.companylawclub.co.uk>
Delia Venables	*Legal Sites and Resources in the UK*. Very practical pages of links regularly updated by Delia Venables.	<http://www.venables.co.uk>
Electronic Immigration Network	Immigration, refugee, and nationality law. Gateway site with links to relevant organisations, case law, tribunal decisions, and databases; UK and international law.	<http://www.ein.org.uk>
Intellectual Property	*The Intellectual Property Office* website hosts a wealth of information concerning intellectual property issues in the UK and EU (patents, designs, trade marks, and copyright).	<http://www.ipo.gov.uk>
Law Bore	Primarily an educational resource but the Pro version is profession-facing and offers links to legal resources, articles, and useful online tutorials for researching the law.	<http://www.lawborepro.net>

Law Society	Latest offerings on policy, law reform, and education and links to legal resources in the UK, Europe, and abroad.	\<http://www.lawsociety.org.uk\>
intute – Law	*intute – Law* catalogues a host of legal Internet sites with evaluative abstracts of website content and links to the home pages.	\<http://www.intute.ac.uk/socioalsciences/law\>

CASE LAW	*Transcripts, law reports, and summaries of cases*	
BAILII	UK portal, the *British and Irish Legal Information Institute* offering access to transcripts of cases from the High Courts and Court of Appeal, from 1996.	\<http://www.bailii.org\>
Court Service	Database of selected High Court judgments (full-text transcripts from 1998 and links to tribunals, many with their own judgments); full text of Practice Directions from July 2000; extensive array of Court forms, leaflets, and guidance.	\<http://www.hmcourts-service.gov.uk\>
European Court of Human Rights – HUDOC database	Full-text judgments and decisions from 1959. Aims to be comprehensive but there are omissions. Includes pending cases, text of European Convention, and Rules of the Court.	\<http ://www.echr.coe.int\>
European Court of Justice	Full-text judgments of the European Courts of Justice from 1954 and First Instance from 1989, added on day of delivery.	\<http://eur-lex.eu/en/index.htm\>
House of Lords	Full-text transcripts of all judgments delivered from 14 November 1996.	\<http://www.parliament.uk\>
Recent, Current and Forthcoming Law Reports (ICLR)	Summaries of cases in *The Law Reports, Weekly Law Reports*, and *Industrial Cases Reports*. Also access to *Daily Law Notes*, offering briefs of forthcoming cases.	\<http://www.lawreports.co.uk\>
Swarbrick Law Index	Index of cases principally from the *Times* and *Law Society Gazette* abstracts. View by date, legislation, subject, or court.	\<http://www.swarb.co.uk\>

LEGISLATION	*Acts, SIs, Parliamentary material, EU legislation, etc.*	
Acts of Parliament and SIs	In their ORIGINAL form. Full-text statutes from 1987, SIs from 1996 published by *The Stationery Office*.	\<http://www.opsi.gov.uk\>
Civil Procedure Rules 1998	Full text, updates, and related materials are available on the Lord Chancellor's Department website.	
Eurlex	Full text of all EU legislation, preparatory legislation, consolidated texts, and treaties. *Official Journal* (C and L series), from 1998.	\<http://eur-lex.eu/en/index.htm\>

LEGISLATION	*Acts, SIs, Parliamentary material, EU legislation, etc.*	
Government Information	Links to central and local government departments, agencies and services and to some NGOs.	\<http://www.direct.gov.uk\>
Parliament	Full-text of parliamentary materials including Bills, *Weekly Information Bulletin*, recent *Hansard* debates, etc. from 1997.	\<http://www.parliament.uk\>
UK Statute Law Database	The official revised version of all UK Primary legislation from 1267 up to date to 2001. Secondary legislation is in its original form.	\<http://www.statutelaw.gov.uk\>

PUBLICATIONS	*Online versions of major publications*	
Bar Code of Conduct	. . . and other Rules and Guidance.	\<http://www.barcouncil.org.uk\>
Bar Directory	The official directory, searchable by barrister or chambers.	\<http://www.legalhub.co.uk\>
Crown Prosecution Service	Publications including Code for Crown Prosecutors, the Victims and Witnesses Charter, and recent CPS reports.	\<http://www.cps.gov.uk\>
Electronic Law Journals	Gateway to UK law journals, electronic and paper. Some with links to full text, abstracts, and contents pages.	\<http://elj.warwick.ac.uk\>

Law Commission for England and Wales	Click Publications for summaries or full text of recent reports, consultation papers, annual reports, and *Law Under Review*.	<http://www.lawcom.gov.uk>
UK Official Publications on the Internet	Links to full text of UK official documents, including White Papers, Command Papers, research briefs, etc. Search by title, date, publishing department, or category.	<http://www.official-documents.co.uk>

5.5 Search strategies using electronic resources

5.5.1 First principles

Searching an online legal database requires a different approach to that which many users employ when searching the Internet. On the Internet we tend to type any combination of keywords into the search box and click *Search*. In fact, 80 per cent of searches carried out on the Internet use just one keyword. Another common approach is to type a sentence into the search box, much as you would when using the 'natural language' search engine, *Ask*.

We adopt this approach because whatever we search for on the Internet, we nearly always obtain a large set of results: *recall* is very high. We often find, however, that the *relevance* of many of these results is actually very low. If we were to search again using slightly different keywords, we would be very likely to find other websites that did not appear when we first searched: our original search has not been very *precise*.

When conducting legal research we need to adopt a more accurate and controlled approach to searching electronic legal sources; we cannot afford to miss any relevant results but nor do we have time to plough through a large set of results to find what we need. To do this, we need to devise a search strategy that uses carefully selected keywords combined in such a way as to maximise *recall, relevance*, and *precision*.

5.5.2 Basic search strategies for electronic sources

Legal research technique is dealt with in more detail in **Chapter 3**. What follows here relates more specifically to searching electronic databases.

5.5.2.1 Analyse the problem: what exactly are you looking for?

Spend some time identifying clearly the information you are trying to find. Is the solution likely to be found in case law, legislation or is it a procedural matter? This will help you to decide which database to search and the keywords you might use.

5.5.2.2 Choose which database you are going to search

It is very important to know the contents of the legal databases you have access to. There is little point in searching for a case dating from 1977 on *Lawtel*, for example, as the case law database began in 1980. Similarly, if you wanted the full text of a law report in *Criminal Appeal Reports* you will only find it on *Westlaw* as it is a Sweet & Maxwell publication and will not appear on a *LexisNexis* product.

Which database is the best one to use? It depends on what you need. A good method for finding out which database to use is to ask yourself what *type* of question you are faced with. Is it legislative or procedural? Might it involve finding case law? If you are faced with a very general problem and you don't know where to begin, then use a general source. An encyclopaedia of law such as *Halsbury's Laws* is an excellent starting point.

When, during the year, does the law prohibit one from shooting snipe?

The word 'prohibit' hints that the answer is probably to be found in legislation and we might therefore use a legislative database but as there may be case law or procedure involved, it is probably best to start with a general source such as *Halsbury's Laws*.

5.5.2.3 Select the keywords

Search engines will find all occurrences within the text of the words you enter into the search box. If you enter a word that does not exist on the database or you misspell a word, you will get no results. If you enter too common a word, you will get too many results. Selecting the correct combination of keywords is crucial.

Which words define the problem you are researching? From our example, these might be:

- words offered to you by the problem itself (*shooting, snipe*);
- alternatives to those words (*shoot, bird, wild bird*); and
- concepts behind those words (*game, close season, licensing*).

Search engines are good at finding facts, names, and concrete entities; they are poor at classifying problems into concepts. Try to convert the problem into equivalent concrete keywords—the name of a case, the title of a statute, etc.

5.5.2.4 Combine the keywords in a 'controlled' search

After selecting our keywords, we need to combine them in a search that will maximise *recall*, *relevance*, and *precision* (see **5.5.1**). To do so we make use of a range of tools.

Boolean operators (or 'connectors') AND, OR, and NOT

Search phrase	. . . will find . . .	Use it to . . .	Notes
shoot AND *snipe*	. . . records containing the words *shoot* and *snipe*	. . . combine keywords, **narrowing** the search	Many databases assume an AND if no connector is entered (e.g., *close season* will find *close* AND *season* rather than the phrase *close season*).
Search phrase	. . . will find . . .	Use it to . . .	Notes
shoot OR *game* OR *bird*	. . . records containing the words *snipe* or *bird* or *game*	. . . search for alternative keywords, **widening** the search	Useful for searching for alternative concepts (e.g., *copyright* OR *patents* OR *designs* OR *intellectual property*).
snipe NOT *bird*	. . . records containing the word *snipe* provided it does *not* contain the word *bird*	. . . exclude keywords, **narrowing** the search	Use rarely and with caution as it excludes records that may actually prove relevant.

Most databases allow several operators to be combined into one search. *Brackets* may be needed to group complex phrases and refine the search even further.

> e.g., *shoot AND (snipe OR bird)*
> e.g., *shoot AND (snipe NOT bird)*

Wild card characters/truncation

Wild cards, such as the asterisk * or the exclamation mark !, allow the user to search for different permutations of a word ending. Most databases use an asterisk * but some use other characters such as an exclamation mark !, a question mark ?, a percentage sign %, or a dollar sign $. Conveniently, the two largest databases, *LexisNexis* and *Westlaw,* use an exclamation mark !

5.5.2.5   Ensure the search form is completed correctly before clicking *Search*

Database providers have made their products easier to search by providing search forms but one of the most common user errors is not completing the form correctly, or entering incorrect truncation on keywords.

Search phrase	. . . will find . . .	Use it to	Notes
licen!	. . . records containing the words *licence, licensing, licensed, licensee, etc.*	. . . replaces one or more letters, searching for alternative keywords, **widening** the search	Particularly useful for obtaining plurals to words (though some databases do this automatically).
licen*e	. . . records containing the words *licence* or *license*	. . . search for alternative keywords, **widening** the search	Allows for uncertain spelling (US v UK English, in this example). Might also be used where a hyphen may appear in the text, e.g. *self* incrimination.*

5.5.2.6   Display a list of results . . . and search again!

After performing a search, databases usually display the results as a list of 'hits' with links to the full text of the record. If the result list you have retrieved is too big (or too small) or you cannot find the information you need, you should go back and search again. Think about your keywords:

- too many results? *Narrow* your search. Add another keyword using an AND;
- too few? *Widen* your search—think of alternative keywords the text might use and add them using an OR;
- results not relevant? Find a result from the list, that is relevant, select keywords from that record and combine them in a new search.

5.5.3   Updating your findings

After finding an answer on the database, you must check that the information you have found is up to date. Changes to legislation, case law, and commentary are rarely incorporated into the online text immediately and you are usually required to check elsewhere on the screen for updating information. The availability of updates also varies from one database to another and it may be necessary to 'migrate' to a different source to check that the law is current. You need to consider:

(a) *How the service actually displays updated material.* Is the updated information included in the text (*Lawtel UK* case database) or do you need to scroll to the bottom of the text (*Halsbury's Laws*)? Do you need to click an update button (*LexisNexis*) or a coloured flag *(Westlaw)*?

(b) *How often the service is updated.* If the database is updated daily, does this apply to the WHOLE database or just a part of it? Case law on *Lawtel* is updated daily, for example, but articles are added on a weekly basis.

As a general rule, case law and legislation are usually updated on a daily basis or regularly (i.e., 'within a few days') on an online service. Practitioner texts and loose-leaf works available online are usually only updated when the printed text is published. The online service may offer frequent *commentary* but this does not form part of the text of the work and it does not mean that the online version is more up to date.

CD-ROMs are updated infrequently. Check the front screen when you first log on for information about when the disk was last updated.

EXAMPLE

How do you go about changing a child's surname when the name was first registered incorrectly and where the divorced parents are in dispute as to what the correct form should be?

Stage of legal research: the question	*The answer . . .*
1. Analyse the problem: what *exactly* are you looking for?	The *procedure* for changing a minor's surname. Any relevant *legislation* and *case law*. The question assumes we *CAN* change the name but we must check *IF* we can.
2. Choose which database you are going to search.	The procedure may involve *legislation* and *case law*. Faced with such a general question, *Halsbury's Laws* online might be best placed to offer an answer . . .
3. Select keywords. What words most accurately define the problem you are researching? (i) words offered to you in the written text (ii) alternatives to those same words (iii) concepts behind those keywords	Keywords we could search on here might be: (i) child, changing, surname (ii) children, change, changes, name, forename (iii) registration of names; divorce
4. Join keywords using appropriate connectors and wild cards . . .	Join keywords with AND connector to narrow the search down; use a wild card to search for variations on the keywords: *child! AND chang! AND name!*
5. Ensure search form is completed correctly before clicking *Search*.	Ensure *Halsbury's Laws* is selected as the source to search and check keywords are entered correctly.
6. Display a list of results . . . and search again!	Around 20 results are returned in the 'hit list'. The keywords for each result indicate that paragraph 1274 within the title *Children* may offer an answer. However, you could:
(i) too few results?	(i) widen the search by using the OR connector in place of an AND; or search on fewer keywords by removing one
(ii) too many results?	(ii) narrow the search by adding another connector and keyword, e.g. *AND parent!*
(iii) not relevant?	(iii) choose keywords from results that are more relevant and search again
7. Update your findings.	Scroll to the bottom of the paragraph or click UPDATE to the left; the update information for *Halsbury's Laws* appears at the bottom of the screen and incorporates the text of the Cumulative Supplement and monthly Noter-up. The service is updated monthly.

5.5.4   More advanced searching

5.5.4.1   Fields

Databases are made up of 'records'—for example, a case summary on *Lawtel* or the full text of a law report on *LexisNexis*. Usually, those records are further divided into 'fields' (such as case name, citation, etc.) that are themselves searchable. If you retrieve too many results searching the full text, try *narrowing* your search by confining it to a specific field (such as the 'catchwords' field for case law or the statute title field for legislation) where the words would only appear if they were pertinent to the main text.

5.5.4.2   Proximity searching

Searching for several keywords joined by an AND can be a problem on a full text database, as one keyword may appear at the beginning of the record and the other, in an entirely different context, right at the end. Proximity searching allows the user to define how close together the keywords should be, thereby *narrowing* the search. On *LexisNexis,* to find the phrase "close season" in close proximity to "snipe", enter the search: "close season" w/n snipe, where 'w' is for 'within' and 'n' is the number of words.

5.5.4.3   Phrases

Databases vary in how they search for phrases. If you were to enter *close season* into *LexisNexis* or *Justis,* it would find records containing the exact phrase. On *Lawtel* it would search for *close* AND *season,* unless you specified otherwise. Other databases may assume an OR between the words. Each search produces different results, so if you wish to search for a phrase (or an exact word and no other variations of it), always use double quotation marks " " around the keywords. For example, *"consumer protection"* finds only documents in which these two words appear next to each other rather than anywhere within the text of a database record.

You can also combine the use of the exclamation mark! wild card, and double quotes to search for derivatives of words next to each other—*"unfair! dismiss!"* finds *unfair dismissal* and/or *unfairly dismissed.* (See table at **5.5.5.5.**)

5.5.5   Problematic searches

There are a few situations in which you should be aware of the limitations of electronic searching and the foibles of the particular database you are searching.

5.5.5.1   Hyphenated words

Databases vary as to whether they treat a hyphen as a space or a character. Use an OR to ensure you retrieve all variations, e.g., *trademarks* OR *trade marks* OR *trade-marks.*

5.5.5.2   Stop words

Most databases will not search for very common words such as *the, is, of* or *have.* Thus, *breach of confidence* will produce an error or too many results; use double quotation marks around the phrase, i.e. "breach of confidence".

5.5.5.3   Section numbers

When searching for a particular section of an Act, it is usually better to search on a specific field (see above). If you must search the full text, avoid using the word 'section' or the abbreviation 's'. Those terms may or may not be used in the text and inputting the section number alone will suffice. Trying to specify sub-sections is similarly counterproductive. Use proximity searching, as the section number might appear before or after the title of the Act, e.g. *employment* w/4 *1998* w/157) to find s. 7 of the Employment Act 1998.

5.5.5.4 Capital letters

While many databases are not case-sensitive, some do retrieve different results if you enter your keywords entirely in capital letters. This can be useful for organisation names and abbreviations but is otherwise confusing. It is good practice to enter keywords in lower case and the Boolean operators AND, OR, and NOT in capitals. You can then see immediately if you've entered your search terms and connectors incorrectly.

5.5.5.5 Boolean truncation and wild cards

	Lawtel	Westlaw	LexisNexis
Distinguish between search phrase with and without AND? (e.g., *firearms offence or firearms AND offence*)	No (assumes AND)	No (assumes AND)	Yes
Connectors allowed	AND, OR, NOT	AND, OR, NOT, w/n	AND, OR, NOT, w/n
Assumes plural? (e.g., looks for *vehicles* as well as *vehicle*)	No	Yes	Yes
What wild cards are used?	* at start or end of word (e.g., **legal* would search for illegal, legality, etc.) ? replaces single character " " allows exact phrase searching, e.g. *"professional negligence"*. () e.g. (*dog* OR *animal*), (*firearm* AND *ammunition*)	* replaces single character ! truncates word " " allows exact phrase searching	* replaces single character ! truncates word " " allows exact phrase searching
Possible to search for words in proximity?	No	Yes. w/n (where n is a number) searches for terms within that many words of each other. eg *alcohol w/4 bloodstream*	Yes. w/n (where is a number) searches for terms within that many words of each other, e.g. *alcohol w/4 bloodstream*

6

Researching words and phrases

6.1 Introduction

Sometimes, a legal problem comes down to the precise meaning of a word or words. The uncertain words may be in an act or regulations; or they may occur in a contract, insurance policy, lease, etc., between the parties. Conversely, you may be drafting a document and trying to find an expression which will have the legal effect you want without any risk of unwanted side effects.

You will already know something of the interpretation of statutes and documents, the various approaches (literal, mischief, etc.) and subrules *(eiusdem generis,* etc.). Those may be needed if all your research fails to resolve the ambiguity. However, the initial question is whether the law has already defined the term used, giving it an authoritative interpretation.

6.2 Checklist

There are a number of questions to bear in mind:

(a) Does the act or document provide its own definitions? If the expression is defined, does any uncertainty remain?

(b) Does the Interpretation Act 1978 help? It lays down some very basic clarifications (e.g. masculine includes feminine, England includes Wales, etc.), but it only applies to statutes.

(c) Has any other statute or case provided a definition? Check specialist dictionaries and other sources—see **6.3** below. If you find a definition, is it applicable to your problem? A definition of, say, 'child' in an Act dealing with succession is unlikely to be thought applicable to the construction of the same word in a statute on, say, employment conditions or education. On the other hand, Acts on the same subject (e.g. tax) have to be read together, including their definitions, so that, for example, 'income', has consistent meaning throughout. But two Acts on different subjects may sometimes be arguably on legally comparable subjects; if so, their definitions may be worth borrowing for the purposes of your argument.

(d) Would ordinary dictionaries help? They are quite often produced in court—see **6.3.7**, below.

6.3 Where to look for definitions

6.3.1 Dictionaries of words and phrases

These are multi-volume compilations, with updating supplements, which aim to include every word or phrase which has been judicially or statutorily defined. They give detailed citations and cross-references, examples of usage, and other helpful information. The two key works are:

(a) *Stroud's Judicial Dictionary*, published by Sweet & Maxwell, gives numerous entries for each word or phrase, mostly in just a line or two, with citations.

(b) *Words and Phrases Legally Defined*, published by LexisNexis, gives fewer entries for each term, but gives them fully in the context of the judgment or other authoritative statement, with citations.

It is advisable to consult both works to ensure that you have not missed anything; make sure you also look at their supplements.

6.3.2 *Halsbury's Laws* Index

The final Index volume of *Halsbury's Laws* contains not just an ordinary index but also a substantial section devoted to words and phrases. These sometimes include a phrase missed by the legal dictionaries mentioned above. If you find your term here, once you have looked up the reference in the relevant subject volume, check for updates in the annual cumulative supplement volume and then in the loose-leaf *Current Service*.

Halsbury's Laws is on the *LexisNexis* database, but the Index volume is not included, so it is not possible to browse the list of words and phrases; you can, however, run a search across the whole work for definitions of your word or phrase. You would not want to retrieve every occurrence of what might be a fairly common word or phrase, but you could try to focus the search by asking for permutations of the various words that mean 'define' within ten or so words of the term you are trying to interpret (see **6.3.5** below).

6.3.3 *The Law Reports* Pink and Red Indices

The ten-year, cumulated index and current year's index to *The Law Reports* (see **4.11.2**) have a section of words and phrases as defined in any cases in the many report series covered. It is located under the letter 'W' for 'Words and phrases'. It makes it possible to trace the interpretation of a particular expression over the years or decades, which could be helpful. An electronic version of these indexes can be found on *JustCite* (see **5.3.2**).

6.3.4 *Current Law*

Current Law is a good source for very recent definitions. The latest monthly part of *Current Law Monthly Digest* cumulates all the words and phrases for the year so far; for previous years, check the *Current Law Year Books*.

6.3.5 Online sources

Databases such as *LexisNexis* and *Westlaw* can be used to search for definitions across multiple series of law reports and/or legislation in force, although this can be time-consuming if you are not a skilled database searcher. To reduce the number of irrelevant search results, try the following as the basis of your initial search strategy, adding or excluding further words as required:

- on *LexisNexis*: [the word] w/10 construe! or defin! or mean! or interpret!
- on *Westlaw* the "w" is not required: [the word] /10 construe! or defin! or mean! or interpret!

There is one obvious pitfall in the above examples: they exclude the word "construction", which can refer to the interpretation of a word, but of course more usually refers to building work. So they will exclude building law cases, but might also miss cases in which the word "construction" is used to mean interpretation of a word or phrase.

6.3.6 General law dictionaries

Rather than authoritative legal definitions with citations to case law and statute, these provide general definitions of legal terms and concepts, including lawyers' Latin. They include *Jowitt's Dictionary of English Law, Wharton's Law Lexicon,* and the *Oxford Companion to Law.*

6.3.7 Ordinary dictionaries

As has already been mentioned, legal interpretation might eventually depend on the general dictionary definition if nothing more authoritative can be found. This definition can be used to establish the accepted meaning of a word, on the assumption that Parliament (or the parties) had that meaning in mind. An example is *R v Fulling* [1987] QB 426, which shows this can be done even where there is a definition in the statute, provided the definition is not exhaustive. The *Oxford English Dictionary* is the standard source.

EXERCISE 10   WORDS AND PHRASES

1. Find the most recent judicial explanations of:
    (a)   'car park';
    (b)   'grievance';
    (c)   'family life'.
2. An Act requires a notice to be 'displayed outside' premises. Is it sufficient to stick it to the inside of the window of the building so that it is visible outside but remains inside?
3. What do *'purger une hypothèque'* and *'Übertragung einer Schuld'* mean in foreign legal documents? (see 6.4)
4. Peter insured his factory against damage from 'flood, bursting or overflowing of water tanks, apparatus or pipes'. While moving some office furniture, his employees dropped a heavy metal cabinet on to a water pipe, which fractured, flooding the office and causing extensive damage to the firm's records. Peter's insurers say this loss is not within the insured perils. Advise him.

6.4 Foreign legal vocabulary

Nowadays, lawyers may be expected to have to translate legal terms from and to other European languages. There are professional legal translators who specialise in this work for big transactions, court documents, and so on. However, where it is just a term or concept in, say, a letter to or from an overseas lawyer, it may suffice to refer to a foreign legal dictionary. Most law libraries have such dictionaries, covering at least the major European languages.

The European Union's official multilingual thesaurus, EUROVOC, gives equivalents of terms used in EU law in twenty-one European languages, including English. It is on the Internet at <http://europa.eu/eurovoc/>.

6.5 *Pepper v Hart* research: using *Hansard*

Since the House of Lords decision in *Pepper v Hart* [1993] AC 593, it has been permissible, subject to limitations, to cite in court what was said in Parliament during the passage of a Bill as an aid to statutory interpretation. Researching *Hansard* is a task which you may well be asked to do as a pupil. As it is a topic for which it is not feasible to provide practical training during the BVC, you may well feel unprepared when asked to do it—even experienced practitioners who have not done it before can find themselves at sea. This short section can do no more than highlight some of the practicalities. But help will be at hand: if you are based in London you will almost certainly have to use Lincoln's Inn Library, which holds the specialist Parliamentary collection on behalf of the four Inn libraries, and whose experienced staff are always willing to offer expert guidance. Even if you are based outside London, they are happy to offer help over the phone.

The practicalities covered answer the following frequently asked questions:

- When might I or should I do it?

- What materials do I need to do it?

- Can I do it online?

- Where can I get the necessary hard-copy materials?

- How long does it take?

- How much do I need to know about Parliamentary procedure?

- What is the best way to get started?

- Are there any tips for finding my way around *Hansard*?

- If I cannot find any debates on the section, am I going wrong?

- If I find any relevant material, are there any formalities for putting it before the court?

6.5.1 When might I or should I do it?

Lord Browne-Wilkinson in *Pepper v Hart* itself (at p. 640) set out three criteria which have to be met if recourse to *Hansard* is to be taken:

- legislation is ambiguous or obscure, or leads to an absurdity;
- the material relied upon consists of one or more statements by a Minister or other promoter of the Bill, together, if necessary, with such other Parliamentary material as is necessary to understand such statements and their effect; and
- the statements relied upon are clear.

Once there is the possibility of the first criteria being met, then it will almost always be necessary to carry out *Hansard* research. It may indeed be professionally negligent not to do so. However, this research can be time-consuming (see **6.5.5**). If a matter is urgent and there is not time to do it, any advice involving statutory interpretation given in an opinion or in a conference should make that clear.

However, *Pepper v Hart* has since been considered by the House of Lords on several occasions, and you should be aware that its applicability has been qualified in some circumstances. The following are some of the leading cases:

- *Melluish (Inspector of Taxes) v BMI (No. 3) Ltd.* [1996] 1 AC 454 (relevance of adjacent provisions).
- *R v Secretary of State for the Environment, Transport and the Regions, ex p Spath Holme Ltd* [2001] AC 349 (consolidation Acts, and enabling provisions to make Statutory Instruments).
- *R (Westminster City Council) v National Asylum Service* [2002] 1 WLR 2956 (use of Explanatory Notes on the Bill).
- *Wilson v First County Trust (No. 2)* [2004] 1 AC 816 (Human Rights Act compatibility cases).
- *McDonnell v Christian Brothers Trustees* 1 [2004] AC 1101 (overruling pre-*Pepper v Hart* cases).
- *Harding v Wealands* [2007] 2 AC 1 (latest HL discussion).

6.5.2 What materials do I need to do it?

Typically, you will need the following materials:

- A copy of the Act in question *as it was originally passed* (*Current Law Statutes* is best—its annotations may help before you even start; otherwise, from the official Stationery Office (Queen's Printer) copies).
- A copy of the relevant *House of Commons Sessional Digest*, which gives the dates for each stage of the Bill, and lists the prints of the Bill (useful, but not essential)—first published for session 1983–1984.
- The Bill, as reprinted, incorporating amendments during its passage—usually two complete prints for the Commons and three for the Lords.
- The Explanatory Notes accompanying the Bill (one for the Commons and one for the Lords) and for the Act—these were first provided from Parliamentary session 1998–1999.

- House of Commons *Hansard*.
- House of Commons *Standing Committee Debates* (from session 2006–2007 called *Public Bill Committee Debates*).
- House of Lords *Hansard*.

You may also need the following materials that precede the Parliamentary debates on the Bill, either as general background on the Bill or because they are referred to in the debates:

- Any Law Commission report, or reports from Royal Commissions or official inquiries;
- Departmental consultation papers (green papers) and Government white papers; and
- Draft Bills and Select Committee reports on Draft Bills: many Government Bills now receive 'pre-legislative scrutiny' by a Select Committee of the Commons or of the Lords or by a Joint Committee; the procedure was first introduced in 1998.

Such materials can often be identified in the general note or annotations on the Act in *Current Law Statutes*.

6.5.3 Can I do it online?

The short answer is: if you want to, you can for Acts passed from 2007 onwards; before that if you have to, you can but only for Acts passed from 1998.

All of the materials listed above are only available online (free of charge on the Parliament website <www.parliament.uk>) in complete form from session 2006–2007 onwards, i.e. in relation to Acts passed from 2007 onwards. This was the first session in which all the Bills and their amendments were put up and retained on the website. Although *Pepper v Hart* research can be done without the benefit of having the Bills, it is (even) more time-consuming (see **6.5.5** and **6.5.7**). If you did need or want to research an Act before 2007 online, the earliest you could go would be for Acts passed in 1998, since the *Standing Committee Debates* are only available online from session 1997–1998, and your research would be dangerously incomplete without them. Commons *Hansard* is available online from 1988–1989, and the Lords from 1994–1995, so partial research online from those dates would theoretically be possible, but in any event, *Pepper v Hart* research is one area of legal research where using the printed materials is considerably more convenient than using material on a screen.

6.5.4 Where can I get the necessary hard copy materials?

In London, Lincoln's Inn Library (which is open to barristers of any Inn) has a complete set of all the Parliamentary materials, except that its run of *Standing Committee Debates* only starts with session 1983–1984; they can advise on the best place to go if earlier ones are needed. All the other Inn libraries do have the main Commons and Lords *Hansard*, and Inner and Middle Temple libraries have some of the Bills, but it will usually be necessary to go to Lincoln's Inn to complete the research, if you do not go there in the first place.

Outside London, only the largest central public reference libraries and official publications collections in university libraries are likely to hold the necessary materials. Again, Lincoln's Inn Library can advise.

6.5.5 How long does it take?

Not all pupil supervisors may have had to do this for themselves. They may have un-realistic expectations as to how long it might take. If, as is typical, you only need to research a single section in a single Act, then the main factor is the size of the Act, since that dictates the volume of debates that have to be trawled. As a very rough guide: for a very short Act with only, say, half a dozen sections, an hour may be enough; for a very large Act, such as the Planning or Housing or Insolvency Acts, you should allow at least half a day. But other complications can arise: you may need to search more than one section, or there may be related provisions in successive Acts; also bear in mind that if the Act is before 1984 and you are planning to use Lincoln's Inn Library, you may well have to go off to another unfamiliar library for the *Standing Committee Debates*.

6.5.6 How much do I need to know about Parliamentary procedure?

There are numerous complications and exceptions, some rare, others less so, but you need to know at least the basic pattern of Parliamentary stages for a typical Government Bill. A Bill may start in either House. If the Bill starts in the Lords (it will have 'HL' after its title in the prints for both Houses), the following applies *mutatis mutandi*:

- Commons first reading: purely formal, no debate.
- Commons second reading: general debate on the principle of the Bill, usually on a single day; no amendments at this stage.
- Commons committee stage: detailed clause-by-clause consideration, usually off the floor of the House in a Standing Committee (from 2006–2007 a 'Public Bill Committee'), over several days.
- Commons report stage: also known as the 'consideration stage'; further amendments, often more than one day.
- Commons third reading; usually purely formal with no debate; even if there is a debate, no further amendments would be made.
- Lords first reading: as for the Commons.
- Lords second reading: as for the Commons.
- Lords committee stage: not taken by a 'committee' as such, but by the whole House, usually on the floor of the House, or sometimes elsewhere physically in another room (a 'Grand Committee'); otherwise as for Commons.
- Lords report stage: as for the Commons.
- Lords third reading: unlike the Commons, a substantive stage with further amendments, but usually only one day.
- Commons consideration of Lords amendments: usually a brief stage when the Commons have to approve any amendments made by the Lords; usually last stage, but if disagreement with the Lords, then:
- 'Ping-pong': Lords will usually withdraw offending amendment.

6.5.7   What is the best way to get started?

Is it a consolidation Act?

Before starting, check whether your Act is a consolidation Act: such an Act will have as its long title at its head, for example, 'An Act to consolidate the Badgers Act 1973, the Badgers Act 1991 and the Badgers (Further Protection) Act 1991', or 'An Act to consolidate the enactments relating to company insolvency . . . ' Such Acts, designed to tidy up the statute book, do not change the law and go through a special Parliamentary procedure, during which there are no further debates on their substantive provisions. You will need to trace the derivation of your section back to the Act in which it originally appeared, and then direct your researches to the debates on that Act.

Has the provision been inserted by a later Act?

If you have been using a version of the Act that presents the text in amended form, e.g. *Halsbury's Statutes*, check that the relevant provision has not been inserted by a later Act—if so, it will appear in square brackets or have a capital-lettered section number, e.g. 17A. Look then at the notes to see which Act inserted it, and research that.

Look at the Bills

The next step is to look at all of the prints of the Bill—usually five in all. Note the clause number for the provision ('sections' in Acts are 'clauses' in Bills) in each print and the stage to which it relates—it may not start out as the same number as the section in the Act, and may change as the Bill is amended. Knowing the clause number at each stage makes it easier to find any debate on the provision when leafing through *Hansard* for that stage. At the same time, check whether there are any material differences in the text of the provision in the successive versions of the Bill as compared to the Act. If there is a change, you will know there must have been an amendment, so there must have been debate. But if the text is identical to the Act throughout, that does not mean there was no debate—there may have been debate on an *unsuccessful* amendment.

6.5.8   Are there any tips for finding my way around *Hansard*?

Running order

The sessional indexes to *Hansard* will give all the references to the debates. Even if you just have the dates of each stage, e.g. from *House of Commons Sessional Digest*, the debates for each stage can readily be found. The *Standing Committee Debates* are arranged by Bill in the first place. The difficulty, particularly when a stage lasts several days, is finding when your clause was reached, especially if, as often can happen, the clauses are not taken simply in sequential order. In the Commons, look at the very start of the debate at the stage in question: there is usually a motion on the order of consideration of clauses, which gives the running order. The official bound volumes of *Standing Committee* debates (cream-coloured volumes) have a clause index. In the Lords, the Bills come with 'marshalled lists of amendments' which are reprinted each day of the stage: from this you can see the running order and on which day your clause was reached, as well as seeing before you get to *Hansard* whether any amendments were indeed tabled.

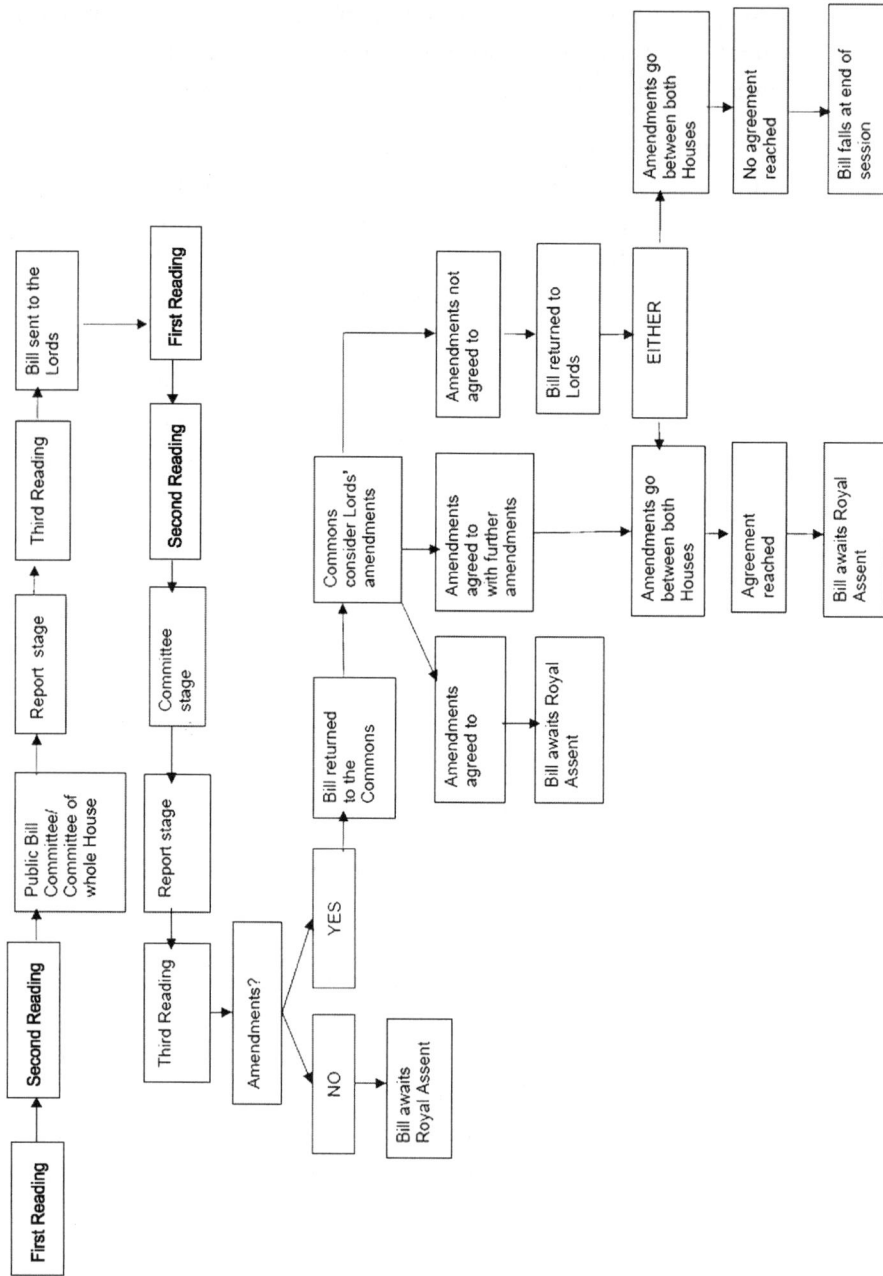

Figure 6.1 Example of a Bill originating in the Commons.

Note that other than at the second readings in each House, debates are entirely generated by amendments: if no amendments to the clause in question are tabled then there is no debate on it. Note also that entirely fresh clauses may be inserted as amendments at any stage, right up to the Lords' third reading.

If from looking at the Bills an amendment is known to have been made
If when looking at the Bills you found it had been significantly amended at a particular stage, look first at the debates for that stage—all may become clear. However, you may still need to look at all the earlier and later stages, too. Even if the provision is in its final form at that stage, there may have been debate on an earlier unsuccessful amendment, or there may be a later unsuccessful attempt to overturn the amendment, generating debate.

Ministerial statements
Remember that you are looking for *Ministerial* statements (the second criterion in *Pepper v Hart*). If you are uncertain whether the person speaking is a Minister, look back until you find when the person first spoke in the debate—at that point, *Hansard* will identify the speaker as a Minister. There is also a list of Ministers at the front of each bound volume of *Hansard*. In the case of second reading debates, look first at the start when the Minister introduces the Bill, and then at the very end when the Minister (often a different Minister) winds up the debate. You only need to look at the debates in between if you need to elucidate something the Minister says in the winding-up speech.

6.5.9   If I cannot find any debates on the section, am I going wrong?

Provided you are satisfied that you found the debates at each stage, and have examined them systematically, the answer is almost certainly no. At the committee stage, each clause has to be agreed, even if there are no amendments and so no debate. So you should at least find one line when the clause in question was approved (e.g., 'Ordered that Clause 25 stand part of the Bill' in the Commons; simply 'Clause 25 agreed to' in the Lords). At the other stages, other than second reading, if there were no amendments tabled to the clause, there will be no debate. It is very common, especially in large Acts, for provisions to be enacted with no debate whatsoever. You should also realise that even if debate is found, it may well be of no assistance to you, still less to the court. Cases where what has been found in *Hansard* has been decisive to the outcome, are rarer still.

6.5.10   If I find any relevant material, are there any formalities for putting it before the court?

In criminal cases, there is provision for this in the *Consolidated Criminal Practice Direction* (<http://www.hmcourts-service.gov.uk> and as an appendix to *Blackstone's Criminal Practice*)—at para II.20 for the Court of Appeal and para IV.37 for the Crown Court. This stipulates the number of copies, on whom and by when to be served, and so on. It also mentions that copies must be from the 'Official Report', i.e. *Hansard* itself, though rarely could it be otherwise. It does not mention that the copies should be from the official *bound* volumes as issued by the Stationery Office, rather than from the daily or weekly parts. The bound volumes contain revisions (editorial rather than substantive) and there are adjustments to the column numbering.

In civil cases, there is no longer equivalent express provision in the practice directions accompanying the CPR. The editors of *Blackstone's Civil Practice* (2008 edn, para 71.49) merely suggest that reasonable advance notice must be given to the other parties and the court. In the Court of Appeal, the extracts will need to be included in the bundle of authorities in accordance with PD 52, para 15.11.

Reading and interpreting a case

7.1 Introduction

This chapter is about case law. Its chief purpose is to give guidance to the reader on how to read a case in order to identify, extract, and where necessary apply its *ratio decidendi*. All those training for the Bar have in theory read many cases at the academic stage, and so have learned to do this. But you may not ever have given much comprehensive thought to the process of reading a case, or to identifying exactly what the *ratio* of it is. Also, anecdotal evidence suggests that there are some students who have got by to a very large extent using case books, which contain only digests of cases, or simply by reading the headnote of a case, which contains a short statement of what the reporter considers to be its *ratio*, but which may or may not be accurate, particularly after the case has been interpreted by a court in a later case.

Yet a barrister who is arguing a point of law before a judge, or seeking to persuade the judge to distinguish or to apply a case, needs to be able to analyse case law more deeply than that. Only a detailed study of a case and exactly what the judge(s) said in that case will enable you to identify and express clearly the arguments based on that case that you will put forward on behalf of your client. The *ratio* of a case is often found only through a very detailed study of not just what the judge said, but of what he or she must be taken to have meant in the light of previous decisions, and the particular facts of the case.

So, with apologies to those who are already well versed in the art of case reading, let us take it through in stages.

7.2 Judicial precedent

It is not possible to think about finding the *ratio* of a case, or especially applying or distinguishing it, without being aware of the doctrine of judicial precedent. This is another matter than almost everyone picks up at the academic stage, but a quick reminder will do no harm.

7.2.1 The doctrine

The doctrine of judicial precedent is often stated in a Latin principle: *stare decisis*—to stand by what has already been decided. This means that once a court has decided a point of law, other courts are bound to follow it, unless they have the power to alter it by overruling, or unless they are permitted to reach a different conclusion (more on this below). So a decided case becomes a precedent, and that precedent is almost certainly binding on any court that is equal or lower in the hierarchy. A judge cannot make a correct decision on a point of law without first examining case law in order to determine whether there is a precedent which is binding on him or her. This doctrine is self-imposed by the courts; it has never been legislated.

7.2.2   The hierarchy

7.2.2.1   The European Court of Justice

A decision of the European Court of Justice on the interpretation of EC legislation, and the validity and interpretation of EC regulations, is binding on all English courts.

7.2.2.2   The House of Lords

A decision of the House of Lords is binding on all lower courts, and it is not bound by the decision of any lower court. But the House of Lords is not bound by its own previous decisions. It will, however, not overrule its previous decisions as a matter of course; it will only do so rarely and after very careful consideration. This ensures that mistakes can be rectified without the need for legislation. It seems likely that this position will remain unchanged when the Constitutional Reform Act 2005 comes into force and the Supreme Court replaces the House of Lords as a judicial court.

7.2.2.3   The Court of Appeal

The Court of Appeal is bound by any decision of the House of Lords, unless it can distinguish it, or unless it was reached *per incuriam* (by carelessness or mistake, for example by failing to take account of a relevant precedent). However, in an interesting development, the Court of Appeal recently decided in *R v James; R v Karimi* [2006] 1 All ER 759 that it should regard itself as bound by a decision of the Privy Council rather than a conflicting decision of the House of Lords, because the composition of the Privy Council had been nine law lords, who were clearly intending to overrule their own previous decision in the House of Lords.

Whether the Court of Appeal is bound by its own decisions is less clear. It decided in *Young v Bristol Aeroplane Co Ltd* [1944] KB 718 that it will normally be so bound except in three circumstances:

(a) the previous decision was reached *per incuriam;*

(b) there are previous decisions which conflict with each other (this does happen, although in theory it should not); and

(c) its previous decision has been overruled expressly or implicitly by the House of Lords.

However, the Court of Appeal retains a discretion in criminal cases to refuse to regard a previous decision as binding, which it will exercise occasionally.

7.2.2.4   The High Court

A High Court judge is bound by the Court of Appeal and House of Lords. If faced by conflicting decisions, he or she must follow the decision of the higher court, or, if they are of equal status, the later in time. A decision of a High Court judge at first instance is binding on all lower courts, but not strictly on another High Court judge. It is therefore possible and not uncommon to get conflicting decisions at first instance. However, the decision of another High Court judge is strongly persuasive, and a judge will not readily decline to follow it.

7.2.2.5 Lower courts

The decisions of all judges in higher courts are binding on all lower courts, including a circuit judge sitting in the crown court or the county court, magistrates, and tribunals.

7.2.3 When is a case binding?

A case is only binding to the extent that it decides a point of law. No court is bound by any other court's decision on a pure question of fact. The extent to which a case is binding depends on identifying and extracting its *ratio decidendi* (or *ratio* for short). There is more on this in **7.3** below. Any part of a court's reasoning that is not part of the *ratio* is known as an *obiter dictum*—something said 'by the way'. *Obiter dicta* are not binding, though they may be persuasive.

7.2.4 Overruling and reversing

When a decision of a lower court is altered by a decision of a higher court on appeal in the same case, then that decision is said to have been reversed.

When a decision of a lower court is altered by a higher court in another case, so that it is no longer binding precedent, then it is said to have been overruled.

When a decision is overruled, the effect is retrospective. That is to say, the previous decision is taken never to have been the law, rather than to have been the law up to this point. This makes it possible for the higher court to reach the opposite conclusion on the facts of the case before it. However, the decision in the overruled case stands.

7.2.5 Distinguishing

The chief way in which a court avoids being bound by a precedent is by distinguishing it. If a case contains a decision on a point of law, the court will probably have first decided a principle and then made a decision on the facts of the case by applying that principle. The decision on the principle is undoubtedly binding law, assuming the case has then been decided by applying it. But if in the end the court decided the case without applying that principle, then what the court had to say remains *obiter*. A previous decision is, however, only binding if it is indistinguishable on the facts from a later case. If the two cases have some significant factual differences, the judge in the later case may be able to distinguish the former case. He or she is then saying that the previous case, although it contains a binding point of law, does not bind him or her on the facts of this case, and so he or she is free to establish a new precedent.

For example, in a previous case a court was faced with the question 'is the defendant liable to the claimant in these circumstances?' It held that facts A, B, and C existed, and concluded that when facts A, B, and C exist, the answer will as a matter of law be 'Yes'. In the present case, if the judge, faced with the same question, finds that facts A, B, and C exist, he or she will be bound. But if he can find that facts A and B exist, but not C, he will not be bound. He or she may then decide that the answer is 'No'. He or she will also not be bound if he or she decides that facts A, B, C, and D exist, D being a fact that did not exist in the previous case, and a fact which makes a difference.

Alternatively, he may find that facts A, B, and C exist, but that on closer examination, there are two kinds of fact B: B1, and B2. In the previous case, facts A, B1, and C existed, but in this case, facts A, B2, and C exist. If B1 and B2 are significantly different, then again he or she is not bound and may decide that the answer is 'No'.

7.2.6 Persuasive precedents

A precedent may not be binding, but that does not mean it can be ignored. Many non-binding precedents are, nevertheless, highly persuasive. A non-binding decision by the House of Lords on a point of law is, for example, so strongly persuasive that it will be very difficult indeed to persuade the Court of Appeal, let alone a judge, to depart from it. Courts will take into account *obiter dicta,* decisions of lower courts, decisions of commonwealth courts, dissenting judgments, and give them such weight as they see fit. The Court of Appeal will not infrequently be persuaded to a decision by the *obiter dicta* of a lower judge.

7.3 The *ratio* of a case

7.3.1 What is the *ratio* of a case?

There are differing views on what the *ratio* of a case actually means. The strict view is that the *ratio* of the case is to be found only in any decision and reasoning on a pure point of law, and no case is binding to the extent that it decides a question of fact. However, very few cases turn entirely on a question of law, just as very few turn entirely on a question of fact. The great majority involve points of mixed law and fact, and it is very difficult to persuade a judge to decide a case differently to a reported case when it is almost identical on the facts, even if there is not a fully binding point of law.

So it is submitted that for practical purposes it is best to consider the *ratio* of a case to be the reasoning that has led to the conclusion. If the Court of Appeal, for example, has interpreted a piece of legislation in a certain way, and has applied this interpretation to the facts of the case before it to reach a conclusion on those facts, then that interpretation is part of the *ratio* and is binding on a lower court in a subsequent case. But if the Court of Appeal has then managed to decide the case without relying on its interpretation, so that it would have reached the same conclusion even without that interpretation, then that interpretation is not part of its *ratio* and is not binding on any lower court.

7.3.2 Discovering the *ratio* of a case

It is often quite difficult to discover the *ratio* of a case. It may need close examination and analysis. This is because the judge rarely sets the *ratio* out expressly. He or she is concerned with deciding the case before the court and giving reasons. He or she has little thought to helping judges in subsequent cases. Even if he or she does attempt to state it, the correct view is that the *ratio* of a case is what a later court decides it to be, not what the judge who decided the case perceived it to be. The *ratio* has to be dug out from all the dicta and reasoning contained in the judge's judgment. Some of what he or she says will be *ratio,* some will be *obiter.*

A court in a previous case was again faced with the question 'is the defendant liable to the claimant in these circumstances?' It found that facts A, B, C, D, and E existed, and decided that for that reason the answer was 'Yes'. It may be tempting to assume that all of facts A, B, C, D, and E must be present before the answer can as a matter of law be 'Yes'. But it may be that on closer analysis of the judge's reasons, only facts A, B, and C were material to the eventual conclusion, and facts D and E were no more than persuasive. Then what the judge had to say about facts D and E is *obiter,* and the *ratio* is only that facts A, B, and C must be present before the answer will be 'Yes'. Alternatively, the judge may have said that although facts A, B, C, D, and E existed, he or she did not think fact D was essential. It would be tempting then to assume that only facts A, B, C, and E must be present before the answer can as a matter of law be 'Yes'. But a later court, on closer analysis, may conclude that the judge did in fact give more weight to fact D than he said he did, and that the *ratio* is really that all five facts must be present before the answer is 'Yes'.

It can therefore often be important, when reading a case, to separate those facts which truly form the *ratio* of the decision, because the decision would not have been the same without them, from those which were merely persuasive, and pointed the judge in the direction of the decision, but in the end have not resulted in that decision.

7.3.3 Altering the *ratio* of a case

Sometimes the *ratio* of a case may be altered by another case. For example, a judge decides that facts A, B, C, and D are present and that the answer is therefore 'Yes'. In another case, a judge finds that facts A, B, and C are present, but not D. Nevertheless, he or she does not distinguish the first case, but decides that the answer is still 'Yes'. The law is now that only facts A, B, and C need be present before the answer will be 'Yes'.

It is not unusual for the Court of Appeal to be faced with previous decisions of lower courts, or maybe even of its own, which at first sight seem to be in conflict with each other. What it will often then do is to reconcile the conflicting decisions, by discovering a common principle which was not clearly enunciated by the previous judges, and by applying it so as to produce a valid distinction which justifies all the previous decisions and the differences between them. The *ratio* of all previous decisions must now be read in the light of the Court of Appeal's 'explanation'.

7.3.4 The *ratio* when there is more than one judgment

If a case is decided in the Court of Appeal or the House of Lords, there may well be more than one judgment. If every member of the court says the same thing in different words, then the *ratio* of the case is clear. But what if they do not?

First, if the court does not reach a unanimous conclusion, then the *ratio* will only be found in the judgments of those in the majority. If the minority judge(s) agree with the reasoning on any issue with the majority, what they have to say is still *obiter*, because it is not what has led them to their individual conclusion.

If two or more judges reach the same conclusion but for different reasons, then only the reasoning of the majority can form the *ratio* of the case. If all three members of the Court of Appeal come to the same conclusion, but two of them reach that conclusion for reason A, and the other for reason B, then the *ratio* is based on reason A. If there are three different reasons, then the case has limited value as a precedent, because there is no binding *ratio*. If the House of Lords decides a case by a majority of three to two, but only two of the majority decide as they do for the same reasons, then again there is no clear *ratio* in the case. There must be a majority of the whole court on the *ratio* before there is a binding precedent.

It is not uncommon for judges in the Court of Appeal to give a single judgment of the whole court. There is then only a single *ratio* and this is as good as three separate judgments, each giving the same reasons. But it is also not uncommon for judges in the Court of Appeal and the House of Lords to give separate judgments, some of which consist only of the words 'I agree'. This means that the judge agrees only with the conclusions of his colleagues, not necessarily with their reasons. The *ratio* may then be hard to determine, or there may be none. If, however, he or she says 'I agree with Bloggs LJ for the reasons he gives', then there is no problem.

Sometimes a judge says 'I agree and would just like to add . . .'. He or she then addresses certain issues only. His or her reasoning on those issues may help to determine the *ratio,* but on issues which he does not address, his judgment is of no help.

7.4 Some test questions

Try these questions to see if you are able to apply the principles explained above. The answers and their explanations are given at the end of this chapter.

7.4.1 Question 1

A High Court judge is deciding a case which involves a point of law on which there is no binding authority. Which of the following statements is correct?

[A] He or she should always follow a decision of a High Court judge rather than an *obiter dictum* of the Court of Appeal.

[B] He or she should follow the decision of a fellow High Court judge if he or she can find no good reason to differ.

[C] If there are conflicting Court of Appeal decisions he may choose which he prefers.

[D] He should follow an *obiter dictum* of the House of Lords rather than an *obiter dictum* of the Court of Appeal.

7.4.2 Question 2

A High Court judge is deciding a case involving a point of law which has previously been dealt with in a Court of Appeal decision. In which of the following circumstances will he or she be bound by that decision?

[A] The Court of Appeal decision is just about distinguishable.

[B] The Court of Appeal decision was later reversed by the House of Lords.

[C] The Court of Appeal decision was later changed by an Act of Parliament.

[D] The Court of Appeal decision was regarded as highly dubious by the House of Lords in a later case.

7.4.3 Question 3

You are advising a client on a matter involving a point of law and you come across several Court of Appeal cases which include persuasive *obiter dicta* in favour of your client's position, but also one High Court case which seems to decide the point against your client. You should:

[A See if you can distinguish the High Court case making use of the Court of Appeal *dicta*.

[B] Ignore the High Court case and advise on the basis of the Court of Appeal cases.

[C] Advise your client that his case is unarguable.

[D] Advise your client that in the light of the Court of Appeal *dicta* his case is strong.

7.4.4 Question 4

A judge is deciding a case on a point of law which has previously been considered by the Court of Appeal and the House of Lords in different cases. The Court of Appeal decided that the defendant was liable to the claimant because facts A, B, and C existed. The House of Lords decided that the defendant was liable because facts A, B, and D existed and doubted that fact C was relevant. In which of the following circumstances is the judge NOT bound by previous precedent?

[A] He or she finds facts A, B, C, and D exist.

[B] He or she finds facts A, B, and C exist, but not D.

[C] He or she finds facts A, C, and D exist, but not B.

[D] He or she finds facts A, B, and D exist, but not C.

7.4.5 Question 5

In 2008, a circuit judge is deciding a case on a point of law which has previously been considered as follows:

(1) In 2003, the Court of Appeal decided in favour of the claimant because facts A and B existed.

(2) In 2004, a High Court judge decided in favour of the defendant because facts A, B, and C existed.

(3) In 2005, a High Court judge decided in favour of the claimant because facts A, B, C, and D existed.

(4) In 2006, the Court of Appeal decided in favour of the claimant because facts A, B, and C existed.

(5) In 2007, a High Court judge decided in favour of the defendant because facts A, B, C, D, and E existed.

In which of the following circumstances should the judge find in favour of the defendant?

[A] He finds facts A and B exist.

[B] He finds facts A, B, and C exist.

[C] He finds facts A, B, C, and D exist.

[D] He finds facts A, B, C, and E exist.

7.4.6 Question 6

In a case involving the interpretation of the Unfair Liability Act 2007, the House of Lords ruled in favour of the defendant. The Law Lords were unanimous that the claimant could only succeed if he could show that for the purposes of the Act a warehouse was a 'workshop' but a forklift truck was *not* a 'vehicle' and a portacabin was *not* a 'building'. The Law Lords decided as follows:

Lord Able: a warehouse is a workshop, a forklift truck is a vehicle, a portacabin is not a building.

Lord Boot: a warehouse is not a workshop, a forklift truck is a vehicle, a portacabin is not a building.

Lord Cobbler: a warehouse is a workshop, a forklift truck is a not a vehicle, a portacabin is a building.

Lord Dupe: agreed with Lord Cobbler for the same reasons.

Lord Egg: agreed with Lords Able and Boot 'for the reasons they give'.

Which of the following interpretations of the Unfair Liability Act has been decided as a matter of law?

[A] A warehouse is a workshop.

[B] A forklift truck is a vehicle.

[C] A portacabin is not a building.

[D] All of these.

7.5 Analysing cases

We are now going to take two short cases and analyse them, looking at the reasoning of the judges, working out what the *ratio* of each case is, and understanding the distinction between them. As it happens, they are tax cases, but do not be put off by that. There are no points of specialist tax law involved. In fact, they both turn on a judicial examination of the concept of 'a dwelling house' and what those words mean in a certain context. The cases are *Batey (Inspector of Taxes) v Wakefield* [1982] 1 All ER 61 and *Lewis (Inspector of Taxes) v Lady Rook* [1992] 1 WLR 662, and both are in the Court of Appeal. Only the judgments are printed; the facts and the relevant law are all included in the judgments, so you need no more. After each case there appears a commentary. Because of the need to refer in the commentaries to particular sections of the judgment, the format of the judgment has been altered, and they are given paragraph numbers in the modern neutral citation style. In the original reports, of course, you would have to refer to passages by page numbers and marginal letters.

7.6 *Batey v Wakefield* [1982] 1 All ER 61

Batey v Wakefield was heard in the Court of Appeal on 22 June 1981. Judgment was delivered on the same day.

7.6.1 The judgments

FOX LJ:

[1] This is an appeal from a decision of Browne-Wilkinson J relating to capital gains tax. Mr Wakefield, the taxpayer, purchased about one –and –a half acres of land in 1957 near Marlborough in Wiltshire. At that time there were various buildings on the land; they consisted of, or included, brick loose boxes, a forage store, and a garage with a room above. Those buildings were sold off by the taxpayer not long after he acquired the land. As a result of those and further sales, the amount of land which was owned by the taxpayer from 1966 to 1974 was about 1.1 acres.

[2] In about 1959, the taxpayer built a dwelling house called 'Paddocks' on the land; that dwelling house consisted of about eight rooms. The house was built for occupation by the taxpayer and his family. Because of the demands of his work, the taxpayer was not originally able to live at Paddocks all the time; during the week he lived in a flat in London with his wife and daughter. Paddocks was therefore left unattended, except at weekends when the taxpayer and his family lived there.

[3] There were a number of burglaries in the neighbourhood, and Paddocks itself was burgled once. So the taxpayer decided that since he and his family were not living in the house during the week, he must have a caretaker at Paddocks to look after it. He therefore employed a caretaker-gardener, together with his wife as a housekeeper.

[4] For them, in 1966, he built on part of the 1.1 acres a chalet-bungalow called Paddocks Lodge, which had one main bedroom; precisely what the other accommodation was, I am not certain. Paddocks Lodge had a detached garage of its own, and access from a different road from that giving access to Paddocks itself. It was separated from Paddocks by about the width of a tennis court and by a yew hedge which had been established before the building of Paddocks Lodge. Paddocks Lodge was occupied free of rent and rates by the caretaker-gardener and his wife and son, in return for work done at Paddocks. The General Commissioners found that the occupation of Paddocks Lodge was intended to enable the caretaker and his wife to perform the duties of their employment with the taxpayer.

[5] By 1974 it was no longer necessary for the taxpayer to live in London, so he took up full-time residence at Paddocks. The need for the caretaker therefore no longer existed.

[6] In about March of 1974, the taxpayer sold Paddocks Lodge with about 0.2 of an acre of land, for some £18,000, which gave rise to a capital gain of some £11,895. Since the sale of Paddocks Lodge the taxpayer and his family have continued to live in Paddocks. The properties had always been separately rated.

[7] For completeness, perhaps I should mention that in 1967 the taxpayer made an election under the statute to treat Paddocks as his main residence. The Crown claims capital gains tax on the gain of £11,895 on the sale of Paddocks Lodge.

[8] I come now to the statutory provisions. Section 29(1) and (2) of the Finance Act 1965, which is the material statute for the purposes of this transaction, provides as follows:

'(1) This section applies to a gain accruing to an individual so far as attributable to the disposal of, or of an interest in—(a) a dwelling-house or part of a dwelling-house which is, or has at any time in his period of ownership been, his only or main residence, or (b) land which he has for his own occupation and enjoyment with that residence as its garden or grounds up to an area (inclusive of the site of the dwelling house) of one acre or such larger area as the Commissioners concerned may in any particular case determine, on being satisfied that, regard being had to the size and character of the dwelling-house, the larger area is required for the reasonable enjoyment of it (or of the part in question) as a residence.'

'The gain shall not be a chargeable gain if the dwelling-house or part of a dwelling-house has been the individual's only or main residence throughout the period of ownership, or throughout the period of ownership except for all or any part of the last twelve months of that period.'

[9] Then I should mention sub-s (5), which deals with the case of a dwelling house part of which is used for the purposes of trade; sub-s (8), which deals with the position of a husband and wife, and provides that where they are living together there can only be one residence for both; sub-s (12) deals with apportionments of consideration where a person disposes of a dwelling house, only part of which is his only or main residence. Subsection (10) deals with what were referred to as 'granny flats'; it does not determine the question which is in issue in the present case.

[10] The decision of the commissioners, so far as material, was as follows:

'We . . . found that a dwelling house could consist of more than one building on the same site not being contiguous buildings. "Paddocks Lodge" was occupied in conjunction with "Paddocks" having been built specifically for staff purposes. It could equally have been occupied by the children or aged parents of the family. We were satisfied that 1.1 acres was a reasonable area of land for a dwelling house of the character of 'Paddocks. We were satisfied that the taxpayer's intention was to make additional accommodation available for his staff or the better enjoyment of his own dwelling house. We found that by building "Paddocks Lodge" for the caretaker/gardener and housekeeper the taxpayer was doing no more than increasing his reasonable enjoyment of his residence. We found that the disposal of "Paddocks Lodge" was a disposal of part of [the taxpayer's] dwelling house which had been his only or main residence throughout the period of ownership and that the gain which he made on the sale of "Paddocks Lodge" was therefore exempt from capital gains tax . . . '

[11] The Crown appealed from that decision. Browne-Wilkinson J upheld the decision of the commissioners and dismissed the appeal.

[12] In effect, the argument of the Crown is this, that one must ascertain whether what has been disposed of is part of a dwelling house. The lodge is quite a separate physical dwelling, actually used as a separate dwelling house by a separate family; it cannot, therefore, be part of another dwelling house, namely Paddocks. It is said that an independent dwelling house used by a separate household, like Paddocks Lodge, cannot be part of another dwelling house; and it is said, therefore, that the decision of the commissioners must be bad on the face of it.

[13] I do not for myself feel able to accept that. In approaching these matters, there are two propositions which seem to me to be correct. First, it seems to me that in the ordinary use of English, a dwelling house, or a residence, can comprise several dwellings which are not physically joined at all. For example, one would normally regard a dwelling house as including a separate garage; similarly it would, I think, include a separate building, such as a studio, which was built and used for the owner's enjoyment. Indeed, I think a living room could be in one building and bedrooms in another; that might be inconvenient, but I see no reason why they should not together constitute a single dwelling house for the purposes of this statute.

[14] Secondly, if a dwelling house contained a staff flat which is self-contained and with, for example, its own access, I see no reason why that cannot accurately be called part of the larger dwelling house. It seems to me that that is exactly what it is; it is physically part of the dwelling house and its user is for the purpose of serving the dwelling house as a residence.

[15] What, then, is the position of a building which is itself a house but which is physically separate from the dwelling house of which it is said to form a part? That is Paddocks Lodge in the present case. The fact that it is physically separate from what I might call the main dwelling house, Paddocks, seems to me to be irrelevant. As I have indicated, separate buildings can together form the residence; similarly, a self-contained residence may form part of a dwelling house. I can see no logical reason why a house which is physically quite separate should not form part of another residence or dwelling house. For example, a flat over a coach house in a stable yard which is occupied by servants is, I think, none the less part of the main dwelling house even though it is physically separate from it and I think that, as a matter of the ordinary use of English, it would be so described as being part of the main dwelling house.

[16] I do not think that one can approach the matter in a piecemeal way; a dwelling house can consist of more than one building. I agree with the judge that what one is

looking for is the entity which in fact constitutes the residence of the taxpayer. I can see no difference in principle between a coachman's flat in the stable yard used for the purpose of serving the main house and a bungalow such as Paddocks Lodge, built on the comparatively small area of land held with Paddocks for the purpose of serving Paddocks. It is, it seems to me, a question of degree in each case. The question is what are the true constituents of the residence which is in question?

[17] The judge, in his judgment, said this ([1980] STC 572 at 577):

'On the commissioners' findings, the lodge was built and occupied to provide services and caretaking facilities for the benefit of the main house. The lodge was occupied by the taxpayer through his employee, who was employed for the purpose of promoting the taxpayer's reasonable enjoyment of his own residence. In those circumstances, bearing in mind the fact that the buildings are very closely adjacent, it seems to me proper to find that the lodge was part of the residence of the taxpayer . . . '

I agree with that. What has to be determined is the identity of the dwelling house. The fact that it comprised separate accommodation in which staff, or children, or guests may be accommodated does not, in my view, determine conclusively that such accommodation is not part of the dwelling house. It may be a factor, but it is no more. It is, as I have indicated, a matter of degree in every case whether a separate building does or does not in truth form part of the residence in question. That question is one for the commissioners to determine. The court can only allow an appeal from the commissioners if their decision is shown to be wrong in point of law. I see no reason for saying that the commissioners misdirected themselves in law in the present case, and I am quite unable to say that no reasonable tribunal, properly directed, could have reached the conclusion which they did.

[18] Therefore, despite the very helpful and able argument of counsel for the Crown, I do not feel able to interfere with the determination of the commissioners. I think the judge reached the right conclusion, and I would dismiss the appeal.

OLIVER LJ:

[19] I entirely agree and do not feel that I can usefully add anything.

STEPHENSON LJ:

[20] Is also agree.

7.6.2 Commentary

If we work through the judgment of Fox LJ, we can see how it is put together.

7.6.2.1 The facts

In paragraphs [1] to [7], the judge is setting out the facts. This is not of course necessarily a statement of all of the facts—they have been selected by the judge. But that is useful for two reasons: you can avoid having to read unnecessary factual material, and you know which facts the judge regards as relevant. These are likely to be the facts that have led him to his conclusion, or which were persuasive. You may in due course decide that they are part of the *ratio* of the case.

Do not, however, assume that this statement of the facts will *only* contain relevant facts, nor that you will not find relevant facts elsewhere in the judgment. Where, as here, the judge is delivering the judgment *extempore*, perfection in this respect cannot be expected of him!

7.6.2.2   The law

The judge then sets out the relevant statute law in paragraphs [8] and [9].

The law is simply contained in Section 29(1) of the Finance Act 1965, and as we shall see, the case turns on the construction of this Section, or more accurately, two words in this Section: 'dwelling house'. The rest of it turns out to be material only insofar as it determines the undisputed outcome of the case once this point of law has been resolved.

7.6.2.3   The commissioners' decision

Then in paragraph [10] the judge sets out the decision of the commissioners by quoting from their written decision. Note that only their conclusions are set out here—this passage does not contain any reasons, or the full *ratio* of their decision. At this point the judge makes no comment on it, as he might do in some cases. He is still continuing to set out all the relevant background material before he starts to say what he thinks.

7.6.2.4   The appeal

There is then a very short paragraph [11] in which the appeal route is stated. Note that Fox LJ is the third judge to consider the case. The decision of Browne-Wilkinson J is not referred to further at this point; we discover that he reached the same conclusion as the commissioners, but not whether he did so for the same reasons. Some of his reasons appear later in paragraph [17].

7.6.2.5   The Crown's argument

In paragraph [12] Fox LJ then outlines the argument on behalf of the Crown (the Inland Revenue). The Crown seems to have adopted an all-or-nothing argument: that an independent household in a separate building can never be part of another dwelling house.

7.6.2.6   The conclusion and reasons

Fox LJ then starts to set out his conclusion and reasoning. This begins at paragraph [13] and continues to the end of the judgment at paragraph [18]. Note that we are now about two-thirds of the way through the judgment, and everything said so far is simply by way of introduction. We know therefore that decision and the *ratio* of the case will be found exclusively in the few paragraphs still to come.

The judge makes his decision clear in three short statements:

(a) The first sentence of paragraph [13]—'*I do not feel able for myself to accept that*'.
(b) The sentence '*I agree with that*' in paragraph [17]. The judge is adopting the reasoning of Browne-Wilkinson J.
(c) The final paragraph [18].

The rest of this section contains the judge's reasons, and within it you will find both the legal proposition decided by this case and its *ratio*.

This section, however, subdivides. In paragraphs [13]–[16], the judge is dealing with his conclusions and reasons on the issue of law. In paragraph [17], he is dealing with his conclusions and reasons on the facts.

7.6.2.7   The legal issue and conclusion

The question of law in this case was 'What is a dwelling house?'; or more specifically, 'Can a dwelling house consist of more than one building?'

The conclusion is not of course a complete definition, but a partial definition: the case decided as a matter of law that a 'dwelling house' for the purposes of the statute could consist of more than one building.

The court did not of course decide that a dwelling house *must* consist of more than one building. Nor did it decide that more than one building will *always* amount to a single dwelling house. There is a further question of fact to be decided—whether the separate buildings in any given case do or do not amount to a single dwelling house.

7.6.2.8 The *ratio*

The legal *ratio*, that is the reasoning that led to the conclusion on the point of law, is found in paragraphs at [13] to [16].

There are four propositions mentioned by the judge:

(1) A dwelling house, or residence, can comprise several dwellings which are not joined:

[13] . . . First, it seems to me that in the ordinary use of English, a dwelling house, or a residence, can comprise several dwellings which are not physically joined at all. For example, one would normally regard a dwelling house as including a separate garage; similarly it would, I think, include a separate building, such as a studio, which was built and used for the owner's enjoyment. Indeed, I think a living room could be in one building and bedrooms in another; that might be inconvenient, but I see no reason why they should not together constitute a single dwelling house for the purposes of this statute.

(2) A self-contained staff flat within a single dwelling house can be part of that dwelling house:

[14] Secondly, if a dwelling house contained a staff flat which is self-contained and with, for example, its own access, I see no reason why that cannot accurately be called part of the larger dwelling house. It seems to me that that is exactly what it is; it is physically part of the dwelling house and its user is for the purpose of serving the dwelling house as a residence.

(3) There is no logical difference between that and a staff residence in a separate building:

[15] . . . I can see no logical reason why a house which is physically quite separate should not form part of another residence or dwelling house. For example, a flat over a coach house in a stable yard which is occupied by servants is, I think, none the less part of the main dwelling house even though it is physically separate from it and I think that, as a matter of the ordinary use of English, it would be so described as being part of the main dwelling house.

(4) What one must look for is the entity which in fact constitutes the residence of the taxpayer, and its true constituents:

[16] I do not think that one can approach the matter in a piecemeal way; a dwelling house can consist of more than one building. I agree with the judge that what one is looking for is the entity which in fact constitutes the residence of the taxpayer . . . The question is what are the true constituents of the residence which is in question?

Propositions (1), (2) and (3) are steps in the judge's reasoning process, and contain the reasoning that led to the conclusion that a dwelling house can in law consist of more than one building. But proposition (4) is also important. In effect here, the judge states as a matter of law the approach that must be adopted when determining the factual issue in each case. This is therefore also part of the *ratio*. The judge says the same thing again in slightly different words in paragraph [17]: '*What has to be determined is the identity of the dwelling house.*' The judge doubtless meant to say the same thing, but he changed 'residence' to 'dwelling house', which is a slip that is picked up in the later case of *Lewis v Lady Rook*.

7.6.2.9   The decision on the facts

There is no appeal to the Court of Appeal on a question of fact, only on a question of law. So the issue to be decided was *not* 'Is Paddocks Lodge part of the dwelling house?' but 'Was the decision that Paddocks Lodge was part of the dwelling house open to the commissioners?' The court can only overturn their decision if:

(a) it was wrong in law, that is because they reached it through a misunderstanding of the concept of a dwelling house; or

(b) it was wrong in law because they applied the wrong test; or

(c) it was irrational, that is because no reasonable tribunal, properly directed, could have reached the conclusion which they did.

Here, the Court upheld the decision on the facts.

7.6.2.10   The *ratio* on the facts

There can be no binding *ratio* on the facts because the Court did not decide the factual issue. However, if one can identify the facts which were persuasive to the commissioners and which the Court believed were relevant, what the Court said about them will be sufficiently persuasive to need distinguishing in any subsequent case in which the decision is different.

Here one might well say that the following facts were persuasive:

(1) The buildings were very closely adjacent (paragraph [17])—separated by about the width of a tennis court and a yew hedge (paragraph [4]).

(2) Paddocks Lodge was occupied by an employee (paragraph [17]).

(3) The employee paid no rent (paragraph [4]).

(4) The employee was employed for the purpose of promoting the taxpayer's reasonable enjoyment of his own residence (paragraph [17]).

7.6.2.11   *Obiter dictum*

Anything that is not part of the *ratio* is strictly *obiter,* but there is a good example of an *obiter dictum* in paragraph [17], when the judge says that the fact that there is separate accommodation for staff or guests does not determine conclusively that that accommodation is not part of the dwelling house but then adds that '*it may be a factor but it is no more*'. The implication is that in other cases, the separateness of the accommodation may tend to point away from its being part of the dwelling house.

7.6.2.12   Agreement by the other judges

Oliver and Stephenson LJJ agree with Fox LJ. There is potential to argue that they agree with the conclusion but not necessarily the reasons. But in the light of the issues to be determined in this case it is highly probable that they can be taken to agree with everything Fox LJ said, and so the *ratio* of his judgment is the *ratio* of the whole Court of Appeal's decision.

7.7   *Lewis v Lady Rook* [1992] 1 WLR 662

Lewis v Lady Rook was heard in the Court of Appeal on 30 January 1992. Judgment was reserved and delivered on 19 February 1992.

7.7.1 The Judgments

BALCOMBE LJ:

[1] This is an appeal by the Crown from a decision of Mervyn Davies J [1990] STC 23 dated 5 December 1989 affirming a decision of the General Commissioners for Sevenoaks that the respondent taxpayer was entitled to relief from capital gains tax on the disposal by her of 1 Hop Cottages, Newlands, Crockham Hill, Kent, on 30 August 1979.

[2] The facts as found by the General Commissioners are set out in para 5 of the case stated as follows:

'(1) On 6th June 1968 the taxpayer purchased the property known as Newlands, Crockham Hill, Kent for £34,501. s(2) Included in the purchase were two cottages known as Nos 1 and 2 Hop Cottages (formerly an oasthouse) on the south boundary of the property. (3) The total acreage of the property owned by the taxpayer on 30th August 1979 was 10.5 acres. The distance between the nearest points of No 1 Hop Cottages and Newlands is approximately 569 feet (175 metres). (4) The main house Newlands has a large hall, an imposing landing, a very large dining room, a drawing room, a playroom, a further reception room making four in all, eight bedrooms, one used as a billiard room, a kitchen, a pantry, a scullery and a silver room. (5) No 1 Hop Cottages comprised a dining room, a lounge, a kitchen, two bedrooms and a bathroom. No 2 Hop Cottages next door had similar accommodation. (6) Before the taxpayer purchased Newlands and Nos 1 and 2 Hop Cottages, No 1 Hop Cottages had been occupied by Mr and Mrs Foster. Mr Foster worked in the garden of the main house and Mrs Foster helped in the main house. When the taxpayer was on the point of completing the purchase of Newlands Mr Foster died. Mrs Foster remained at No 1 Hop Cottages after the purchase but never worked for the taxpayer. (7) Mrs Foster paid the taxpayer a contribution of £1.12per week which was the amount she had always paid ever since the taxpayer purchased the property. She paid this in respect of No 1 Hop Cottages and in respect of No 2 when she moved. She was 75 years of age at the time of the appeal hearing. (8) In early February 1973 Mrs Foster vacated No 1 Hop Cottages and moved into No 2 Hop Cottages. Since purchasing Newlands, the taxpayer had renovated No 2 Hop Cottages (which at the date of purchase had no bathroom and outside sanitation). In February 1974 the taxpayer's gardener moved into No 1 Hop Cottages. In February 1978 the gardener vacated No 1 Hop Cottages. (9) By contract dated 30th August 1979 the taxpayer sold No 1 Hop Cottages for £33,000. The sale proceeds helped to finance the conversion into residential accommodation of the Coach House which was immediately adjacent to the main house and which had previously been used for storing hay in the loft with two garages below. After vacating No 1 Hop Cottages the taxpayer's gardener moved in the Coach House. The taxpayer was elderly, lived alone in the main house and needed someone close at hand; hence the reason for the gardener's move. (10) The greenhouses, tool shed and compost heaps used in connection with the main house garden were situated between the main house and No 1 Hop Cottages and convenient to No 1 Hop Cottages. The greenhouses and the potting shed were located approximately half way between No 1 Hop Cottages and the main house. (11) During the taxpayer's ownership of it, No 1 Hop Cottages had never been screened from the main house so that the taxpayer could see the lights in the cottage and could flash a light if she needed help. She also had a ship's bell which she could ring and which could be heard from the cottage which she would use if she needed help. This had happened more than once. It was very convenient to come up through the garden to the house and it was not convenient by the road.'

[3] The relevant statutory provisions are to be found in ss 101 and 102 of the Capital Gains Tax Act 1979 (the 1979 Act). Section 101, so far as relevant, is in the following terms:

'(1) This section applies to a gain accruing to an individual so far as attributable to the disposal of, or of an interest in—

(a) a dwelling-house or part of a dwelling-house which is, or has at any time in his period of ownership been, his only or main residence, or

(b) land which he has for his own occupation and enjoyment with that residence as its garden or grounds up to the permitted area.

(2) In this section "the permitted area" means, subject to subsection (3) and (4) below, an area (inclusive of the site of the dwelling-house) of one acre.

(3) In any particular case the permitted area shall be such area, larger than one acre, as the Commissioners concerned may determine if satisfied that, regard being had to the size and character of the dwelling-house, that larger area is required for the reasonable enjoyment of it (or of the part in question) as a residence.'

Section 102, so far as relevant, provided at the material date:

'(1) No part of a gain to which section 101 above applies shall be a chargeable gain if the dwelling-house or part of a dwelling-house has been the individual's only or main residence throughout the period of ownership, or throughout the period of ownership except for all or any part of the last twelve months of that period.

(2) Where subsection (1) above does not apply, a fraction of the gain shall not be a chargeable gain, and that fraction shall be . . . '

The rest of s 102 is concerned with the calculation of the amount of the relief and that is not in issue on the present appeal.

[4] The issue is whether No 1 Hop Cottages formed part of a dwelling house which was the taxpayer's only or main residence.

[5] The General Commissioners' findings are contained in para 9 of the case stated as follows (at 26):

'We the Commissioners who heard the appeal, having considered the parties' contentions and the evidence before us, found that No 1 Hop Cottages formed part of the entity which comprised the dwelling-house of Newlands. We considered that during Mrs Foster's residence at No 1 Hop Cottages the exemption should not apply and we found that accordingly an apportionment should be made and a figure of £2,855.10 of tax paid . . . '

[6] The judge upheld the commissioners' findings, although on grounds which formed no part of the commissioners' decision. His conclusions are contained in the following passage from his judgment (at 31):

'I now look at the facts of this case with a view to deciding whether or not No 1 Hop Cottages is within the entity constituting the taxpayer's residence. There are the following considerations: (i) The cottage is about 190 yards from Newlands House. (ii) The cottage is rated separately from Newlands House. (iii) At a relevant time it was occupied by a gardener employed by the taxpayer, (iv) His work took him up the path from the cottage to the lawn and vegetable garden, the boundaries of which were less than 100 yards from the cottage: see in this connection para 10 of the case stated [at 26] as quoted above [at 27]. (v) The taxpayer, elderly and living alone, placed reliance on a presence in No 1 Hop Cottages: see the case stated [at 26] para 11 as quoted above [at 27]. Taking these considerations into account it seems to me that the entity constituting the taxpayer's residence included No 1 Hop Cottages because the taxpayer's way of living embraced use not only of Newlands House itself with its gardens but also of the cottage of the gardener who attended to the gardens. That the cottage is about 190 yards distant from the house is, to my mind, not of paramount importance in the context of the Newlands set-up; that is, of the way of life led by the taxpayer. It is a matter of degree. In these circumstances I do not feel able to say that the commissioners came to an unsound determination.'

[7] The Crown maintains that no reasonable tribunal of fact, properly directing itself, could have reached the conclusion that No 1 Hop Cottages (the cottage) and Newlands together formed one dwelling house which was the taxpayer's residence.

[8] It is to be noted that s 101(1)(a) refers to 'a dwelling-house . . . which is . . . his . . . : residence'. The Crown would wish to argue from the reference to a dwelling house (in the singular) that the buildings which form a taxpayer's dwelling house under s 101(1)(a)

cannot include buildings apart from the taxpayer's main house which themselves form a separate self-contained dwelling house. Mr Warren, counsel for the Crown, accepted that this argument was not open to him before us because of the decision of this court in *Batey v Wakefield* [1982] 1 All ER 61, although he reserved the right to argue the point in a higher court.

[9] Since *Batey v Wakefield* is the first of three reported cases in which a question arose similar to that in the present case, it will be convenient to consider those cases before turning to the arguments in the present case.

[10] In *Batey v Wakefield* the main house (Paddocks) was a four-bedroomed house set in 1.1 acres of land. On a part of that land the taxpayer built a chalet bungalow (Paddocks Lodge) for occupation by a caretaker/gardener. Paddocks Lodge had one main bedroom, its own garage and separate access from the road. It was separated from Paddocks by the width of a tennis court and a little more. It was built behind an established yew hedge. The taxpayer subsequently sold Paddocks Lodge which sale gave rise to a capital gain and the question was whether that gain was exempt from capital gains tax under the provisions of the Finance Act 1965 corresponding to ss 101 and 102 of the 1979 Act. The General Commissioners decided that the gain was exempt. The Crown appealed. The appeal was dismissed, both at first instance by Browne-Wilkinson J (1980) 55 TC 550 and by this court (Stephenson, Oliver and Fox LJJ) [1982] 1 All ER 61. Browne-Wilkinson J said, 55 TC 550, 556:

'The difference between the two sides depends on whether one stresses the words "a dwelling house", as the Crown suggests, or the words "a residence", as the taxpayer suggests. In the ordinary use of the words, if one looks at a man's residence it includes not only the physical main building in which the living rooms, bedrooms and bathroom are contained, but also the appurtenant buildings, such as the garage and buildings of that kind. One is looking at the group of buildings which together constitute the residence. It is true, as the Crown says in this case, that s 29 [of the Finance Act 1965] draws a distinction between a dwelling house, which is dealt with by sub-s (1)(a), and the land occupied and enjoyed with the residence as its garden or grounds, which is separately dealt with by sub-s (1)(b). Therefore the dwelling house referred to in sub-s (1)(a) does not include the whole of its curtilage. But in my judgment sub-s (1)(a) is including in the dwelling house some other buildings which are appurtenant thereto; for example, the garage, the potting shed and the summer house, which otherwise would not come within s 29 at all . . . In my judgment the commissioners were right in saying that what one has to look at and discover is: what was the residence of the taxpayer? For that purpose, you have to identify the dwelling house which is his residence. That dwelling house may or may not be comprised in one physical building; it may comprise a number of different buildings. His dwelling house and residence consists of all those buildings which are part and parcel of the whole, each part being appurtenant to and occupied for the purposes of the residence. The Crown does not go so far as to maintain that a building separate from the main can never be part of the dwelling house. If that be so, then it seems to me that the commissioners directed themselves rightly in seeing whether the lodge was itself appurtenant to and occupied for the purposes of the building occupied by the taxpayer. On the commissioners' findings, the lodge was built and occupied to provide services and caretaking facilities for the benefit of the main house. The lodge was occupied by the taxpayer through his employee, who was employed for the purpose of promoting the taxpayer's reasonable enjoyment of his own residence. In those circumstances, bearing in mind the fact that the buildings are very closely adjacent, it seems to me proper to find that the lodge was part of the residence of the taxpayer, and accordingly the gain falls within the exemption in s 29(2).'

[11] Fox LJ, with whom the other members of the court agreed, said [1982] 1 All ER 61, 64:

' . . . what one is looking for is the entity which in fact constitutes the residence of the taxpayer. I can see no difference in principle between a coachman's flat in the stable yard used for the purpose of serving the main house and a bungalow such as Paddocks Lodge, built on the comparatively small area of land held with Paddocks for the purpose of serving Paddocks. It is, it seems to me, a question of degree in each case. The question is what are the true constituents of the residence which is in question? . . . What has to be determined is the identity of the dwelling house. The fact that it comprised separate accommodation in which staff, or children, or guests may be accommodated does not, in my view, determine conclusively that such accommodation is not part of the dwelling house. It may be a factor, but it is no more. It is, as I have indicated, a matter of degree in every case whether a separate building does or does not in truth form part of the residence in question. That question is one for the commissioners to determine.'

[12] The next case in the sequence is *Markey (Inspector of Taxes) v Sanders* [1987] 1 WLR 864. There there was a main house with outbuildings in 12 acres of land. The taxpayer built a detached three-bedroomed bungalow some 130 metres away from the main house and separated from it by a paddock. The bungalow, which was occupied rent-free by staff, had its own garden, and was also screened by trees and separated by a ha-ha from the main house. The issue was whether the main house and the bungalow together formed a dwelling house which was the taxpayer's residence. The General Commissioners held that they did. This decision was reversed by Walton J on appeal. He considered *Batey v Wakefield* [1982] 1 All ER 61 and said [1987] STC 256 at 263, [1987] 1 WLR 864 at 869:

'The way in which it was put by the Court of Appeal, therefore, was that one had to look to see whether the separate building was one which was "very closely adjacent"; and so I think one can lay down fairly simply the conditions which have to be satisfied before a taxpayer can claim that a building which is not the part of his main residence where he himself ordinarily resides does for the purposes of the Capital Gains Tax Act 1979 fall within that description. The first condition is that the occupation of the building in question must increase the taxpayer's enjoyment of the main house. That is a necessary but clearly not a sufficient condition. The second condition, and again I take this at the moment straight from the Court of Appeal, is that the other building must be "very closely adjacent" to the main building; and, once again, that is a necessary but not sufficient condition.'

Then, after rejecting a test based on the words 'curtilage' and 'appurtenant' as used by the judges in *Batey v Wakefield*, he said at pp. 870–2:

'Now I myself would prefer to ask: looking at the group of buildings in question as a whole, is it fairly possible to regard them as a single dwelling house used as the taxpayer's main residence? I prefer to put it in that way because the concept of "very closely adjacent" does not of itself indicate that the scale of the buildings must be taken into consideration, which appears to me to be fairly obvious: for what would be "very closely adjacent" were one dealing with the sale of no 7 Paradise Avenue, Hoxton, might very well be quite different from what those words would mean if one were considering the sale of Blenheim Palace. Of course, those are two absurd examples at either end of the scale, but the fact that buildings can vary as much as those two vary indicates quite clearly that "very closely adjacent" is perhaps in itself too imprecise, whereas if one takes the test that I suggest, which I think is fully in line with the spirit of the decision of the Court of Appeal, it becomes very much easier to see what one is really talking about . . . What is said by counsel for the taxpayer, who has taken every conceivable argument on the part of the taxpayer, is that the test of "very closely adjacent" is an elastic test and that it is one which must be left to the commissioners to determine. I entirely agree that it is an elastic test, but merely because it is an elastic test does not mean that the commissioners are entitled to apply it absolutely regardless of the facts. Following up his way of putting it, there comes a time when the elastic snaps and the court is entitled to say, "You have gone too far." It is no use the commissioners describing in great detail what is clearly recognisable as an elephant and then concluding that it is a giraffe: it just does not work. So it seems to my mind that something has gone wrong here, but I am totally unable to determine precisely what it is . . . Whilst I do not put it in the forefront of my reasons, it does strike me that it would be a very curious circumstance indeed that where a house, including the ground on which it stands, is allowed (as it were) free of capital gains tax up to one acre (and there has been no determination by the commissioners that any area greater than one acre would be proper in this case, although I understand that the Revenue is prepared to concede that the gardens, which do exceed the one acre, do qualify for relief) a house which is sited well over an acre's worth of land away from the main residence and separated from it by a paddock which is not part of the ground so allowed could nevertheless be deemed to be part of it. It seems to me that that really is a totally absurd conclusion.'

[13] The last case in the series is *Williams (Inspector of Taxes) v Merrylees* [1987] 1 WLR 1511. In that case, a lodge some 200 metres from the main house was held by the General Commissioners to be part of a dwelling house which was the taxpayer's residence, being 'within the curtilage of the property of and appurtenant to' the main house. Vinelott J dismissed an appeal by the Crown, although expressing doubts that he would himself have reached the same conclusion. He considered both *Batey v Wakefield* [1982] All ER 61 and *Markey v Sanders* [1987] 1 WLR 864. He doubted whether it was possible to spell out of the decision of the Court of Appeal in *Batey v Wakefield* [1982] 1 All ER 61 two distinct conditions each of which must be satisfied before a separate building can be considered part of a dwelling house.

[14] I have to say that I do not find the current state of the authorities very satisfactory, and it is hardly surprising that different sets of General Commissioners have reached conclusions which are not always easy to understand.

[15] In these circumstances, it is necessary to go back to the words of the statute. What has first to be determined is what in the particular case constitutes the 'dwelling house'. This is an ordinary English word of which the definition in the *Shorter Oxford English Dictionary,* 3rd edn (1944), rev. 1973, is 'a house occupied as a place of residence'. That dwelling house can, following the decision of this court in *Batey v Wakefield,* consist of more than one building and that even if the other building itself constitutes a separate dwelling house. Nevertheless, I agree with what Vinelott J said in *Williams v Merrylees* [1987] 1 WLR1511, 1519:

'What one is looking for is an entity which can be sensibly described as being a dwelling house though split up into different buildings performing different functions.'

[16] How, then, can that entity be identified in any given case? First, attention must be focused on the dwelling house which is said to constitute the entity. To seek to identify the taxpayer's residence may lead to confusion because where, as here, the dwelling house forms part of a small estate, it is all too easy to consider the estate as his residence and from that to conclude that all the buildings on the estate are part of his residence. In so far as some of the statements made in *Batey v Wakefield* suggest that one must first identify the residence they must, in my judgment, be considered to have been made *per incuriam.*

[17] In all the cases to which I have referred, there has been an identifiable main house. Where it is contended that some one or more separate buildings are to be treated as part of an entity which, together with the main house, comprises a dwelling house, Mr Warren submitted for the Crown that no building can form part of a dwelling house which includes a main house, unless that building is appurtenant to, and within the curtilage of, the main house.

[18] At first I was inclined to the view that this introduced an unnecessary complication into the test, even though this was the way in which Browne-Wilkinson J approached the problem in *Batey v Wakefield,* 55 TC 550. On reflection I have come to the conclusion that this is a helpful approach, since it involves the application of well-recognised legal concepts and may avoid the somewhat surprising findings of fact which were

reached in *Markey v Sanders* [1987] 1 WLR 864, *Williams v Merrylees* [1987] 1 WLR 1511 and, indeed, in the present case. In *Methuen-Campbell v Walters* [1979] QB 525, 543–44 Buckley LJ said:

'In my judgment, for one corporeal hereditament to fall within the curtilage of another, the former must be so intimately associated with the latter as to lead to the conclusion that the former in truth forms part and parcel of the latter. There can be very few houses indeed that do not have associated with them at least some few square yards of land, constituting a yard or a basement area or passageway or something of the kind, owned and enjoyed with the house, which on a reasonable view could only be regarded as part of the messuage and such small pieces of land would be held to fall within the curtilage of the messuage. This may extend to ancillary buildings, structures or areas such as outhouses, a garage, a driveway, a garden and so forth. How far it is appropriate to regard this identity as parts of one messuage or parcel of land as extending must depend on the character and the circumstances of the items under consideration.'

[19] That passage was cited with approval by all the members of this court in *Dyer v Dorset CC* [1989] QB 346, all of whom emphasised the smallness of the area comprised in the curtilage. This coincides with the close proximity test to which the other cases refer: 'very closely adjacent' in *Batey v Wakefield* 55 TC 550, 551 per Browne-Wilkinson J, approved in the same case by Fox LJ [1982] 1 All ER 61, 64, and adopted by Walton J in *Markey v Sanders* [1987] 1 WLR 864.

[20] This approach also avoids the difficulty to which Walton J referred in the final passage cited from his judgment in *Markey v Sanders*. Since under Section 101(2) and (3) the 'permitted area' of garden and grounds which is exempt from capital gains tax is limited to one acre or such larger area as the commissioners may determine as required for the reasonable enjoyment of the dwelling house as a residence, it does seem to me to be remarkable that a separate lodge or cottage which by any reasonable measurement must be outside the permitted area can nevertheless be part of the entity of the dwelling house.

[21] If the commissioners in the present case had applied what in my judgment was the right test: 'Was the cottage within the curtilage of, and appurtenant to, Newlands, so as to be a part of the entity which, together with Newlands, constituted the dwelling house occupied by the taxpayer as her residence?'—I do not see how they could have reached the decision which they did. The fact that the cottage was 175 metres from Newlands, that Newlands was on the northern boundary and the cottage on the southern boundary of the 10.5 acre estate, and that they were separated by a large garden with no intervening buildings other than the greenhouses and tool shed (as is apparent from the commissioners' findings and the plans and photographs which were before us as they were before the commissioners) leads me to the inescapable conclusion that the cottage was not within the curtilage of, and appurtenant to Newlands, and so was not part of the entity which, together with Newlands, constituted the taxpayer's dwelling house.

[22] In my judgment, Mervyn Davies J also adopted an incorrect test when he referred to 'the entity constituting the taxpayer's residence' as Mr Milne QC for the taxpayer conceded. However, for present purposes it is sufficient to say that, if the commissioners had properly directed themselves, they could not have reached the conclusion that the cottage and Newlands together formed one dwelling house which was the taxpayer's residence.

[23] Accordingly I would allow this appeal.

RALPH GIBSON LJ:

[24] I agree that this appeal should be allowed for the reasons given by Balcombe LJ to which I can add nothing.

STUART-SMITH LJ:

[25] I also agree.

7.7.2   Commentary

We will again start by working through the judgment of Balcombe LJ. We can see that once again the other members of the Court of Appeal have agreed with him, so his is the only judgment which carries the decision and the *ratio*.

7.7.2.1   The facts

The judge begins with the appeal history (paragraph [1]), then goes on to the facts, this time taking them from the decision of the commissioners (paragraph [2]). This is logical, because it is the commissioners who have found the facts: neither the judge nor the Court of Appeal have heard any evidence, so they are in no position to make any new findings of fact. The commissioners' statement of the facts is the most authoritative statement there can be.

7.7.2.2   The law

Then the statutory provisions are set out in paragraph [3]. This time the relevant section is Section 101(1)–(3) Capital Gains Tax Act 1979, which is a successor to s. 29(1) Finance Act 1965; it is not identical, but has the same effect.

7.7.2.3   The issue

A very short paragraph [4] setting out the factual issue to be determined comes next.

7.7.2.4   Commissioners' decision

Next in paragraph [5], the judge sets out the commissioners' conclusion; simply the basic decision, with no reasons.

7.7.2.5   The judge's decision

Then the conclusion of the judge is set out a little more fully in paragraph [6], quoting from his judgment, and giving some of his reasons, as well as his overall conclusion on the issue. The judge reached the same conclusion as the commissioners but for different reasons. His *ratio* has therefore overridden theirs as far as precedent is concerned. He says that the distance between the cottage and the main house is not of paramount importance; rather, it is the taxpayer's way of living that should be the determining factor, and on the facts found by the commissioners, the taxpayer's way of living embraced both the main house and the cottage.

7.7.2.6   The Crown's contention

In paragraphs [7] and [8], the judge sets out the Crown's contention. It is important to note that the Crown did not argue that the commissioners were wrong in law. They were bound by *Batey v Wakefield*, as indeed was the judge, and as also are the Court of Appeal. So the Crown indicated that it would like to argue that the law was wrong in the House of Lords, but for now was bound to contend either that the commissioners applied the wrong test, or that their decision was wrong on the facts. As we shall see, these two arguments are linked. Once the Court decides the correct test, it can consider what conclusion the commissioners would have reached on the facts if they had applied it, and reverse their decision if necessary.

7.7.2.7   Case law

At this point, the structure of the judgment differs substantially from that in the previous case. In *Batey* no other cases were considered, but here the judge reviews three previous decisions: *Batey v Wakefield* (paragraphs [10] and [11]), *Markey v Sanders* (paragraph [12]) and *Williams v Merrylees* (paragraph [13]). The first is a Court of Appeal decision and so will be binding on any issue of law; the other two are first instance decisions, but are nonetheless persuasive, and the judge will try hard not to overrule either of them.

We will consider the judge's reasoning later, but this part of a judgment always needs to be looked at carefully. The cases that are reviewed will contain *ratio* and *dicta*, all of which might well be incorporated into the judge's reasoning in this case, and form part of its *ratio* in due course. It is important to look at the judge's review of these cases to see what he says about each of them. When advising a client, this part of the judgment is also the most fertile for finding arguments in support of your client's case.

In each of the first two cases, the judge states the facts (or an abbreviated version of them) and then quotes substantial sections of the judgments. He does not, however, go on yet to indicate any of his own views about them. He is simply setting out more law, by way of preliminary material which he will draw upon to reach his conclusions and give reasons. This is rather unusual. In most judgments a judge will comment on the cases he is referring to as he goes along.

7.7.2.8   *Batey v Wakefield*

We have already studied the decision of the Court of Appeal in *Batey v Wakefield*, but it is worth noting that the judge gives rather more weight to the reasoning of Browne-Wilkinson J at first instance than he does to Fox LJ. Note, too, that Browne-Wilkjnson J used the word 'appurtenant', which does not appear in Fox LJ's judgment. We shall see the significance of this word shortly.

Let us remember too the outcome in *Batey v Wakefield*: the lodge was distant from the main house by the width of a tennis court and a hedge (perhaps 30 metres?) and was held to be part of a single dwelling house.

7.7.2.9   *Markey v Sanders*

The separate bungalow in this case was 130 metres away from the main house and was held on appeal not to be part of a single dwelling house comprising both buildings. The judge reversed the decision of the commissioners, so he had to explain why they were wrong in law or reached a decision that could not be justified on the facts as found.

We can see that the judge was looking for a test to help determine when a separate building could be part of another dwelling house. He rejected a test based on the words 'curtilage' and 'appurtenant', and instead attempted to find more law in *Batey v Wakefield*. He came up with two conditions to make a single dwelling house of two buildings: firstly, the occupation of the building in question must increase the owner's enjoyment of the main house, and, secondly, it must be very closely adjacent to it. The first test was doubtless satisfied, but applying the 'very closely adjacent' test, he came to the conclusion that the commissioners reached a conclusion on the facts which no reasonable commissioners could have reached. He accepted that this was an elastic test, but (maintaining the metaphor) decided that the commissioners had stretched the elastic to breaking point. He therefore reversed their decision. In other words, *Batey v Wakefield* was distinguished.

7.7.2.10   *Williams v Merrylees*

In this case, the lodge was 200 metres away from the main house. The commissioners concluded that it was part of a single dwelling house, applying a test of whether it was 'within the curtilage of and appurtenant to it'. But this time the judge felt unable to reverse their decision as being irrational, though he doubted it. He also rejected the approach of the judge in *Markey v Sanders*.

7.7.2.11 Comment of the judge

After this review of the cases, the judge for the first time comments in paragraph [14]. Not surprisingly, he finds the state of the law unsatisfactory. Different judges have approached similar factual situations in different ways, and their conclusions on the facts are hard to reconcile. In particular, the judge in *Williams v Merrylees* reached a decision similar to that in *Batey v Wakefield*, doubting the *ratio* of *Markey v Sanders*, yet on facts which might have seemed more similar to those in *Markey v Sanders*, and the judge in this case had adopted a different approach to either of those cases, using the test of the taxpayer's way of living.

7.7.2.12 The legal conclusion and the *ratio*

Next, Balcombe LJ comes to the point and sets out his decision on the law (paragraphs [15] to [20]). He is faced with cases which conflict in their reasoning and seem to have produced inconsistent decisions on the facts. So he is seeking a legal *ratio* which can justify all the previous decisions; in other words he is seeking to reconcile them.

Batey v Wakefield decided that a dwelling house can be more than one building, but gave little guidance as to *when* a dwelling house can comprise more than one dwelling. What is needed is a test, which can be applied in any future case (including this one) and which will not be inconsistent with any of the previous cases (if possible). This is what the judge attempts to provide.

So the question of law to be decided is: 'When is a dwelling house that consists of more than one building or household a single dwelling house?'

The judge answers the question with three propositions:

(1) That there must be an identifiable main house (see paragraph [17]). The law that is about to be propounded is only applicable in such a situation. A further test will need to be developed in the future when the two buildings said to comprise a single dwelling house are of equal status.

(2) No building other than the main house can form part of a dwelling house unless it is appurtenant to, and within the curtilage of, the main house:

[17] . . . *Where it is contended that some one or more separate buildings are to be treated as part of an entity which, together with the main house, comprises a dwelling house, Mr Warren submitted for the Crown that no building can form part of a dwelling house which includes a main house, unless that building is appurtenant to, and within the curtilage of, the main house.*

[18] . . . *On reflection I have come to the conclusion that this is a helpful approach, since it involves the application of well-recognised legal concepts . . .*

(3) In applying this test to the facts, it is necessary to focus attention on an entity which can be described as the taxpayer's dwelling house, and *not* his residence:

[15] . . . *I agree with what Vinelott J said in* Williams v Merrylees . . .

'*What one is looking for is an entity which can be sensibly described as being a dwelling house though split up into different buildings performing different functions.*'

[16] *How, then, can that entity be identified in any given case? First, attention must be focused on the dwelling house which is said to constitute the entity. To seek to identify the*

taxpayer's residence may lead to confusion . . . In so far as some of the statements made in Batey v Wakefield *suggest that one must first identify the residence they must, in my judgment, be considered to have been made* per incuriam.

These are therefore the points of law to be derived from this case and constitute its legal *ratio.*

However, the judge goes on to give some further explanation on the meaning of curtilage. He does this by citing a passage from *Methuen-Campbell v Walters*, in paragraph [18]:

' . . . for one corporeal hereditament to fall within the curtilage of another, the former must be so intimately associated with the latter as to lead to the conclusion that the former in truth forms part and parcel of the latter. . . . How far it is appropriate to regard this identity as parts of one . . . parcel of land as extending must depend on the character and the circumstances of the items under consideration.'

This passage was further cited with approval in another case, *Dyer v Dorset CC*, referred to in paragraph [19], and both cases emphasised that the area comprised within the curtilage is small. Balcombe LJ is then able to use this point to reconcile the cases which used the 'curtilage and appurtenant' test with those which used the 'very closely adjacent' test, by pointing out that it is likely to come to much the same thing. This enables him to avoid overruling any previous case.

7.7.2.13   The decision and *ratio* on the facts

Having formulated a test, Balcombe LJ then looks at what happens when it is applied to the facts, in paragraphs [21] and [22]. This naturally leads to the judge setting out his conclusion on the facts.

In this case, the Court of Appeal did decide that the commissioners' decision had been wrong in law. Balcombe LJ says in paragraph [20] that if they had applied the test he has now established, they could not reasonably have come to the conclusion they did. This therefore entitles the court to reverse the decision on the facts, and find for the Crown.

The *ratio* on the facts is clearly set out. It must be noted that certain facts are in common with those in *Batey v Wakefield*:

(1) The cottage was occupied by an employee.

(2) The employee was housed there to promote the taxpayer's reasonable enjoyment of her own residence.

It is not clear on the given facts whether the gardener paid rent or not. But none of the above facts would justify any distinction being made between this case and *Batey*.

However, there were several identified facts on which the judge felt able to distinguish *Batey*:

(1) The distance of the cottage from the main house—175 metres.

(2) They were at opposite boundaries of the estate.

(3) They were separated by a large garden with few intervening buildings. The judge clearly identified this as a persuasive fact, the implication being that open space between them links them less closely than a series of other buildings would.

There was a further persuasive fact on which the judge expressed a view *obiter*, namely that . . . 'it does seem to me remarkable that a separate lodge or cottage which is outside the permitted area can nevertheless be part of the entity of the dwelling house.' (Paragraph [20].)

7.7.2.14   Agreement by the other judges

This time there can be no doubt that there is a *ratio* to be found in the decision of the Court of Appeal as a whole, because Ralph Gibson LJ expressly agrees for the same reasons as Balcombe LJ, and so at least two have adopted the same *ratio*. So, too, probably has Stuart-Smith LJ, even though he does not actually say so.

7.8   Answers to test questions

For the questions, see **7.4** above.

7.8.1   Question 1

The correct answer is [B]. Although the decision of another High Court judge is not binding, nevertheless it is sufficiently persuasive that there must be a good reason to differ. Answer [A] is wrong because neither the decision of the other judge nor the *obiter dictum* is binding, and so neither will *always* take precedence. Answer [C] is wrong: in this case the judge must follow the later decision. Answer [D] is wrong: the judge might well prefer an *obiter dictum* of the House of Lords, but he does not have to.

7.8.2   Question 2

The correct answer is [D]. It does not matter how dubious the House of Lords felt the Court of Appeal decision to be; if they did not overrule it, it is still binding law. The words 'just about' in answer [A] are a red herring; if the case is distinguishable, it is distinguishable. Answers [B] and [C] are wrong because in each case the Court of Appeal decision is no longer good law.

7.8.3   Question 3

The correct answer is [A]. This is what you should do in the circumstances. Answer [B] is wrong because the High Court case is binding law and cannot be ignored. Answer [C] is wrong because it is too pessimistic and probably involves a breach of your duty to do the best you can for your client. Answer [D] is wrong because it is too optimistic and you would be misleading your client.

7.8.4   Question 4

The correct answer is [C]. Answer [A] is wrong because the judge is bound both by the House of Lords and by the Court of Appeal: facts A, B, C, and D or A, B, and D will lead to the same result. Answer [B] is wrong because the judge is bound by the Court of Appeal. Answer [D] is wrong because the judge is bound by the House of Lords. Only in answer [C] is there a factual difference, the absence of fact B, sufficient to enable the judge to distinguish the other decisions.

7.8.5   Question 5

The correct answer is [D]. We need first to track the legal effect of the five decisions. The judge in 2004 distinguished the decision of Court of Appeal in 2003. The judge in 2005 distinguished the decision of the judge in 2004. The Court of Appeal in 2006 overruled the decision of the judge in 2004. Therefore, as the law now stands, the claimant wins if facts A and B exist, or facts A, B, and C, or facts A, B, C, and D. It follows that facts C and D are no longer relevant. The judge in 2007 distinguished the decision of the Court of Appeal in 2006.

So, answers [A], [B], and [C] are wrong because in each case the judge is bound by the Court of Appeal decision in 2006 to find in favour of the claimant. Only in the situation described in answer [D] should the judge find in favour of the defendant, because facts C and D being irrelevant, he should follow the judge in 2007, and hold that adding fact E to facts A and B is sufficient to distinguish all the earlier decisions.

7.8.6   Question 6

The correct answer is [B]. We are looking for the overall *ratio* of the House of Lords decision. We can observe quite easily that the Lords ruled unanimously in favour of the defendant. Only if they found for the claimant on three issues out of three would the decision go the claimant's way. Each Law Lord found for the defendant on at least one issue. So we now look to see whether any three of them ruled in favour of the defendant for the same reason.

Lords Able, Cobbler, and Dupe all agreed that a warehouse was a workshop, but that was a decision in favour of the claimant, so cannot be part of the *ratio*. Answer [A] is therefore wrong. Lords Able, Boot, and Egg all agreed that a portacabin was not a building, but that, too, was a decision in favour of the claimant, so answer [C] is wrong. Lords Able, Boot, and Egg were also all agreed, however, that a forklift truck was a vehicle. That was a decision in favour of the defendant, and produced the overall result in favour of the defendant, so that is the *ratio* of the case, and is binding law. Answer [B] is therefore correct. Answer [D] is wrong by default.

8

Practical legal research: a summary

8.1 The purpose of this chapter

The preceding chapters of this manual have set out in detail the legal research process. This chapter is intended to serve two purposes: to summarise the key points contained in the earlier chapters, and to emphasise the distinction between academic research and practical research.

8.1.1 What is 'practical' legal research?

The important hallmarks of a practitioner's research are these:

(a) A practitioner may start the research with a textbook, but will base the advice to the client on primary sources (that is, cases, statutes, or statutory instruments), unless there is no primary source which adequately answers the question.

(b) Research carried out by a practitioner has a very narrow focus: the practitioner will search only for the law which is needed to answer the specific questions which have to be answered in order to deal with the specific matters on which the client needs advice. As Chapter 6 of the *Opinion Writing* manual makes clear, the law is a means to an end, not the end itself.

(c) A practitioner's research must be quick ('time is money'), but it must also be accurate (since getting it wrong may well amount to negligence).

8.1.2 Identifying the issues

The first step is, of course, to digest the facts of the problem. Once you have done this, the next step is to identify the issues which need to be researched. In some cases, your instructing solicitor will already have done this, and your instructions will contain a series of questions for you to answer. Even if this is so, you should consider whether there are any other questions which the solicitor should have asked you. In other cases, the solicitor will seek general advice and so you will have to identify the specific questions yourself.

Remember that some problems with which you may be faced might involve basic principles of law and so need little or no legal research (though you may still need to check that there have been no significant changes in the law of which you are unaware), or else the problems may raise purely factual questions which involve no law (and so require no legal research).

8.1.3   What sources should I use?

If the problem is one where you need to do some legal research, you must first decide what source(s) you are going to use.

In most cases, there will be more than one starting point to solving the problem. It will often be the case that another user of the library has got the source you wish to consult or the website you want to use is down, and so you will have to think of an alternative. All libraries have lists (usually on computer), arranged according to subject-matter, of the titles they hold. There is also the list of practitioner books in **Appendix 1**.

8.1.4   Textbooks

If you are unfamiliar with the area of law in question, you will probably want to start the research process by using a textbook. You should use textbooks written for practitioners, not those written for students. For example, *Chitty on Contracts, Clerk and Lindsell on Torts, Charlesworth on Negligence* or 'loose-leaf' works (such as *Harvey's Industrial Relations and Employment Law* and *Butterworths Family Law Service*). The latter may look rather off-putting at first, but they function in exactly the same way as ordinary textbooks. If you cannot identify an appropriate practitioners' text, or the one you want is not available, *Halsbury's Laws of England* is often a good starting point.

Unless you are looking for commentary on a particular case or a particular statutory provision (in which case, you will use the table of statutes or table of cases in whichever book you are using), the best starting point in any textbook is the index. This is the essential tool which enables you to find the part of the book you are looking for. To use an index you need to be able to formulate the question which you are trying to answer by using words which are likely to be found in the index. This involves identifying 'keywords'. If you cannot find the word(s) you are looking for, try to reword the question. To take a rather trite example, you might have to look for 'taxi' instead of 'cab'. In many practitioner textbooks, there is also a detailed table of contents which can be a useful aid to navigation within the text. We have already seen that practitioners base their answers on primary sources, and so the use of textbook(s) at the start of the research process must be seen merely as a means of locating the appropriate primary sources.

8.1.5   Primary sources

In some instances, you might want to bypass textbooks and go straight to the 'primary' sources (in other words, statutes, statutory instruments or cases). You might know, for example, that the basic law governing a particular subject is statutory, and so the statute is likely to provide the starting point you need. For example, the statutory provisions relating to unfair dismissal are in the Employment Rights Act 1996, so you might decide to start your research there. However, you should only start the research process with primary sources if you are already familiar with the area of law in question; if you are not, it is much better to start with a textbook, which will help you to understand the particular topic you are researching.

If you want to find a statute, you should ideally choose an annotated version, since this will give you assistance in interpreting the Act. *Current Law Statutes Annotated* contains commentary written when the statute was first enacted (including Hansard references to Parliamentary debates for *Pepper v Hart* research). However, *Halsbury's Statutes* has two advantages over *Current Law*. First, the volumes are periodically reissued; this means that where the statute has been amended, the amended version is shown, and the footnotes take account of cases decided after the enactment of the statute. Second, there is a very useful Cumulative Supplement which gives up-to-date information about the statutes printed in the main volumes and in the loose-leaf binders which contain more recent statutes. Many textbooks also reprint statutes, although the commentary will often be in the main body of the text and not in the form of annotations to the statute itself. When you are trying to find your way around a statute, remember that the list of sections (headed 'Arrangement of Sections') at the start of each Act will help you to find the section(s) you need.

If you are looking for case law, the starting point will often be to use a textbook. When reading cases themselves, it is best to use the official law reports published by the Incorporated Council for Law Reporting (the *Weekly Law Reports*, the *Appeal Cases*, etc.) or the *All England Law Reports*. However, do not forget that there are several very useful 'specialist' series of law reports. For example, the *Industrial Relations Law Reports*, the *Family Law Reports*, the *Criminal Appeal Reports*, and the *Justice of the Peace* reports.

8.1.6 Electronic resources

You should also be aware of the range of electronic databases available for legal research. Quite a lot of information is available free of charge on the Internet, including statutes from 1996 (<http://www.opsi.gov.uk/acts.htm>) and statutory instruments from 1997 (<http://www.opsi.gov.uk/stat.htm>), House of Lords decisions from 1996 (<http://www.publications.parliament.uk/pa/ld/ldjudgmt.htm>) and judgments from the Civil and Criminal Divisions of the Court of Appeal, and from the Administrative Court, are available for free on the Bailii (British and Irish Legal Information Institute) database (<http://www.bailii.org/>). There are also various online subscription services, such as *LexisNexis Butterworths* (which includes an electronic version of the *All England Law Reports*, *Halsbury's Laws of England*, and *Halsbury's Statutes*), *Westlaw*, and *Lawtel*.

If you know the name of the case or statute you are looking for, you can simply enter that name into the database (or the citation, if it is a case); otherwise, you have to decide what words you are going to ask the computer to search for. Each database has its own rules regarding how searches should be phrased, but all search engines perform the same basic function of looking for words or phrases. Remember, too, that if you ask the computer to look for negligen* (the * is called a 'wild card') it will look for 'negligent', 'negligently', 'negligence'.

Searching for combinations of words will also make your research more focused. For example, if you are trying to find cases on sentencing in theft cases, you will get far too many hits if you just look up 'theft' or if you just look up 'sentencing'. If you confine your search to the catchwords or to the headnotes and search for theft AND sentenc* you should get a far more manageable number of hits.

Another way of defining your electronic search to get a more manageable number of hits is to ask the computer to look for words within a specified distance from each other. For example, if you are looking for cases involving theft in breach of trust, you could ask the computer to look for 'theft' within 10 (say) words of 'trust' (this might be written as <theft w/10 trust>).

8.1.7 Finding relevant material

Once you have found the law you are looking for, you must be able to sort through it. You will generally find more law than you need in order to answer the particular question you are dealing with. You therefore have to be able to distinguish between what is relevant and what is irrelevant. The acid test of relevance is whether the source you have found actually helps you to answer the question or whether it is merely background material.

If, when you are giving your advice, you cite a case, it must be clear what proposition you derive from it. It is a mistake to cite cases without making it clear what proposition of law is to be derived from each case you are citing.

8.1.8   Interpreting the law

In some cases, the law will be so clear that only one interpretation is possible. However, this will not always be so.

When reading a statute, you should always look to see if there is a definition section which gives specific definitions to particular words or phrases used in the statute. You should also look for relevant case law on that section.

In an area governed by case law, you may well have to distil the relevant legal principles from dicta in a series of cases.

When you have found relevant case law, it may be necessary to consider whether the facts of the case upon which you are advising can be distinguished from the facts of the authorities you have found. If there are conflicting authorities, it may be necessary to predict which is more likely to be followed.

If you cannot find a clear answer to the problem you are researching, it may well be that you can find a case (or series of cases) setting out a narrow principle which you can then use to establish a wider principle.

Textbooks will often show how various authorities relate to each other (for example, summarising the effect of a line of cases), pointing out any inconsistencies and suggesting ways in which apparently conflicting case law can be reconciled.

8.1.9   Following through between sources

You must also be able to 'follow through' from one source to another. For example, if a textbook sets out a proposition of law which seems to answer the question you are researching, and the book cites a particular case as authority for that proposition, you should ensure that the case really does say what the textbook asserts. It is rarely sufficient (although very tempting!) to rely on what textbooks say about primary sources.

8.1.10   Updating

For the practitioner, one of the most important stages of the legal research process is the updating stage. Giving advice or making submissions to a court based on out-of-date law may well amount to negligence on the part of the researcher. It is therefore essential that you take all reasonable steps to ensure that your answer is current.

For example, where you have found the primary sources upon which your answer is based through use of a textbook, check how up to date the textbook is and whether there is a supplement to it (this will give you an idea of the period which your subsequent updating should cover).

If your answer is based on a statute, make sure that the statute was in force at the relevant time (i.e., that at the relevant time, it had been brought into force and had not been repealed) and that it has not been amended. Doing statute-based research in *Halsbury's Statutes,* it is important to remember to check not only the hardback annual cumulative supplement but also the loose-leaf noter-up service binder.

If your answer is based on case law, it is important to check the 'status' of the case(s) on which your answer is based (e.g., that the case on which your advice is based has not been overruled, or distinguished in a case that is similar to the one in which you are advising). If you are doing the research using paper sources, you can check *Current Law* and/or the 'Cases Judicially Considered' section of the *Law Reports Index*.

If you are doing research electronically, remember that you still have to do some updating. Exactly what you have to do depends on how up-to-date the particular source is and whether it contains an updating facility. The online version of *Halsbury's Laws* is updated regularly and contains all the text that is in the annual cumulative supplement and in the loose-leaf noter-up service binder which updates the supplement. *LexisNexis Legislation* is kept up to date, showing the amended version of statutes and statutory instruments quite soon after the changes are enacted; there is a 'stop press' button which gives brief information about changes which have not yet been incorporated into the database.

A useful electronic source for checking the currency of case law is *Westlaw*. The 'case analysis' section of the summary often includes details of cases which cite the case you are currently looking at: this includes references to cases in which the present case has been considered, applied, distinguished or even overruled. It is important to carry out such checks even if you are using a source that is regularly updated, such as *Lawtel* (which has new cases added quickly but does not usually indicate in a case summary whether that case has subsequently been applied or overruled).

8.1.11   Using the law that you have found

Once you have done all this, you need to be able to summarise the relevant law and apply it to the facts of the case you are dealing with, so that you can give accurate and succinct advice to your client.

A barrister does not carry out abstract legal research. The purpose of the research is to give the best advice you can to your client, or to ensure that the strongest possible case is put before the court on behalf of your client. You must therefore apply the law to the facts of the case in a realistic and practical way. Your advice must not be an essay on the law: it must be specific to the case in which your advice is sought.

You must attempt to answer all the questions or issues raised in your instructions. It may or may not be possible to give a definite answer. If you are unable to give a categorical answer, you must try to assess the likely result and the degree of probability that the court will come to the conclusion you suggest.

Each answer you reach must be 'satisfactory' in the sense that it has a reasonable prospect of being upheld by the court.

8.2   Notes to pupil supervisor

In most cases, your pupil supervisor will not require you to produce a full opinion, but rather the notes which could form the basis for an opinion. The notes must be clear, concise, and accurate. The following guidelines may help you:

(a) You may write in note form (rather than writing complete sentences which conform with the rules of grammar) if you wish to do so, but do remember that the result must be intelligible to another reader (in this case, your pupil supervisor).

(b) Your answers must be 'satisfactory', in the sense of being sustainable given the present state of the law which applies to the questions you are answering.

(c) Your answers must be supported by relevant authority (usually, statutory or case law):

(i)   Only cite relevant authority, as the citation of irrelevant sources adds to the length of your notes and tends to create confusion. Something is relevant only if it actually makes a difference to your answer.

(ii) Show *how* the authority you cite is relevant. This will involve relating that authority to the facts of the case in which you are advising. When you are citing precedent, you will normally find it easier to show its relevance by referring to a particular dictum rather than simply referring to the case as a whole. If you do not set out your legal reasoning, your pupil supervisor cannot check the soundness of your reasoning.

(iii) Correct citations must be given for each primary source to which you refer. For example, a statutory instrument should be cited thus: the Criminal Defence Service (Very High Cost Cases) Regulations 2008 (SI 2008/40). A case should be given its full citation, for example *Amjad v Steadman-Byrne* [2007] EWCA Civ 625, [2007] 1 WLR 2484. Where a particular dictum is referred to, it should be located: for example, 'per Sedley LJ at para 17'; in older cases, where there is no 'neutral citation' (i.e., the first half of the citation used in the example), the dictum is located by reference to the page number of the report being referred to). If you do not give the correct citation for the authority which supports your conclusion, your pupil supervisor will not be able to find that authority quickly.

(iv) Verbatim quotation of statutes and judgments should be kept to a minimum. If the passage upon which you wish to rely is very short, or the precise words are crucial, then you will have to write it out in full. Otherwise, you should simply distil the essentials, which will involve paraphrasing the material rather than copying it out.

(v)   You should always cite 'primary' sources (i.e., statutes, case law, etc.) in preference to 'secondary' sources (textbooks, articles, etc.). However, if there is no authority, or there are conflicting authorities, then it may be appropriate to cite academic opinion. In that case, you should wherever possible refer to a source which could be cited in court (that is, a textbook written for practitioners rather than students, or an article in a publication which is aimed, at least in part, at practitioners).

(d) Finally, some guidance on the incorporation of background detail in your notes. If you are unfamiliar with an area of law, it may well be that you will have to do a certain amount of background reading before you can put the questions which you have to answer into context. However, your notes should contain only reasoned answers to the questions which are posed (expressly or by implication) in your instructions. Otherwise, you will find that you are writing a legal essay, not the notes which form the starting point for an opinion.

8.3 Summary

To summarise, these are the basic steps of legal research:

(a) Analyse the issues raised by your instructions so that you can identify what questions of law (if any) have to be answered.

(b) Classify the questions (e.g., magistrates' court procedure, criminal law, tort, highways). This will help you to decide what source(s) to look for. Remember that if the source you want is unavailable, there is almost certain to be another one that you could use.

(c) Decide what word(s) you are going to look up in the index or on the database ('keywords' or 'catchwords'). To do this, you must be able to formulate the question(s) you are trying to answer and then see what keywords appear in that formulation. If the word you are looking for is not in the index or database, try to think of another one.

(d) If you have found what you are looking for, distil what you have found. Set out the statement of law and the authority for that statement.

(e) Ensure that the law you have found is up to date. Is the statute in force? Has the statute been amended? Has the statute been repealed? Has the case you have found gone on appeal to a higher court? Has the case been considered, followed, distinguished or overruled by a later case?

(f) Check that you have answered the question(s) completely. If not, look for other relevant sources, distil the contents and check that what you have found is up to date.

(g) Summarise the relevant law, apply it to the facts of the case you are dealing with, and advise the client.

8.4 Criteria by which you may assess your legal research

To assess the standard of your performance in carrying out a legal research exercise, you may use or adapt the following basic criteria. In carrying out legal research, you should be able to:

- identify the specific issue(s) of law involved;
- identify appropriate primary and, where appropriate, secondary source(s) for resolving those legal issues, citing the source(s) correctly;
- ensure that your answer is up to date;
- show clearly and concisely, and in a format that is easily traceable, the research route by which you reached the up-to-date answer(s); and
- apply the law correctly to resolve all legal issues contained, explicitly or implicitly, in the question.

There now follows a worked-through example, demonstrating the legal research process from beginning to end.

8.5 A sample exercise in legal research

There is no single 'right' way of conducting legal research. However, we now consider one way of approaching a particular exercise. It is not the only approach that is possible.

So that the rest of this chapter has the greatest general value, we are going to assume that specialist books are not available and that the researcher has access only to

Halsbury's Laws of England and *Halsbury's Statutes* or to the online versions (*Halsbury's Laws* and *Legislation* on the *LexisNexis Butterworths* website). It should be borne in mind, however, that the method of research would be very similar using other sources.

RE JOHN AND JANE HAYWARD

Instructions to Counsel to Advice

Counsel is instructed on behalf of Mr and Mrs Hayward. They recently purchased the freehold of a plot of land in Kent. This land has been used as an apple and pear orchard for over 100 years. Together with their two children (Emily and Rachael), they moved into a large mobile home which they brought onto the land.

Shortly after the mobile home was moved into the orchard, the local authority wrote to Mr and Mrs Hayward saying that this represented a change in the use of the land (by introducing a residential element onto land which should be used for wholly agricultural purposes). However, Mr and Mrs Hayward have refused to remove the mobile home. They say that they could not afford to buy a house as well as the orchard and so they have no choice but to live in the orchard.

The local authority have now issued proceedings in the County Court seeking an injunction requiring Mr and Mrs Hayward to remove the mobile home from the orchard.

Counsel is instructed to appear at the hearing of this application and to use best endeavours to prevent the granting of the order being sought by the local authority.

Before going to the hearing, you need to know what approach the court will take to this application.

For the purposes of considering the legal research aspect, we will focus on just one particular question—namely, whether, in dealing with the application for an injunction, the court applies the usual 'balance of convenience' test (the *American Cyanamid* test) or applies a different test that is specific to the subject matter of the application.

The starting point is to classify the problem. It could be 'civil procedure'/'civil litigation', or it could be 'planning law'. If it is the former, the research process could start in a textbook such as *Blackstone's Civil Practice*. If it is the latter, the starting point would be a textbook on planning or, if a specialist text is not to hand, *Halsbury's Laws of England* (or the electronic version of *Halsbury's* on the *LexisNexis Butterworths* website).

Another way of classifying a problem is to consider whether the answer is likely to be found in statute law (an Act of Parliament or a statutory instrument) or in case law. If the former, the research could be done in a source such as *Halsbury's Statutes or Halsbury's Statutory Instruments* (or *Legislation* on the *LexisNexis Butterworths* website). If the latter, a search in the *Law Reports Index* or a search of a case law database (such as *LexisNexis Butterworths* website or *Westlaw* or *Lawtel*) could be employed.

Let's assume that we are going to classify this as a problem of planning law, and that we are going to carry out the research using *Halsbury's Laws*.

If we are using the paper version, the best starting point is the two-volume *Consolidated Index*. When using an index, we have to try to think in the same way as the people who compiled the index. In other words, a series of words: the main keyword, followed by a sub-keyword, followed by sub-sub-keywords. We must be prepared to try different orders for the words. For example, we may find the answer by looking up 'planning—injunctions—criteria', or it may be 'injunctions—planning—criteria'.

In fact, in the *Consolidated Index* of *Halsbury's Laws,* you will find:

PLANNING

    Breach of planning control
        Injunction restraining: 46,585

These keywords thus take us to paragraph 585 in volume 46.

Using an electronic source, the order of the words does not matter unless we select a search option which requires that the search terms appear in a particular order.

Let's try *Halsbury's* on *LexisNexis Butterworths* (using the quick search on the home page). We begin by searching for 'planning and injunction'. That results in 58 hits (research done in January 2008). To refine the search, a solution is to use 'proximity' searching. For example, the search 'planning w/10 injunction*' looks for any instances where the word 'planning' occurs within 10 words of 'injunction/s'. Alternatively, it is possible to confine the search to a single volume of *Halsbury's* (using the 'browse' option)—in this case, the relevant volume is *Town and Country Planning*. Searching for 'planning and injunction' in that one volume yields only 18 hits, of which the eighth (headed 'injunctions') is obviously the relevant one. The text contains the following:

---

585. INJUNCTIONS.

Where a local planning authority[1] considers it necessary or expedient for any actual or apprehended breach of planning control[2] to be restrained by injunction, it may apply to the court[3] for an injunction, whether or not the authority has exercised, or is proposing to exercise, any of its other statutory powers[4] relating to enforcement.[5] On such an application the court may grant such an injunction as it thinks appropriate for the purpose of restraining the breach.[6] If the court grants an interim injunction, it may exercise its discretion not to require a local planning authority to give an undertaking in damages.[7] Rules of court may provide for such an injunction to be issued against a person whose identity is unknown.[8] Without prejudice to the court's power to make an order for service by an alternative method or an order dispensing with service,[9] an applicant for such an injunction must, in the claim form, describe the defendant by reference to (1) a photograph; (2) a thing belonging to or in the possession of the defendant; or (3) any other evidence, with sufficient particularity to enable service to be effected.[10] The applicant must file[11] in support of the application evidence by witness statement or affidavit:

- (a) verifying that he was unable to ascertain, within the time reasonably available to him, the defendant's identity;
- (b) setting out the action taken to ascertain the defendant's identity; and
- (c) verifying the means by which the defendant has been described in the application and that the description is the best that the applicant is able to provide.[12]

There is no requirement that an injunction has to be confined to the area in respect of which an enforcement notice has been issued.[13]

Authority (statutory and/or case law) for each of the propositions of law contained in the main text is set out in the footnotes, along with cross-references to other parts of *Halsbury's*. The footnotes for this paragraph (taken from the electronic version of *Halsbury's*) contain the following text (of which only footnotes 1–8 are reproduced):

---

1   As to local planning authorities see para 28 et seq ante.

2   For the meaning of 'breach of planning control' see para 551 ante.

3   For these purposes, 'the court' means the High Court or the county court: Town and Country Planning Act 1990s 187B(4) (s 187B added by the Planning and Compensation Act 1991 s3).

4   I.e. any of its powers under the Town and Country Planning Act 1990 PtVII (ss 171A–196C) (as amended): see para 551 et seq ante, para 586 et seq post.

5   Ibid s 187B(1) (as added: see note 3 supra). For general policy guidance as to injunctions to restrain breaches of planning control see ODPM (ex-DOE) Circular 10/97 Enforcing Planning Control—Legislative Provisions and Procedural Requirements Annex 5; and as to the status of such guidance see para 9 ante. [. . .]

6   Ibid s 187B(2) (as added: see note 3 supra). The court has jurisdiction to grant interim injunctions and mandatory injunctions to enforce actual breaches of planning control: *Runnymede
Borough Council v Harwood, Croydon London Borough Council v Gladden* (1994) 92 LGR 561,
[1994] JPL 723, CA (applied in *South Hams District Council v Halsey* [1996] 3 PLR 38, CA). Once
an injunction has been granted, it cannot be discharged except where there has been a significant change of circumstances since the order was made: *Salisbury District Council v Le Roi*
[2001] EWCA Civ 1490, [2002] 1 P & CR 501, CA. Similar considerations apply to its suspension
pending a further planning appeal: see *Waverley Borough Council v Lee* [2003] EWHC 29 (Ch),
[2003] All ER (D) 30 (Jan); further proceedings [2003] EWHC 941 (QB), [2003] All ER (D) 64 (Mar).
The jurisdiction of the court under the Town and Country Planning Act 1990 s 187B (as added)
is an original, not a supervisory, jurisdiction, and in all cases the court has to decide whether
in all the circumstances it is just and proportionate, in the Convention sense, to exercise its
discretion under that provision to grant the relief sought against the particular defendant:
*South Buckinghamshire District Council v Porter, Chichester District Council v Searle, Wrex-
ham County Borough Council v Berry, Hertsmere Borough Council v Harty* [2003] UKHL 26,
[2003] All ER (D) 312 (May), affg [2001] EWCA Civ 1549, [2002] 1 All ER 425, [2002] 1 WLR 1359,
CA (a case involving enforcement action against four gypsy families living in mobile homes in
breach of planning control and enforcement notices; for a discussion of the competing objectives of protecting the environment and whatever countervailing rights the families had see
[2001] EWCA Civ 1549 at [38]–[41] per Simon Brown LJ; and see further para 7 the text and
notes 24–26 ante). Cf *Tonbridge and Malling Borough Council v Davis* [2003] EWHC 1069 (QB)
at [40], [2003] All ER (D) 177 (May) per Stanley Burnton J (judicial loyalty (and not merely defer-
ence) to the lawful decisions of the elected executive branch of government required (other
things being equal) the enforcement of the Secretary of State's decision) (affd [2004] EWCA
Civ 194, (2004) *Times*, 5 March, [2004] All ER (D) 426 (Feb) where the dictum of Stanley Burnton
J is explained at [23]); *Buckinghamshire County Council v North West Estates plc* [2002] EWHC
1088 (Ch) at [29], [2003] JPL 414 per Jacobs J (prima facie the court should exercise its discretion to grant an injunction to enforce compliance with an enforcement notice when asked to
do so since the planning authority is the democratically elected body entrusted with planning
control; it is for the respondent to demonstrate why an enforcement notice beyond challenge
should not be enforced by way of injunction); *St Albans District Council v Daniels* [2003] EWHC
2485 (QB), [2003] All ER (D) 230 (Oct) (as a matter of principle, when exercising its discretion
under the Town and Country Planning Act 1990 s 187B (as added) the court should have at
the forefront of its consideration the need to bring present and defined breaches of planning
control to an end); *Epping Forest District Council v Mason* [2002] EWHC 1532 (QB), [2002] All
ER (D) 110 (Jul) (differing considerations applying to the grant (1) of an interim injunction to
prevent anticipated breach of planning control by bringing caravans onto a site and (2) of a
permanent injunction requiring the removal of the defendants from the site and the carrying
out of restorative works); *Mid Bedfordshire District Council v Brown* [2004] EWCA Civ 1709 at
[25], [2004] All ER (D) 310 (Dec) (judge's decision to suspend injunction pending determination of the planning application held not to have taken proper account of the vital role of the
court in upholding the important principle that its orders are meant to be obeyed and not to
be ignored with impunity). As to the exercise of discretion see also *North West Estates plc v
Buckinghamshire County Council* [2003] EWCA Civ 719, [2003] All ER (D) 304 (May) (judge correct in accepting validity of enforcement notice at face value and granting mandatory injunction ordering removal of workshop); *Brent London Borough Council v Dowman* [2003] EWCA
Civ 920, (2003) 147 Sol Jo LB 904, [2003] All ER (D) 309 (Jul); *Tewkesbury Borough Council v
Appleton* [2004] All ER (D) 131 (Oct) (injunction against a group of travelling showpeople; the
court indicated its willingness to commit the defendants to prison if the injunction was not
obeyed); *Maldon District Council v Hammond* [2005] All ER (D) 92 (Jul), CA. For a case with
multiple defendants see *Hillingdon London Borough Council v Guinea Enterprises Ltd* (1998)
76 P & CR 338.

7   See *Kirklees Metropolitan Borough Council v Wickes Building Supplies Ltd* [1993] AC 227,
[1992] 3 All ER 717, HL; *Uttlesford District Council v Sanders* [2005] All ER (D) 79 (Aug).

8   Town and Country Planning Act 1990 s 187B(3) (as added: see note 3 supra); and see CPR
Sch 1 RSC Ord 110 r 1(1), Sch 2 CCR Ord 49 r 7(1). See eg *South Cambridgeshire District Council v Persons Unknown* [2004] EWCA Civ 1280, (2004) *Times*, 11 November, [2004] All ER (D)
112 (Sep) [. . .]

UPDATE

585 Injunctions

NOTE 6—See *Bromley LBC v Maughan; South Cambridgeshire DC v Gammell* [2005] EWCA Civ 1429, [2006] 1 WLR 658 (where an injunction had been granted in breach of planning control by persons unknown, a person moving on to the land who learned of the injunction was in breach of it and in contempt of court).

This information in the electronic version of *Halsbury's* is also contained in the paper version, using a combination of the updates for Vol 46, para 585, in the 2007 *Cumulative Supplement* and the *Noter-up* section of the *Current Service Noter-up* loose-leaf binder.

From this we learn that there is a specific injunctive power in relation to planning matters (footnote 5 reveals that the power is contained in s 187B(1) of the Town and Country Planning Act 1990 (added by the Planning and Compensation Act 1991, s 3)) and that there is a highly relevant House of Lords case called *South Buckinghamshire District Council v Porter* [2003] UKHL 26.

The summary of the case is necessarily rather terse in *Halsbury's*, so we need to look at the case itself. If we are using the online version of *Halsbury's* and there is a hyperlink, we could jump straight to the *All England* report of the case. If not, we would have to search for the case by name or citation. Or we could simply go to the paper version and read the case there (using the citation in *Halsbury's* or finding the citation in, for example, *Current Law* or the *Law Reports Index*).

This is the headnote to the report of *South Bucks District Council v Porter* [2003] 2 AC 558 (this is the most authoritative report of the case). It reads as follows:

Planning—Planning control—Breach—Local authority's application for injunction—Gipsies occupying mobile homes on own land in breach of planning control—Whether court obliged to consider likely effect of injunction and any penalties for infringement on gipsies' right to respect for home and family life—Whether environmental considerations outweighing gipsies' human rights—Town and Country Planning Act 1990 (c 8), s 187B (as inserted by Planning and Compensation Act 1991 (c 34), s 3)—Human Rights Act 1998 (c 42), s 6(1), Sch 1, Pt 1, art 8.

In three cases local planning authorities applied successfully to the court under section 187B of the Town and Country Planning Act 1990 for injunctive relief against the defendants, who were gipsies, to prevent them from living in mobile homes and caravans on land acquired by them for that purpose but for which planning consent had been refused. The defendants appealed on the ground that in granting the injunctions the court had failed to consider, in addition to any relevant planning considerations, the likely effect of the orders on their human rights in accordance with section 6(1) of the Human Rights Act 1998 and the Convention scheduled to that Act. The Court of Appeal allowed their appeals.

On appeal by the local planning authorities—

Held, dismissing the appeals, that section 187B of the 1990 Act conferred on the court an original and discretionary, not a supervisory, jurisdiction, to be exercised with due regard to the purpose for which it was conferred to restrain actual or threatened breaches of planning control; that it was inherent in the injunctive remedy that its grant depended on the court's judgment of all the circumstances of the case; that, although the court would not examine matters of planning policy and judgment which lay within the exclusive purview of the authorities responsible for administering the planning regime, the court was not obliged to grant relief because a planning authority considered it necessary or expedient to restrain a planning breach; that the court would have regard to all, including the personal, circumstances of the case, and, since section 6 of the 1998 Act required the court to act compatibly with a Convention right as so defined, and having regard to the right guaranteed in article 8, the court would only grant an injunction where it was just and proportionate to do so; and that, accordingly, the planning authorities' applications would be determined on that basis (post, paras 20, 27–31, 37–42, 49–50, 53, 55–59, 63–67, 71, 73–74, 75–77, 84–89, 92–93, 95, 98–104).

Mole Valley District Council v Smith (1992) 90 LGR 557, CA and *Hambleton District Council v Bird* [1995] 3 PLR 8, CA distinguished.

Decision of the Court of Appeal [2001] EWCA Civ 1549; [2002] 1 WLR 1359; [2002] 1 All ER 425 affirmed.

This headnote confirms the relevance of the case and points to the paragraphs of the judgment which set out the court's reasoning.

We found this case through the updating process using *Halsbury's Laws* and so it is likely to be the up-to-date answer. However, it is worth double-checking. Electronically, we could use a source such as *Westlaw*. Again, we know the name of the case, and so we can search for that specific case either using keywords from the name of the case or else the citation of the case. The case analysis on *Westlaw* includes information about instances where the case in question has been subsequently considered.

Entering the name or citation of the case on *Westlaw* and then clicking on the 'case analysis' link reveals a section entitled 'appellate history' (which shows that the House of Lords upheld the decision of the Court of Appeal) and a section entitled 'cases citing this case', which shows that *Porter* has been distinguished in two cases, applied in eight cases, followed in three cases and considered in four others. In one of those cases, *Tunbridge Wells BC v Redford* [2004] EWHC 3410, it was held that the court could not sanction a state of affairs to exist whereby a person served with enforcement notices simply ignores them; in that case, the fact that the defendants would have to vacate their home did not militate against the grant of the relief sought since they had had ample opportunity over many years to regularise their affairs. It is of course unlikely that a decision of the House of Lords would be reversed (since the House only departs from its own earlier decisions in exceptional circumstances). However, it is always worth checking the history of a case (even a House of Lords case, since that decision may well have been applied, or distinguished, in a case similar to the one in which you are instructed).

If the updating were to be done using paper sources, *Current Law* would be a good choice. Searching for cases reported in the current year requires you to look at the *Cumulative Table of Cases* in the latest monthly part (research for previous years can be done in the *Current Law Case Citators*).

8.5.1   Analysis of the sources

It is often the case that the researcher finds a lot of material which ends up being discarded. But it is important to be thorough in the research process or else you might miss material that is highly relevant.

The next stage is to reduce the material you have found into more manageable proportions by summarising the key points.

The *Porter* case sets out a number of factors to be taken into account:

(a) The judge should not grant injunctive relief unless he would be prepared, if necessary, to enforce the order by committing the defendant to prison in the event of a breach of the order.

(b) The judge must therefore consider the question of hardship to the defendant and his family if they are required to move.

(c) This has to be set against countervailing considerations, such as the need to enforce planning control in the general interest and the planning history of the site.

(d) The degree and flagrancy of the alleged breach of planning control might well prove critical.

(e) If conventional enforcement measures have failed over a prolonged period of time to remedy the breach, the judge will be readier to grant an injunction; on the other hand, an injunction may not be appropriate where enforcement action has never been taken, unless there is some urgency in the situation which justifies the pre-emptive avoidance of an anticipated breach of planning control.

(f) The extent to which the planning authority can be shown to have had regard to all the material considerations and to have properly posed and approached the Article 8(2) questions as to necessity and proportionality before seeking injunctive relief.

(g) The degree of environmental damage resulting from the breach and the urgency or otherwise of bringing it to an end.

The final stage is to apply the law you have found to the facts of the case in which you are advising, so that you can produce an answer. That answer might be along the following lines:

Section 187B of the Town and Country Planning Act 1990 (inserted by s 3 of the Planning and Compensation Act 1991) empowers a local planning authority to seek an injunction to restrain an actual or threatened breach of planning control. It has this power whether or not it has exercised, or is proposing to exercise, any of its other statutory enforcement powers. The exercise of this power was considered by the House of Lords in *South Buckinghamshire District Council v Porter* [2003] UKHL 26; [2003] 2 AC 558. In that case, it was held that the judge should consider a number of factors. These factors include consideration of the hardship which would be caused to the defendants and their children if they are required to move from what is now their home (a factor made all the more weighty by the operation of Article 8 of the European Convention on Human Rights).

Detailed evidence from Mr and Mrs Hayward about the question of alternative accommodation (or the lack of alternative accommodation) would therefore be very useful. The hardship to the defendants and their family has to be balanced against other considerations, such as the need to enforce planning control as a matter of public interest. The judge will also consider the degree and flagrancy of the alleged breach of planning control (and so it might be relevant how prominent the mobile home is in the orchard). Although s 187B specifically provides that there is no requirement that the planning authority must have tried using other enforcement methods before seeking an injunction, the judge may be more reluctant to grant an injunction where the local authority has not tried other methods first. It should be borne in mind that the court will not sanction long-term failure to comply with planning enforcement notices *(Tunbridge Wells BC v Redford* [2004] EWHC 3410), and so Mr and Mrs Hayward will be expected to comply once they have had a reasonable opportunity to regularise their housing arrangements.

8.5.2 Research route

The purpose of a research route (which should be as concise as possible) is to show how you found the primary sources (i.e., the cases and statutory materials) that are cited in your answer, and to show how you ensured that those primary sources were up to date.

A record of the research route to support the answer in **8.5.1** might look something like this:

Sources

LexisNexis Butterworths: Halsbury's Laws.
Westlaw: Cases.
Law Reports: Appeal cases.

Method

*LexisNexis Butterworths—Halsbury's—*Browsed volume titles:
>selected Town and Country Planning.
>opened Town and Country Planning, volume 46; Browsed index:
>opened 5: 'Enforcement'> opened section (8): 'Injunctions'
>para 585–planning authority may apply for injunction to restrain breach
>Footnote 5 cites s 187B of the Town and Country Planning Act 1990
>Footnote 6 refers to *South Buckinghamshire District Council v Porter* [2003] UKHL 26.
*Westlaw—*case locator—search by citation
–'[2003] UKHL 26'> *South Buckinghamshire DC v Porter* reported at [2003] 2 AC 558
Law Reports—Appeal Cases [2003] Vol. 2
Read full judgment

Updating

Halsbury's, para 585
— checked update section. Refers to one case, not relevant.
— hyperlink to s 187B 1990 Act—section inserted by s 3 Planning and Compensation Act 1991.
— hyperlink to that section: in force for all purposes by 2 January 1992.

Westlaw-

–*South Buckinghamshire DC v Porter:* Used case analysis link: distinguished in two cases, applied in eight cases, followed in three cases, and considered four others. Clicked on hyperlinks to check summaries of these cases; only one was relevant: *Tunbridge Wells BC v Redford* [2004] EWHC 3410.

8.5.3 A further exercise

The instructions in the case of Mr and Mrs Hayward may well require you to research a number of other issues. Even if the immediate threat of an injunction can be averted, how should Mr and Mrs Hayward go about applying for planning permission to keep a mobile home in their orchard? What criteria will the local planning authority use when determining that application? Try to answer these questions using either a planning text or *Halsbury's Laws* (online or paper). Remember that your answer should identify, and be based upon, relevant primary sources (i.e., cases, statutes, or statutory instruments), and that you should apply the law you find to the facts of the case in which you are advising.

8.6 And, finally, some useful tips

You might find this non-exhaustive list of tips helpful in carrying out your legal research. You may like to add to the list as you do your own research and discover for yourself useful shortcuts.

8.6.1   Paper sources

(a) If you are unfamiliar with an area of law, it is often best to start with a paper source rather than an electronic source: it is generally easier to browse through a paper source to get an overview of a subject.

(b) Once you have formulated the legal question(s) you are trying to answer and you have found an appropriate textbook, it is usually best to start with the index at the back of the book rather than the contents pages at the front, unless the contents pages are very detailed.

(c) Do not forget to go through the updating process: e.g., check to see if the textbook you are using has a supplement. Remember that even if there is a supplement, it is likely to be at least a little out of date, so check the supplement to see when it was issued and update from then; similarly, even loose-leaf publications can be out of date, so check to see when the publication was last updated.

(d) If your answer is based on a statute or statutory instrument, check that it was in force at the relevant time.

8.6.2   Electronic sources

(a) Remember that in most databases you can make your search more efficient by the use of 'Boolean searches', i.e. using connectors such as AND, OR, NOT.

(b) Sometimes the use of brackets is needed in a search, e.g. '(transfer OR transaction) AND illegal' if you are not sure whether the appropriate noun is 'transfer' or 'transaction'.

(c) You can narrow your search by using 'proximity searching', e.g., looking for one word within (say) ten words of another word, e.g. <solicitor w/10 negligence>.

(d) Truncation (use of 'wild cards') enables you to look for words with a common stem; with most databases, the symbol to use is an asterisk (*), with others it is an exclamation mark (!). For example, neglig* would find negligent, negligently, negligence.

(e) The best way of searching for a particular section of a statute, e.g. s. 246 of the Insolvency Act 1986, is usually to search for: 246 AND insolvency AND act AND 1986.

(f) If you want to find out whether a particular word appears in the file you have currently opened, click on 'edit'—'find' and type in the word you are looking for.

(g) Be aware that you can find links to useful sites containing legal information from sites such as <http://www.venables.co.uk/sites.htm>, <http://www.kent.ac.uk/lawlinks/>, <http://www.intute.ac.uk/socialsciences/law>, or the City Law School site <http://www.lawbore.net>.

(h) If you want to copy information from the Internet (or a CD-ROM) into a word-processed document, highlight the text you want to copy by dragging the cursor over the relevant text with the left-hand mouse button held down; then you have three options: click on 'edit', then 'copy', and then go to your word-processed document and click on 'edit', then 'paste' (or click on the paste icon); or press 'ctrl' and the letter 'c' simultaneously, then go to your word-processed document and press 'ctrl' and the letter 'v' simultaneously; or press the right-hand mouse button, highlight 'copy' and click with the left-hand mouse button, and when you are in your word-processed document, press the right-hand mouse button, highlight 'paste', and click with the left-hand mouse button. If you want to eliminate formatting from the text you are copying (e.g. you want to remove hyperlinks) you can select 'edit'—'paste'—'unformatted text'.

(i) Remember that a case reported in one set of reports may be referred to in a later case that is not reported in the same set of reports: *Westlaw* or *Lawtel* are good sources for tracking down the later case.

Overview of a civil case

9.1 Introduction

This chapter outlines the different contexts in which you will be working and what may be required of you at the different stages of a case by setting out the main stages in a civil case, explaining the different roles of the solicitor and barrister, the work done by the solicitor at each stage, the stages at which the barrister will generally be consulted, and the work done by the barrister at each of these stages.

9.2 Stages in a civil case

9.2.1 Introduction

Civil disputes cover a broad range of cases including those involving general common law, family matters, insolvency, Chancery claims, and claims to statutory tribunals such as employment tribunals. The steps set out here relate to those in the most common types of common law cases taken in the High Court and County Courts, e.g., suing for debts and damages in tort and contract. This is not a civil litigation manual and does not cover the detailed rules but rather the main stages in a civil case and the work to be done by the lawyers at each stage. The Woolf reforms implemented as the Civil Procedure Rules 1998 (CPR) in 1999 made major changes to the terminology used and procedure followed in both courts, simplifying them and attempting to cut the cost and delay of litigation in many cases. This has been done by introducing the concept of 'proportionality' by which the court will attempt to balance the need for disputes to be resolved as quickly and as cheaply as possible, with the need for cases to be properly prepared and fairly heard. Although the changes have altered what is required or possible at any particular stage of a case, the main stages in the preparation of a case remain the same.

9.2.2 Main stages

The conduct of a civil case through the courts can be divided into seven main areas of work from the time the client first sees a lawyer, to the closure of the client's file:

(a) *Before action:* involves analysis of the case and decisions by the client and the lawyer, in particular whether court action is appropriate and how the costs will be paid. In some cases, some urgent action may need to be taken, e.g. a tenant claiming to have been unlawfully evicted may seek an injunction to be reinstated, pending determination of his or her right to remain by a full trial.

A big change introduced by the Woolf reforms in certain standard cases is the introduction of the concept of 'pre-action protocols', which requires parties to exchange a fair amount of information before initiating proceedings. A number of such 'protocols' have been implemented for specific areas of work, e.g. personal injury and clinical negligence. It is envisaged that such 'protocols' will be written for as many standard types of cases as possible. In areas where no protocol exists, parties are required to follow the general spirit of the protocols. The idea is to break down the present adversarial and secretive approach and promote settlement as early as possible.

(b) *Initiating proceedings:* involves deciding which court to use, the drafting and issue of proceedings, and exchange of statements of case by the parties.

(c) *Interim:* involves all the intermediate steps between the exchange of statements of case and the trial, some taken automatically and some requiring applications to the court. These steps are largely concerned with determining what issues will be fought and collecting the evidence to support the allegations by both sides.

(d) *Trial:* involves the preparation immediately before the trial and the actual day(s) of the trial.

(e) *Enforcement:* involves the winning party taking formal steps to force the losing party to obey the order of the court where there is any failure to do so.

(f) *Appeal:* involves any party dissatisfied with the court's judgment or order considering whether an appeal is possible and appropriate and taking the formal steps necessary to appeal.

(g) *Payment of costs:* involves ensuring all costs of the litigation have been assessed, where appropriate, and been paid to the relevant person or authority.

Clearly, the first four of these areas of work occur in succession. However, the parties may decide not to proceed further or to discontinue the case at any time during the process, for example, if the parties agree to settle the case. A case may not involve enforcement or appeal. Payment of the various costs of litigation occur throughout the process.

9.2.3 Civil Procedure Rules

The Civil Procedure Rules 1998 set out in some detail how cases are to be conducted and prepared for trial. Important concepts introduced by these rules in April 1999 which affect the work of both barristers and solicitors are:

(a) The 'overriding objective' which the court and parties must bear in mind throughout. One of the principal concepts is that of 'proportionality' by which the court, parties, and lawyers must, throughout the case, deal with the case expeditiously and efficiently and keep the preparation involved proportionate to the value and importance of the case.

(b) The use of pre-action protocols (see (a) in **9.2.2**). These result in the costs of a case being moved earlier, as much of the information will have been exchanged before proceedings are even issued. It also sometimes means that barristers are more involved in cases before proceedings are issued (see **9.3.5**).

(c) Case management by the courts. The idea behind this is that the control of the timescale and costs of the litigation should be vested in the courts. This is done partially through tracking of cases (see (d)) where the steps allowed in preparation are kept commensurate with the value and importance of the case. It is also done by 'procedural' judges keeping an eye on cases and, where necessary, having case management hearings with the lawyers to ensure that the case is proceeding in a way which is efficient and cost effective.

(d) Tracking of cases. There are three tracks, each with its own set of rules to ensure that the cost and speed with which the case comes to trial is proportionate to the value and importance of the case. The three tracks are:

(i)   Small claims (basically, where the value of the claim is £5,000 or less, with some exceptions). The way in which cases are dealt with in the small claims track is very different from the fast-track. The procedure is very simple. The hearing is informal and strict rules of evidence do not apply. A party who wins his or her case will not have his legal costs paid. Such cases are therefore frequently conducted by litigants in person.

(ii) Fast-track (basically, where the value of the claim is £15,000 or less but over £5,000). This is a slightly more detailed procedure with limited steps to ensure sufficient disclosure of documents, witnesses, and expert evidence (where relevant) and a trial date set for 30 weeks after the case has been allocated to this track. In addition, the time for the trial will be limited to one day. These rules attempt to ensure that the case does come to trial as quickly as possible and the costs of preparation are controlled.

(iii) Multi-track (basically, where the value of the claim is more than £15,000). This is a more detailed procedure, which allows for more detailed disclosure and preparation of evidence to reflect the greater complexity of the case. In addition, judges are more likely to become actively involved in managing the case through procedural hearings such as 'case management conferences' (held early on to determine the main issues, steps to be taken in preparing the case, etc.), 'listing hearings' (to assist the parties and court in the decisions necessary for fixing the date for trial), and 'pre-trial reviews' (to set out how the actual hearing will be conducted, e.g. the length of time for speeches, witnesses, etc.).

Thus, the amount of work involved in the interim and trial stages (see (c) and (d) in 9.2.2 above) will vary depending on the 'track' to which the case is allocated and the specific requirements of the individual case.

9.3 Roles of solicitor and barrister

9.3.1 The bar is a referral profession

Although there are now some cases where clients have direct access to barristers, the Bar is a referral profession which, generally, gets its work from solicitors. A solicitor will use counsel for specialist advice or advocacy either because the solicitor lacks the relevant expertise or rights of audience or because it is more cost-effective for the solicitor to use a barrister than to do the research or advocacy personally. The solicitor decides when to use a barrister and if he or she fails to instruct counsel when it is necessary, the solicitor may be liable to the client in negligence.

9.3.2 Solicitors' work

The level of expertise and specialisation of solicitors' firms varies enormously, from a firm which offers a broad range of legal services, from drafting wills to acting for defendants in criminal cases, to one which specialises, e.g. doing largely personal injury work. In any firm, work will be done by the partners, who must be solicitors, employed solicitors, and paralegals who are often qualified legal executives. Most firms will assign the contentious and non-contentious work to different people. The litigation department may also be divided into criminal, family, and civil, with solicitors specialising in one or two areas, e.g. personal injury and housing. In many firms, the litigation department has people with expertise in numerous areas ranging over commercial, landlord and tenant, employment, family, financial services, etc. Paralegals usually do the more routine aspects of civil litigation such as service of documents or sitting behind counsel and taking notes in a hearing.

Technically, a client instructs a firm of solicitors to act. Barristers may be instructed directly by clients under the Professional Client Access Rules which includes largely professionals (e.g., accountants, valuers) or under the Public Access Rules whereby lay clients may instruct barristers in certain types of cases. All correspondence and instructions or briefs to counsel will be in the firm's name. Once the other side has been notified that solicitors are acting, it is improper for any other lawyer to communicate with the client directly (although there is nothing wrong with the parties dealing with each other directly). When court proceedings are issued, the firm (but not the individual solicitor) is on the record at court as acting for the client in the particular proceedings and will remain so until this is altered or the case is concluded or withdrawn. Although the firm as a whole technically acts for the client, an individual solicitor will usually conduct the case. Most firms will try to ensure that the solicitor who first sees the client takes the case on and sees it to completion.

The individual solicitor with conduct of the case will decide when to consult a barrister. Within the seven areas of work set out above, barristers will frequently be involved in pre-action, initiating proceedings, interim work, the trial, and appeals. In addition, they need to be able to justify costs where the court assesses costs summarily at the end of the hearing rather than doing a detailed assessment later. This is likely to happen where interim applications are made prior to the hearing. However, barristers are rarely involved in enforcement.

9.3.3 Dealing with costs

Prior to taking any steps, including instructing counsel, the solicitor must explain the costs of litigation to the client and ascertain how they will be paid.

9.3.3.1 Ascertaining the costs

The bulk of the costs will be the fees to cover the work done by the solicitor and any barrister involved. The bulk of the solicitor's fees will usually be calculated on the basis of an hourly charge, with even small firms charging at least £100 an hour. Barristers' fees are usually calculated on a piecework basis, for a particular opinion or statement of case or court appearance. The level of the fee depends on the seniority of the barrister doing the work and its complexity, and is agreed between the solicitor and the barrister's clerk, but the minimum charge even for a junior barrister on a short application would be £100. In addition to the 'legal fees', expenses are incurred such as court charges and the costs of obtaining expert reports. The client must be made aware of the fact that every consultation with the solicitor, and every step taken in the case, adds to the costs. The solicitor must also make clear that if the case is lost, the client may be liable for the other side's costs because the general rule is that costs 'follow event' and the loser will be ordered to pay the winner's costs. However, the court rarely orders the loser to pay all the winner's costs. The solicitor should therefore also advise the client that, even if he or she wins, he or she is likely to be liable for some costs.

9.3.3.2   Methods of payment

The method of paying costs in civil litigation is changing rapidly. The client may simply pay privately, i.e. pay the costs from his or her own pocket. He or she may be asked to pay 'on account' (i.e. a sum upfront, calculated to cover a certain amount of work) and/or pay as he or she receives the invoices for work done by the solicitor. Expenses other than solicitor's fees (e.g., barrister's fee, court fees, expert's fees, etc.—called 'disbursements') are paid by the solicitor and the money recouped from the client. If the client wins his or her case, the other side may be ordered to pay his or her costs. However, this may not be ordered, so the client may still be liable for all of his or her own costs, and in any event, will almost certainly have to pay some of his or her own costs.

Alternatively, the client and solicitor may enter a conditional fee agreement (CFA) whereby, if the client loses, no legal fee will be charged by the solicitor, but if the client wins, the solicitor is entitled to payment of the usual rate plus a success fee. Such agreements with the solicitor will cover only the solicitor's fee and not 'disbursement' costs such as expert's fees or the barrister's fees which the client will pay in the normal way. A client conducting litigation on a conditional fee basis remains potentially liable for the other side's costs if the claim is unsuccessful, but this liability can often be covered by insurance. Some people have legal expenses insurance whereby the costs are met by the insurance company. This is called 'before the event' insurance, and is increasingly common as part of motor insurance and household insurance policies. Even if no such insurance has been arranged before the event that results in litigation, 'after-the-event' insurance is available and increasingly popular. It can be obtained even during the litigation process. The premium payable will depend on the risk taken by the insurance company (i.e., the amount of cover sought and the strength of the case).

Finally, some people qualify for public assistance by way of legal aid or its replacement, help under the Community Legal Service. The manner in which public funds are made available for litigation is changing dramatically. The new method requires firms to apply to the Legal Services Commission to obtain a franchise. This franchise enables the firm to conduct publicly funded work on the basis of being given a budget from public funds for each period for which the firm has a franchise. The old method required firms to apply to the Legal Aid Board in each case and often for each step in the case, and if the Board approved the application, a 'legal aid certificate' was issued by the Board. As old cases are completed, this method will gradually disappear.

9.3.4   Instructing and briefing counsel

The solicitor with conduct of the case will also decide which barrister to consult and when 'booking' the barrister will officially deal through the clerk to the barrister's chambers. Most solicitors build up a 'stable' of several barristers in any one field of work whom they use regularly because they are good, fast, efficient, get on well with clients or with whom they have a particularly good rapport. Solicitors new to litigation or a particular area of work without such a 'stable' will select on the basis of recommendations of those working in the firm, solicitors working in the same field or, possibly, the clerk of a set of chambers which the solicitor has used. Lacking such recommendations, a solicitor may select on the basis of the specialisation of the chambers which can be obtained from the various directories.

A solicitor will use a range of barristers from very junior barristers for fairly simple matters, generally because it is cost-effective, to very senior Queen's Counsel for their highly specialist knowledge and advocacy skills on particularly complex cases. The cab-rank rule (see paras 601–607 of the Code of Conduct for the Bar) requires barristers not to refuse to do work except for specified reasons which include lack of expertise, inadequate time and opportunity to prepare, and lack of proper fee. Within the rule, when taking on work for the barristers in their set, clerks do try to take into account the work preference of the barristers. However, in early years of practice most barristers have no particular area of expertise and will usually take a broad range of cases.

9.3.5 The barrister's involvement

A barrister's involvement in any civil case is limited to doing specific tasks as requested by the solicitor. The three types of tasks which solicitors will usually ask a barrister to undertake are:

- advising on:
  — merit and/or quantum,
  — difficult or obscure points of law,
  — evidence;
- drafting documents, e.g. statements of case, affidavits;
- advocacy at:
  — interim hearings,
  — trial.

The solicitor consults the barrister separately on each specific step. Most solicitors will want continuity of barrister throughout a case so, for example, will ask the same barrister who advised on the merits at the beginning to draft the statement of case and do the advocacy at the trial. In the civil brief in **Chapter 13**, the same barrister has been instructed at three stages: to draft a Defence; advise on merits; and appear at an interim hearing. However, if the solicitor is not satisfied with the work done at any stage, he or she may ask someone else or decide to do the work personally. A solicitor may also use barristers of different call for different aspects of the same case, e.g. one of very junior call for simple interim hearings but a more senior barrister for advising on evidence and the trial. Finally, briefs for interim hearings or for trial may pass from one barrister to another because the original barrister briefed is not available, e.g. when he or she is 'double-booked' because a case is taking longer than expected.

The solicitor is responsible for paying any fee charged by a barrister. The solicitor pays the barrister's fee and recoups the money from the client. If the barrister's fee is not paid, the barrister pursues the solicitor and not the lay client. The traditional way in which a barrister charged the fee was on a piecework basis (e.g. a fee for an opinion or a fee for the advocacy at an interim hearing). However, barristers now also enter conditional fee agreements with solicitors which operate on the same basis as conditional fee agreements between lay clients and solicitors (i.e., no fee if the case is lost but an additional success fee if the case is won). Such an agreement can cover all areas of work done by the barrister or be limited to specific areas of work. This means that the barrister has to do a 'risk assessment' when deciding whether or not to accept instructions from a solicitor.

Doing such an assessment can be very complicated and further consideration of this is beyond the scope of this manual.

9.3.6 Form and content of instructions or brief

Although solicitors may consult counsel by phone on occasion, it is more usual for them to consult in writing or by email. Technically, a solicitor 'instructs' counsel to advise or draft documents and 'briefs' counsel to attend hearings. The solicitor will send a fresh set of 'instructions' or 'brief' each time the barrister is consulted. Instructions or briefs from solicitors should include copies of all relevant documents, follow a fairly standard format (see **13.1** for an example) and include:

(a) The heading which sets out the names of the prospective parties if proceedings have not yet been issued or the title of the case as drafted if proceedings have been issued.

(b) The party for whom counsel is instructed or briefed.

(c) A list of the documents enclosed.

(d) The name of the instructing firm and the name, reference, and extension of the particular solicitor conducting the case within the firm.

(e) A brief summary of the case which should identify the relevant issues, information, and documents and explain the solicitor's opinion, advice to the client, and steps taken to date.

(f) Specific directions as to what work the barrister is instructed or briefed to do, for example to advise on merit and quantum or represent a client at a hearing.

(g) A 'back sheet' which contains the heading, the barrister's name and chambers address, the solicitor's firm name, address, telephone number, fax number and e-mail address, the reference or name of the individual solicitor dealing with the case, and the words 'Community Legal Service' if the client is publicly funded, or counsel's fee where briefed to appear on a hearing for a private client. If counsel is instructed on a condition fee basis this will be noted in the brief.

9.3.7 Returning the work and endorsing the brief

The barrister does the work as instructed or briefed and returns the instructions or brief to the solicitor with all the enclosed documents and an endorsement on the back sheet of the work done, the date, and the fee. The endorsement is important as it is the statement of the work done. Where an opinion or draft is enclosed with the returned brief (as in the case of *Lowe v Mainwaring* at **13.2**), the endorsement merely signifies the work done, the date, and the counsel who did it. Where court hearings are attended, it is important to ensure that the endorsement fully and accurately sets out the order made or the settlement reached. It should contain all the relevant details, including the date, the judge, and the order made and be signed by counsel. An example of such an endorsement after a hearing in a criminal case is shown at **14.2**. Writing a full attendance note for the solicitor can be very useful and impress him or her.

The barrister usually retains none of the papers once the work under any particular set of instructions or brief has been completed. When solicitors instruct or brief counsel they should include any previous instructions or briefs, together with their enclosed documents and any written advice or opinion. However, it is important for a barrister to keep a copy of any written work done for the solicitor and a note of any relevant detail about the case, e.g. factual analysis of the case or legal research done, for future reference, as the barrister may be instructed again on the case.

9.3.8 Solicitors and barristers as client's agent

Solicitors and barristers act as the client's representatives and as such the rules of agency apply. The actual authority of the solicitor conducting the case will depend on the instructions of the client and the solicitor should obtain specific instructions from the client before taking any step. The actual authority of the barrister at any stage will be limited to the work required by the current set of instructions or brief. Both solicitor and barrister may be liable to the client if they act outside their actual authority.

The apparent authority of solicitor and barrister to bind the client may be wider or narrower than their actual authority. The solicitor's apparent authority will extend to accepting service on behalf of the client and progressing the case to trial. It will also extend to making admissions and, in certain circumstances, compromising or settling the case. The barrister's apparent authority extends to speaking for the client in court and may also extend to making admissions and settlements on behalf of the client. If either the solicitor or barrister bind their lay client by acting within their apparent authority but beyond their actual authority, they will be in breach of their professional duty to the client and liable to them.

9.4 Pre-claim stage

9.4.1 The barrister's involvement

A barrister's involvement at this stage is usually confined to being:

- instructed to advise on merit and/or quantum; and
- briefed to appear in court to obtain pre-action orders.

In both situations, the solicitor will have dealt with the legal costs and how these will be paid. The solicitor will almost invariably have interviewed the client, should have obtained full details of all relevant matters and sent instructions or a brief to counsel including all the relevant information and documents. How much barristers will become involved with satisfying pre-action protocols (see (a) at **9.2.2**) remains to be seen.

9.4.2 Opinion on merits and/or quantum

9.4.2.1 Generally

The solicitor will seek counsel's opinion if he or she wants a second opinion of the case, feels further legal research or a more expert view is required to assess the case or it is required, e.g., by the insurance company where the client has legal expenses insurance.

Prior to seeking counsel's opinion, the solicitor should have obtained full information from the client on personal details, the problem, details of any loss suffered, and the solution the client is seeking. The solicitor should have discussed with the client what the best course of action is, given the remedy the client is seeking, taking into account all the relevant factors including:

- the solicitor's provisional view on the merits of the client's case;
- the position of the potential defendant(s) (e.g., easily located, in the country, financially good for the sum to be claimed, likely to pay up if proceedings are issued);
- the time it will take to bring proceedings to trial if necessary; and
- whether some other alternative, such as mediation or complaint to an ombudsman, might be more appropriate.

Having reached a provisional view that litigation is at least worth investigating, the solicitor may then seek counsel's opinion by sending instructions setting out clearly all the relevant information, the solicitor's own view and advice to the client to date and any steps already taken, for example an attempt may have been made to mediate or settle the case which has failed. The instructions should set out clearly what advice is sought from counsel.

The date of receipt of instructions in chambers will be noted on the instructions. Once the barrister has written the opinion, which should be signed and dated by counsel, it will be returned to the solicitor, together with the original instructions to counsel with the back sheet properly endorsed with the fee and the date the work was completed. One of the criticisms of barristers is the time taken to return written advice. It is important, therefore, to ensure you develop efficient methods which enable you to achieve a reasonable turnaround time. With ever more efficient methods of communication being used (e.g., fax, email) what is a 'reasonable' turnaround time gets shorter and shorter.

Although the instructions to counsel will rarely be shown to the lay client, solicitors frequently do either give or show a copy of counsel's opinion to the lay client. The client will then make a decision on whether or not to issue proceedings. Depending on the type of case and client, the solicitor may call the client in for an interview and give or show the client a copy of the opinion. Alternatively, a copy of the opinion may just be sent to the lay client, with a covering letter setting out the solicitor's view and seeking the client's decision.

9.4.2.2 Case analysis: advising on the merits and/or quantum

Context

Even where you are asked to advise before proceedings have been issued, your analysis is focused on what will happen at trial: what issues will be fought and what is the likelihood of success (i.e., will your client win and, if so, get the remedy he or she is seeking?).

When advice is being sought at this preliminary stage, the solicitor will have been conscious of not taking any steps which might cost the client and be wasted because the advice is not to proceed. Thus, the instructions may not contain, for example, expert reports, all the necessary documentation or much in the way of evidence, e.g. proofs from witnesses. The solicitor may also have felt that, in the circumstances, despite the additional cost to the client, a conference with counsel might be advisable prior to any written advice being given. However, if the instructions do not suggest a conference, counsel should advise on the basis of the information in the brief. Clearly, if essential information has not been provided, counsel could contact the solicitor to obtain this before advising.

Consider the stage the case has reached. Is there any urgency? For example, is the limitation period about to expire. If it is a case where a pre-action protocol applies, has this been followed? From the tone of the instructions, how knowledgeable about civil procedure is your instructing solicitor? In addition to advising on the merits and quantum, what procedural aspects should you also include in your advice?

Analysis

Your analysis should be focused on the allegations which will be included in the client's statement of case, any possible counter-allegations by the potential defendants, and how these allegations will be proved in court. On the basis of this analysis, you must evaluate the client's case and form an opinion on the likelihood of the court finding in your client's favour.

You should be considering in as much detail as possible:

(a) What cause(s) of action will form the basis of the client's claim and what facts will be used to support the cause(s) of action? Thus, for example, if the claim is based on negligence, what precisely will you allege are the breaches? In addition, you must consider how the potential defendant is likely to defend the case, e.g. will he or she simply deny the breaches or also plead contributory negligence by your client? You are thinking forward to how you will draft your client's statement of case, which issues are likely to be disputed in the defence, and therefore the issues which the court will have to decide.

(b) What evidence exists to support or counter the allegations which will be contained in the statements of case? Your analysis of the evidence must be thorough, detailed, and precise. You need to be clear what evidence the solicitor has already identified and what further evidence should be collected. It is essential that your analysis is firmly focused on the allegations which are likely to be disputed and will need to be proved.

Having done this analysis, you then need to evaluate the case. Consider the allegations which need to be proved. Who bears the burden of proof? How likely is it that the court will find for your client on the allegations? How difficult and/or expensive will it be to collect the evidence? What remedy is your client likely to get if he or she wins?

Finally, consider any procedural points which need to be highlighted for your instructing solicitor, given your analysis and evaluation of the case.

Presentation

The opinion must be practical and accessible to the reader. The lay client will want to know his or her chances of succeeding and what the court will award if he or she does win. The solicitor will want to be able to understand quickly what your conclusions are, why you have reached those conclusions, and the action you advise be taken. This means that your opinion must be structured and written in language which clearly sets out:

- *your conclusions:* on the case overall and on the individual issues which will be fought;
- *your reasoning:* identifying the cause(s) of action, the allegations of fact and evidence on which you have relied in your evaluation of the case;
- any advice on further evidence to be obtained; and
- any procedural steps of which the solicitor should be advised.

For more information on writing opinions, see the *Opinion Writing* manual.

9.4.3   Making applications before issue

There are a variety of orders which can be obtained prior to issue. Most of these are done by application to the court for a hearing at which the matter can be determined on the basis of written evidence. Although solicitors may have the right to appear on such an application, counsel is frequently instructed. The more common of these orders are set out below.

9.4.3.1   Injunctions

A client may require an immediate court order to be protected from an alleged wrong. Thus, for example, the client's neighbour may be doing building work which is undermining the client's house and an application is made to court to order the neighbour to cease the building work until the case can be determined at trial. Another client may fear that property relevant to his claim (e.g., a pirated video) held by the wrongdoer may be destroyed and a search order will be sought to permit the client to search and seize the property pending trial. A third client who fears that the wrongdoer will dissipate assets or transfer them out of the country so as to render judgment hollow, may seek a freezing injunction to freeze those assets.

9.4.3.2   Orders to assist collection of evidence

In order to ascertain whether or not a client has a sufficiently good case to issue proceedings, it may be necessary to obtain documents or inspect property which is in someone else's possession. If access is refused, an application can be made in certain circumstances for a court order that inspection be given.

9.4.3.3   Making the application

In these situations, particularly where injunctions are sought, counsel may receive extremely short notice of the hearing (e.g., an hour), and very little written information from the solicitor (sometimes only the back sheet). The written evidence which forms the basis of the application is that of the client but will be drafted by the barrister or the solicitor. Counsel may be asked to make the application on the basis of the written evidence drafted by the solicitor. Alternatively, counsel may also be instructed to advise in conference (where time is short, the whole thing may be done in one telephone call) and/or draft the written evidence (faxed to the solicitor's office). If time is very short, the written evidence may be drafted outside the court door. Indeed, the matter may be so urgent that a telephone application can be made for the injunction.

Where a detailed order is also sought (e.g., an injunction), counsel should have a draft order ready to present to the court. Again, this may have been prepared by the solicitor or by counsel. Clearly, care must be taken in the drafting of the order to ensure that it does give the client the protection sought and is within the court's powers.

Those attending court should, in theory, include the barrister, the solicitor, and the lay client. However, often the solicitor will not attend. If the case is sufficiently straightforward there may be no representation from the solicitor's firm. Alternatively, the solicitor may send an 'outdoor clerk', i.e. a file-carrier from the solicitor's office who may be extremely bright and *au fait* with the client and the case, or a part-timer who has no idea about the case and very little, if any, legal knowledge. In addition, there is strictly no need for the client to attend, as he or she will have no role to play in the hearing (the evidence being that contained in the written statement). However, if possible, it is desirable for the client to attend in case something unexpected arises. Thus, the barrister at the hearing may have access to fairly comprehensive information where both the solicitor and the lay client attend. However, he or she may equally have to rely solely on information from the brief including the written evidence.

At court, there may be attempts to settle the matter, either just the immediate application or the whole matter. Although the solicitors may have been negotiating prior to this, once at the court door, negotiations will usually be between counsel. Thus, the barrister needs to be aware of the wider context of the case and be ready to receive and process information very quickly indeed. If a settlement is reached, the barrister should ensure that he or she knows exactly what has been agreed and that it is within the client's instructions. Clearly, this will be extremely difficult, if not impossible, where the client is not present and the solicitor is represented by an uninformed 'outdoor clerk'.

9.4.3.4   Case analysis: pre-issue applications

Context

As explained above, when instructed on a pre-issue application, you may be instructed to draft the documents which form the basis of the application or be instructed to make the application on the basis of documents drafted by someone else. In either case, you need to ensure that all the relevant documents are available for the hearing. What precisely is required depends on the urgency of the application and whether or not it is being made without notice to the other side. You need to check the relevant Civil Procedure Rules as to what documents are required. For most applications, even those made without notice to the other side, the applicant (as the prospective claimant) is required to have a claim form, particulars of claim, application notice, evidence to support the application (either a witness statement or affidavit, depending on the type of application), and a copy of the draft order sought in the proper format. Sometimes, e.g. for injunctions, the draft order is also supplied on disk so that it can be readily adapted by the court.

If you are briefed to make the application on the basis of documents drafted by someone else, check that copies of all relevant documents are included in your instructions and that they are in the required format. If you are instructed to draft relevant documents, ensure you are clear what documents must still be drafted. Generally, you will be instructed to draft the order and possibly witness statement/affidavit. However, you may also be instructed to draft the particulars of claim.

Whether you are just instructed to make the application or have also been instructed to draft the documents, you will need to be clear what the application is for and why it is being made now, what your client's case is, and what, if any, prior contact there has been with the (proposed) defendant(s). The instructions may contain minimal evidence about the case as a whole at this stage, e.g. just that contained in the witness statement or affidavit and exhibits, for much the same reasons as set out above (see **9.4.2**). The information and evidence in the instructions will be focused mainly on that required for the particular application.

Analysis

Your analysis should cover both:

(a) *THE case:* you need to be clear what cause(s) of action your client is relying on, who the defendants are, what facts are alleged by your client which support the cause(s) of action against each defendant, and what evidence there is at this point to prove those facts. All these should be clear from the particulars of claim and the witness statements (or affidavits), and exhibits if already drafted. If these have not yet been drafted, the information should be contained in the instructions from the solicitor and documents enclosed (e.g., statements from the client taken in interview). The extent to which the court will focus on the merits of the main case depends on the type of application being made and the test which the court applies in determining that type of application (see below). However, whatever the application, you must understand why your client's case is pleaded as it is (i.e., what the allegations of fact are and how they support the cause of action) and the evidence currently available.

(b) *THIS application:* you need to be clear about what the client is seeking; what test the court will apply in determining whether or not to grant the application; whether the application is opposed or not; what, if any, notice has been given to the other side and the reasons why no notice or short notice has been given; and, what evidence is available to the court in the witness statements or affidavits and exhibits on which to determine the application. This should be clear from the witness statements or affidavits and exhibits and the draft order, if already drafted. If these have not yet been drafted, the information should be contained in the instructions from the solicitor and documents enclosed (e.g., statements from the client taken in interview).

Once you have done this detailed analysis, you must formulate the arguments which can be used both for and against the granting of your client's application. In doing this, you must focus on the issues that will concern the court in determining the application. This will include considering every element of the test that the court will apply, being clear which aspects will be disputed and which will be of most concern to the court and will therefore require more attention in your argument. In addition, you need to consider the precise wording of the order very carefully as you will be required by the court to justify the order as drafted.

You also need to evaluate the arguments, ensuring that you are focusing on your strongest arguments and ready to deal with any weaknesses in the case. If necessary, consider what your 'fall back' position will be (i.e., if you cannot persuade the court to grant the order as drafted, what amendments might you suggest to get the most for your client?).

If the application is without notice to the other side, you need to consider carefully your duty of full and frank disclosure and ensure that you have identified any matters which professional conduct requires you draw to the courts' attention in the absence of the defendant (see the *Advocacy* manual and *Civil Litigation* manual on this).

Finally, ensure that you are prepared to deal with costs if this is necessary. What are the rules on costs on this type of application? Have you all the relevant information from the solicitor (e.g., a schedule of costs, if this is required)?

Presentation

Ensure you know the order in which the judge will hear the submissions and tailor your submission accordingly. Thus, for example, if you are instructed for a defendant to oppose an application for an interim injunction, the judge will hear the applicant first. You need to be ready both to respond to the applicant and to make any additional points you feel are important to raise on behalf of your client.

Judges deal with numerous applications, often in a very short time. You must therefore ensure that you present your case clearly and concisely, focusing on the decisions that the judge has to make in the order he or she will make them. Thus, for example, if the application is made without notice to the other side, the court will want that issue addressed first in order to determine whether or not the application should proceed in the absence of the defendant(s). Only then will the court be interested in considering the test to be applied in determining the application.

Consider which matters may be of concern to the judge and which you wish to draw to the judge's attention and ensure you focus on these. Take very careful note of the arguments which are raised by your opponent and be ready to counter them with your strongest arguments. Alternatively, be clear when a strong argument by your opponent cannot be rebutted and acknowledging this will add credibility to the other arguments on which you do rely.

Skeleton arguments are required in many instances. In any event, a skeleton argument is a useful tool to assist you. If you have time, draft a skeleton argument and have a copy ready to hand to the judge (for further advice on drafting skeleton arguments, see the *Drafting* manual).

Ensure that you have all the papers in order suitably marked so that you can refer to specific documents quickly.

Once the judge has heard the submissions and states his or her decision on the application, if an order is granted, you must note the precise wording and check that it is within the power of the court to make and is enforceable. You must also make sure that the costs of the application have been dealt with and (where necessary) that a certificate for counsel has been granted. You should also be clear who must draft and serve the order.

Once outside court, you should ensure that the solicitor (or whoever attended from the office) and the lay client (if attending) understand exactly what has been ordered, both in terms of the substantive order and as to costs. The brief should be properly endorsed (see **9.3.7**).

9.5 Instituting proceedings

9.5.1 Introduction

If the client decides to take proceedings on the basis of the solicitor's advice or counsel's opinion, any of the requirements of a relevant pre-action protocol not already satisfied should be completed before issue. Even in cases where no pre-action protocol exists, the spirit of these protocols must be followed (see (a) at **9.2.2**). Failure to follow a particular protocol or the spirit of protocols, may result in the client, even if he or she wins in the end, having to pay costs incurred by the other side which would not have been incurred if the protocol had been followed. At a very minimum, a 'letter before action' should be sent to the proposed defendant or his or her solicitors, warning that proceedings will be issued if the client's claim is not satisfied. The client will have to pay court costs if no such letter is sent and the defendant satisfies the claim on receipt of the court documents and argues that this would have been done if warned of the impending proceedings. The proper court documents must also be drafted, served and, where necessary, filed with the court.

A barrister will rarely be involved in writing the 'letter before action' but may be consulted on satisfying the pre-action protocol and will frequently draft court documents. In addition, there are a variety of orders which may be sought early in the litigation process and the barrister may be briefed to obtain these (see above).

9.5.2 Court documents

9.5.2.1 The claimant's case

Claims are commenced by issuing a 'claim form' and 'particulars of claim'. The claim form always contains basic information such as the name and address of solicitors acting for the claimant. The particulars of claim set out the facts (but not generally the law or evidence) of the claimant's case sufficient to inform the defendant of the nature of the case which has to be met. The particulars of claim may be set out on the claim form or in a separate document. Whether or not a separate document is needed depends on the complexity of the case, generally only simple cases do not require a separate document.

It is vitally important that the statement of the claimant's case (the particulars of claim) is properly drafted as it sets out the issues which the claimant wishes the court to consider and the remedies being sought. It is usual to instruct counsel to draft the particulars of claim. The instructions from the solicitors should contain all the relevant information and documents. If counsel has already advised on the merits and/or quantum, the instructions seeking this advice and the advice given should be included in the instructions to draft the statement of the claimant's case.

When counsel has drafted the particulars of claim, his or her clerk will then arrange for the instructions together with the draft document to be returned to the solicitor. The solicitor (or a clerk in the firm) will then complete the formal documentation. This includes completing the claim form and the client or solicitor signing a 'statement of truth' verifying the content of the particulars of claim. The solicitor will also arrange for sufficient copies to be sent or taken to the court where they are stamped (the date of issue). Service on the defendants will be arranged by the court or by the solicitor by posting or personal delivery (by clerk or process servers).

Once served, the defendant will have a set period of time to respond by serving a defence. If the defendant fails to respond within the period, the claimant, in many cases, can get 'judgment in default' (i.e., of the defendant responding). This is a routine step in which the barrister will not be involved. A defendant who does respond may also consult a solicitor, who in turn may instruct counsel to draft the statement of his or her case.

9.5.2.2   The defendant's case

Counsel instructed to draft a response to particulars of claim should receive a proper set of instructions with all the relevant documents and sufficient information for the drafting of a defence and, where appropriate, a counterclaim (where the defendant, in addition to a defence, has a claim against the claimant) and/or an additional claim against another person (where the defendant alleges someone else is wholly or partly responsible for any damages which the claimant may obtain against the defendant). The barrister will return the instructions with the relevant documents which have been drafted to the solicitor who will serve them on the relevant parties. Strict time limits apply and counsel must ensure that the necessary work is done in sufficient time for the solicitor to keep to those limits.

9.5.2.3   Reply by claimant

Where the defendant makes a counterclaim, which is relatively common, the claimant must serve a defence to that claim. If the defendant merely serves a defence, the claimant only needs to serve a 'reply' if the defence raises a good answer to the claimant's claim. The need for a 'reply' is rare. The barrister who drafted the initial statement will almost invariably be instructed to draft the subsequent responses. Again, there are time limits for these to be served.

9.5.2.4   The statements of case

The particulars of claim, defence, counterclaim, defence to counterclaim, and any reply constitute the 'statements of case'.

If any of the parties consider that the statement of case served on them does not give sufficient information to enable them to prepare their case properly, he or she may request further information. The further information provided will be available at trial.

9.5.2.5 Case analysis: drafting statements of case

Context

The statements of case set out the issues to be determined by the court and the parties are confined to arguing the issues in dispute as set out in the statements of case. Although all statements of case can be amended throughout the litigation process, there are limits on the amendments which can be made and there are cost implications for a party seeking amendments. Thus, it is very important that counsel draft the statements of case carefully.

Analysis

In drafting particulars of claim, you must ensure that you have done sufficiently detailed and precise analysis to enable you to draft both the statement of the client's case and the relief sought as strongly and clearly as possible. The analysis is much the same as that set out in **9.4.2** (opinion on merits and/or quantum). Consider whom to join as parties, in particular whom should be joined as defendants and how all the parties should be named on the particulars. Ensure that you have considered all possible cause(s) of action (e.g., the claim may be brought in contract and tort) and determined which should be pleaded, and the allegations of fact to be included to prove each element. Check that you have included all the remedies desired by and available to your client (e.g., if damages and an injunction are sought, both of these are included). Check that all the requirements on content contained in Civil Procedure Rules are satisfied (e.g., if your client is seeking aggravated or exemplary damages, the particulars of claim must include a statement to that effect and the grounds for claiming them).

In drafting defences, you must ensure that you have identified each and every allegation made in the particulars. You must then consider very carefully what your client's version of events is. You then need to consider each allegation in turn and decide how the defence will respond to it: admit it (where it is clear from your instructions and the evidence that it is true); deny it (where it is within your client's knowledge that it is not true and he or she has a positive case to the contrary); or require the claimant to prove it (where it is not something on which your client can comment because it is outside his or her knowledge or any evidence to the contrary). Finally, you must consider very carefully your client's positive case (i.e., his or her alternative version of events to that which appear in the particulars of claim) and ensure that you include any additional facts on which the defendant intends to rely. Check that all the requirements on content contained in Civil Procedure Rules are satisfied (e.g., if your client is relying on the expiry of any limitation period, details must be set out in the defence).

When acting for a defendant, your client may also contend that he or she has a counterclaim or that someone else is wholly or partially responsible for the claimant's losses. Drafting a counterclaim against the claimant or a claim against a new person (a 'third party') is the same as drafting particulars of claim (see above). If the counterclaim also amounts to a set-off, this must be included in the defence.

Presentation

Any statement of case, whether it is particulars of claim, defence, counterclaim, or claim against a third party, must be set out clearly and concisely and comply with the Civil Procedure Rules both in the content and format. Your draft statements of case must be signed and dated by you before you return them to the solicitor. The solicitor must then have the statement of case verified by a statement of truth signed by the lay client or solicitor.

Examples of statements of case can be found in the civil brief in **Chapter 13**. Detailed consideration of this is beyond the scope of this manual and you are referred to the *Drafting* manual.

9.5.3 Applications to the court

9.5.3.1 Introduction

In any civil proceedings, there are a variety of applications which the parties can make to shorten the process or obtain payment or some form of court order without having to wait for the full hearing. Although some of these can be used at any stage in the proceedings, they will more commonly be employed relatively early in the process and before much of the evidence has been collected.

Applications are usually heard by judicial officers known as Masters (in the High Court in London) and District Judges (in a County Court and the High Court outside London). Although solicitors have rights of audience in these matters, they often instruct counsel. The hearing will generally be in public but often in a smaller room than a courtroom, with counsel being invited to sit rather than stand. The Master or District Judge will hear argument from counsel for both parties on the basis of the statements of case served to date and written evidence. Counsel may have drafted the statements of case and also have been instructed to draft the written evidence for the hearing. However, applications often have to be made on the basis of statements of case and written evidence drafted by someone else, whether it be the solicitor or another barrister. The most common of the applications in which counsel may be involved are set out below.

9.5.3.2 Summary judgment

The claimant may apply to the court for 'summary judgment' where there is no real prospect the defence will succeed and therefore no real need for trial. The defendant may also apply for summary judgment where the claimant's case has no real prospect of success. The purpose of this process is to dispose of the case without the expense and delay of a full trial. In drafting the written statements and doing the advocacy at the hearing, counsel will need to balance the need to present the best case for the client with the fact that, as the purpose is to dispose of the case without extra expense, the application will be made at a stage before much of the evidence has been collected.

9.5.3.3 Interim payments

Although there are now procedures to attempt to bring cases to trial much faster than in the past, the interim payment procedure recognises that even this delay may cause hardship to a claimant and allows an application for early payment of at least some of the money being claimed. An interim payment will be ordered only where it is clear that the claimant will be at least partially successful and it would be unjust to delay immediate payment of that entitlement.

9.5 3.4 Security for costs

A defendant who considers he or she has a strong case may be worried that, though he or she will win at trial, the claimant will be unable to pay his or her costs. In certain circumstances, a defendant can apply to the court for an order that the claimant give 'security for costs', usually by paying a specified amount into court. There is no general right to obtain such security merely because an individual is impecunious. The applicant must satisfy the test in the Civil Procedure Rules (see the *Civil Litigation* manual).

9.5.3.5 Other orders

The orders which can be sought prior to issue can equally be sought after issue and before the full hearing (see **9.4.3** above).

9.5.3.6 Case analysis: applications to court

Context

Given that proceedings have been issued and served, the defendant(s) will be aware of the claim against them and the remedies sought by the claimant. The context varies according to the purpose of the application, which range from seeking to stop the claim in its tracks (summary judgment), through to getting money up front before the trial (interim payment), and to ensuring the claimant can pay the costs if the defendant wins (security for costs). It will also depend on the point in the litigation process at which the application is made. Although most of these applications will be made early on in the process, when little if any evidence has been collected or exchanged, they may also be made later in the process when much more of both sides' cases have been revealed.

Analysis

The process of analysis for these applications is much the same as for those made pre-issue (see **9.4.2.2**). Generally, the only difference will be that you are likely to have more information about the case.

Presentation

The considerations in respect of presentation for these applications are much the same as for those made pre-issue (see **9.4.2.2**). The only difference will be that, generally, a court file will exist which contains documents already filed and served. There will be no file available in a hearing before a Queen's Bench Master.

9.6 Interim stage: preparing the evidence

9.6.1 Introduction

Once statements of case have been exchanged, the issues between the parties have been defined and they now move to collecting and preparing their evidence for trial, including any relevant documents, real evidence (e.g., goods which are claimed to be faulty), expert reports, and witness statements.

The evidence at trial is that of all the parties, and the solicitor for each party must ensure that he or she collects all the evidence relevant to his or her client's case and exchanges evidence and information with the other parties where mutual disclosure is required or appropriate.

9.6.2 Obtaining information from other parties

There are formal steps by which all parties are obliged to exchange information about their evidence. This will be done by the solicitor, sometimes with counsel's assistance. The steps involved include the following.

9.6.2.1   Disclosure

This is the process by which the parties exchange information about the potential documentary evidence which they hold. All parties are obliged within a set time period to make a list of all relevant documents (even those they themselves do not intend to use at the trial) which are or have been in their possession, custody or power and serve the list on the other parties, who then have the right to inspect all those still in possession and for which privilege is not claimed. Inspection may be by exchange of photocopies of documents or actual inspection at the solicitors' offices. From this exchange of lists and inspection, both sides collect the documents and information contained in them which may form evidence for or against them. The process, which it is essential to carry out carefully, can be extremely tedious and, fortunately, counsel is rarely involved in it, unless problems occur as in the case of *Lowe v Mainwaring* at **13.3**. Frequently, the process is done by each side sending photocopies of their relevant documents to the other side. Theoretically, the costs of the copying are borne by the side receiving them. However, to avoid unnecessary bureaucracy, it is also common for each side to undertake to pay these costs and, if the cost is low or comparable on either side, the parties then waive the right to enforce the undertaking.

9.6.2.2   Requests for further information

A party can request 'further information' from other parties on matters which are reasonably necessary and proportionate to enable the party to understand the case he or she has to meet or to assist in the preparation of his or her case. The request could be for clarification/further information of the statements of case (see **9.5.2.4**) or other matters, such as witness statements. The requests and answers form part of the bundle of documents used at trial and counsel is likely to be involved in drafting both.

9.6.2.3   Notice to admit facts

The length and cost of trial will depend to a degree on the number of disputed issues which need to be determined. The statements of case limit the issues to those which the defendant denies or does not admit (i.e., puts the claimant to proof). A party may attempt to limit the issues further by seeking admissions from the other side through the formal process of serving a notice to admit. A party who fails to admit facts in response to such a notice may have to bear the cost of proving them at trial. Counsel may be asked to draft notices and replies.

9.6.2.4   Exchange of witness evidence

Within a set period, parties must simultaneously exchange both witness statements and expert reports of all those they intend to call and are basically confined at trial to the evidence in the statements and reports exchanged. The actual wording of them is therefore very important and counsel will frequently be involved in the drafting of them. The solicitor then arranges the exchange with the other parties.

9.6.3   Advising on evidence

9.6.3.1   Generally

The solicitor may seek counsel's advice on evidence at any stage in the litigation process, either through formal instructions seeking written advice or a conference with counsel, with or without the lay client. Even where this is done in conference, counsel is frequently asked to confirm the advice in writing. Counsel's involvement in collecting and preparing the evidence for trial is usually confined to advising on the strengths and weaknesses of the evidence and what further evidence should be collected.

9.6.3.2   Case analysis

Context

As explained above, you may be asked to advise on evidence at any stage in the proceedings and this will dictate the amount of information you have and the period which the solicitors have to act on your advice. Generally, the disputed issues will have been identified and there will be some information on which to gauge the overall strength of the case. Documents may have been inspected and expert reports and witness statements obtained. At this point, you are focusing on precisely what evidence will be used, i.e. which documents to include in the court bundle, whether any additional witnesses are needed, and the precise content and format of witness statements and expert reports.

Analysis

Check that the solicitor has sent you all the relevant materials to enable you to advise properly. From the statements of case, you should determine precisely what issues are disputed and on whom the burden of proof lies to prove the various allegations of fact on those issues. Consider whether any of the issues could be clarified or narrowed by the use of requests for further information or notices to admit. Consider whether any amendments are necessary to the statements of case in light of the evidence.

You then need to review the evidence available on each issue and decide what evidence to tender on each of those issues. It is helpful to make a list of the issues at this point and in respect of each issue, consider the evidence available. Are there any gaps? In particular, identify the matters on which it is essential that evidence is tendered on your client's behalf to make out your case and ensure there are no gaps. Consider what form the evidence will take on the various issues (witnesses of fact, expert opinion, documentary, and/or real evidence) and any formalities which need to be fulfilled to be able to tender the evidence in this form.

In respect of potential documentary evidence, consider whether full disclosure has been given by both sides. Do you want the authenticity of any document challenged? Consider which documents relate to which issues. Where documents or real evidence are to be relied on, consider who will produce them.

Consider what matters call for expert evidence, check that the expert instructed has the relevant expertise to give opinion evidence on these matters and that the report contains relevant evidence, including copies of any articles, literature, etc., on which the expert relies for his or her views. Check that the directions in respect of experts has been followed (e.g., if a meeting was directed, has this happened?) and that the report complies with the Civil Procedure Rules on content and format. If there is a single joint expert or an expert report from the other side, are there matters on which it might be useful to put written questions to the expert?

Consider what witnesses of fact need to be called. Go through the proofs of each witness, checking the issues on which he or she can give useful evidence. Note any gaps where the proof does not cover matters on which it appears the witness could give evidence. When you have considered all the proofs, check whether there are any issues on which there is no or insufficient oral evidence. Consider whether or how these gaps can be filled (e.g., by other existing witnesses or a new witness). Note if there are any particular difficulties in respect of any of the witnesses, e.g. reluctant to give evidence or may be confused when giving evidence. The solicitor, having taken the original statements from the witnesses may be in a better position to gauge this than you. Where you have been provided with witness statements, ensure they comply with the Civil Procedure Rules on content and format. Check that any directions have been fulfilled, e.g. witness statements exchanged.

Having considered what is available, you need then to decide what evidence should be tendered. For example, there may be several witnesses who can give evidence on the same facts. Consider whether all of them are needed and, if not, which should be called. Similarly, check which documents should be put before the court and what advice you might give on the preparation of the bundles for use at trial.

When advising on the evidence to be collected and the evidence to be available for the hearing, you should be acutely aware of the overriding principle of 'proportionality' (see (a) at **9.2.3**). This involves two aspects. First, the amount of time involved and difficulty in obtaining the evidence. The actual work of collecting the evidence falls to the solicitor who will interview witnesses to obtain statements, ensure all the relevant documents and items of real evidence are assembled, and, where necessary, instruct and obtain a report from an expert. You must weigh up the need to have all relevant evidence available for the hearing with the feasibility of the solicitor actually being able to produce it in the time available. Second, collecting and preparing the evidence increases the client's costs. The solicitor charges for any work done on the case. In addition, there will be 'disbursement costs' incurred which will be passed on to the client where a charge is made to the solicitor to obtain information, copy documents, advice, etc., from others. Experts will charge for their work, as will counsel. You must therefore also weigh up the need for the evidence against the cost of obtaining it.

Presentation

An advice on evidence must be practical and accessible to the solicitor. He or she will want to be able to understand readily what further evidence needs to be collected and why it is needed. He or she will also want to be able to identify readily what evidence you advise should be tendered at court and the reasons for your decisions. This means that your opinion must be structured and written in a way which clearly sets out:

- what further evidence needs to be collected;
- what evidence should be tendered at trial;
- any formalities which must be satisfied to ensure the evidence can be tendered; and
- any procedural steps which should be followed.

For more information on writing opinions, see the *Opinion Writing* manual.

9.6.4 Drafting witness statements

9.6.4.1 Generally

Until recently, all witnesses except expert witnesses gave evidence orally at trial. The solicitor drafted statements (or 'proofs' as they were sometimes called) for use by the advocate in court as the basis for questioning in examination-in-chief. These statements or proofs were not revealed to the other side and the evidence of the witness-in-chief was what was said orally at the trial. Any errors or omissions in the statements or proofs could therefore be rectified by counsel's careful questioning in court.

In virtually all cases now, witness statements must be in a particular format and exchanged prior to the hearing. The statements themselves stand as the bulk of the witness's evidence-in-chief. The actual wording of the witness statements is therefore incredibly important. The witness signs it as an acknowledgement that he or she accepts the truth of its contents and the solicitor should, therefore, ensure that the witness has the opportunity to check and amend the contents prior to signing and exchange.

9.6.4.2   Case analysis

Context

Although the witness statement is technically that of the witness, it is usually drafted by the solicitor or barrister. The Bar's Code of Conduct (para 705) prohibits 'witness coaching' and sets out some guidance for discussing the evidence with witnesses. Generally, you will be instructed to draft statements on the basis of the solicitor's instructions and enclosed documents, including records of interviews with the client, letters, client's files, and attendance notes by the solicitor. Alternatively, you may be instructed to 'polish' a statement drafted by the solicitor.

Analysis

The statement represents the witness's evidence-in-chief and should cover all the issues in the statements of case on which this witness can give evidence. You therefore need to determine from the statements of case precisely what issues are in dispute and the allegations of fact made by each side. You then need to consider each witness in turn and determine which allegations of fact they can deal with in their evidence. In addition, clarify what first-hand evidence the witness can give and what evidence is hearsay. Although hearsay evidence is now admitted in civil cases and it can be included in the witness statement, the source of it should be set out in the witness statement and you should be conscious that it will be given less weight than first-hand evidence. Finally, consider what, if any, documents or real evidence support this witness's evidence and ensure that reference to it is included in the statement. Check that appropriate formalities have or will be fulfilled, e.g. hearsay notices served on the other side where appropriate.

Presentation

At trial, the witness statement will become the witness's evidence-in-chief. It is therefore written in narrative form in the first person, as if written by that witness. Getting the style or tone of the language right in a witness statement can be difficult as, while technically it is supposed to be the words of the witness, generally the language used is slightly more formal than the language many witnesses would use when questioned. Any documents or real evidence which the witness will produce must be formally marked and exhibited to the witness statement. The witness statement must also fulfil the formal requirements as to form and content. For further guidance on drafting witness statements, see the *Drafting* manual.

9.6.5   Experts and their reports

9.6.5.1   Generally

The success of many cases will depend on the expert evidence. Thus, for example, in personal injury cases, the court will usually determine the extent of the claimant's injuries on the basis of medical evidence. In building disputes, the parties may rely on the opinion of surveyors, e.g. as to the extent of disrepair and what is required to rectify it. Expert evidence is basically opinion evidence of a suitably qualified or experienced person. Experts can differ in their opinions. In order to prevent the trial disintegrating into the swapping of numerous expert opinions, parties are usually each confined to a certain number of experts, frequently one or two. In addition, the procedure has for a number of years encouraged the parties to limit as far as possible the need for experts to be called at trial by directing exchange of expert reports and meetings of experts to attempt to limit the issues and have the reports agreed if possible. The Woolf reforms have increased the limitations on numbers of experts, including requiring the appointment of a single joint expert's report (i.e., no oral testimony) in fast-track cases generally.

Obtaining expert evidence can be a complicated task which requires great skill to choose the right experts, instruct them properly, and ensure that their evidence is well presented.

A barrister's involvement in obtaining expert evidence will depend on the level of expertise of the instructing solicitor. The solicitor may be new to this area of work and look to the barrister for advice throughout, including seeking advice on which expert to instruct. However, most solicitors who specialise will have a 'stable' of experts on which they can rely and will be sufficiently au fait with the area to instruct them. The solicitor will obtain the report and the barrister will have no involvement with the expert prior to the evidence being given in court. The only exception to this is where the expert evidence is complicated or in an area not known to the barrister. In such a case, a conference may be held with the expert for the barrister to ensure that he or she has sufficient understanding of the evidence to deal with it properly at court.

The basis of expert evidence is the reports which the experts will write themselves. The report will be considered by the solicitor, who may also seek the barrister's view of it, to ensure that it covers all relevant matters and does not include irrelevant ones. If an expert report is not favourable, the lawyer (solicitor or barrister) can discuss the contents of the report with the expert. Clearly, there are professional conduct issues in the lawyers becoming too involved in the drafting of the report and attempting to 'rework' the opinion of the expert. If the expert's view is genuinely not favourable to the client, the lawyers need to decide whether or not to seek the opinion of another expert. The report of the first expert remains privileged and will not be shown to the other parties. However, if the other parties have discovered that the expert has been consulted, there is nothing to stop them from calling that expert to give evidence.

9.6.5.2   Case analysis

Context

As can be seen from the above, the contexts in which you may be instructed to deal with experts and expert evidence are many and varied. The two main areas on which you are likely to become involved are advising on the report and questioning experts in court.

Analysis

In either situation, advising on an expert report or preparing to question an expert in court, you need to check precisely what issues call for expert opinion evidence, that the expert has the relevant expertise (qualification and/or experience) to give the evidence, and that the report does cover the issues on which expert opinion is required. You also need to understand fully and in detail what the expert opinion is and the expertise on which it is based. This includes understanding all technical terms used and any diagrams or plans. It also includes understanding the basis of the expert's expertise (i.e., his or her experience and any other sources which inform his or her view such as journals, custom in the trade, etc.) and why he or she has the opinion he or she does in respect of this case.

To assist you in dealing with experts, keep information or ensure easy access to information on areas of expertise common to your practice, for example copies of relevant books, websites, and diagrams to assist in deciphering reports, e.g. medical dictionaries, surveying terminology, etc.

Once you thoroughly understand the expert evidence fully, identify any gaps and ambiguities in the report and the issues to which they relate. Check that any directions of the court in respect of experts has been or will be fulfilled and that the report satisfies the requirements of the Civil Procedure Rules on both form and content.

Presentation

Advice on an expert report will usually be contained in an advice on evidence generally. See comments above on this. Dealing with experts at trial will form part of preparation for trial. See comments below on this.

9.7   The trial: final preparation and hearing

9.7.1   Introduction

Having gone through the stages of exchanging statements of case to define the issues to be tried and collecting and exchanging the evidence as required by the rules, the final preparations for trial involve ensuring that all the parties, witnesses, and lawyers attend court properly prepared and that the evidence is put into a format which is convenient for all, including the judge.

9.7.2   Trial dates and timetables

Cases assigned to the small claims and fast-tracks will almost invariably be given trial dates when allocated to that track. In cases where no trial date has been given (in multi-track cases and some fast-track cases), a trial date will have to be obtained from the court. In addition, in both fast-track and multi-track cases, a few weeks before the trial date, the court will make directions as to the evidence to be called, the documents to be used (see **9.7.4**), how the trial should be conducted (trial timetable which will include limitations on the amount of time for each step in the trial), and any other matters it considers are required to prepare the case for trial. Where it is intended that counsel act as advocate, he or she should be involved in providing the information to the court on which decisions as to trial date and directions for trial are made (whether done in writing or by way of a procedural hearing at court).

9.7.3   Witnesses

It is the solicitor's duty to ensure that the witnesses attend court on the hearing day. The solicitor should therefore make sure that all the witnesses (and the client, if not also a witness) are given as much information as possible about likely hearing dates and, when it is actually fixed, the precise date. If there is any likelihood that a witness will not attend, the solicitor should consider compelling attendance by issuing and serving a witness summons.

9.7.4   Trial bundles

The claimant's solicitor must, within a set number of days before the date fixed for the trial, prepare and lodge with the court copies of all the documents which will be used or referred to at the trial by the claimant or defendant (the defendant's solicitor having given notice to the claimant's solicitor). The division of labour becomes more complicated where there is a claim and counterclaim (i.e., the defendant taking on the role of claimant in respect of the counterclaim).

The purpose of preparing and lodging the bundles of documents is to ensure that they have been put into a usable format for the court. The rules set out the number and format (e.g., paginating) of bundles to be lodged; the principal documents lodged include:

- the claim form and all statements of case;
- a case summary and/or chronology where appropriate;
- all requests for information and the answers;
- all witness statements with an indication of whether the contents are agreed;
- all expert reports with an indication of whether the contents are agreed;
- all documents which any of the parties wish to have before the court.

The claimant's solicitor will arrange for sufficient copies of the bundles to be provided for all parties (the other parties paying a reasonable fee for their copies). Each party will usually have three or four copies, one for the solicitor, one for counsel, one for the witness and, possibly, one spare.

Ensuring that the bundles contain all the relevant documents and are compiled in accordance with the rules is an extremely important but tedious task. Fortunately, counsel's only involvement in this will be to advise on which statements, reports, documents, etc., are to be included.

9.7.5 Briefing the advocate

9.7.5.1 The brief

Where the solicitor has decided not to do the advocacy personally, his or her choice of counsel will depend on a variety of factors, including the type of case, its complexity, and whether counsel has been involved in the preparation stages. Whoever the solicitor decides to use should be properly briefed (see **9.3.6** for general format) and should include copies of the following:

- any bundles lodged at court;
- all previous advice and opinions of counsel; and
- any additional proofs of evidence from witnesses (i.e., updating their statements).

The detail in the brief will depend on counsel's previous involvement. Thus, where counsel has been actively involved, and the documents enclosed include previous opinions and advice, the brief itself may be relatively short as counsel is au fait with all the detail.

9.7.5.2 The brief fee

The barrister's fee for the case will depend on his or her standing and the complexity of the case. It is agreed on the basis of a 'fee' of £x for the first day (a sum which includes preparation time) and a 'refresher' of £y (a lower sum than the fee, a daily charge) for subsequent days. Although technically the full fee is payable once the brief is delivered even if the case settles or folds before then, in practice many barristers agree to accept no fee if, e.g., the case settles before a deadline date which is calculated to give them time to prepare.

Where a conditional fee agreement has been made between the barrister and solicitor, the brief will be so marked.

9.7.5.3   Delivery of brief/acceptance by counsel

Ideally, where the trial is of any substance, briefs should be delivered to counsel at least two weeks before the hearing date.

While some solicitors are very professional and do ensure counsel has the brief in adequate time, some more often than not deliver it very late. On the reverse side of the coin, barristers who have been booked to do the hearing may become unavailable, e.g. because of being 'part heard' (i.e., in the middle of a case which has overrun its estimated time). Counsel's clerk should notify the solicitor as soon as the problem arises so the solicitor can choose another barrister to take the brief. Some chambers are very good at notifying solicitors and some delay the notification, hoping the barrister will in the end be free. The clerk may suggest someone else in chambers to take over. The advantage of this is that counsel taking over has more opportunity to discuss the case with counsel who was initially briefed.

9.7.5.4   Preparation for trial by the advocate: case analysis

Context

The brief you receive from the solicitor should contain all the documents set out in **9.7.5.1**. In addition, your instructing solicitor should confirm that all the witnesses and experts have been warned and, where necessary, witness summons have been issued to compel attendance.

The focus of your preparation is on your submissions, in particular your closing submission and your questioning of the witnesses. If you are familiar with the case, in particular have given an advice on evidence just prior to trial, you can build on the analysis done at that stage. In addition, you will at this stage have all the evidence on which the opponent relies which you may not have had when you gave the advice on evidence. If you are not familiar with the case, you will need to do the analysis from scratch.

Analysis

Check that you have received all the relevant documents. The analysis will follow much the same lines as that set out in **9.6.3.2**, **9.6.4.2**, and **9.6.5.2**, but this time it will also include consideration of the other side's evidence (i.e., identifying the strengths and weaknesses of their evidence).

You must ensure that you are clear which issues the court will have to determine, i.e., the issues in dispute and the factual allegations by each side on those issues, and the evidence which will be used by you and your opponent on those issues. Evaluate the strengths and weaknesses of your case on the basis of this analysis.

From your analysis and evaluation, the important areas of the case will have emerged. You then need to work out how you are going to present the case, focusing on the relevant issues, using the strengths and avoiding or neutralising the weaknesses. This is often called developing a 'theory of the case'. Basically, it is your client's 'story' told through your submissions and the evidence of the witnesses which gives a logical and convincing account of how the events in the case are likely to have happened in a way which is favourable to your client's case. It must be plausible and firmly based on the legal principles and evidence. However, it will rely on inferences and generalisations to fill the gaps which always exist in cases (given they are generally based on what people remember of an event which occurred sometime in the past). You need to be clear what inferences you wish the court to draw and the generalisations (premises which rest on the general behaviour of people or objects) on which you rely to persuade the court to accept your explanation.

For example, you might have a case where your client, a 65-year-old woman fell while in a fast-food hamburger restaurant just after a 19-year-old employee had washed the floor. She alleges that she slipped on a wet floor. The restaurant alleges that she was not paying attention to where she was going. The case turns on whether or not the floor was wet and whether this caused the fall. One could use the 'generalisations' that washing floors is a routine task and that most 19-year-olds would find it boring and that when someone finds a task boring they may not do it properly. The inference you would be seeking the court to find is that the floor was not dried properly in this case.

The 'theory of the case' must be a coherent story which is consistent with the legal principles and all the evidence which will be heard by the court. It should include consideration of both the overall story and the 'characterisation' of any relevant witnesses (as done in the example above).

Having developed a 'theory of the case', you then need to consider the contents of your closing speech, the issues which will concern the court and how you will use your 'theory of the case' to persuade the court to find for you. You then need to consider each witness in turn and determine what you must draw out in questioning, both in examination-in-chief of your own witnesses and in cross-examination of the opponent's witnesses. You must also consider at what point documents and real evidence will be introduced.

Presentation

Determine what speeches are allowed by counsel, e.g. if you are for the defendant, will you be allowed an opening and a closing or just a closing speech (more likely). Decide the contents of both, keeping your submissions/arguments for the closing speech.

Counsel should consider whether a skeleton argument is required. This may have been included in the case management directions, or it may be required by a specialist court guide. Skeleton arguments are generally required for High Court trials (and in the Court of Appeal). Otherwise, it is a matter of professional judgment based on the complexity of the issues. Skeletons should be served on the other side and filed at court 24 or 48 hours before the hearing (except for the Court of Appeal, when they must be lodged early on in the process).

As witness statements generally stand as evidence-in-chief, oral examination-in-chief is severely restricted in civil cases. You will need the court's permission if you wish to expand or introduce new matters which have arisen since the exchange of witness statements. You will also need to inform your opponent. Knowledge of the general practice of the particular court is helpful on this as some courts are more restrictive in allowing oral examination than others.

Consider the witness statement of each of the opponent's witnesses. First consider whether or not you should cross-examine that witness. If there is no purpose to it, don't do it! You must 'put your case'. You must challenge all material parts of the evidence given by a witness which your client (or his or her witnesses) does not accept. Be clear which points you must 'put' to the witness. Then identify the evidence on which you can build (i.e., are helpful to your case or neutral and may support your theory of the case) and the areas on which the witness is damaging (e.g., evidence which directly contradicts your theory of the case). Then plan the order in which you will cross-examine, building on the favourable before moving on to the aspects with which the witness is likely to disagree.

Finally, consider how you will 'tab' the bundle (mark the documents for easy access by you in the trial). Make notes as appropriate to assist you both in the submissions and in the questioning. This may include highlighting the witness statements, documents, expert reports, etc. Also plan how you will take notes during the trial, e.g. during questioning of witnesses, to ensure that you can cross-examine or re-examine effectively and precisely.

9.7.6 The trial

When counsel is instructed as the advocate at trial, there may or may not be a representative of the instructing solicitor's firm present. The representative may be the solicitor, where the case or the client is worth a reasonable amount, or a 'file carrier' who may or may not know anything about the case or the law.

At trial, the advocate has control of and responsibility for the conduct of the case. There are numerous matters which require some attention immediately before going into court, e.g. there may be last-minute checking of information, updating of statements, reassuring witnesses who are nervous, ensuring the court has the advocate's name, etc. It is the advocate's duty to ensure the smooth running of the case—that all the witnesses are present, all the documents are before the court and available for those who need them, e.g. witnesses when giving evidence, etc. It is also important to make sure that witnesses have read their statements before giving their evidence.

Once the hearing has started, the advocate will be fully occupied either addressing the court or dealing with witnesses. It is an important part of the barrister's duty to take careful notes during the trial even where the attendant solicitor (or representative) is also taking notes. It is the barrister's own notes on which he or she will rely if questions arise later as to precisely what happened. The barrister may cross check with the solicitor. However, it is not possible to turn constantly to the solicitor (or representative) for their notes and the quality of their notes varies enormously.

Once all the evidence has been called and the closing speeches given, the court will deliver judgment. This may be done immediately or, where the case has been long or complex, may be reserved by an adjournment to the next day or to a much later date where the judge requires more time to consider it. Counsel should take a full note of the judgment and endorse the brief properly (see **9.3.7**). Counsel should also check that any orders are within the court's power, the details are accurate and that he or she understands the judgment or order in detail.

The advocate for the successful party will ask for costs. It is important that the court makes orders on all the costs before it, including any which are outstanding from interim hearings. In addition, the court should deal with the summary assessment of costs if it is a fast-track trial, or make an order for detailed assessment, including the detailed assessment of any public funding costs.

The judgment and/or order of the court cannot be enforced until it is formally drawn up. This will usually be the task of the court. Counsel must ensure that his or her notes and endorsement are sufficient for the solicitor to check that the court has done the task properly before serving the order on the party against whom it has been made.

9.8 Settlement during the process

A very high percentage of cases never get to trial but settle at some stage along the way. Although there is nothing preventing the parties themselves from negotiating a settlement, once proceedings are issued, negotiations are usually conducted through the lawyer, usually the solicitor. Counsel may be involved in negotiations, most frequently at the court door prior to the full trial or possibly at interim hearings. All such negotiations should be conducted on a 'without prejudice' basis which means that they cannot be revealed to the court if settlement is not reached.

A defendant who wishes to put some pressure on the claimant to settle can use one of two devices. If the claimant's claim is for money (damages or a debt), a 'payment in' (now called a 'Part 36 payment') to court may be made. Under this procedure, the defendant pays a sum into court which the claimant can then accept, which ends the matter, or refuse, in which case the case will still go to court. However, if the claimant does not win more than the sum paid in, he or she will have to pay the defendant's costs from the date of the 'payment in'. Where 'payment in' is not possible, e.g. the claim is not for money or raising the money would require the sale of an asset which would be unreasonable to do prior to acceptance of the offer, the defendant can make an offer in a 'Part 36 offer'. This procedure may also be used by claimants. The contents of the letter cannot be revealed at trial prior to judgment but will be used in much the same way as a 'payment in' for costs. Counsel may be asked to advise on the level or format of the offer or its acceptance.

9.9 Enforcement

Many parties against whom judgments are given or orders are made comply with them without any further steps being required. However, if a party fails to comply, further formal steps are required to force compliance, e.g. the issue by the court of a warrant for possession to instruct the bailiffs to evict a person whom the court has ordered to deliver up possession or a warrant of execution to instruct the bailiffs to seize goods and sell them to obtain money a person has been ordered to pay. All of this falls to the solicitor and the barrister is rarely, if ever, involved.

9.10 Appeal

A party may wish to appeal a decision of the court, e.g. because judgment has been given against them or because, although an order has been made in their favour, they disagree with the terms set by the court. Counsel will frequently be involved both in advising on whether or not to appeal and in drafting the grounds of appeal.

9.11 Costs

The costs incurred which form the subject of a costs order include court fees, lawyers' fees, and other costs such as photocopying costs and expert witness fees. Although the general rule is that 'costs follow the event', which means that the losing party is ordered to pay the winning party's costs, this is not always the case and the court may refuse to make the order, e.g. where there has been a 'payment in' which has not been exceeded at trial.

Even where a costs order is made, the winning party will rarely have all of his or her costs paid by the loser. There are three different methods for determining the actual amount which the loser must pay:

(a) Under 'agreed' costs the parties agree how much of the winner's costs the loser will pay.

(b) 'Summarily assessed' costs are used in 'fast-track' cases where, immediately after giving judgment, the court assesses and states the costs payable.

(c) 'Detailed assessed' costs are used where the solicitor whose client's costs are being paid submits a bill of costs to the court and a court officer decides the costs which should be allowed, reduced or disallowed on either a 'standard' or 'indemnity' basis. The 'standard' basis is the usual basis used and allows a reasonable sum in respect of all costs reasonably incurred, any doubts being resolved in favour of the paying party. The 'indemnity' basis, under which all costs are allowed except in so far as they are unreasonable, is far more generous and is ordered against the loser only in exceptional cases.

The solicitor has overall responsibility for keeping a record of all the costs incurred, including the barrister's fees, paying the various expenses, including the barrister's fees, having the bill assessed where a costs order is made, and getting payment from the paying party and/or the client and/or the Community Legal Service.

Where a costs order is made, the winning party still has to pay his or her solicitor the full amount of the bill and is reimbursed by the losing party paying what was agreed or assessed. However, the winning party may feel that the bill is too high and have it assessed (which may be done on the indemnity basis). Only the amount allowed on assessment is payable. Counsel's brief fee will generally be what was agreed between the clerk and the solicitor. Although technically still payable by the solicitor to the barrister, the solicitor will only recoup from the client what was assessed as reasonable. In light of this, the barrister needs to decide whether or not to press for the full amount of the assessed amount, particularly where these solicitors regularly instruct the barrister.

A barrister who has entered a conditional fee agreement with the solicitor will be paid in accordance with that agreement, generally nothing if the case is lost and a success fee if the case is won.

Anatomy of a criminal case

10.1 Introduction

The purpose of this chapter is not to act as a textbook on criminal procedure, nor as a guide to criminal advocacy. Rather, its function is to set out the stages of a case in which counsel may be involved so that this involvement can be put in its proper context as regards fact management (or case analysis, as it is sometimes called). Further details regarding the procedure adopted by the criminal courts may be found in the *Criminal Litigation and Sentencing* manual and in the *Advocacy* manual, as well as specialist practitioner texts such as *Blackstone's Criminal Practice* (published annually).

The popular picture is of the barrister acting as an advocate in the courtroom. However, counsel's role is necessarily much wider than that. This chapter sets out some of the tasks which a barrister instructed in a criminal case may have to perform. You should compare and contrast this chapter with **Chapter 9** (especially **9.3**), which deals with civil cases.

Although counsel may be briefed only for a particular stage in a case, real life does not exist in tidy compartments. For example, counsel may be instructed to apply for bail but, in the course of talking to the client about the bail application, may be asked questions about what plea the defendant should enter or (in cases where there is a choice) which court should try the case. It is therefore vital for the barrister to be able to take an overview of the case as a whole.

Although reference is made to the role of the Crown Prosecution Service, most of this chapter is written from the perspective of a barrister representing the defendant. This is because barristers in private practice are generally required to have gained several years' experience in the criminal courts as defence advocates before being instructed to prosecute cases.

10.2 Role of the defence barrister

A barrister only represents a defendant if 'briefed' to do so by a solicitor. Solicitors themselves have complete rights of audience in the magistrates' court, and so there is nothing a barrister can do there that a solicitor cannot.

In the Crown Court, any solicitor may appear at the hearing of an appeal (against conviction and/or sentence) from a magistrates' court and at the sentencing hearing which follows a committal for sentence by a magistrates' court, provided that the solicitor is from the firm of solicitors which represented the defendant in the magistrates' court. Solicitors who have been granted Rights of Audience in the Higher Courts may also conduct Crown Court trials and appear at pre-trial hearings in the Crown Court.

If a barrister is instructed, the brief (generally entitled 'Instructions to Counsel') usually consists of a short introduction to the case, written by the instructing solicitor, together with a 'proof of evidence' (i.e., a written statement) from the defendant. In the criminal brief in **Chapter 14**, the same barrister has been instructed at three stages of the same case but this will not necessarily be what happens in practice.

At the early stages of a case, the brief sent to the barrister may consist of very little. Indeed, there will be cases where the barrister is the first lawyer the defendant sees in connection with this particular offence. In that case, the brief may consist of only a 'back sheet' (i.e., a piece of paper containing the name of the defendant, the court in which that defendant is appearing, and the name and address of the solicitors).

When the barrister meets the client, it is necessary to go through the proof of evidence (assuming there is one) with the client. It may be that there are things the client wishes to correct or to add. Where the barrister is taking instructions from the client at court (shortly before the hearing), there may only be a short time available and counsel should give priority to eliciting information which is relevant to the hearing which is about to take place. For example, if the reason for the appearance is to make a bail application, then the information which counsel needs to draw out first from the client should relate to matters which are relevant to bail. Other matters can be dealt with after the more important information has been discovered.

By the time the case is ready for trial, counsel should have a much fuller brief which contains not only a proof of evidence from the client, but also statements from any witnesses whom counsel is to call in support of the defence case. In the case of Crown Court trials, defence counsel will also be in possession of the written statements made by the witnesses whom the prosecution intend to call (as the sending of these statements to the defence is an integral part of the process whereby the case is transferred to the Crown Court). In the case of magistrates' court trials, counsel for the defence *may* have copies of the witness statements made by the prosecution witnesses; if the offence is one which is triable either way (i.e., triable either in the magistrates' court or in the Crown Court), counsel will at least have a summary of the prosecution case. If defence counsel has not received copies of the prosecution witness statements in a magistrates' court case, he or she should ask CPS to supply such statements, since the Attorney General has issued guidance to the effect that the defence should receive the prosecution witness statements for all summary trials.

If the solicitor has not already done so, defence counsel should make sure that the defendant looks through the statements made by the prosecution witnesses and so has a chance to comment on those statements; this may give counsel very useful ammunition with which to cross-examine those witnesses when the time comes.

In the magistrates' court, where counsel has been instructed on behalf of the defendant, no representative from the solicitor's office will be present. If the defendant brings witnesses who have not made statements to the instructing solicitor, counsel will have to take statements from those witnesses.

In the Crown Court, a representative from the instructing solicitor should be present, although this will usually be an 'outdoor clerk' (i.e., a representative who is not legally qualified).

10.3 Criminal Defence Service

Since April 2001, publicly funded representation for defendants has been available through the Criminal Defence Service (established by the Access to Justice Act 1999).

Representation through the Criminal Defence Service is granted only if it is in the interests of justice. The following factors are taken into account:

- whether the defendant would, if convicted, be likely to lose their liberty or livelihood or suffer serious damage to their reputation;
- whether the determination of any matter arising in the proceedings may involve consideration of a substantial question of law;
- whether the defendant may be unable to understand the proceedings or to state their own case;
- whether the proceedings may involve the tracing, interviewing, or expert cross-examination of witnesses on behalf of the defendant; and
- whether it is in the interests of another person that the defendant be represented.

As well as satisfying this 'merits' test, the defendant must also satisfy a 'means' test for cases to be heard in the magistrates' court. Where the defendant is in receipt of income support or income-based jobseeker's allowance, the means test is satisfied automatically. In the remaining cases, account is taken of the defendant's annual income. The means test is due to be extended to Crown Court cases.

10.4 Crown Prosecution Service

In all but very minor cases, the Crown Prosecution Service (CPS) will be involved in the decision whether or not to charge a suspect. In more serious cases, where the police will oppose the grant of bail, the police will charge the suspect but only after having received advice from a Crown Prosecutor on whether there is sufficient evidence to charge the suspect and, if so, with what offence(s). In other cases, the suspect will be released on bail, pending a decision by CPS whether or not to proceed with the case (and, if the decision is in favour of proceeding with one or more charges, CPS will issue a written charge and requisition, requiring the suspect to appear before a magistrates' court).

In the magistrates' court, the CPS is represented by a Crown Prosecutor or by an 'agent' (that is, by a solicitor or barrister instructed by the CPS); in the Crown Court, the CPS will usually be represented by a barrister (although increasing numbers of Crown Prosecutors are conducting Crown Court trials).

In the magistrates' court, the CPS file takes the place of the brief for the prosecutor. In the Crown Court, prosecuting counsel receives a brief which is very similar in form to the brief sent to counsel for the defence. The file or brief, as the case may be, will contain an introduction written by a Crown Prosecutor, copies of written statements made by the witnesses to be called on behalf of the prosecution, and details of the defendant's previous convictions (if any).

In the Crown Court, a representative from the CPS should be available to assist counsel, and the police officer in charge of the case will also be present. In the magistrates' court, the prosecutor will be alone, although the police officer in charge of the case will be present for the trial (but not for any hearings which precede the trial).

10.5 Stages of a criminal case: a thumbnail sketch

To help you make sense of the rest of this chapter, this section aims to provide a thumbnail sketch of criminal procedure in so far as counsel may be involved.

Where proceedings were commenced by the issue of a 'written charge' and a 'requisition' requiring the suspect to attend court (the procedure established under s. 29 of the Criminal Justice Act 2003 to replace, in the case of public prosecutions, the laying of an information and the issue of summons as a way of commencing criminal proceedings), counsel is likely to attend only for the trial itself. This is because the question of bail does not arise (and so remand hearings, where the question of bail is addressed, do not take place).

The other method of commencing proceedings is to arrest and charge the suspect. Under s. 24 of the Police and Criminal Evidence Act 1984, a police officer may arrest a suspect for any offence, subject to a test of necessity (for example, to allow the prompt and effective investigation of the offence, or to prevent any prosecution for the offence being hindered by the disappearance of the suspect). A suspect who has been arrested will usually be interviewed at the police station. At the police station, the suspect is entitled to legal advice; that advice will invariably be provided by a solicitor, not by a barrister. If the suspect is to be charged with an offence, that will either happen at the police station (the police having first sought advice from a Crown Prosecutor) or else the papers will be sent to the CPS, who will decide whether to charge the suspect and, if so, with what offence (in which case, the CPS will commence proceedings through the issue of a written charge and requisition). If the suspect is charged at the police station, he or she may either be granted bail by the police or else be held in custody until the next sitting of the magistrates' court (when the magistrates can be asked to grant bail to the defendant). If police bail is granted, counsel may attend remand hearings but, assuming the prosecution do not subsequently oppose bail, the grant of bail is a formality and so there is little for counsel to do.

However proceedings were instituted, a Crown Prosecutor will decide whether those proceedings should be continued. In coming to this decision, the Crown Prosecutor will have regard to the strength of the evidence against the suspect and to whether it is in the public interest to continue the prosecution. In complex cases, the CPS may seek the advice of counsel.

If proceedings were commenced by the arrest and charge of the suspect, and police bail was withheld, counsel may be instructed to attend the magistrates' court to make an application for bail on behalf of the defendant. In many cases, however, the first bail application will be made by a solicitor. Where the prosecution wish to oppose the grant of bail, the bail application will be resisted by the CPS representative. If that application for bail is unsuccessful, counsel may be briefed to return to the magistrates' court a week later to make a further bail application, as in the criminal brief of *R v Costas Georgiou* at **14.1**.

If bail is withheld by the magistrates after the second application for bail, counsel may be asked to return to the magistrates' court to reapply for bail if there is a material change in circumstances (enabling a further bail application to be made) or there may be an appeal against the refusal of bail by the magistrates; this appeal is to the Crown Court. In the Crown Court, bail will be opposed by a barrister instructed by the CPS or by a Crown Prosecutor.

In addition to the remand hearings in the magistrates' court, counsel may, if the offence is triable either way, be instructed to attend the magistrates' court to represent the defendant at the 'mode of trial' or 'allocation' hearing: at this hearing, the defendant is asked to indicate whether he intends to plead guilty or not guilty to the 'either-way' offence(s) with which he is charged. If the defendant gives no indication or indicates an intention to plead not guilty, the next step is for the decision to be taken whether the case should be heard in the magistrates' court or in the Crown Court; if the defendant indicates a guilty plea, he or she is deemed to have entered a guilty plea (and so the court will either pass sentence or commit the defendant to the Crown Court, which has greater sentencing powers). Again, the prosecution will be represented by a Crown Prosecutor or by a solicitor or barrister instructed by the CPS.

In some cases, prosecuting counsel may be asked to advise on evidence and/or on the question of disclosure to the defence of material which the prosecution have but which they do not intend to use at the trial. Defence counsel may be instructed to advise on the contents of (or even draft) the statement of the defence case which (in the case of Crown Court trials) must be served on the prosecution.

Next, counsel may be instructed to appear at the trial itself. This trial will be in the magistrates' court if the offence is a summary one or if the offence is triable either way but both the defendant and the magistrates agreed (at the mode of trial hearing) to summary trial; if the offence is triable only on indictment, or the offence is triable either way and the mode of trial hearing resulted in a decision in favour of trial on indictment, the trial will take place in the Crown Court. In the magistrates' court, the prosecution will be conducted by a Crown Prosecutor or by a solicitor or barrister instructed by the CPS; in the Crown Court, the prosecution will usually (but not invariably) be represented by counsel.

Wherever the defendant is tried, if he or she either pleads guilty or is found guilty, counsel will have to make a plea in mitigation on behalf of the defendant before sentence is passed.

At the conclusion of the case, it may be necessary for defence counsel to advise the defendant on the possibility of appeal against conviction and/or sentence. Where the trial took place in the magistrates' court, that appeal will normally be heard in the Crown Court (although an appeal on a point of law may be made to the High Court, by way of case stated or by means of an application for judicial review). Where the trial took place in the Crown Court, appeal lies to the Court of Appeal (Criminal Division).

10.6 The stages in greater detail

Having set out an overview of criminal procedure, it is necessary to examine some of the stages in more detail.

10.6.1 Bail application

In most cases, on the first occasion that a defendant appears before the magistrates' court charged with a particular offence, representation will be provided either by a duty solicitor or by a solicitor from the firm which later instructs counsel. An application for public funding may be made at the time of that hearing.

There will be occasions, however, where the barrister is the first lawyer the defendant meets in connection with this offence. It may be, for example, that the defendant agreed to be interviewed by the police without a lawyer being present and, after being charged with an offence and finding that police bail was withheld, contacted a firm of solicitors he or she has used before. If there is insufficient time for a solicitor from that firm to see the defendant prior to the first court appearance, counsel may receive instructions by telephone or fax (or even email) to go to the magistrates' court. In that case, it will be for counsel to take initial instructions from the defendant, to give preliminary advice, and to make a bail application.

The role of defence counsel when attending court to make a bail application involves a number of elements, including preparation, advice, and advocacy.

In particular, counsel will have to:

(a) *Take instructions from the client:* If a proof of evidence from the defendant is included in the brief, it is important to check with the client that it is complete, accurate and up to date; if there is no proof of evidence, it is up to counsel to elicit all the necessary information from the defendant. In deciding what questions to ask the defendant, counsel should consider the factors set out in the Bail Act 1976, Sch 1 (e.g., risk of absconding, committing offences while on bail or interfering with witnesses, all of which are assessed in the light of such matters as the nature and seriousness of the present offence, the defendant's previous convictions (if any), the defendant's community ties and record of answering bail in the past).

(b) *Advise the client:* If this is the client's first court appearance, he or she may need reassurance; it may therefore be necessary to explain to the client what will happen in court. It is highly likely that the client will ask counsel to advise on the probable result of the bail application. Furthermore, the client may seek advice about other aspects of the case. Where such advice is given, a short note of the advice given should be endorsed on the brief, signed and dated by counsel (so that the solicitor knows what counsel has said to the client).

(c) *Address the court in favour of bail:* Assuming the prosecution oppose the grant of bail, the prosecutor addresses the court first and explains to the court the grounds upon which the prosecution say that bail should be withheld. Counsel for the defence then replies to those submissions and will try to show that the prosecution objections to the grant of bail have no foundation or that those objections can be overcome by the imposition of conditions on the grant of bail. No witnesses are called (unless a surety comes forward, in which case that person will usually have to give evidence to show that he or she is a suitable surety). The submissions to the court should be based on the matters that the court is required to consider under the Bail Act 1976.

(d) *Advising the client on challenging refusal of bail:* If bail is withheld, counsel should advise the defendant (and, later, communicate this advice to the instructing solicitor) on any steps which might be taken to increase the chance of bail being granted (e.g., the provision of a surety) and/or whether an application for bail should be made to the Crown Court.

The role of the prosecutor is rather more limited. He or she simply makes a speech opposing the grant of bail. In doing this, the prosecutor will usually have to rely on notes contained in the CPS file; those notes are based on information supplied by the police. The police officer in charge of the case is unlikely to be present at the bail application.

There may occasionally be some scope for negotiation between defence counsel and the prosecutor. It may be that the prosecutor will agree not to oppose the grant of bail if the defendant agrees that the grant of bail should be subject to certain conditions.

If the first bail application is unsuccessful, the defence may make a second application to the magistrates a week later. This is so even if the second application says nothing different from the first application (although the advocate making the application will normally try to find something different to say). Once the magistrates have heard two fully argued bail applications, however, they can only hear a further application if there is a material change in circumstances (i.e., the defence can put forward an argument which has not been put forward already).

Where bail has been refused by the magistrates following the second fully argued bail application, it may be appropriate to make a further bail application in the Crown Court. The procedure in the Crown Court is very similar to that in the magistrates' court (that is, the prosecutor sets out the reasons for opposing the grant of bail and defence counsel then replies to those submissions). However, the defendant will not be present and the CPS will usually (but not always) be represented by counsel.

If the offence is triable in the Crown Court, the case may be sent to the Crown Court for trial after the first appearance in the magistrates' court. If the magistrates refuse bail, any further application for bail will therefore have to be made in the Crown Court.

10.6.2   Mode of trial

Where the defendant is accused of an offence which is triable either way (that is, triable in either the magistrates' court or the Crown Court), counsel may be asked to advise the client on which court should try the case. This advice will almost always be given orally, and will generally be given just before the mode of trial hearing itself (unless it was given at an earlier remand hearing).

At this stage (if not before), the client may well need advice on plea, since the mode of trial hearing in court begins with a 'plea before venue' hearing. The defendant is asked to indicate whether he or she intends to plead guilty or not guilty to the 'either-way' offence(s) with which he or she is charged. If the defendant indicates an intention to plead guilty, then he or she is regarded as having pleaded guilty. At that point, the magistrates will either proceed to sentence (if necessary, after an adjournment for a pre-sentence report to be prepared by a probation officer) or else commit the defendant to the Crown Court for sentence (the Crown Court having greater sentencing powers than the magistrates' court). If, on the other hand, the defendant either indicates an intention to plead not guilty, or gives no indication as to the intended plea, the magistrates then proceed to determine the question of mode of trial.

At the mode of trial hearing, the magistrates have to decide whether the case is suitable for summary trial. The key question is whether, in the event of the defendant being convicted, their sentencing powers would be adequate to deal with the case. If the magistrates decide that the case is not suitable for summary trial, only trial in the Crown Court is possible. If the magistrates decide that the case is suitable for summary trial (i.e., they 'accept jurisdiction'), the defendant is asked where he or she wishes to be tried. This is because, in the case of an offence which is triable either way, the defendant has an inalienable right to choose to be tried on indictment (that is, at the Crown Court).

During the mode of trial hearing, the prosecution and the defence both have the right to make representations regarding the appropriate mode of trial. If the defendant wishes to elect trial on indictment, there is little point in the defence making any representations, because of the defendant's right to choose Crown Court trial. If, on the other hand, the defendant wants to be tried in the magistrates' court but the prosecution are seeking trial in the Crown Court, counsel for the defendant will first have to try to persuade the magistrates that the case is suitable for summary trial.

In advising the client on whether or not to elect Crown Court trial in the case of an 'either-way' offence, counsel will need to be aware of the various arguments for and against the two types of trial. Jurors tend to be less 'case-hardened' than magistrates, which may explain why the acquittal rate is slightly higher in the Crown Court than in the magistrates' court. Where it is likely that the defence will seek to have some of the prosecution evidence (such as a confession) ruled inadmissible, Crown Court trial is preferable because matters of admissibility are dealt with by the judge in the absence of the jury; this separation of functions is not possible in the magistrates' court, where the justices are triers of both law and fact (although it should be borne in mind that, under the Courts Act 2003, it is possible to ask a bench of magistrates to make a pre-trial ruling to decide any question as to the admissibility of evidence or any other question of law relating to the case; this pre-trial ruling is binding on the trial court, and so if evidence is ruled inadmissible in a pre-trial ruling, that evidence is inadmissible at the trial and the magistrates who try the case will hear nothing about that evidence).

Another factor relevant to the choice between magistrates' court and Crown Court trial is that trial in the magistrates' court is a little less formal (and so maybe a little less daunting for the accused) than jury trial; trials in the magistrates' court also tend to be considerably shorter than trials in the Crown Court. Another advantage of magistrates' court trial is that there is a cap on the sentencing powers of the magistrates (although this advantage is largely negated by the power of the magistrates' court to commit the defendant to the Crown Court for sentence).

10.6.3 Advising the prosecution

Counsel who has been briefed to prosecute in a forthcoming Crown Court trial may be asked by the CPS to advise on the evidence (and sometimes to draft or redraft the indictment) before the trial takes place. This involves examining the witness statements made by the prosecution witnesses in order to see how strong the prosecution case is; counsel has to consider if the case can be improved (e.g., advising that the police take further statements from existing witnesses, to fill gaps or clarify ambiguities, or advising that further investigations be made).

The advice given must be both realistic and practicable. It must be remembered that the police do not have limitless resources (and are not endowed with psychic powers!).

Where the trial is to take place in a magistrates' court, these matters will almost invariably be considered by a Crown Prosecutor, not by a barrister in private practice.

10.6.4 Advising the defendant

Counsel for the defence may be asked to advise on evidence prior to a Crown Court trial. This advice will often be given orally, during a conference with the client, rather than in writing; such conferences usually take place in counsel's chambers (or in a prison if the defendant is in custody). Any advice must be realistic and practicable: where the defendant is represented through the Criminal Defence Service, further enquiries involving considerable expense are unlikely to be covered by public funds. (See **14.3** for an example of a written advice in the case of *R v Costas Georgiou*.)

Prior to a magistrates' court trial, it is very rare for defence counsel to have a conference in chambers or to give written advice. The conference usually takes place in the court building, shortly before the trial is due to begin.

The function of the pre-trial conference (whether held in counsel's chambers or, just before the trial is due to start, in the court building) may include some or all of the following elements:

(a) *Taking instructions from the client (i.e., gathering information):* By the time of the trial, counsel will be in possession of a proof of evidence from the defendant which sets out the client's version of events. However, it is still useful to get the client to go through his or her side of the story: the solicitor may have missed something, or the defendant may remember something new. Whilst it is unethical, and therefore forbidden, for counsel to 'coach' the defendant (that is, to suggest evidence which the defendant might give), there is no objection to counsel questioning the client closely on the evidence he or she will be giving. It is helpful for the defendant to go through the evidence he or she will be giving in court and to prepare for cross-examination by the prosecutor.

Where counsel is in possession of the witness statements made by the prosecution witnesses, the defendant should also be asked to comment on what those witnesses say (so that counsel can decide what questions to ask them by way of cross-examination). It may be that the solicitor has already performed this task, so that the defendant's proof of evidence contains comments on the prosecution evidence; even then, it can be helpful to ask the defendant if there is anything he or she wishes to add to those comments.

(b) *Advising the defendant on plea and tactics:* Where the client has not received full advice on plea (from the solicitor, or from counsel on a previous occasion), it may be necessary for counsel to advise the defendant (based on what the client has said about his or her side of the story) on plea. It may be, for example, that the defendant has indicated an intention to plead guilty but then says something which amounts to a defence (e.g., a person accused of theft says that he or she did not realise that the property belonged to someone else).

It may also be necessary to advise on tactics, for example, what lines of cross-examination to pursue and what evidence to call.

(c) *Taking instructions on matters relevant to sentence:* Counsel should be careful to have all the information needed to make a plea in mitigation. Instructions should therefore be taken on matters which would be relevant to sentence. This is so even where the client is going to plead not guilty, since (in the event of the defendant being convicted) there may not be time for a further conference between the defendant being convicted and the moment counsel has to start the plea in mitigation.

(d) *Advising on sentence:* Whether the defendant is going to plead guilty or not guilty, it will almost always be necessary to give advice on the sentence which is likely to be imposed in the event of conviction. Counsel will therefore have to be familiar with the relevant Guidelines (issued by the Sentencing Guidelines Council).

Counsel representing a defendant at an early stage of the proceedings should always be prepared to give advice about later stages of the case. On occasions, for example, counsel may be instructed to attend the magistrates' court to make a bail application, or for the mode of trial hearing, and may be asked for advice then by the defendant. Provided counsel is sufficiently well acquainted with the background to the case, there is no objection to such advice being given (although a short note setting out the advice given should be endorsed on the brief, so that the instructing solicitor, and any barrister involved in the case at a later stage, knows what was said). However, where the advice is given without full knowledge of the prosecution case and the defence response to that case, it should be made clear to the client that the advice is only provisional and may change if new information comes to light.

10.6.5   Pre-trial disclosure

A particularly important aspect of advising on evidence concerns the rules which govern pre-trial disclosure. The rules which apply to the prosecution are different from the rules which apply to the defence. The disclosure rules are contained in the Criminal Procedure and Investigations Act 1996 (as amended by the Criminal Justice Act 2003). Further details can be found in the *Criminal Litigation and Sentencing* manual and in *Blackstone's Criminal Practice*. As regards disclosure by the prosecution, a further distinction has to be drawn between material that the prosecution will be using as part of their case and material which they will not be using.

10.6.5.1   Pre-trial disclosure by the prosecution

If an offence is triable either way, the prosecution must (if the defence so request) supply the defence with a summary of the prosecution case or with copies of the statements made by those persons to be called as prosecution witnesses. This must be done (assuming the defence request advance information) before the mode of trial hearing (see **10.6.2**) takes place. If the case is to be tried in the Crown Court, copies of the statements made by the witnesses whom the prosecution intend to call at the trial must be supplied to the defence (if this was not done prior to the mode of trial hearing). Guidelines from the Attorney General stipulate that the defence should normally receive the prosecution witness statements prior to any trial in the magistrates' court.

Where the prosecution wish to use a witness whose statement has not already been served on the defence, a 'notice of additional evidence' (including a copy of the witness statement) must be served on the defence prior to the trial.

The prosecution are also under a statutory duty to disclose material other than the statements of the persons they will be calling as witnesses. Under the Criminal Procedure and Investigations Act 1996, the prosecutor must disclose to the accused any prosecution material which might reasonably be considered capable of undermining the case for the prosecution against the accused or of assisting the case for the accused. This applies to all trials (whether in the Crown Court, the magistrates' court or the youth court).

It follows that by the time of the pre-trial conference (at the latest), counsel for the accused should be aware both of the case to be met and of any material that has come to the attention of the prosecution and which undermines their case or supports the defence case.

10.6.5.2   Pre-trial disclosure by the defence

The Criminal Procedure and Investigations Act 1996 imposes a compulsory duty of disclosure on the defence, but this compulsory duty applies only to trials in the Crown Court. This disclosure takes the form of a 'defence statement'. This has to:

(a) set out the nature of the accused's defence, including any particular defences on which he or she intends to rely;

(b) indicate the matters of fact on which the accused takes issue with the prosecution;

(c) set out, in the case of each such matter, why the accused takes issue with the prosecution; and

(d) indicate any point of law (including any point as to the admissibility of evidence or abuse of process) which the accused wishes to take, and any authority on which he or she intends to rely for that purpose.

Where the accused wishes to rely on an alibi, the defence statement must give full particulars of the alibi and of any witnesses the accused believes are able to give evidence in support of the alibi. The defence must also supply the prosecution with details of any witnesses they propose to call and details of any experts who have been instructed by the defence (whether or not the expert is to be called a defence witness). The accused is required to serve an updated defence statement prior to trial (or a notice saying that there are no changes to the original statement).

In the case of summary (i.e., magistrates' court or youth court) trials, the Act enables the defence to make voluntary disclosure of their case.

If the defence fail to comply with the compulsory duty of disclosure prior to Crown Court trial, or if the defence case at trial differs from that disclosed to the prosecution (whether the disclosure was compulsory or voluntary), then adverse inferences can be drawn by the jury or magistrates, as the case may be.

The Bar Standards Board has given guidance on the involvement of counsel in the drafting of defence statements. The guidance makes the point that it will normally be more appropriate for instructing solicitors to draft the defence statement, since counsel will generally have had little involvement in the case at this stage. Nonetheless, there is no reason why a barrister should not draft a defence statement. However, counsel must ensure that the defendant:

- understands the importance of the accuracy and adequacy of the defence statement; and
- has had the opportunity of carefully considering the statement drafted by counsel and has approved it.

10.6.6   Preliminary hearings in the Crown Court

The Criminal Procedure and Investigations Act 1996 requires preliminary hearings to take place before all Crown Court trials. The nature of the hearing differs according to whether or not the trial is likely to be lengthy or complex. However, in both cases, the purpose of the preliminary hearing is to ensure that the issues in the case are defined before the start of the trial and to reduce the number of cases where the defendant was due to be tried on a 'not guilty' plea but then pleads guilty at the start of the trial (giving rise to what is sometimes called a 'cracked trial').

10.6.6.1   Complex or lengthy trials

Under the Criminal Procedure and Investigations Act 1996, s. 29, which applies to Crown Court cases which are likely to be complex or lengthy, the judge may order a preparatory hearing to take place. The purpose is to identify the issues in the case, to see how the jury can be assisted to understand those issues, to expedite the trial, and to assist the judge's management of the trial.

To this end, the judge can make rulings on the admissibility of evidence or other questions of law likely to arise in the trial. The judge can also order the prosecution to prepare a document setting out the principal facts of the Crown's case, the witnesses who will speak to those facts, and any propositions of law the Crown will rely on. The prosecution can be ordered to prepare the evidence in a form that is likely to aid comprehension by the jury. Finally, the prosecution can be ordered to provide a written notice, detailing any documents the truth of which the prosecutor believes the defence should admit.

The judge can then order the defence to give written notice of any points of law they will be raising and to state which of the documents referred to in the notice from the prosecutor the defence are prepared to admit; where the defence are not willing to admit the truth of any such documents, they must explain why this is so.

10.6.6.2 Other cases: the Plea and Case Management Hearing

In the case of Crown Court trials other than those which are likely to be complex or lengthy (in other words, the majority of cases), s 39 of the 1996 Act enables a pre-trial hearing to take place. Such a hearing is known as a 'plea and case management hearing' (PCMH), the full agenda for which can best be seen from the detailed form that has to be completed as part of the process (see Annex E of the *Consolidated Practice Direction*).

At this hearing, the defendant is asked to enter a plea. If he or she pleads 'guilty', the judge proceeds to the sentencing stage (if necessary, with an adjournment for a pre-sentence report). If the defendant pleads 'not guilty', a date is fixed for the trial.

Where the defendant pleads 'not guilty', prosecuting and defence counsel are expected to inform the court of matters such as: the issues in the case, the number of witnesses to be called, any points of law likely to arise (including questions on the admissibility of evidence), and whether any technical equipment (such as video equipment) is likely to be needed. It follows that it is very important that, by the time of this hearing, the factual and legal issues in the case should have been identified. (See **14.3.1** for the issues in *R v Costas Georgiou*.)

At this hearing, the judge is empowered to make rulings on the admissibility of evidence and on any other questions of law which are relevant to the case. These rulings are binding for the whole of the trial unless there is an application for the ruling to be altered, but such an application can only be made if there has been a material change in circumstances since the ruling was made.

As we have seen, under the Courts Act 2003, a magistrates' court is also able to make pre-trial rulings on the admissibility of evidence or any other question of law relating to the case, and those rulings are binding on the magistrates who eventually try the case.

10.6.7 Trial

Defence counsel and the prosecutor may attend court expecting a trial to take place. However, a trial will not take place if either the defendant pleads guilty to the charge(s) or the prosecution accept a plea to a lesser offence. In the Crown Court, any negotiations with the prosecution regarding the acceptance of a plea of guilty to a less serious offence than that charged will usually take place at the plea and case management hearing. Where the case is to be heard in the magistrates' court, such negotiations will usually take place just before the trial.

We have already seen that counsel for the defence may have to give advice to the defendant at the conference which takes place immediately before the trial.

During the trial itself, counsel is involved in three main tasks:

(a) *Making speeches:* In the magistrates' court the prosecutor usually makes an opening speech but no closing speech, whereas counsel for the defence will usually make a closing speech but not an opening speech; in the Crown Court, both the prosecution and the defence are usually entitled to make both an opening speech and a closing speech (although the defence often forgo the right to make an opening speech). As well as these speeches, it may be necessary for counsel to address the court on the admissibility of certain evidence or to make (or, if prosecuting, to respond to) a submission that there is no case to answer.

The purpose of the prosecution opening speech is to prepare the jury or magistrates for the evidence they are about to hear. The prosecution case is summarised so that the jury or magistrates can put the evidence they are about to hear in context.

The purpose of the closing speech is to highlight the strengths of one's case and, where possible, to minimise the impact of any weaknesses. The defence, for example, will stress any doubt in the prosecution evidence and any explanation which the defendant has given for apparently incriminating evidence.

A submission of no case to answer may be made by the defence at the end of the prosecution case. The essence of the submission is that the evidence adduced by the prosecution is so weak that no reasonable tribunal (jury or bench of magistrates) could convict the defendant on the basis of that evidence.

(b) *Examination-in-chief:* This means getting the witness to tell the story (answering questions such as 'Who?', 'When?', 'Where?'). Care must be taken not to 'lead' the witness (that is, to suggest answers to the questions being put or to ask a question which can be answered with a simple 'yes' or 'no'). Before going into court, counsel must have decided what he or she hopes to achieve with the particular witness, since the examination-in-chief should only bring out evidence which is relevant to the case. Counsel will always be in possession of a written statement from the witness (which obviously forms the basis of the questions which will be put to the witness). Counsel should also be alert to any inadmissible evidence which is contained in the witness's written statement (e.g., references to previous dealings between the defendant and the police, unless such evidence has been ruled admissible) so that those areas can be avoided in the questioning.

Examination-in-chief can also be used to anticipate questions which may be put to that witness in cross-examination. For instance, in a case involving identification evidence, prosecuting counsel would, in examination-in-chief, ask a witness who claims to have identified the defendant as the perpetrator about the circumstances of that identification (e.g., distance, lighting, obstructions to view, etc.). The answers to these questions may well make it more difficult for counsel for the defence to cross-examine effectively on the matters.

The defendant has been present in court throughout the trial and so has heard the evidence of the prosecution witnesses. The defendant may be asked, in examination-in-chief, to comment on what he has heard (for example, 'You heard Miss Jones say . . . What do you say about that?').

(c) *Cross-examination:* This means probing the story told by the witness. In the Crown Court, counsel for the defence will be in possession of the written statements made by the prosecution witnesses; in the magistrates' court, counsel for the defence will usually have sight of the prosecution witness statements. However, the prosecution never have sight of the written statements made by witnesses for the defence. Obviously, it is easier to prepare a cross-examination if one has advance notice of what the witness is going to say.

Cross-examination essentially focuses on inconsistencies and on the probing of weaknesses:

(i)   inconsistencies between what the witness is saying now and what he or she has said in the written statement;

(ii)   inconsistencies in the evidence which the witness has given to the court (e.g., in the course of the witness's testimony, the colour of the getaway car changes from dark blue to black);

(iii) inconsistencies between what this witness has said and what another witness says;

(iv) inconsistencies between what this witness is saying and the theory which counsel has formed about the case he or she is presenting;

(v) inconsistencies between what the witness is saying and what common sense suggests actually happened (e.g., a witness who says that a car was travelling at 70 mph and that it braked sharply and stopped within a distance of 15 metres cannot be correct);

(vi) exposing weaknesses in the other side's evidence (e.g., establishing that the witness was some distance from the scene of the crime and that there were obstructions to their observation). Does the witness have a motive for misleading the court?

It is important that in cross-examination you 'put your case'. In other words, if a witness called by your opponent may be able to comment on part of your case, the witness should be given the chance to do so. In the case of counsel for the defence, this will include putting to the witness those parts of the witness's evidence which differ from, or are inconsistent with, the defendant's account of what happened.

The fact management process which is fundamental to trial preparation is discussed in detail in the next chapter. Many practitioners have in mind their closing speech from the moment they start to prepare the case (but note that, in the magistrates' court, the prosecutor does not have the automatic right to make a closing speech). In thinking about your closing speech, you are asking yourself how you are going to persuade the jury (or magistrates) to come to the result that you want them to come to. In other words, how will you persuade them to accept your 'theory of the case'? This will determine what evidence you put before the court through the examination-in-chief of your witnesses, and what questions you ask in cross-examination of your opponent's witnesses.

Much of the case analysis process involves consideration of strengths and weaknesses: the strengths and weaknesses of your case, and the strengths and weaknesses of your opponent's case. Your task is to think about ways of emphasising or maximising the strengths of your case and ways of improving, or minimising the effect of, the weaknesses of your case; also, to see if you can reduce the effect of the strengths, and increase the impact of the weaknesses, of your opponent's case.

This process can be expressed as a series of questions:

Strengths of your case

- What evidence supports your case?
- How might your opponent try to undermine the evidence that supports your case?
- How might you be able to prevent your opponent from undermining the evidence that supports your case?

Weaknesses of your case

- What evidence weakens your case?
- How might you reduce the impact of the evidence that weakens your case?
- How might your opponent try to prevent you from undermining the evidence that weakens your case?

Strengths of your opponent's case

- What evidence supports your opponent's case?
- How might you try to undermine the evidence that supports your opponent's case?
- How might your opponent try to prevent you from undermining the evidence that supports their case?

Weaknesses of your opponent's case

- What evidence weakens your opponent's case?
- How might you increase the impact of the evidence that weakens your opponent's case?
- How might your opponent try to prevent you from increasing the impact of the evidence that weakens their case?

10.6.8   Plea in mitigation

A plea in mitigation is required if the defendant either pleads guilty or is found guilty. Sentence is usually passed, either immediately or after an adjournment for preparation of a pre-sentence report, by the court which convicted the defendant. However, if the defendant is convicted in the magistrates' court of an offence which is triable either way, the magistrates may (if they decide that their sentencing powers are insufficient to deal with the case) commit the defendant to the Crown Court to be sentenced (the Crown Court having greater sentencing powers); in that case, the plea in mitigation is delivered in the Crown Court. It should be borne in mind that, where sentence is being passed in a magistrates' court following an adjournment, the magistrates who sentence the defendant will probably not be the same ones that convicted him.

If sentence is passed immediately after the defendant has been convicted following trial (i.e., the defendant pleaded not guilty but was convicted), the prosecutor will simply tell the court about any previous convictions recorded against the defendant. If the defendant pleaded guilty, or the defendant is being sentenced at a hearing which takes place after the trial at which he or she was convicted, the prosecutor will also have to explain to the court precisely what the defendant did.

The next step is for defence counsel to make a plea in mitigation on behalf of the defendant. The essence of a plea in mitigation is to draw the court's attention to any mitigating factors relating to the offence itself and to emphasise personal mitigating circumstances relating to the offender.

The plea in mitigation will be based on information gathered from the client (in the proof of evidence and in things said by the client prior to the hearing) and, in many cases, on information contained in a pre-sentence report prepared by a probation officer. A list of the client's previous convictions (if any) should be in the brief; if not, the list can be obtained from the prosecutor. Counsel should check that the defendant agrees that the list of previous convictions is correct and that the defendant is content with the comments made by the probation officer in the pre-sentence report. Counsel should be prepared to probe the client for details of mitigating factors relating to the offence itself or to the client's personal circumstances.

Before advising the client on likely sentence or presenting a plea in mitigation, counsel should ensure that he or she is familiar with the approach taken by the courts to sentencing for the particular offence(s) of which the defendant has been convicted. If the 'entry point' (i.e., the type of sentence taken as a starting point) is a custodial sentence, counsel should indicate that he or she is aware of this before trying to persuade the court to impose a lesser sentence. A useful source of guidance may be found on the website of the Sentencing Guidelines Council (<http://www.sentencing-guidelines.gov.uk/guidelines/index.html>) and in publications such as *Blackstone's Criminal Practice*.

10.6.9 Appeals

10.6.9.1 Appeals from the magistrates' court

Most appeals from the magistrates' court are heard by the Crown Court. An appeal against conviction takes the form of a complete rehearing of the case. The prosecution will be represented by counsel instructed by the CPS or by a Crown Prosecutor. Counsel for the defence may or may not have represented the defendant in the magistrates' court.

Leave to appeal is not required. Because the appeal takes the form of a rehearing, the Crown Court is not concerned with what happened in the magistrates' court; one corollary of this is that a witness who was not called in the magistrates' court can be called in the Crown Court and a witness who was called in the magistrates' court need not be called in the Crown Court. This means that both sides may reconsider any tactical decisions (regarding which witnesses to call) which were taken prior to the trial in the magistrates' court.

Similarly, the hearing by the Crown Court of an appeal against sentence imposed by the magistrates' court takes the same form as the original sentencing hearing in the magistrates' court, with a prosecution summary of the facts followed by a plea in mitigation by the defence advocate.

When advising the defendant whether or not to appeal to the Crown Court, counsel should warn the defendant that the Crown Court has the power to increase the sentence imposed by the magistrates' court, up to the maximum which the magistrates could have imposed; this is so even if it is only the conviction (and not the sentence) which is the subject of the defendant's appeal.

Alternatively, in a case which involves a point of law or jurisdiction, the defendant may appeal instead to the High Court. This can be done in two ways. The first is to ask the magistrates to 'state a case' for the opinion of the High Court (known as 'appeal by way of case stated'); the magistrates duly summarise their findings of fact and their rulings on the law and the High Court considers whether the magistrates reached the correct conclusion. The second way is to apply for judicial review of the decision of the magistrates' court; this method is particularly appropriate where the magistrates exceed their powers in some way or behaved unfairly. The prosecution can also appeal to the High Court by way of case stated, or seek judicial review, on a point of law or jurisdiction and thereby challenge an acquittal by a magistrates' court.

10.6.9.2 Appeals from the Crown Court

Appeals from the Crown Court against conviction and/or sentence lie to the Court of Appeal (Criminal Division).

Sometimes the appellant is represented by the same barrister who appeared in the Crown Court, sometimes a different barrister is chosen. In any event, counsel for the appellant has to examine the notes which were taken during the trial by counsel for the defence to see if any errors occurred during the course of the trial. Particular attention has to be paid to any rulings made by the judge during the course of the trial (e.g., rulings on the admissibility of particular evidence) and to the judge's summing-up of the case to the jury. As far as the latter is concerned, counsel should consider whether the judge stated the law correctly and whether the judge summarised the case for the prosecution, and the case for the defendant, accurately and fairly. Similarly, the comments made by the judge when passing sentence should be scrutinised with care, to ensure that the correct sentencing principles were applied.

If errors were made in the course of the trial and/or in the summing-up, or when sentence was passed, grounds of appeal have to be drafted; these grounds are attached to an 'Advice on Appeal' written by counsel, in which the errors are identified and any relevant case law set out. This is an important document, since it forms the basis of the decision by a Court of Appeal judge whether or not to give leave to appeal.

Once an application for leave to appeal against conviction has been lodged, a transcript of the summing up and any other rulings made by the trial judge will be sent to the barrister who drafted the grounds of appeal; counsel then has the chance to 'perfect' the grounds of appeal (that is, to relate those grounds to the transcript).

If leave to appeal is granted, counsel also has to submit a 'skeleton argument' to the court prior to the hearing of the appeal.

The hearing of the appeal itself takes the form of argument by counsel for the appellant and counsel for the respondent; no evidence is heard except in exceptional cases (e.g., where the conviction is said to be unsafe in the light of evidence that has emerged after the trial).

11

The fact management process

11.1 Introduction to the fact management process

At the heart of the practitioner's work are facts: an incident has occurred or must be prevented from occurring, a person injured, property damaged or likely to be damaged, and loss threatened or sustained. From the first moment of receiving a brief until the last stage of trial, it is the facts of a case that will be the basis of the practitioner's work. 'Facts' are the basis of any evidence given, any speeches made and any questions asked. It is the barrister's ability to manage the facts, to understand their implications, and to use them as the basis of argument, which will be crucial to the success of a case.

The majority of cases involve disputes of facts, not, despite the emphasis in academic training, disputes about questions of law. The ability of barristers to carry out the task of managing facts has in the past been developed by experience, and until the development of the vocational course for the Bar, very little attempt had been made to consciously define and develop this skill. Very few texts have sought to unravel the fact management process in order to teach others how to carry it out on a step-by-step basis. However, it is generally recognised that the ability to prepare a set of papers effectively depends on:

- the need to have a clear picture of what you are preparing for;
- being able to identify what is relevant to your task;
- identifying what the issues are;
- recognising what can and cannot be proved;
- evaluating the strength of the case accurately; and
- putting together, from the information available, the most compelling argument on your client's behalf.

The working approach advocated in this chapter, the C.A.P. approach (Context, Analysis, Preparation), applies these intellectual skills in a practical and structured process to case preparation. The C.A.P. method of preparing a case demonstrates, on a step-by-step basis, every stage in the process—from initial understanding of the legal and factual context, to detailed analysis of issues and evidence, and finally the construction of persuasive and pertinent arguments to present to a tribunal, a client, or, in negotiation, an opponent. The chapter also illustrates some of the techniques which can be used to aid analysis and the presentation of a case. Thorough case preparation can be achieved by many different working methods and it is usual for these to develop and change with time and experience.

While some may think of this as an objective science, the process involves more than applying a logical method of analysis and presentation. Resourceful barristers also use lateral thinking to identify alternative interpretations of the facts. One's own perception of how witnesses see and describe events and their effectiveness as witnesses will influence a decision about whether they should be called at trial or how to question them. Finally, the ability to use different methods to communicate information in a clear and persuasive way calls for creativity and thought about how to present the facts in the best light. These qualities are part of the practical aspects of fact management which cannot be separated from the more objective tasks of collecting facts.

You will find that your own ability to analyse and evaluate factual situations, and to use the results to communicate persuasively, develop best through conscious application and reflection on how effective the results were. You will have regular opportunities to do this in the practical training exercises on which you will work while studying the Bar Vocational Course. If you are able to take the opportunity of giving advice through pro bono schemes, or to undertake representation through organisations such as the Free Representation Unit you will develop further and faster. You will also find yourself developing your abilities further when you move into practice or any other legally related career.

11.2 Starting from scratch—defining basic terms

11.2.1 'Agreed' facts

Every problem will contain 'facts': who the parties are, the history of the situation, what transpired on certain dates, etc. '*Agreed facts*' are those facts which are conceded by your opponent and are not therefore issues in the case. In criminal cases, they may sometimes be set out in a 'formal admission' (see Chapter 1 of the *Evidence* manual). More often, practitioners simply tell the court, 'It is not in dispute that . . . '. In civil cases, the statements of case will disclose what is agreed between parties. Put simply, if a fact is 'admitted', that fact is not in issue and no evidence has to be adduced to prove it.

It is important to note down what facts are agreed between the parties. It helps to narrow down the issues of a case and will be likely to shorten the length of a trial. It may also assist in a negotiation situation to be able to start from some common ground between the parties.

11.2.2 Facts and evidence

When a 'fact' has been agreed, or can be proved by a witness or document, that fact is then considered to be 'evidence' in the case, and can be taken into account in determining the strengths and weaknesses of the case. The distinction is important: some facts are incapable of proof and (if not agreed) should not be relied upon as part of the case.

11.2.3 Disputed facts and facts in issue

If a fact is in dispute between the parties, that is, the opponent does not 'agree' it, it is deemed to be a '*disputed fact*' in the case. In civil cases, you can determine what the 'disputed facts' are by looking primarily at the court papers, although documents and correspondence may bring up other facts that are not agreed. The statements of case (particulars of claim and defence) will show which facts are 'denied' or simply 'not admitted'. If a fact is 'not admitted', the party seeking to prove the fact will have to adduce evidence. By stating 'no admissions are made as to . . . ', the other party is saying, 'I will not adduce evidence to contradict this fact but I reserve the right to cross-examine your witnesses to test their evidence on this point'. If a fact is 'denied', the party relying on that fact will have to adduce evidence to prove it and the opponent will probably bring evidence to contradict it.

It is easy to confuse *'disputed facts'* and *'facts in issue'*. First, bear in mind that it is common for a case to contain many disputed facts. Of these, there will be some that are crucial in the sense that they support points that must be proved in law in order for the case to be successful. It is these facts, i.e. the facts which are not agreed by the opponent and which must be proved in law, that become the 'facts in issue'. For example, D is accused of assaulting the owner of a public house after D and his friend asked to play a game of pool. D's story is that he arrived at the bar 15 minutes after his friend on the evening in question; the prosecution say that he arrived sometime before his friend. The time and sequence of arrival are 'disputed facts' between the parties in the sense that there is no agreement as to who arrived first and at what times they arrived. But bringing evidence of the truth of one version or the other is not relevant to proving the elements of the criminal offence of assault and will not affect a successful outcome. Therefore it is not a 'fact in issue'.

The facts in issue will be determined by what legal elements (in a criminal case) or prima facie requirements (in a civil case) apply. For example, in a contract case where C is suing D for breach of contract and resulting loss, the parties may agree that a contract was made, and the terms of that agreement. However, D disputes that a breach occurred and naturally disputes causing losses. As breach and causation are two of the prima facie requirements for a successful action in contract (and the facts on these two matters are disputed), these become the 'facts in issue' in the case. C will only win the case by producing evidence on these issues to prove that his version of the facts was correct and is therefore entitled to judgment in his favour.

It is important to bear in mind that 'facts in issue' (sometimes called 'factual issues') can be a general heading containing several separate issues. For example, in a criminal case, the identity of the defendant might be in issue. One element of the identification evidence concerns the colour of his hair. One witness says that he had fair hair, another that he had brown hair. The colour of the hair is therefore a fact in issue. Its proof will affect whether the prosecution have proved their case in that identification of the defendant as the offender is an element of the offence. It will assist in identifying all the factual issues to divide the case into fairly broad factual issues first and then look at the facts which are in dispute within each of those main issues. This is covered in more detail later on in the chapter.

11.2.4 Legal issues

These are the questions of law which will have to be answered in the case:

- What are the potential causes of actions or offences?

- What are the potential defences?

- What are the potential legal outcomes?

- What procedural and evidential questions arise?

In tort and contract cases, there are established frameworks to work from, e.g. elements that the claimant must prove in order to establish a prima facie case. In criminal cases, the prosecution must prove the elements of an offence, and in some cases, the absence of a defence. Of the host of legal issues that apply to a case, only some will need to be formally proved since often there will be no dispute between the parties on some of the relevant issues. Later on in this chapter, we look at establishing legal frameworks and defining the issues to be resolved.

11.2.5 The 'theory' of the case

After the barrister has identified a framework of the legal and factual issues in a case and done the necessary legal research, a picture should start to emerge. For each case, it is necessary for you to consider a 'theory' of the case, that is, your explanation of how the events of the case are likely to have happened. The 'theory' of the case will influence the nature of the evidence that will be required for a successful resolution and will also be the base for the advocacy in the case. For example, in the civil brief of *Lowe v Mainwaring* in **Chapter 13**, the claimant (tenant) alleges damages were caused by the failure of the defendants (also tenants) to keep an external pipe in good order. In representing the defendants, one theory might be as follows.

The duty was owed by the landlord (not the defendants) under the lease. If any duty was in fact owed by the defendants, there was no breach of the duty as the pipe was properly insulated and, in any event, the damage which the claimant suffered, if proved, was not caused by the flood of water from the pipe but from the pre-existing financial difficulties.

In a straightforward case, the theory may be fairly clear, and based solidly on legal and factual certainties. But often the law may not be clear, all the facts may not be available, or there may be gaps in the evidence. In those cases, you will need to develop arguments which link the facts and evidence which are available into a persuasive explanation of your client's version of events.

Developing a 'theory' is covered in more detail later in this chapter.

11.3 The C.A.P. approach

Having identified the intellectual elements of fact management skills in **11.1**, there are a number of practical techniques which barristers may use to produce a well-prepared case. Regardless of the task which a barrister might be asked to undertake—to advise on the merits, appear in court, or advise in conference—it is crucial to absorb and analyse the facts of the case. Without a uniform approach and structure to this process, thoughts and theories can become confused. Adopting a logical yet flexible framework will not only minimise the chances of missing important pieces of information, but will maximise productivity in terms of your time and effort.

The C.A.P. approach is a step-by-step method of preparing and analysing a case. All barristers develop their own practical styles of working, with or without attaching formal names or titles to their working methods. In order to study the necessary stages, the C.A.P. approach sets out the three main stages involved in efficient preparation:

- Context;
- Analysis;
- Presentation.

Each stage contains tasks and questions which must be answered before moving on to the next stage. The time necessary for each step depends on the complexity of the case and the specific task you are instructed to do. The advantage of taking an overview of the preparation process is that it enables the student to see how the process develops, from the first reading of the facts, through to the analysis of evidence needed in order to present a successful case. As you gain experience, it is hoped that the C.A.P. framework will allow you to determine selectively what is required by means of thorough preparation for any given case.

In **Chapter 12**, the C.A.P. approach is applied to the civil case *of Lowe v Mainwaring* to illustrate the process at different stages in the life of a case when a barrister might become involved, i.e., giving advice on merits, drafting, and appearing in an interim application.

The C.A.P. approach is applied to a criminal action in **Chapter 14**, based on the brief for the defence in the case of *R v Costas Georgiou*.

It should be remembered that the C.A.P. approach is only one method of achieving a well-prepared case as discussed in **11.1**. Even while following the C.A.P. approach, the tasks within each stage can be done by using any number of techniques, e.g. lists, charts, mind-maps, graphs. As examples, a set of proforma charts which can be used as part of the C.A.P. approach are included at **11.8**. While their use is by no means prescriptive, they may be helpful in clarifying the various steps involved in thorough case preparation.

11.3.1   The three stages of C.A.P.

Stage 1: The context of the case

(a) Understand the stage of the proceedings: your role and instructions, and the objectives.

(b) Understand the problem: e.g., the history of the situation, nature, and cause of the problem.

(c) Collect the 'facts'.

(d) Identify the agreed facts and facts in dispute: i.e., those facts which are disputed between the parties, for example, by use of a chart to set out the facts, queries, and each party's version.

(e) Identify the legal framework: in a criminal case, this would be the elements of the offence, possible defences, sentence, jurisdiction, and procedure. In a civil case, this would be the elements required to obtain or refuse the remedy sought.

Stage 2: Analysis of issues and evidence

(a) Analyse the issues:

   (i)   Identify the factual issues: i.e., those disputed facts which are not agreed by the opponent and which must be proved in law for a successful outcome.

   (ii)   Identify the legal issues by applying the facts to the legal framework.

   (iii)   Identify a potential 'theory' of the case.

   (iv)   Identify the gaps and ambiguities in the facts.

(b) Analyse the evidence:

   (i)   Analyse the strengths and weaknesses of your case and that of your opponent.

   (ii)   Establish 'proof'—turning facts into 'evidence'.

Stage 3: The presentation of the case or argument

(a) Revisit the chosen theory and select a theme.

(b) Consider how to support the legal framework.

(c) Consider how to carry out your instructions.

(d) Consider the intended audience: e.g., who will be reading your work or listening to you, and the best method of conveying information.

(e) Ensure that this process enables you to carry out your client's instructions.

11.4   Stage 1: context

11.4.1   Introduction

When you receive a set of papers, they will contain varied information. The first task is a simple one of comprehension. Specialist terminology may be used in a report (for example, to describe a part of a machine used in factory production) and you may need to consult a glossary or trade manual for a full understanding of the term. This occurs frequently with medical terms used in expert reports, e.g. diagnosis of a condition, and practitioners must understand the meaning of the term and its application in the particular context. There is a glossary covering medical terms in **Appendix 2** to this manual.

Increasingly, information is presented in numerical form and you will need to be able to analyse bank statements, sets of accounts, and possibly graphs or statistics. It is likely that you will be expected to verify any figures you have been given. Indeed, in planning for a negotiation or considering a proposed settlement package you would be expected to make accurate calculations without the need to call for an accountant, except in fairly complex cases. (See **Chapter 15** on dealing with figures.) Understanding a variety of information is only part of the task. It is also important that you develop an ability to present that information to others using various modes, and for a variety of purposes (see **Chapter 16**).

11.4.2 Understanding the stage of the proceedings, your instructions, role, and the objectives

Just as the facts in a case must be viewed in the context of all the surrounding information, they can be and are interpreted differently according to the standpoint of the interpreter. Before beginning a factual analysis, it is important to understand the stage that the case has reached, what you have been instructed to do and why, and what your client is hoping to achieve.

Your view of the past and present situation will be influenced by whether you are representing the claimant or defendant, prosecution or defence, employer or employee, a consumer or a manufacturer. As you read the papers, it is important to approach them with an objective frame of mind. In some cases, proceedings may have already begun before you become involved in the case. In other cases, the 'present' situation is one where there is a threat of future harmful events and the 'future' solution will be some type of preventative action.

11.4.2.1 The stage of the proceedings

Fact management skills cannot be divorced from civil and criminal procedure and require a thorough knowledge of the legal process. **Chapter 13** provides an overview of the stages of a civil case and **Chapter 14** gives an outline of a criminal case. Ascertaining what stage of the process a case has reached is a crucial starting point and it is wise to make a written note of when proceedings were issued, served, previous court orders made, etc., prior to embarking on further analysis of the case.

Your approach will differ according to your instructions and the development of the case to date. For example, it is common for barristers to be instructed to write an advice on evidence. This is the particular 'task' which is requested, but it can occur at different stages in the life of a case. In a civil case, advice is often requested when a solicitor is preparing for trial and wishes to know if there are any gaps in the evidence or whether to call for further evidence. It is also common for such an advice before disclosure of documents occurs or after an initial wave of disclosure has been completed, or both (see *Civil Litigation* manual on disclosure). Advice may be requested prior to any proceedings being issued, to ascertain whether there are sufficient grounds to support a claim, and if so, the appropriate parties to be sued. In this case, you will be advising only on the evidence available at that particular time. Advice on evidence may be requested at any time before the trial.

Understanding the procedural and factual history will assist you to appreciate the task requested, define successfully your objectives for the task, and to resolve the problem.

11.4.2.2 Your instructions, role, and objectives

It is perhaps stating the obvious to point out the necessity of understanding the parameters of your instructions to ensure that the advice sought is in fact given, and the requested performance completed to the letter. However, the fact is that in the process of digesting a multitude of facts, documents, events, and statements, particularly in a complex case, it is easy to lose sight of the specific task that has been requested.

Is your role to be the sole counsel who will see the case from beginning to end? Or are you one of several counsel who will represent the client on a variety of ancillary matters? As a junior barrister, it is common to find that you are briefed to appear on a bail application in a criminal case, or an interim hearing in a lengthy and complex civil case. The task involves one small part in the process, and it may be difficult or even impossible in the time available to understand fully the 'past' of the case. While spending hours reading through files in preparation for a hearing is laudable, two points should be remembered.

First, unless you recognise where in the litigation process you (and the court hearing) are, you will be reading the papers with the wrong purpose. A legally qualified schedule sponge, soaking up facts without a reference point achieves nothing. Time would be better spent analysing the arguments that may be made, both for and against, at the hearing.

Second, you will often find that these arguments (particularly in protracted cases) will have already been considered as part of the general strategy for the case. The senior barrister with overall responsibility may have specific thoughts about the hearing for which you have been instructed. In these cases, it would be unwise to decide that the brief is yours to handle independently; the hearing may not achieve its real purpose (either long-term or short-term). The danger lies in highlighting the wrong areas, or giving away points unnecessarily because your involvement prevented you from seeing their long-term significance. In short, determine your role properly in the context of the size of the case and the stage it has reached. Consultation with the instructing solicitors and the senior barrister (if there is one) is advised.

In answering 'Why are you instructed to do this task?' you will need to identify your objectives, which you should realise by now may differ from those of the client. Superficially, your objective may be to win the case or succeed at a particular hearing. Of the several aims that you might have, the most obvious is not necessarily the only one or even of primary importance. In carrying out your task, be it written work or attending hearings, there may be latent as well as manifest reasons for your working methods. For example, when a barrister in court asks his or her own witness, 'What is your name and address?' the manifest purpose is to put on record who the witness is and his or her residence. The latent purpose is usually to settle the witness in the witness box by asking easy and comfortable questions. There may be other latent purposes, for example, to show the judge or jury that the witness comes from a deprived part of the city (if this is part of your theory or theme of the case).

One further point about objectives borrows a page from advocacy skills. Be sure that in clarifying your objectives and expectations, you have considered your audience. It is common for barristers to speak in front of magistrates, judges, juries, administrative or employment tribunals. Thought should be given to their expectations, agenda, and what methods of persuasion will produce the most successful results.

11.4.3   Understanding the problem

To understand the context of a case, it is essential to understand fully the history of the parties (civil), or background information about the client (criminal), and how the situation arose. For every client and fact situation, there is a past, present, and future. Once you see how and why the problem arose, it will assist you in identifying how to deal with the present problem, and possible solutions for the future. In the civil context, parties may have enjoyed a good business relationship in the past which one or both parties wish to continue in the future. In a criminal case, the defendant's financial situation leading up to the alleged offence may provide an insight into the circumstances.

11.4.3.1   Looking at the cause of a problem

A crucial part of understanding a problem is appreciating the cause. Why has it occurred? What circumstances led to the problem? If an effective solution is to be found, what circumstances must be avoided to prevent recurrence? For example, your client has asked that a court order be obtained allowing him to have contact with his children on a Sunday, rather than the present arrangement on a Saturday. You will need first to investigate why this issue has arisen between the parties. More specifically you would wish to know:

- whether Saturday contact had been agreed or was the subject of a court order;
- whether the agreement or order had worked well, and the history of any difficulties;
- what the nature of any problems had been;
- whether changing the day is considered by the client and/or child carer to make arrangements easier or more difficult;
- how the children have responded;
- whether the children wish to maintain contact;
- why your client wants to see the children on Sundays, e.g. to go to church, because of a work schedule, etc.;
- whether the children want to change to Sunday—any conflict with their activities or school projects;
- if the proposal has been refused, the possible reasons; and
- whether there are any other difficulties between the parties which may be masked by this dispute.

Once this information has been digested, you will then be in a position to understand fully the problem and consider appropriate ways of solving it which will meet the client's objectives.

The process of 'understanding' a problem is achieved by a combination of using your individual sense of perception and intellect. Just as the results of computer output are only as accurate as the data which has been put in, the range and accuracy of facts fed into the human mind will affect the conclusions made from them. You will find that developing an approach or structure for posing generic questions (who did what to whom, when, where, and with what result?) will focus your mind on collecting the crucial facts and appreciating how and why a problem has arisen, thus paving the way to reaching a solution that is appropriate on the facts and desired by the client.

11.4.3.2 The client's objectives

One may wonder why, in a study of fact analysis, the client's objectives, or even those of the barrister, are a part of the process. Simply put, understanding the client's objectives impacts the way the problem-solving process is managed and influences the way facts can be interpreted. As you read the papers, a mental picture emerges of the appropriate ways to resolve the problem. The client's objectives may or may not be reflected in the papers. Alternatively, you may find after a conference that the client holds different or additional objectives that will require a rethink on the best method of resolving or presenting the case.

The barrister's day-to-day contact with the legal system and the constant approach to problems solely from a legal standpoint can easily allow his or her own objectives to influence the understanding of the problem and the client's objectives. For example, you may decide that the best course of action would be to negotiate a settlement or seek arbitration to avoid a court hearing. However, your client may want a public investigation (or a day in court) and/or be opposed to settlement where no commercial benefit can be seen in settling the case, for example where the client is a supplier of faulty goods but has already received full payment. Your task is to identify your client's values and interests, to know the extent to which your own objectives may affect a proposed resolution, and base your factual analysis on the strengths and weaknesses of the case.

It should be remembered that clients may have non-legal as well as legal objectives; these may or may not be articulated. Some stated objectives may eclipse the true interests that the client has but, for whatever reason, has not verbalized. Rather than taking statements at face value, strive for more thorough questioning which may reveal additional reasons for their objectives and which may improve the strength of their position.

It is not too soon, even at this stage of reading the papers, to bear in mind possible resolutions to the problem. In civil cases, while some disputes will ultimately go to trial for final resolution, this may not be in the client's best interest. Various forms of alternative dispute resolution (ADR), such as arbitration and mediation, are becoming more popular as costs escalate and the delays of bringing an action to trial increase and are actively encouraged by the Civil Procedure Rules. Arbitration is common in construction cases and is increasingly used in commercial and civil cases. Mediation, the process whereby a mediator attempts to bring the parties together into an agreed resolution, is often preferable to a contested trial in family and child cases and neighbour disputes. Further, there are other remedies that might be suggested by the facts, including use of internal employee complaint procedures, filing formal complaints with an agency such as the Commission for Racial Equality, or with the local authority. In criminal cases, the client's circumstances may indicate that the best solution would be long-term medical treatment and you may wish to raise with the solicitor the possibility of investigating this option on behalf of the client.

11.4.4 Collecting the facts

The next stage is to collect all the relevant facts in the case. In practice, this work is divided between the barrister and the solicitor. The degree of factual information included in the instructions to counsel will vary according to the type of case (civil or criminal), the size of the case, the stage in the proceedings and the task which you are asked to do. In the early stages, you may have only a proof of evidence from the client, and possibly a few witness statements. In civil cases, this may be sufficient to provide an advice on the merits, although it would be insufficient for providing, e.g., an advice on evidence and quantum. Where you are briefed to appear at an interim hearing and have been sent copies of the drafts and relevant witness statements, there may be no need to acquire further information, unless the facts require clarification. In defending a criminal case, the defendant is likely to be best placed to provide more information about witnesses, particularly about potential alibi evidence. Prosecuting counsel often request additional information from, e.g., police who were at the scene or otherwise involved in the matter.

In some cases, your written instructions to counsel may be minimal. You may need to ask what has taken place in previous conferences between the client and solicitors. If so, you will want to ensure that you understand exactly what was said or done, as different interpretations can easily arise when discussions are relayed second-hand. If the need for information or clarification can best be met by requesting a conference with the client, this is appropriate, but you will want to bear in mind that conferences increase the costs in a case and should only be requested when the information cannot be obtained by other, less expensive means.

Once you have understood the contents of your brief, and held a conference (if necessary), you can begin to clarify in your own mind precisely what is said to have occurred. It is crucial to develop a critical and questioning approach to all information which you receive. Remember that the information that is missing is as important in the context of the situation as what has been said or written. It is not sufficient merely to identify the gaps in the information or inconsistencies in the facts. You must attempt to fill the gaps by acquiring more information and ask, 'Why might these inconsistencies exist?'

It is also important to remember that fact-finding is an ongoing process. New facts will become available at different stages in a case, for instance, on disclosure of documents. As new facts emerge you must keep an open mind; your view of the case may need to be reconsidered and your original conclusions reassessed and possibly modified. You may never possess all the facts in a case.

11.4.4.1 Methods of collecting facts

Rather than start with a group of assorted facts, which at this stage may not bear a great degree of logical order, it is more helpful to approach collection with a structure or framework of main questions to be answered. The facts that are presently available can then be filled in, and the areas where more information is needed, or ambiguities exist are highlighted. Regardless of what task is requested, e.g. to advise, draft, or appear as an advocate, you will find that most practitioners undertake several routine steps in preparing a case. These preparatory steps are important because they assist in understanding the events and problem generally, and the schedules and charts produced as a result (if the information they contain is agreed) are often given to the court in hearings and at trial to assist the court's understanding of the case. As there is always that possibility, strive for accuracy, clarity, and neatness as you prepare them. There are several methods which can be used, though the purpose of all of them is the same: to ensure that every aspect of the problem is explored thoroughly and from every angle. As you gain experience you will no doubt devise your personal methods of asking these important questions of who, what, where, why, and how?

11.4.4.2 Construct a chronology and *dramatis personae*

Listing the people involved and the events in the order in which they occurred clarifies what happened, assists understanding, and can be invaluable as the basis of an opening speech. Increasingly, an agreed chronology is handed up to the judge at the start of both civil and criminal trials which provides a structure for the presentation of the case.

11.4.4.3 Draw a plan of the *locus in quo*

The *locus in quo* simply means the place where the events occurred. It can be represented by maps, floor plans, or other types of drawings. The first plan which you prepare should be entirely uncontroversial: either delete any points which are in dispute or, if they are included, ensure that they are clearly identified as in dispute. The rationale for this is that, where a plan is produced that makes assumptions about facts which are yet to be proved, the plan tends to become fixed in the mind as the true factual scenario and may prevent you from keeping an open mind to consider other possible explanations. An 'undisputed' plan can also be useful in a client conference where asking the client to explain his or her version of events will test the credibility of the client's evidence.

You also need to devise ways to represent in the plan the areas about which you do not yet have enough information to present the data accurately. For example, in the plan of a bank robbery, you are told that a witness was on the opposite side of the road, but at this stage of the case you do not know precisely where. Guessing the position and marking it on the plan is inaccurate and could lead to subconsciously assuming its truth without obtaining further factual information. Mark it in a way that shows there is doubt, or delete it until further facts are known. Until the location is certain, it is impossible to assess the witness's line of view, obstructions, etc.

It may also be helpful to draw a series of plans. Following the first which is uncontroversial, additional plans may then show various alternative explanations of what might have occurred.

11.4.4.4 Organise by sorting

This method, based on the five basic questions of who, what, why, where, and how, will assist you to categorise main areas. In **Table 11.1**, column 1 contains main categories of questions; column 2 lists possible answers (or possibilities which may lead to answers). You will note that the suggestions in column 2 are appropriate to different factual situations.

Table 11.1 **Sorting method**

Column 1	Column 2
1. Who did what to whom?	Names, addresses of parties, witnesses.
2. With whom does the problem occur?	Friend, employer, supplier.
3. When does the problem occur?	Date, time, season.
4. Where does it occur?	Work, home, public place.
5. In what situation?	Drunkenness, anger, lack of funds, lack of supplies, etc.
6. Is there a pattern?	When contact is refused, when maintenance is unpaid, when supplies are scarce.
7. What triggers it?	Smell, noise, rain?
8. What results from the problem?	. . .

11.4.4.5 Flowcharts

Some practitioners prefer to use general-style, blank flowcharts which provide an overview of the case as well as prompt heads of information which will be needed. The chart shown in **Figure 11.1** is an overview of a civil case. It could be used in its present form in fairly straightforward cases. More complex cases will require a more extensive system of collection and organisation of the facts.

LOSS/REMEDIAL RELIEF

PERSONAL INJURY

Nature?
Medical prognosis
    Present?
    Future?
Full recovery?
Residual disability?
Special damages — list
Expert's report

LOSS OF INCOME

Gross income before and after?
Net income before and after?
Benefits previous and present
Minimise loss:
    Steps could/should have
    been taken?
        Why?
        What effect?
Proof?
Expert opinion needed?

LOST PROFIT

Expected profit?
How calculated?
Why was it lost?
    Property damage?
    Reputation/good will?
How to prove?
Expert opinion needed?
Minimise loss:
    Steps could/should have
    been taken?
        Why?
        What effect?

DAMAGED/LOST PROPERTY

Nature?
Value before and after?
How to prove?
Expert opinion needed?

DOCUMENTS/EXHIBITS

List

Where are they?

Who has them? (Cl, Def,
    Third Party)
What can each prove?

Admissible?

EVENTS

Date/Time/Period

Place

Conditions (weather, etc.)

Map/Plan?

WITNESS TO EVENT

Who?

Relationship to client?

Position (if applicable)?

Statement given?

OTHER WITNESSES

Who?

Relationship to client?

Position?

Proof given?

To whom?

When?

Who has copy?

What does each say?

What facts does each prove?

Go on to fact analysis

CLIENT INFORMATION

Who?

Address

Public funding

Occupation

Current finances

Other—personal

CLIENT'S VERSION

What happened?

Why/Cause?

Over what time period?

Action taken by client?

Action by others?

Statement made?

OPPONENT'S VERSION

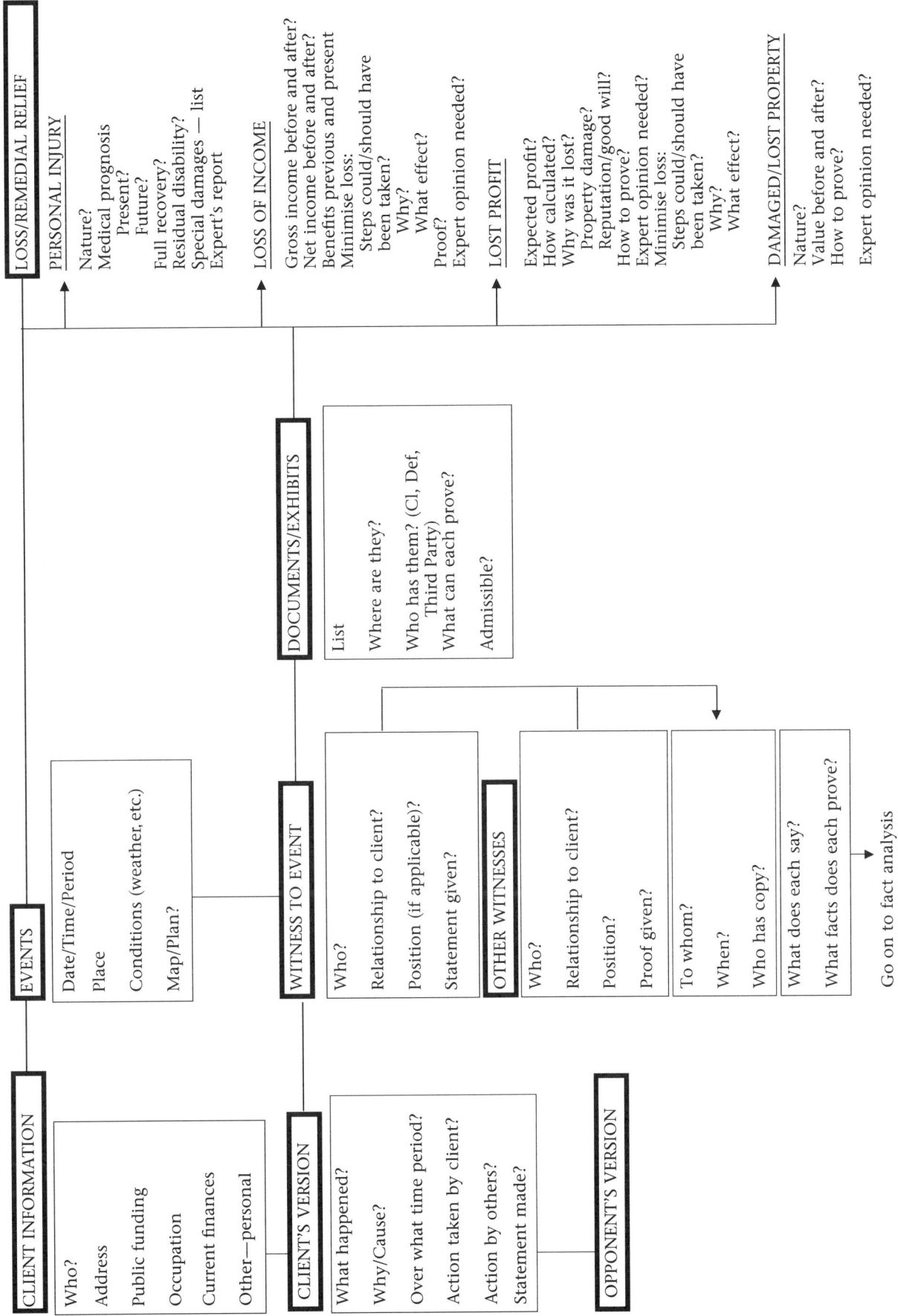

Figure 11.1 Overview of a civil case

11.4.4.6 Checklists

Finally, you may prefer to develop checklists of the information which you will need when you prepare your cases. With experience, you will be able to amend and update your lists to home in on the crucial information, cover new legal developments, and avoid spending time and effort on sorting through information which is not relevant to the issues as hand. Of course, there may be times when papers are received at the last minute and there is not sufficient time to prepare copious checklists. However, if you have developed this structure as part of your working approach, your mind should automatically take you through the generally relevant areas, using the little time which you have to best advantage.

EXAMPLE

An example of the questions that would be included in a checklist in a civil action based on the flowchart illustrated in **Figure 11.1** is as follows:

Personal:
1. Who is your client?
2. Where does he or she live?
3. Occupation?
4. Other personal details?

Event:
5. When and where did the event happen?
6. How does your client say it happened?
7. What did your client do or say at the time?
8. Who heard or saw what your client said or did?
9. Who witnessed it? What do the witnesses say happened?
10. Can they give evidence?
11. What points could each prove? Are they consistent with the client's story?

Exhibits:
12. What exhibits are there?
13. Where are they? Who has them?
14. What can each prove?
15. Who will produce them in court?

Loss or damage:
16. Type of loss suffered?
17. If PI, nature of injury?
18. Medical prognosis?
19. Will there be full recovery?
20. If no, to what extent is disability permanent?
21. What experts have given or should give evidence?
22. What other losses are there, e.g. lost income, lost profit, lost or damaged property, pain and suffering, etc.?

If income lost:
23. What is/was client's gross and net income?
24. What payments were/are being received from State?
25. What steps could/should have been done to minimise loss?
26. Why should they have been taken?

If profit lost:
27. What profit should have been made?
28. How calculated?
29. Why was it lost?
30. What steps could/should have been taken to minimise loss?
31. Why should they have been taken?

If property lost or damaged:
32. What was its value before and after the event?
33. What is its value now?

34. Can it be repaired? If so, what is the cost?
35. What could/should have been done to minimise loss?
36. If so, why should they have been taken?

Insurance:

37. Does client have insurance? With whom?
38. Does the policy cover this loss?
39. Has a claim been made? If so, when?
40. Does the other party have insurance?
41. Does that insurance cover this loss if liability can be proved?
42. Has a claim been made?

11.4.5   Identify agreed facts and disputed facts

Once the basic facts have been digested, you will begin to identify the facts which are agreed between the parties and those which are disputed. It is necessary to crystallise these issues and ascertain, for each disputed fact, both your client's version and that of your opponent. This is an important preliminary analysis which should be recorded in a practical form which can be used later in the fact management process. The way in which this information is presented is a matter of style, although its usefulness may be increased if it is neat and can be used, for example, in discussing the case with the solicitor. A suggested format can be found in **Table 11.8** at the end of this chapter.

EXAMPLE

In the civil case of *Lowe v Mainwaring* (see **Chapter 13**), the defendants are the tenants of the first and second floors of a property. The claimant is the tenant of the ground floor and uses the space to run the Topspin Snooker Hall. A flood occurred from a water pipe outside the building at about the first-floor level, causing damage to the claimant's property. The claimant alleges that the defendants were responsible for the water pipe and their negligence caused the damage. The facts might be recorded as in **Table 11.2**.

Table 11.2 **Record of facts**

A/D	Claimant	Page/ref	Defendant	Page/ref
A	At the time, C was tenant of ground floor, and D were tenants of the 1st and 2nd floors of 83–87 Leeds Road	XX		
A	The pipe located in the 1st floor outside the building burst	XX		
D	Time: it burst between 23 and 30 December 1998	XX	Pipe was repaired within a few hours of bursting on finding it on the 30th	XX
D	D responsible for repairing and maintaining the pipe	XX	Under lease with M. Pike, D *not responsible* for repair or maintenance	XX
D	Pipe was not properly insulated	XX	Properly insulated	XX

This table is further developed at **13.1.1**.

There may be many disputed facts in a case and though it may be a tedious job, it is important that all of them are recorded. From this information, you will be able to determine which of these disputed facts will actually be 'facts in issue' in the case, i.e., facts which are not agreed and which must be proved in law in order to win the case. This will be covered in more detail in Stage 2 of the C.A.P. approach in **11.5**.

11.4.6 Identify the legal framework

Having started with facts, you will need to identify a possible legal framework to which the facts will ultimately be applied. This applies equally whether you are determining the best legal basis for bringing a case, or the best defence. At this stage, the aim is to identify all the legal possibilities which may lead to a resolution of the problem. Later in the analysis process, the framework will be developed and any necessary legal research done.

The process of identifying the legal possibilities may be difficult, particularly where the area of law is an unfamiliar one or several potential legal frameworks are suggested. To start, you will need to list all the possible legally relevant factors which are present. You cannot afford at this point to make snap judgments about the best legal framework or settle for a quickly identified clever answer which may have weaknesses or be less appropriate than another, legal basis for bringing or defending the case.

11.4.6.1 List the potential legally relevant factors

Having taken a preliminary view of the facts, it may be tempting to place them into familiar pigeonholes, e.g. contract, misrepresentation, mistake, theft, etc. While this may assist in providing initial focus, it can be restrictive; the best legal solution may not always come from a textbook framework.

First, list all the factors of the case which may possibly have a legal ramification. The index of *Halsbury's Laws of England* or *Halsbury's Statutes* can be a source for ideas. The general categories in **Table 11.3** have legal relevance in most cases.

Table 11.3 **Relevant factors**

Categories	Legally relevant factors
People and partes	e.g., minor, spouse, joint owner, limited company, professional
Places	e.g., occupier's liability, Factories Act, waterways, party resident in France, leased premises
Objects/items	e.g., animals, children's toy, car window, machine part, stereo (consumer)
Documents	e.g., contract, will, bill of lading, deed
Acts	e.g., negligence, intentional, reckless act
Omissions	e.g., failure to act or deliver or mitigate
Words	e.g., inducement, fraud, misrepresentation
Dates	e.g., limitation

In making this list, you should include everything that underlies or surrounds the facts, as well as actual words that appear in the papers. For example, in a case that concerns a jam jar, even though there is no Jam Jars Act, you will still need to enter 'jam jar' on the list. There are laws relating to the manufacture of jam jars, filling jars either in a factory or at home (if the contents are for sale to the public), labelling them (including

EC regulations), not dealing with jars negligently to cause injury to another, etc. The more comprehensive your list of potential factors, the more pieces are available for choosing a framework.

The completed list of factors can then be organised and grouped together into 'legal frameworks'. The following headings might be used as general categories for grouping factors in a civil case:

- parties;
- cause(s) of action;
- defence(s);
- remedy sought.

Some factors on the list in **Table 11.3** may apply to more than one heading. For example, under 'Acts' you may have: 'Piano owned by client wrongfully taken away from his home.' This factor suggests a possible cause of action (tort of conversion) and also the relief sought (return of piano).

Some potentially relevant factors may not fit easily within one of the headings above but should not be ignored. Retain them in a general category at the end. They may prove useful, for example by revealing a gap in the case you are preparing.

EXAMPLE

An example of how factors might be grouped in chart form is shown in **Table 11.4**. In this case example, the claimants have suffered loss and damage as a result of their neighbour (D1) who is burning industrial waste from a machine-shop business operated on the property. The neighbour rents the property from the landowner (D2) who is aware of D1's activities. Column 1 lists the facts which carry a legal implication. Column 2 contains general issue headings. The space in column 3 is for legal frameworks suggested by the facts; in this case, nuisance and a possible breach of statutory obligation. This procedure is the same in criminal cases to explore bases for the offences which might be charged, and potential defences. While many methods can achieve this analysis, the benefit of the tabular form is the visual analysis on a single page.

Table 11.4 **Grouping legal factors**

Example of grouping legal factors towards developing a full legal framework. In this example, the clients (Mr and Mrs C) are suffering from the burning of industrial waste by a neighbour (D1) who lives on adjoining property and runs a small business. D1 leases the property from a freehold landlord(D2).

Col. 1 List legal factors of the case	Col. 2 Group into general 'issue' headings	Col. 3 Identify potential framework(s)	Col. 4 Notes
1. Neighbour (D1) operates machinery shop in garage as a limited company 2. Leases from landlord (D2) who owns property 3. Clients (Cs) owns the property adjoining D1	→ PARTIES		
4. D1 burns his 'waste' in open fires — sometimes uses outdoor incinerator — fumes and ash to Cs' land and home 5. Burning regular: 4 to 6 pm Monday to Friday including holidays 6. C gives oral and written notice to D1 and D2 — request to stop ignored 7. C believes open burning in breach of council regulation — possible zoning problem — live in residential area	→ CAUSE OF COMPLAINT (CAUSE(S) OF ACTION)	**1. NUISANCE** Elements: (a) Parties (b) Duty of care owed to C (c) Breach (d) Damage caused by D (e) Remedy Damages? Injunction?	
8. C's apple orchard suffered loss of winter apple crop — loss of sale of apples and cider usually sold to local factory (ash fell on buds and caused decay) 9. C's wife suffers burning eyes 10. C's asthma made worse by fumes — even when incinerator used	→ DAMAGE/LOSS	**2. BREACH OF STATUTORY REGULATION** Elements: (a) Parties (b) Statute (c) Breach (d) Damage (e) Sanction (f) Defence?	
11. C wants open burning stopped and restricted incinerator use 12. Damages for C and C's wife — medical condition 13. Loss of income from damage of apple orchard	→ REMEDY SOUGHT		

11.4.6.2   Basic legal frameworks

While it would be unwise to conclude at this stage that a particular framework is the only applicable one, it is often a helpful starting point to consider established frameworks which are suggested from the facts, e.g. contract, tort, a specific criminal offence. For a specific criminal offence, you would focus on the following headings:

- *Offence*: What are the elements of the offence?
- *Defence*: Applicable common law and statutory defences.
- *Penalty*: Sanctions on summary trial, on indictment.
- *Jurisdiction*: Type of offence, e.g. can be tried by magistrates or in the Crown Court; financial threshold e.g. if amount less than £5,000 to magistrates' court.
- *Procedure*: Relevant procedural steps.

Table 11.5 shows how this information could be set out in relation to s. 18 of the Offences against the Person Act 1861.

Table 11.5 **Identifying the legal framework—example in a criminal case: offences against the Person Act 1861, s 18**

Heading	Framework
Offence	Unlawfully and maliciously wound with intent to do grievous bodily harm.
Defences	Factual denial of elements including claiming lawfulness of wounding by reason of self-defence, prevention of crime, protection of property or other persons.
Penalty	Imprisonment up to life. Usual bracket 3 to 8 years. Provocation factor which can be taken into account. Deportation. See EC Treaty, Article 48 and Directive 64/221, arts 3 and 9.
Jurisdiction	Indictable offence. Crown Court only. Class 4 offence.
Procedure	Magistrates commit/transfer to Crown Court. Plea taken at plea and directions hearing. If not guilty, date fixed for jury trial.

For civil cases, the facts may suggest a tort and/or a contract claim. The following preliminary frameworks (**Table 11.6**) set out the elements which would be considered in determining whether a prima facie case is established.

Table 11.6 **Preliminary framework: civil case**

Tort	Contract.
Parties.	Parties.
Accident or cause of complaint.	The contract.
Cause(s) of action (causation).	The terms.
Damage or loss.	Performance.
Remedy sought.	Breach.
	Damage and causation.
	Remedy sought.

Even where an established framework fits the facts well, you should in any event investigate other legal bases to ensure that your chosen framework not only applies to the facts but offers the best opportunity to achieve the client's objectives. In civil cases, it may be wise to plead alternative causes of action, join causes of action, or bring in additional parties for the most effective legal solution.

11.4.6.3 Identify areas for legal research

Additional research may be necessary to determine whether the framework is the most appropriate, for example, to determine whether the specific act complained of is covered by statute or constitutes criminal activity. By stepping back and taking a critical view of the framework, it should be possible to see all the strengths and weaknesses within it and to take decisions where there are options.

If additional research is undertaken, notes of it should be recorded for later use, possibly at trial. At a minimum, the following should be recorded:

- *sources:* including the relevant page or paragraph numbers of textbooks, and full citations of case law;
- *short summary of the relevant legal point;*
- *your view of the answer to the question:* indicating how the point found in research will support a specific fact or issue in the case.

See **Chapters 5** and **7** above.

11.4.6.4 How to choose the best legal framework

Surrounded by a myriad of legal possibilities, it is sometimes difficult to know what particular legal framework should be chosen and why. Having an understanding of alternative ways of assessing the case, as well as using your professional judgment in filling gaps will help you to make the best decision.

11.4.6.5 Which framework makes the best use of the legal and factual strengths? The 'best-fit' approach

If the framework does not provide a single obvious answer, it should nevertheless take you some distance down the road. At a minimum, it should define where there are legal and factual certainties and, if options exist, what the options appear to be. One way to proceed is simply to make an objective valuation of all the legal requirements and relevant facts. The solution that 'best fits' the framework—the one which makes the best use of the legal and factual strengths of the case while placing least reliance on its weaknesses—would be the preferred one. This approach is not suggesting that superficial analysis will do so long as it gives a roughly right answer, but that, on critical analysis of the law and facts, a particular framework would make the best use of the elements in the case.

Even in the 'best-fit' method, the elements which do not sit well with the rest of the framework should not be ignored. They may have some use in reviewing the case at a later stage, or in looking for options for a settlement.

11.5 Stage 2: analysis of issues and evidence

11.5.1 Introduction

Thus far, the potential legally relevant factors have been identified and loosely grouped to suggest a possible legal framework or 'legal basis' to the problem. More than one framework may be suggested. The best legal argument has no point in a court if it is not soundly based on the facts. Equally, the facts of the case need the best legal argument to achieve the best result. Although an analysis of a case should start with consideration of the facts, as the case progresses, the role of law and fact is equally important and the two are closely interrelated. More than that, they are interactive; one moves with the other as more legal or factual input is provided for a case.

11.5.2 Analyse the issues: identify the 'factual issues' and analyse the legal issues by applying the facts to the legal framework

By this stage, you will have identified a possible legal framework and noted what facts are agreed and disputed. From the elements or legal requirements of this framework, you must then determine the 'factual issues' (also called 'facts in issue') of the case. The factual issues will be those disputed facts which, according to the legal framework chosen, must be proved in law for the case to be successful. Where statements of case have already been served, these will specify what issues have to be proved. For example, in a contract case where the claimant (landlord) is suing the defendant (tenant) for failure to maintain a gas boiler under the lease which exploded causing damage to the claimant's property, the analysis might look like **Table 11.7**.

Table 11.7 **Analysis of the issues**

Framework	Facts of client	Disputed/agreed
Parties	Landlord: Mr X; Tenant: Ms Y	Agreed
Contract	By lease dated . . .	Agreed
Terms	Tenant had obligation to maintain	Agreed
Performance	Tenant in occupation, rent paid	Agreed
Breach	On XYZ date, boiler not in order	Denied
Causation	Caused explosion	Agree: explosion Deny: causation
Loss	Damaged property	Loss not mitigated

From this analysis, you will see that the legal and factual issues will be breach, causation, and loss. (The loss is a factual issue as the defendant's case is that the claimant's loss is due to his failure to mitigate.) Each of these factual issues must be formally proved by evidence. Thus, each issue must be fully analysed to determine which facts can be proved and by what means. This information should be recorded for clarity and used later in the case.

The aim is to identify, for each factual issue, the name of the witness who can prove the fact; whether oral or documentary evidence is available; on which party the burden of proof lies; and in a civil case, whether it is specifically raised in the court documents. There are various methods of recording this information and provided the relevant analysis is done, the choice is left to the practitioner. One chart which can be used for this purpose appears in **Table 11.9** at the end of this chapter.

In finding the factual support for a framework, remember that every disputed fact will need to be proved. As the evidence is gathered, you will need to update the chart or list of all facts for which evidence is still required. Some of the possible frameworks identified early on may prove unworkable. While you can normally expect to have enough factual information for a preliminary determination, it is rare to have all the relevant facts before starting work on a case. As more information comes to light, your view on the most appropriate framework may change.

One final word on the interrelation of law and fact. It is vital to select relevant law with a sound knowledge of the facts and then also to consider the facts in the light of the law to ensure coherence. Although law and fact become interrelated, never be deceived into thinking the law has become more important—the evidence, or the proven facts, will always be just as important as the law.

11.5.3   Identify a potential 'theory' of the case

The theory of the case is a convincing and logical account of why and how the events in the case are likely to have happened. It is based on:

- the principles of law that are likely to be used at trial, i.e. the legal solution or framework;
- what has to be proved and/or disproved at trial for the case to succeed; and
- consideration of which facts are capable of being proved and the inferences which can be made from them.

Formulating a theory, though based on the available facts and evidence, sometimes requires a degree of guesswork to fill in the gaps. In a sense, it puts cement between the bricks of the framework to fill in any factual or legal gaps in order to make a cohesive and persuasive story. It is your theory of the case that you hope to convince the fact finder is the true version of events.

The dangers of developing an imaginative theory that is not well founded on the facts cannot be overestimated. The more gaps that are filled by guesswork, rather than proven facts, the weaker the case. It follows that the more that the theory is grounded on persuasive evidence rather than supposition, the higher the likelihood that it will be accepted.

In the context of fact management, developing a theory is an important stage in considering the legal and factual basis for the client's version of events and the chance of successfully obtaining a good resolution. Putting forward a theory is also a basis for persuasive advocacy, used in arguing interim applications and submissions at trial. This is covered more fully in the *Advocacy* manual.

The 'theory' should be an objective analysis of the events, rather than merely the best theory for the client. The opponent will also put forward a theory, and seek to disprove your account, thus it is wise to consider how the other parties may view your theory. Critically analyse the legal and factual weaknesses of the potential theory. Ensure that it is coherent and as capable of proof as possible.

In considering the theory, bear in mind:

(a) The need for the *best* explanation for the client's position from all the possible alternatives. Although alternative theories are possible, it should be remembered that a single explanation is inherently more compelling.

(b) Early in a case, it is desirable to develop provisional theories. The 'theory' may need to be altered as more evidence comes to light with regard to the opponent's defence, disclosure, information received in a criminal case, etc.

(c) Although the theory must be logical, the ultimate form that it takes will be influenced by the 'theme' of the case, which goes beyond logic and may show that your client should be successful on, e.g., moral grounds. Choosing the theme of the case is discussed in Stage 4 (see **11.7**) after factual analysis of the case is completed.

11.5.3.1   Ways to develop the 'theory'

If you are fortunate enough to have a substantial amount of factual information, and sources of proof, it may be possible to identify the best legal framework and develop a theory fairly easily. However, where the factual information is scarce, you will have to construct either partially or wholly a theory of the case, alongside the consideration of the best legal framework. Thus, the phrase 'developing a theory' is sometimes referred to as using theory to identify the most appropriate legal framework, or, as is used here, to fit together how and why the events or problem occurred.

Identifying alternative theories can be difficult, particularly where the area of law is unfamiliar to you. The more experienced you are with an area of law, the easier it becomes to appreciate the range of different theories which may apply. If you are in uncharted waters, there are guidelines to assist you in developing a perspective on the situation.

First, the problem at hand may be analogous to another situation with which you are familiar. In civil cases, consider the basic rights and obligations of the parties; the same legal principles may apply. In criminal cases, consider how analogous conduct is treated by the law and whether defences in those situations may be applicable to the case at hand. Second, consider whether the conduct or acts are of a nature that may be covered by statute. Research in one of the legislation sources may suggest other legal solutions and alternative theories for the case. Finally, bear in mind that there is no need to reinvent the wheel. You may find that merely asking whether someone in your chambers or firm has experience in the area enables them to point you in the right direction. It will very likely save time, may prevent you from going down the wrong path, and also give you a different perspective on the case.

11.5.3.2   Logical and lateral thinking

Many of you have played the game where one word is given and the object is to think of all the different words that can be formed from this one word. There are many variations but the challenge remains the same: to brainstorm, or to use another phrase, to use logical thinking to come up with all plausible answers. In this context, you are presented with a proposition that X happened or did not happen. The challenge is to think logically about all the evidence that exists to support that conclusion, even if purely circumstantial. Your analysis must be based on proved—or provable—facts as far as possible. Beware of emotion, intention, and knowledge elements which are particularly difficult to prove. Remember, too, the weakness of logical thinking: the danger of assuming because a theory is logical, it is actually true.

Lateral thinking asks, not how events are most likely to have happened, but what are all the possible ways in which they *could* have happened, logical or otherwise. It looks for explanation from different, and often unexpected, angles to a problem. An example of reaching a solution by lateral thinking follows:

EXAMPLE

Problem

John states that when he came home, he went into the living room of his house and saw immediately that Victoria was lying naked on the floor, and that she was dead. There was broken glass on the floor and a small pool of water. The window was open, but John could not remember if he had forgotten to close it before he went out.

Logical assumptions and focus for questioning

It is natural to assume and concentrate on:

- Victoria has been murdered or has died from natural causes such as a heart attack.
- Why was Victoria naked?
- Broken glass—if the window had been closed, an intruder could have broken a window or door for entry.

Logical thinkers would pursue more about Victoria, e.g., how she died and why, and about John, e.g., how long he had been gone, whether Victoria was very familiar to him, etc. Stimulate lateral thinking by putting the problem in the centre of a diagram as in **Figure 11.2**. Follow the 'dos and don'ts' around the path and think of new lines of questioning.

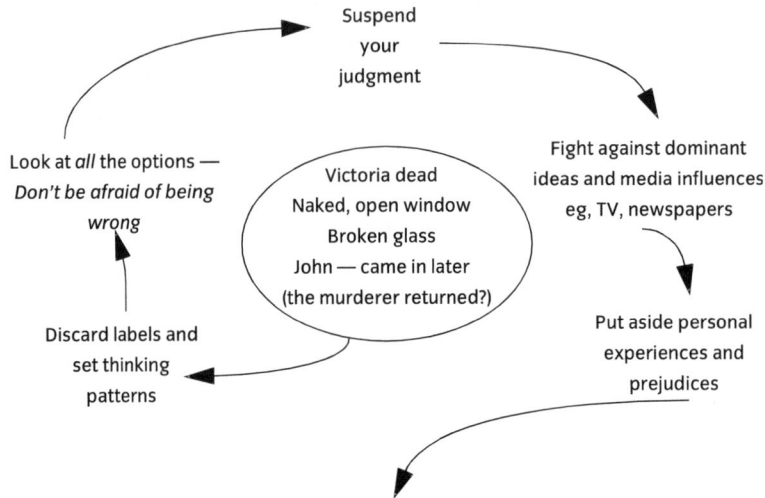

Figure 11.2   Lateral thinking

New lines should include where Victoria lived; whether she was usually clothed and in what type of clothes; who lived with John, including any animals; what objects in the room were made of glass, e.g., vases, ornaments, drinking glasses.

The answer

Victoria is in fact a fish and has died naturally after John's cat knocked the bowl over and ran out through the window!

This, of course, is an extreme example, but does illustrate the trap of simple faith based on assumptions that something is true because it outwardly appears so.

Information rarely arrives in a sequential manner. A piece of information coming in early does not signify that it is particularly important, nor should it prejudice the importance of the other facts arriving later or from unexpected sources.

11.5.3.3   Mind-mapping

Another technique for developing a theory of a case is mind-mapping. When you receive information, your mind processes it in key concepts, interlinking thoughts with other ideas. Each word is received in the context of the words surrounding it, integrating the ideas and concepts to communicate certain meanings. Mind-mapping is a physical picture of the process that is occurring in the mind. Although it can take some time to become proficient at drawing them, the rewards are many as they visually present the structure of the case and indicate where the weaknesses lie.

To start a mind-map, place the main theme or event in the centre. The branches coming out from the centre outline the main characters and events, with descriptive detail forming smaller branches. The more important elements are placed near the centre; the less important ones nearer the edge. There is an example in **Figure 11.3**, which suggests how you might use this technique in preparing a bail application for your client, Costas Georgiou (see **14.1**).

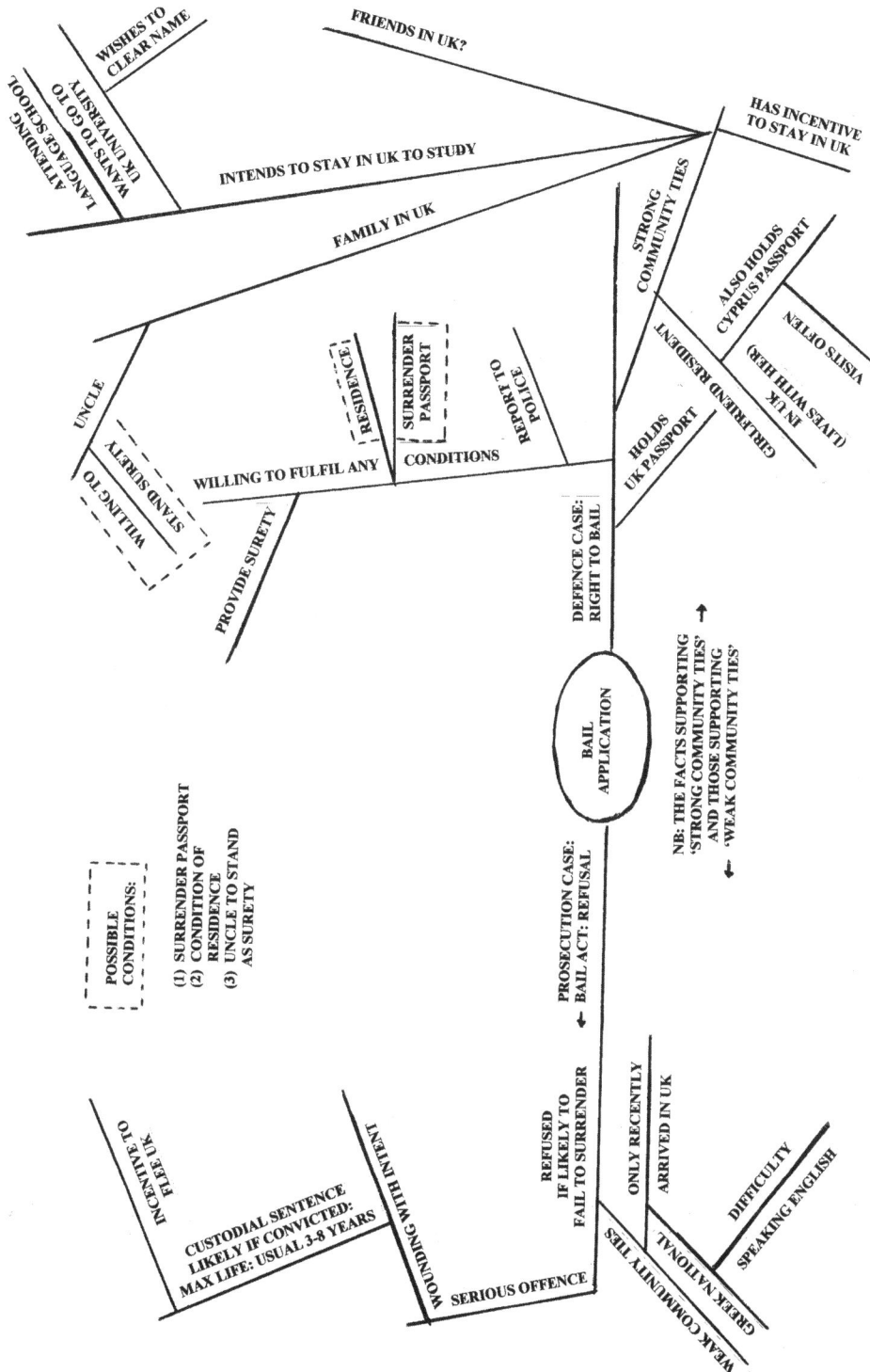

Figure 11.3   Mind-map or concept map of facts for bail application in the case of *R v Costas Georgiou*

11.5.4   Identify the gaps or ambiguities in the facts

The advantage of adopting a methodical approach to analysis and recording is that it tends to highlight any gaps or ambiguities in the fact scenario. Sometimes these are fairly obvious, as where some invoices in a regular pattern of trading are missing which are relevant to the disputed fact. More commonly, these are spotted by putting yourself at the scene—try to picture the story and ask yourself what pieces are missing or unclear. For example, in a fact scenario about a bank robbery, there may be a witness to the robbery. Before the picture can be completed you will need to know where the witness was standing, the direction he or she was facing, any obstructions to a clear view such as cars, signs, weather conditions, personal visual disabilities, etc.

In some cases, the client is able to supply missing information and the most cost-effective way of obtaining this may be by requesting a conference. In civil cases, it may be necessary to serve a request for further information on your opponent (see the *Civil Litigation* manual). Information may be needed from a third party and you will need to ask your instructing solicitor to take a proof of evidence if the identity of the witness is known or seek further witnesses who can provide evidence on a particular issue.

11.5.5   Analyse the evidence: the importance of analysing the strengths and weaknesses

The question which most clients ask their barristers is 'Will I win my case?' The answer will depend on the strength of the evidence, i.e., on what facts can be proved. Before you are in a position to answer the client's questions, you will need to assess:

- what facts must and can be proved by whom;
- from the facts which can be proved (the evidence), the admissible evidence in support of each proposition which must be proved;
- the degree of conflicting or contradictory evidence; and
- whether the evidence is sufficient to satisfy the standard of proof required.

In a civil case, it will be clear from the claim and defence which facts are in issue and therefore must be proved. By identifying which side carries the burden of proof on each issue and assessing the witness statements and documentary evidence which support your case, as well as the contradictory evidence, you will then be in a position to comment on the likelihood of successfully establishing your client's case. While this information can be collated in a number of ways, you may wish to try using the chart in **Table 11.10**. This gives an overview to ascertain easily the strengths and weaknesses of a case. The importance of this assessment process, often called 'assessing the strengths and weaknesses' of the case, cannot be overestimated. It is not only the key result of the fact analysis process but is also essential before you can competently:

- give sound advice on the likelihood of success at trial;
- negotiate effectively on your client's behalf;
- advise on whether to accept a Part 36 payment (payment into court);
- advise on whether further evidence is necessary, and if so, the nature of that evidence; and
- plan the presentation of the case at the trial.

In a criminal case, the prosecution must prove the commission of the offence beyond reasonable doubt. Whether you are briefed for the prosecution or the defence, an analysis will still be required to assess whether the facts, or inferences drawn therefrom, can be established to the required standard of proof for each and every element of the offence. As in civil cases, this evidence must be balanced against the opposing evidence which may weaken the prosecution case.

11.5.6   From facts to evidence—establishing 'proof'

By this stage, you should have identified from the information which you have, the facts which are agreed and disputed, their source, i.e., who or what will (may) be able to prove the proposition, and, where available from the claim or defence and disclosure, the facts which your opponent will be putting forward. Facts become evidence when they are proved. There are various methods of 'proving' a fact: by direct evidence, inferences, and generalisations. Regardless of which form the evidence takes, each required element of the case must be proved.

It is at this point that careful thought will have to be given as to whether, by reason of the rules of evidence, any facts will be (or are likely to be) excluded at trial.

11.5.7   Direct facts versus inferences

Direct evidence is evidence which proves the truth or falsity of a fact, and does not need an inference for proof. Evidence by inference, sometimes called circumstantial evidence, allows proof by virtue of the inference of another fact. The inferred fact may be a required element in the case or, as is more common, may prove a secondary fact, which can in turn infer proof of the required element. The chain of facts which can be inferred before finally proving the required element is not limited, that is to say, a court is unlikely to reject evidence simply because several inferred facts were needed to prove an element. However, where the inferred facts are so remote from proving the element that an extensive chain is needed, there is more risk that little probative weight will be given to the evidence.

The importance of the distinction between direct evidence and evidence proved by inference is significant, but not because one is necessarily more persuasive than the other. A group of inferences—or for television viewers of courtroom drama, the circumstantial evidence—may carry more probative weight than a single fact of direct evidence. The distinction is necessary to recognise where proof can only be through one or more inferences.

It is not uncommon to find in some cases the legal elements of the action or offence have been proved primarily, if not wholly, by inference (or circumstantial) evidence. In these cases, the strength of the inferences and credibility of witnesses become crucial as each offers a piece of the overall picture. Witnesses on both sides will have conflicting evidence of what was seen or what happened. Therefore, how credible, accurate, and persuasive a witness is perceived to be will directly influence the weight which the inferred evidence will have.

11.5.8   Using generalisations to link inferred facts to required elements

Inferences are based on premises assumed to be true. The truth is assumed possibly because it is based on widely accepted knowledge or science. But where this support is lacking it is also possible to rely on a generalisation. Generalisations are based on general life experience which permit a conclusion that something is more likely to be true. As explained by D. A. Binder and P. Bergman, *Fact Investigation*: *From Hypothesis to Proof* (West Publishing Co., 1984, at p. 85), the generalisation becomes the premise which enables one to link the specific evidence (inference) to the final elements which are required to be proved:

A generalisation is then a premise which rests on the general behaviour of people or objects. How does one formulate generalisations? Usually, one adopts conventional wisdom about how people and objects function in everyday life. All of us, through our own personal experiences . . . through knowledge gained from books, movies, newspapers, and television, have accumulated vast store houses of commonly held notions about how people and objects generally behave in our society.

EXAMPLE

To illustrate a case example of how inferences and generalisations operate, take the criminal case of Cassie Charnel who has been charged under the Theft Act 1968, s 1, with stealing a bottle of whisky from Super Stores plc. To establish the case, the prosecution must prove several elements which make up this specific offence. These are:

- Cassie took a bottle of whisky;
- the whisky belonged to Super Stores plc;
- she did so dishonestly;
- at the time, she intended to deprive Super Stores plc permanently of the whisky.

Suppose the Super Stores plc detective has made a statement to the police and that part of it reads as follows:

I saw the defendant take a bottle of whisky from the spirits display. She did not put it in the store's wire basket which she was carrying but instead she put it in an inside pocket in the coat which she was wearing. She went to a checkout and paid for the goods in the basket but made no attempt to pay for the bottle of whisky. She then left the store. I followed her and stopped her in the street outside.

Concentrating on proving the elements of the offence, the crucial facts contained in the detective's statement are that she took the whisky from the display at Super Stores plc, put it in her coat instead of her basket, failed to pay for the whisky at the checkout, and left the store with the whisky. However, there is no direct evidence of this. Rather, they are inferences from the detective's statement to this effect.

The move from the detective's statement to the inference that what he stated was in fact true involves several generalisations:

- in the absence of a motive to lie or opportunity for erroneous observation, a person's account of what he or she has seen is likely to be true;
- the detective had no known motive to lie;
- he had no known opportunity for erroneous observation.

In analysing the evidential support for your case, you will need to consider each fact, whether its proof is by direct evidence or inferences, and what evidence or inference exists to challenge or weaken the proposition. This should highlight where the proof is weak and requires further evidence to strengthen the proposition. It is important in carrying out the analysis that facts do not take on a theoretical superiority, if in reality they cannot be proved to exist, or for evidential purposes they would clearly be inadmissible. Tabulation can be helpful to do this and is illustrated in **Table 11.11**.

11.5.9 Wigmore analysis charts

Another method of analysing evidence is by drawing a chart based on a scheme originally proposed by Wigmore (see J. H. Wigmore, 'The Problem of Proof', *University of Illinois Law Review*, 1913, vol. 8, p. 77). The aim of this method is to identify the chain of proof, including inferences which strengthen or weaken the main proposition to be proved. This method is explained in more detail in **Appendix 3**, along with examples.

While it can be a time-intensive exercise, many people find it beneficial to produce a visual analysis in this way.

11.6 Stage 3: the presentation of the case or argument

11.6.1 Introduction

The last stage in the C.A.P. approach is to prepare the presentation of the case in light of the task which you have been instructed to do. Presentation is a generic term which in practice means:

- making a final decision on the theory and theme of the case;
- determining how you will support the legal framework;
- considering your task and its intended audience;
- preparing the results of your analysis for that task.

11.6.2 Revisiting theories—selecting a theme

After the fact analysis process is completed, you will need to consider the theory chosen earlier and be prepared to amend it as required up until the end of the trial. Having chosen the theory, you will need to select a theme (or themes) to fit the theory of the case. The theme may be defined as the part of the 'story' presented in court which is used because of its persuasive effect.

In an essay entitled 'Lawyers' Stories' (originally presented at the Seminar on Narrative in Culture, University of Warwick, in 1987) in *Rethinking Evidence, Exploratory Essays*, 2nd edn (Cambridge University Press, 2006), Professor William Twining defines theme in the following way:

Sometimes it is used to refer to the overall characterization of the situation or story or some element of it that appeals to a popular stereotype. For example: 'This is an example of a grasping landlord exploiting a helpless tenant'; or 'this is a case of property developers needlessly desecrating the countryside'. Another, more precise usage . . . refers to any element that is sufficiently important to deserve emphasis by repetition. An English barrister (Patrick Bennett QC) gives a vivid account of what he calls 'the mantra', as follows: 'In almost all cases there will be a key factor which has played a dominant role in the case from1 your point of view. It may be stupidity, fear, greed, jealousy, selfishness. Pick your word, inject it into your opening. Put it on a separate piece of paper. Repetition will have a lasting effect. If you have hit the right note and have repeated it often enough, it will echo in the jury's mind when they retire. It will be the voice of the 13th juror. Try to hit the note as soon as possible in opening.'

The theme will be used in opening and closing speeches, and will underpin the questions put to the witnesses. The 'story' should include the items of evidence which support it and exclude any matters that undermine its persuasiveness. Good themes are often very simple. They extend logic and have been defined as the soul or moral justifications of the case, put forward in such a way as to maximise the appeal to the judge or jury.

The theory and the theme must be consistent with each other. The experienced advocate can make the two so consistent that they are virtually indistinguishable. This is done because the better the theme fits with the theory, the greater the moral force of the theory and likelihood of persuading the tribunal of fact to find in your favour. Take, for example, a contested careless driving case in the magistrates' court: a pedestrian steps out onto a zebra crossing, causing the motorist to brake hard and skid. The only substantial dispute on the facts is whether the pedestrian looked to the right before stepping onto the crossing. The defence theme may well be that there is a limit to the care and foresight to be expected of the ordinary competent motorist, especially when faced with a jaywalker. If at the trial it emerged that the pedestrian was late for an appointment, another defence theme might be 'more haste, less speed', and so on.

11.6.3 Supporting your legal framework and reasoning

Whether the law on which your case is based derives from established legal principles or is unsettled, e.g. because previous precedents conflict, a firm basis of legal sources will be required, including any legal research that is necessary to support the chosen legal solution. You may have referred to key statutes or cases in your advice or opinion. You will generally be required to submit a written 'skeleton argument' prior to the hearing. These outlines of the case and the arguments will require legal support for your key propositions. You will be expected to provide your opponents and the court with a list of authorities (e.g., statutes, cases, reports) on which you will rely. Legal research is covered elsewhere in this manual, but a few considerations are included here for thought.

Statute law

If a statutory section is relevant to the legal argument, consider its real role in the case:
- Does the entire section apply to the case, or merely a part?
- Is its effect clear or is its interpretation open to challenge? If so, how could it be challenged?
- What are the relevant principles of statutory interpretation?
- Are there cases interpreting the words of the statute?

Case law

If a case supports your argument, you will want to defend its precedent value; if it does not, you will want to find points on which to challenge or distinguish it, e.g. on the facts, or the application of the principle involved. A case is rarely directly on point and you should consider its real value in constructing the legal arguments supporting the framework. For example:

- On what facts was the decision made?
- What precisely was the ratio as opposed to *obiter dicta*?
- Did all the judges agree? (Which judge gave the principal judgment; what is his or her standing?)
- What was the level of the court making the decision?
- When was the case decided?
- And, finally, of most importance—has the case been subsequently reviewed or over turned?

There is rarely a single case on a particular point. It is more common to find a variety or line of cases. The whole line of cases should be reviewed, not simply to make coherence of the decisions, but also to consider what pattern of thinking can be seen through them and how this will fulfil your purpose.

If appropriate, note the procedural basis on which the decision was made. In some cases, it is not open to the judges to review the facts and their decision is limited to whether the lower decision was properly reached.

Textbooks

While some of the leading textbooks can be quoted in court, and, indeed, judges have been known to adopt passages within their judgments, the support for the legal framework in a case should be based on original sources, rather than textbook comment.

11.6.4 Consider your task and the intended audience

Whether there are any preliminary matters which must be dealt with before you are able to carry out your instructions will depend on the nature of the task requested, the present stage in the proceedings, and the result of your analysis of the case.

In a sense, this is a chicken-and-egg situation, for it is only after you have completed an analysis of the case that it can be determined whether, on the basis of the papers, witness statements, etc. that have been sent by the solicitor, the instructions can be carried out. In some cases, no further information will be needed, save for clarification of confusing points arising in the papers. An example is where you are asked for advice on the merits based on existing facts (which can be proved).

Sometimes, it may be difficult to know what further information to ask for from the solicitor. You should consider the stage of proceedings as this will influence the degree of detail and range of relevant documents which may be required. Where you are briefed to appear at an interim hearing, you will, of course, require support for the arguments to be used at the hearing, and the relevant court documents. However, it would be unreasonable to ask the solicitor to produce documents which are not relevant to the present hearing. An exception might be where the document or evidence to prove a proposition would eventually be needed in any event and preparation for trial is inevitable. Then, it may be prudent to discuss the matter with the solicitor. The point is that requests for further information should only be made where necessary to enable you to carry out your instructions.

Where you have been asked to provide an advice on evidence, it may also be difficult in some cases to know precisely what to advise, particularly if the area of law is an unfamiliar one. By this time, however, the legal framework and factual issues will have been identified and usually a 'theory' of the case developed. These will provide you with a focus to concentrate on what evidence will be needed to bring out the strengths of the case or highlight the weaknesses in the opponent's case. You will also want to consider the nature of the evidence, whether it is consistent in itself and with your client's story, and where more detailed facts may be needed to fill gaps. For example, the history of parties and disputes are often found in more than one medium, e.g. letters, memos, reports, and faxed communications. Many disputes develop over months or years and the client's position will be strengthened if there is supporting evidence over the entire relevant period rather than patchy samples. Even at the stage of preparing for trial, it may be necessary to embark on further disclosure, where, for example, it comes to light that important evidence is in the custody of a third party and previously unseen.

Finally, it may be necessary for counsel to have a site view or product sample in order to appreciate fully the circumstances or how an injury was alleged to have occurred. This is often the case in complex or technical matters, such as engineering, manufacturing or property damage cases. Additional briefing may also be needed in cases involving complicated experts' reports and counsel must prepare the examination of expert witnesses for the hearing.

The manner of 'presenting' your analysis and the case also depends on the intended audience. When you are asked to write an advice or opinion, the audience will likely be limited to your client, the solicitors, and possibly other counsel who may become involved in the case. The knowledge that your written work will not be seen by your opponent (in most cases) allows more flexibility in how you present it. On appearances in court, however, your 'audience' will be the judge whom you are trying to persuade and, unless it is an application without notice, the opponents and their counsel.

Careful thought must be given, not only to the content of presentation, but the best methods of relaying facts and evidence in light of the audience. In studies of how people receive information, it has been shown that the majority of human beings are 'visual', meaning that material shown to them using a visual medium, as opposed to, e.g., an aural medium, has the highest degree of impact and influence. A smaller number of people react more favourably to 'hearing' the information. Therefore, consider whether it might be appropriate to use charts, graphs, or other visual aids in presenting the case.

11.6.5   Preparing the results of your analysis

Your final task will to be make sure that you have everything you need to help you carry out your instructions in a form which will support your presentation. It may be useful to present some of the work you have done in preparation to your opponent or to the court itself. Agreed chronologies, summaries of facts, schedules or plans of the *locus in quo* are frequently handed up before a case begins and can be very compelling and certainly make you appear well prepared and efficient. It is now usual for civil courts to require that lists of issues, skeleton arguments, and lists of the authorities which will be relied on should be submitted before a case begins. The Civil Procedure Rules governing civil cases provide for skeleton arguments to be used in most cases.

If you are instructed to hold a conference or to negotiate it will help you to have some notes with you so that nothing relevant is forgotten. If you are appearing at court, notes about the points you wish to make on each issue will be helpful. Chapter 4 of the ***Advocacy*** manual contains suggestions of the kind of notes you might find useful to prepare for your own use.

Everyone adopts a method of organising information to suit his or her own needs. Many barristers use blue notebooks for all their work done on preparing a case, from notes of conferences with clients, to preparations for trial. One particular form of organising information for trial, described as a 'trial book' is explained in detail in T. Anderson, Schum, and W. Twining's *Analysis of Evidence*, 2nd edn (Cambridge University Press, 2005), Chapter 5.

11.7   The client's choice—acting on instructions

At the beginning of the C.A.P. approach, you became familiar with the client's objectives and what they hoped to achieve. These should not be forgotten as you proceed with your fact analysis and assess the strength of the case. You may be asked for an advice on the merits, or another task which will result in the client needing to take an immediate decision. Your task may alternatively be part of the overall case management. Apart from your client's overall objectives, other criteria such as costs, time efficiency, the desire to avoid stress or risk, the impact on family or business, and the desire to be exonerated may be factors which determine what decision is made. You will need to bear this in mind and ensure that you present the possible solutions to your client in such a way that all the consequences of a particular course of action are highlighted, thus aiding your client to make an informed decision about the next steps.

11.8 Suggested charts

We have seen that the C.A.P. approach identifies the stages necessary for efficient case preparation and that there are varying techniques which can be used to achieve those tasks. The following four charts (**Tables 11.8, 11.9, 11.10**, and **11.11**) can also be used to aid understanding and analysis. The titles refer to the stages in the C.A.P. process.

Table 11.8 Stage 1: Context of the case: identifying agreed and disputed facts

(Note: This form may be used for either civil or criminal cases. 'Ref/page' refers to the source of the statement, e.g. witness statement of J. Bloggs, page 6, para 2.

A = AGREED D = DISPUTED	CLAIMANT'S VERSION OR PROSECUTION VERSION	REF/ PAGE	DEFENDANT'S VERSION	REF/ PAGE	QUERIES/ NOTES
[A]					
[D]					

Table 11.9 **Stage 2: Analysis of issues and evidence: identifying issues and relating evidence to issues**

(Note: This form can be used in criminal cases by changing the reference to the claim and defence.)

Ref	Issue	Para of particulars of claim	Para of defence	Para of reply	Burden of proof	Name of witness	Available oral evidence	Available documen- tary evidence	Notes/ comments, e.g., procedure, evidence, gaps

Table 11.10 **Stage 2: Analysis of issues and evidence: analysing the strengths and weaknesses**

(Note: This form can also be used as the basis for examining and cross-examining witnesses.)

Issue	(a) Evidence in support of C's version	Witness	Page	(b) Evidence which contradicts/ undermines C's version	Witness	Page	(c) Evidence which contradicts/undermines (b)	Witness	Page

Table 11.11 **Stage 2: Analysis of issues and evidence: analysing the evidence proving the case**

ISSUE/ELEMENT:

FACTS IN SUPPORT	WITNESS	INFERNCE IN SUPPORT	CHALLENGE/ WEAKNESS	NOTES

12 The C.A.P. approach in action

12.1 Introduction to Chapters 13 and 14

Once the various stages of the C.A.P. approach have been identified and understood, they should be applied routinely to the preparation of every case until you have developed your own effective methods of preparation. Obviously, the context of every set of instructions will highlight particular aspects and not every stage may be required to be considered for every piece of work.

The following chapters demonstrate through worked examples how using the C.A.P. approach can ensure that you are able to carry out your instructions effectively. **Chapter 13** deals with a civil case, *Lowe v Mainwaring;* **Chapter 14** with a criminal case, *R v Costas Georgiou*. The contents of each chapter are set out on the title page. Each chapter contains a series of instructions in the case at various stages of the legal process at which a barrister is commonly instructed. Each set of instructions is followed by notes entitled '**C.A.P. in action**' which have been prepared as an example of how a barrister might apply each stage of the C.A.P. approach in preparing to carry out his or her own instructions in the context of a civil and a criminal case (see, e.g., **13.1.1** and **14.1.1**).

12.2 Instructions to counsel

Each set of instructions would include a back sheet similar to that shown at **13.1.** After the instructions have been carried out, the back sheet should be returned endorsed to instructing solicitors, together with the completed work (if any). Each subsequent set of papers in the same case, in addition to any new documents, would also contain all the papers previously before counsel, together with a copy of any opinion or case statement previously settled by counsel. For reasons of space, papers have only been duplicated where there is good reason for doing so, for instance, in each case, one back sheet is shown before and after endorsement. Not all back sheets have been printed. The contents of any set of instructions are set out in the 'Instructions for Counsel' prepared by instructing solicitors. These should always be checked to ensure that nothing has been inadvertently omitted.

12.3 The civil brief: *Lowe v Mainwaring*

In this case, counsel is instructed for the defendants on three occasions. The first set of instructions at **13.1** are to draft the defence and a request for further information. The second set of instructions at **13.2** are to advise on the merits of the case; and the last set at **13.3** are to make an application for specific disclosure.

12.4 The criminal brief: *R v Costas Georgiou*

In this case, counsel is instructed for the defence on three occasions. The first set of instructions at **14.1** are to represent the defendant at an application for bail. The next set of instructions at **14.2** are to advise on evidence some months later. Lastly, counsel receives the brief to appear at the plea and directions hearing and to represent the defendant at trial at **14.3**.

12.5 C.A.P. in action notes

The notes, prepared after each set of instructions in **Chapters 13** and **14**, show how every stage of the C.A.P. approach to preparation can be put into practice. The particular technique used in the examples is in no way prescriptive. A variety of methods could be used and everyone will want to develop the method which best suits them. What is important is that preparation should be methodical and accurate so that it is complete and exact and nothing is overlooked which might assist the client or the presentation of his or her case. There is no 'right' way to prepare a case: the test is whether the preparation is effective.

The notes show examples of small chronologies, lists, and tables which can be used to help master the facts and law and identify the issues and evidence in a case using the techniques suggested in **Chapter 11**. You should also refer to the other skills manuals for further assistance in preparing to carry out particular skills.

The majority of barristers keep the notes they prepare in blue books so that a complete record of a case from beginning to end is maintained. If counsel is subsequently instructed, the previous notes can be referred to and built upon, thus saving valuable preparation time.

12.6 Practising the skill

All skills require practice. When you have worked through the examples of the use of the C.A.P. approach in **Chapters 13** and **14**, you should try to apply it for yourself. **Chapter 17** contains a number of self-assessment exercises, including a civil and a criminal brief, which you can use to practise your own skills in applying the C.A.P. approach until they become second nature and you find that you automatically consider each stage as you get to grips with each new set of papers. Once this level of expertise has been reached, you will no longer need to articulate the stage-by-stage process but can concentrate on whether you have acquired the ability to carry out your preparation effectively. This can best be achieved by self-consciously reflecting on your preparation of each case presented to you on the course.

12.7 Criteria by which you may assess your own performance

When you have completed your preparation of any set of papers, you may find it useful to review the list of criteria below to consider which fact management skills you have demonstrated by your preparation and which still require improvement. As these skills are required in all the work you undertake, your performance of other skills will be affected by the level of your fact management skills.

Effective preparation entails the ability to:

- understand data presented in a variety of ways;
- identify gaps, ambiguities, and contradictions in information;
- identify and prioritise the objectives of the client both in terms of practical outcomes and legal remedies;
- place the information in context;
- identify and prioritise the factual issues;
- identify and prioritise the legal issues raised by the facts;
- select possible solutions to the client's problem;
- recognise the interaction between law and fact;
- assess the strengths and weaknesses of a case;
- organise information in a variety of ways:
  — to aid understanding;
  — to prove propositions of law;
  — to assist at trial;
- distinguish between relevant and irrelevant facts;
- distinguish between fact and inference;
- construct an argument from the facts to support the client's case:
  — by developing a theory of the case;
  — by selecting a theme to fit that theory;
- evaluate the issues in response to new information and in the light of tactical considerations.

The civil brief

13.1   Drafting the defence and request for further information

Claim No. WF07 048972

IN THE WAKEFIELD COUNTY COURT

BETWEEN:-

Mr ANTHONY MALCOLM LOWE

<u>Claimant</u>

-and-

(1) Mr HENRY GEORGE MAINWARING

(2) Mrs ELSA ANN MAINWARING

<u>Defendants</u>

<u>INSTRUCTIONS TO COUNSEL</u>

Counsel: Mr BRIAN BARRISTER

Godfrey & Co
27 Cressey St
Wakefield
West Yorks
WF5 3SL

Ref: BB

Date: 30.10.07

IN THE WAKEFIELD COUNTY COURT   Claim No. WF07 048972
BETWEEN:-

Mr. ANTHONY MALCOLM LOWE   <u>Claimant</u>

-and-

(1) Mr. HENRY GEORGE MAINWARING
(2) Mrs. ELSA ANN MAINWARING   <u>Defendants</u>

INSTRUCTIONS TO COUNSEL

Counsel has herewith:
1. Particulars of Claim;
2. Defendants' Lease (only relevant parts reproduced);
3. Relevant correspondence.

Counsel is instructed on behalf of the Defendants, the Tenants of the First and Second Floors of 83–87 Leeds Road, Wakefield. As Counsel will see from the Particulars of Claim, the Claimant is the Tenant of the Ground Floor of this property, which he uses to run a snooker hall business called the Topspin Snooker Hall. It appears that a flood occurred at the premises during the period between the 26th December 2006 and 1st January 2007, while the building was empty for the Christmas holiday.

The flood came from a water pipe on the outside of the building at about First Floor level. It was discovered by Mr Mainwaring when he went to his premises early in the morning to open up. He immediately switched off the water and called a plumber. Obviously, the flood caused damage to our clients' property as well as to that of the Claimant. The damage to our clients' property was relatively minimal. However, the Claimant is claiming very extensive damages, including not only costs of repairs said to be in excess of £19,500, but also loss of profits and loss of what he claims to be the value of the business. Our clients inform us that the snooker hall has been in operation since the flood, and this would seem to be consistent with our clients' evidence that the flood caused them only a small amount of damage. Nevertheless, the Claimant is claiming £145,000, said to be the value of the business which he appears to be alleging has been totally lost as a result of this flood. Regardless of whether or not the business has closed down, Counsel will also see from the papers that in any event the snooker hall appears to have been in financial difficulties before the damage from the flood happened. Indeed, bailiffs called on our clients some time last year mistakenly calling on them instead of Mr Lowe.

Those Instructing are still making inquiries into the facts of this matter, but the Solicitors for Mr Lowe have refused an extension of time for filing the Defence. Clearly most of the information relating to this claim will be in the hands of the Claimant. Counsel is requested to draft a Defence based on the information to hand, and also to draft a Request for Further Information if so advised to obtain such further information as can be obtained by this means.

Should Counsel have any questions on anything raised in these Instructions, please do not hesitate to contact Miss Pemberton of Instructing Solicitors.

Counsel is instructed to settle
the Defence and Request for
Further Information.

IN THE WAKEFIELD COUNTY COURT   Claim No. WF07 048972

BETWEEN:-

Mr. ANTHONY MALCOLM LOWE   Claimant

-and-

(1) Mr. HENRY GEORGE MAINWARING

(2) Mrs. ELSA ANN MAINWARING   Defendants

PARTICULARS OF CLAIM

---

1. At all material times the Claimant has been the Tenant of the Ground Floor (the 'Ground Floor') of a building known as and situate at 83–87 Leeds Road, Wakefield, West Yorkshire, WF4 1AP (the 'building'), where he has traded as the proprietor of a snooker hall.

2. At all material times the Defendants have been the Tenants of the First (the 'First Floor') and Second Floors of the building, where they are and have been trading as upholstery manufacturers.

3. Between 26th December 2006 and 1st January 2007 the Ground Floor sustained severe flood damage when a pipe located at the First Floor level at the rear of and outside the building (the 'pipe') burst.

4. At all material times the Defendants were responsible for maintaining and repairing the pipe.

5. At all material times the Defendants knew or ought to have known that the pipe carried mains water at mains pressure, was not insulated and was not protected against the elements. In the circumstances the pipe was at all material times in a dangerous state of repair. The Defendants knew or ought to have known of the state of the pipe because it was open to view and readily capable of inspection from a fire escape located at the rear of the building.

6. The flood was caused by the negligence of the Defendants, their employees or agents.

PARTICULARS OF NEGLIGENCE

The Defendants, their employees or agents were negligent in that they:

   (a) Failed to insulate or otherwise protect the pipe against the elements whether by lagging or otherwise adequately or at all.

   (b) Failed to inspect, maintain or repair the pipe whether adequately or at all.

   (c) Failed to identify that the pipe was a source of danger to the building and in particular to the Ground Floor of the building.

   (d) Failed to eliminate the danger to the building presented by the pipe by relaying it inside the building.

   (e) The Claimant will further rely upon the doctrine of res ipsa loquitur.

7. By reason of the matters set out above the Claimant has been deprived of his use and enjoyment of the Ground Floor and has suffered loss and damage.

<u>PARTICULARS OF LOSS AND DAMAGE</u>

1. Flooding damage to the Ground Floor £19,503.40

2. Before the flood the Claimant's snooker hall business that he ran from the Ground Floor was worth £145,000. That business has ceased trading as a result of damage caused by the flood and now is of no value. Loss of the value of the business £145,000

3. Before the flood the Claimant's snooker hall business generated profits of £32,000 per annum. As a result of the flood the Claimant's business has ceased trading and the Claimant claims loss of profits from the 1st January 2006 to the date of issue of this claim at the rate of £32,000 per annum equivalent to £87.67 per day. Loss of profits for 293 days £25,687.31

4. Continuing loss of profits at £32,000 per annum.

8. Further, the Claimant claims interest pursuant to the County Courts Act 1984, section 69 at the rate of 8% per annum on such sums and for such periods as the Court thinks fit.

9. The value of this claim exceeds £15,000.00.

AND the Claimant claims:

1. Damages
2. Interest on damages pursuant to the County Courts Act 1984, section 69 to be assessed.

ALISON COUNSEL

<u>Statement of Truth</u>

I believe that the facts stated in these particulars of claim are true.

Signed   A. M. Lowe

Claimant

DATED this 19th day of October 2007

Messrs Fraser & Co, of Bank Chambers, Ripon Road, Wakefield, WF1 9GR, Solicitors for the Claimant who will accept service of all proceedings on his behalf at the above address.

To: The Defendants

and to the Court Manager.

THIS LEASE is made the 17th day of October two thousand and two

BETWEEN

MARGARET PIKE of Grange House, Cleaver Street, Keighley, West Yorkshire, BD21 6EM (hereinafter called 'the landlord') of the one part and HENRY GEORGE MAINWARING and ELS A ANN MAINWARING both of 18 Conniston Road, Wakefield, West Yorkshire, WF6 2UN (hereinafter called 'the Tenant') of the other part

WHEREAS:

In this Lease where the context so admits:

(1) 'the Landlord' shall include the person for the time being entitled in reversion immediately expectant on the term hereby created and 'the Tenant' shall include the successors in title of the Tenant

(2) in the event of the Tenant being at any time more than one individual 'the Tenant' shall be deemed to include also a reference to any of them and any covenant on the part of the Tenant shall take effect as a joint and several covenant

(3) 'the demised premises' means the premises (including the Landlord's fixtures and fittings) more particularly described in the Schedule hereto and all alterations and additions to such premises

(4) 'the conduits' means all ducts cisterns tanks radiators water gas electricity and telephone supply pipes wires and cables sewers drains soil pipes waste water pipes and any other conducting media under or upon the demised premises

(5) 'the Building' means the building of which the demised premises form part

NOW THIS LEASE WITNESSETH as follows:-

1. IN consideration of the rents covenants and conditions hereinafter reserved and contained and on the part of the Tenant to be paid observed and performed the Landlord hereby demises unto the Tenant ALL THOSE premises more particularly described in Part I of the Schedule hereto (hereinafter called 'the demised premises') TOGETHER WITH the rights set out in Part II of the Schedule hereto EXCEPT AND RESERVING unto the Landlord as stated in Part III of the Schedule hereto TO HOLD the same unto the Tenant for the term of twenty one years commencing from the 17th day of October two thousand and two

YIELDING AND PAYING therefore during the said term:

(1) the yearly rent of Eight thousand pounds (£13,000.00) (subject to the provisions for revision contained in Clause 5 hereof) such rent to be paid by equal quarterly payments in advance on the usual quarter days the first of such payments or a proportionate part thereof to be made on the signing hereof . . .

2. The Tenant HEREBY COVENANTS with the Landlord as follows:

(1) To pay the yearly rent and any increased rents as hereinbefore reserved on the days and in manner aforesaid without any deduction . . .

(6) At all times during the said term to keep the whole of the demised premises and the conduits and all Landlord's fixtures and fittings, plant, machinery and equipment therein and all additions and improvements thereto in good and substantial repair and condition (notwithstanding that any want of repair may be due to normal wear and tear) damage by any of the insured risks excepted unless payment of the insurance monies shall be withheld in whole or part by reason solely or in part of any act or default of the Tenant or the Tenant's servants or agents.

3. The Landlord HEREBY COVENANTS with the Tenant as follows:

(1) That the Tenant paying the rents hereby reserved on the days and in the manner aforesaid and performing and observing the several covenants and conditions on the Tenant's part herein contained shall quietly hold and enjoy the demised premises during the said term without any interruption by the Landlord or any person rightfully claiming under or in trust for the Landlord.

(2) To insure and keep insured the demised premises (including all the Landlord's fixtures and fittings plant machinery and equipment now or hereafter in or about the same) subject to such reasonable and usual exclusions and limitations as may be imposed by the Insurers in some insurance office of repute or with Underwriters or through such agency as the Landlord shall from time to time decide in the name of the Landlord with a note of Tenant's interest and that of any mortgagee of the Tenant from time to time notified to the Landlord to be endorsed on the Policy if required by the Tenant in such sum as shall represent the full reinstatement value thereof including Architects' and Surveyors' and other professional fees and incidental expenses against loss or damage by fire and such other reasonable risks which the Landlord shall reasonably consider necessary and against the public liability of the Landlord arising out of or in connection with any accident explosion collapse or breakdown being referred to in this Lease as 'insured risks' . . .

IN WITNESS whereof the parties hereto have set their respective hands and seals the day and year first above written

THE SCHEDULE above referred to

Part I

The Demised Premises

ALL THAT first and second floors of the Building situate at and known as 83–87 Leeds Road, Wakefield, West Yorkshire, WF4 1AP including the floorboards on the first floor but not the joists on which the flooring is laid.

PART III

Exceptions and Reservations out of the Demise

There are excepted and reserved out of this demise all rights and privileges now enjoyed over and against the premises and the particular rights following namely:

(1) The right of the Landlord her successors in title and assigns and all persons authorised by her during the term hereby granted on prior reasonable notice to enter with or without workmen into or upon the premises for the purpose of executing repairs upon the exterior structure of the Building and such installations thereon the proper repair of which is necessary for the protection of the Building.

FRASER & COMPANY
SOLICITORS

Bank Chambers
Ripon Road
Wakefield
WF1 9GR
Tel: 01924 782364
Fax: 01924 807243
Ref: TBC/DH/07.0247

Date: 19th April 2007

Dear Sir,

TOPSPIN SNOOKER HALL, 83–87 LEEDS ROAD, WAKEFIELD

Our Client: Mr A. LOWE

We have been instructed by Mr Lowe, the proprietor of the Topspin Snooker Hall at the above address. The property has been unusable since it suffered severe flooding damage in late December 2006. The cost of repairing the damage to the property and three tables damaged by the flood has been put at £19,503.40. In addition there is an element of continuing loss of profits.

Everyone is denying responsibility for this occurrence, and, if anything is clear, the blame does not rest with our client. We are instructed that the flood emanated from a mains pipe located in your property, and it is our view that the flood would not have occurred in the absence of negligence on your part. We have been instructed to commence proceedings against you without further warning if we do not hear from you in the next 14 days with sensible proposals for settling our client's claim.

A Legal Services Commission certificate was granted on the 6th April 2007 to our client to commence proceedings and the relevant notice is enclosed herewith.

Perhaps we should suggest that you pass this letter to your insurers without delay.

Yours faithfully,

Fraser & Co

Mr and Mrs H. Mainwaring,
18 Conniston Road,
Wakefield,
West Yorkshire,
WF6 2UN

18 Conniston Road,
Wakefield,
West Yorkshire,
WF6 2UN

26th October 2007

Dear Miss Pemberton,

Thank you for agreeing to take on our case, and it was good to speak to you this morning. We don't have many papers relating to this case, but what we have we are sending you with this letter.

My husband Harry runs an upholstery business from the upper floors of 83–87 Leeds Road. Downstairs on the ground floor there is a snooker hall run by Mr Lowe. During Christmas week there was a flood when a water pipe burst at the back of the property. My husband found it when he went in on the 1st. He noticed as soon as he went in through the front door that the place was very damp, and when he investigated he found a pipe on the rear of the building had burst. He immediately telephoned the plumber, who arrived about two hours after he telephoned. In the meantime he stopped any further damage being done by turning off the mains. I arrived at the workshop at about 10 am. The plumber was still working at the back on the pipe. It had happened on the back wall of the first floor, so our property took the brunt of the damage. A lot of water had got in and a fair amount of stock was soaking wet where it had been stored near the rear wall. The floor was awash, and, together with Paula I set to with buckets and mops in drying the place out.

I don't know how Mr Lowe comes to say he suffered such a lot of damage that the repairs will come to over £19,000. Our soiled stock came to about £1,600, of which we salvaged about £500. Although the back wall and floors were soaked, and you have to remember that the pipe was immediately outside our part of the building, after a few days they were back to the same condition they were beforehand, and you would never know that anything had happened. Harry asked the plumber when he arrived how long the water had been escaping, and he was told that it could have been only a few hours.

About six months ago the bailiffs came to our property trying to get arrears of rent. They had called on us by mistake, because when we read the warrant we saw that it was for the ground floor where Mr Lowe's snooker hall is. My understanding is that his business has not been doing at all well for some time, and that, in addition to problems with his rent, he has also had problems with other creditors. I think that most of his claims as set out in the court documents are an excuse for a failing business, and not too much store can be placed on them.

My husband tells me that all the pipes on the outside of the building are insulated, so we don't understand why Mr Lowe is saying that this one was not. Fraser & Co seem to be unsure whether we are in fact responsible for the pipes at the back of the building. Surely they come under the landlord's responsibility as common parts of the building?

As we discussed, we have no insurance against this sort of claim, and we enclose the £1,000 you asked for on account of your costs.

Yours faithfully,

Elsa Mainwaring.

13.1.1 C.A.P. in action

Notes for drafting the Defence and Request for Further Information.

STAGE 1   THE CONTEXT OF THE CASE

(1) THE STAGE OF THE PROCEEDINGS
   (a) What steps have been taken?
        Particulars of Claim filed at Wakefield County Court 19.10.07
   (b) Your Instructions
        Draft Defence and Request for Further Information in order to:

- Clarify issues between parties.
- Protect clients' position.
- Show strength of clients' case.
- Highlight weaknesses of Claimant's case.

(2) UNDERSTANDING THE PROBLEM
   (a) Cause of the problem
        Claimant's business on ground floor at 83–87 Leeds Road, Wakefield, in financial difficulties. He blames financial difficulties on damage to premises caused when water escaped from burst pipe at first floor level on outside of building.
   (b) Clients' objectives
        Resist claim by Claimant. Require Claimant to prove loss and damage.

(3) COLLECTING THE FACTS

   (a) *Dramatis personae*

- Anthony Lowe the publicly funded Claimant and Tenant of Ground Floor and proprietor of snooker hall
- Henry (Harry) Mainwaring 1st Defendant, Joint Tenant of First and Second Floors where he runs an upholstery business on premises
- Elsa Mainwaring 2nd Defendant, joint tenant with husband Harry
- Margaret Pike Landlord of the premises
- Topspin Snooker Hall business carried on by Claimant on Ground Floor
- Fraser & Co Solicitors for the Claimant
- Godfrey & Co Instructing Solicitors for Defendants (Miss Pemberton)
- Paula: helped to dry out Defendants' premises.

   (b) Chronology of events

17.10.02	Lease of First and Second Floors of 83–87 Leeds Road, Wakefield, granted to Defendants by Margaret Pike, Landlord Lease of Ground Floor of building to Claimant
1.1.07	Burst external water pipe discovered at First Floor level of premises and repaired
April 07	Distress Warrant for arrears of rent re Ground Floor premises issued
19.4.07	Letter of Claim sent to Defendants
19.10.07	Date of Particulars of Claim
26.10.07	Defendants Instructed Solicitors

(4)   AGREED/DISPUTED FACTS: GAPS AND AMBIGUITIES

Para. No	Particulars of Claim	Defendants' Version	Notes/Queries
1.	C tenant of ground floor of 83–87 where ran snooker hall	admitted—see Instructions admitted—see letter of 26.10	
2.	Ds tenants of 1st and 2nd floors trading as upholsterers	admitted—see lease admitted—see letter of 26.10	
3.	26/12/06–1/1/07 Ground floor damaged by flood from external pipe at 1st floor level	Burst pipe on exterior 1st floor found 1.1. Probably burst on 1st see letter 26.10	Effect on ground floor? letter suggests that brunt of damage to 1st floor and that minimal
4.	Ds responsible for maintaining and repairing pipe	Landlord's responsibility? See lease preamble cl (4) Tenants' covenants cl 2(6) Schedule 'demised premises' and Landlord's right of entry to repair	Legal basis for allegation? Further legal research needed
5.	Ds knew/ought to have known that pipe carried mains water, not insulated/protected thereby in dangerous state of repair	all outside pipes insulated —see letter of 26.10	No particulars given on why D should have known the pipe carried mains water
6.	Flood caused by Ds' negligence in that failed to: protect against elements, inspect, maintain, repair, identify as danger to building, eliminate danger by relaying pipe inside building	Pipes adequately insulated	
7.	As result C lost use/enjoyment of ground floor suffered loss and damage Flood damage £19,503.40 Loss of value of business £145,000 Loss of profits since 1/1/2007 £25,687.31	Other cause of losses— snooker hall in financial difficulties before flood Snooker hall in operation since flood—see letter 26.10	Level of alleged damage very high. Compared with Ds' damage. What was damaged? How has this figure been calculated? When did business stop running? Net or gross? How were profits calculated?
8.	Interest		

(5) LEGAL FRAMEWORK

(a)   Checklist for Claim in Negligence:

Was duty owed by Defendants? Has there been a breach? Has any breach caused the incident? Has the loss and damage been suffered? Has any breach caused the loss and damage? Is the loss or damage suffered recoverable?

(b)   Areas for Legal Research:

Tortious liability of landlords/tenants towards tenants of building in respect of burst pipes (Clerk and Lindsell *On Torts*, Charlesworth *On Negligence*). Repairing covenants in leases (*Woodfall*).

STAGE 2 ANALYSIS OF ISSUES AND EVIDENCE

(a) THE ISSUES

(1) THE FACTUAL ISSUES

See Stage 1(4) above and Particulars of Claim paras 3, 4, 5, 6, and 7.

(2) THE LEGAL ISSUES

   (i)   Duty: Whether Defendants responsible for maintaining and repairing external water pipe?

   (ii) Breach: Whether outside pipes insulated?

   (iii) Knowledge: Whether Defendants knew or ought to have known of condition of the pipe; whether Defendants knew or ought to have known the pipe carried mains water?

   (iv) Causation: Whether burst pipe caused by negligence of Defendants?

   (v) Causation of loss and damage: Whether any loss or damage suffered by reason of the flood from the burst pipe?

   (vi) Heads of damage: What heads of damage can be proved by the Claimant?

   (vii) The amounts of each head of damage?

(3) THE POTENTIAL THEORY

Duty owed by Landlord, not Defendants under the lease; in any event no breach because pipe insulated, and pipe did not burst because of negligence of Defendants. Further, any loss suffered by Claimant, if it is proved, not caused by flood but by pre-existing financial difficulties.

(4) GAPS AND AMBIGUITIES

See Stage 1(4) above. Also need both clients' dates of birth to comply with PD16, para 10.7.

(b) THE EVIDENCE

At this stage the only evidence available is the lease and the letter of Mrs Mainwaring. Other sources of information are Instructions to Counsel, Particulars of Claim, letter from Claimant's Solicitors.

STAGE 3 PRESENTATION

(1) THE CHOSEN THEORY

See Stage 2(3) above.

(2) CARRYING OUT INSTRUCTIONS

A. Preparing to draft the Defence (see *Drafting* manual).

   (i)   Parties—Paragraphs 1 and 2—Admit.

   (ii) The Incident—Paragraph 3—Admit bursting of pipe, require C to prove effect. Clarify date.

   (iii) Duty—Paragraph 4—Deny. No duty under lease.

   (iv) Knowledge—Paragraph 5—Deny. Allege pipe insulated.

   (v) Negligence/Causation—Paragraph 6—Deny. If anyone's fault Landlord's.

   (vi) Causation/Loss and Damage—Paragraph 7—Deny causation. Require C to prove loss and damage.

B. Planning the Request for Further Information (see *Drafting* manual).

   (a) Re Paragraph 3—How was ground floor damaged?

   (b) Re Paragraph 4—Why does Claimant think Defendants responsible for repair, etc?

(c) Re Paragraph 5—Why should Defendants have known that the pipe carried mains water?

(d) Re Paragraph 7—Insufficient detail of how loss calculated.

(See **13.2** for completed Statements of Case.)

13.2 Advice on merits

IN THE WAKEFIELD COUNTRY COURT   Claim No. WF07 048972
BETWEEN:-

Mr. ANTHONY MALCOLM LOWE   <u>Claimant</u>

-and-

(1) Mr. HENRY GEORGE MAINWARING
(2) Mrs. ELSA ANN MAINWARING

<u>Defendants</u>

INSTRUCTIONS TO COUNSEL TO ADVISE

Counsel has herewith the papers previously before Counsel [only backsheet reproduced] together with:

4. Defence and Request for Further Information as settled by Counsel;

5. Response to the Request for Further Information;

6. Notice of Allocation;

7. Surveyor's Report prepared for the Claimant;

8. Legal Services Commission Certificates for the Defendants [extract only reproduced: both certificates are in substantially the same terms].

Counsel will recall this claim having drafted the Defence and a Request for Further Information. The Claimant's response to the Request appears at enclosure 5. The Defendants' business has not flourished in recent years, and their bank called in their loans some time ago. The effect has been to close down their business as they have been unable to pay their staff. It is hoped that the bank will be paid off more or less in full from sale of stock. The present litigation is a great worry to the Defendants, not least because if there is a substantial judgment against them the likelihood is that it will be enforced against their home, which has a substantial equity of redemption.

Counsel will see that public funding by the Legal Services Commission has been granted to the Defendants subject to a limitation. Counsel is asked to Advise on the Merits in this case for the purpose of removal of the limitation on the Certificate and to advise generally. Instructing Solicitors apologise that it has not been possible to arrange a conference with the Defendants as yet due to the ill-health of Mr Mainwaring.

Counsel is instructed to Advise

Claim No. WF06 048972

Herewith:

(1) Defence

(2) Request for Further Information

B. Barrister

16.11.07

IN THE WAKEFIELD COUNTY COURT

BETWEEN:-

ANTHONY MALCOLM LOWE

Claimant

-and-

(1) HENRY GEORGE MAINWARING
(2) ELSA ANN MAINWARING

Defendants

_____

INSTRUCTIONS TO COUNSEL

_____

Counsel: Mr BRIAN BARRISTER

Godfrey & Co
27 Cressey St
Wakefield
West Yorks
WF5 3SL

Ref: BB

Date: 26.10.07

IN THE WAKEFIELD COUNTY COURT   Claim No. WF07 048972
BETWEEN:-

Mr. ANTHONY MALCOLM LOWE   <u>Claimant</u>

-and-

(1) Mr. HENRY GEORGE MAINWARING
(2) Mrs. ELSA ANN MAINWARING   <u>Defendants</u>

DEFENCE

---

1.   Paragraphs 1 and 2 of the Particulars of Claim are admitted.

2.   Save that it is admitted that the pipe burst, the Claimant is required to prove paragraph 3 of the Particulars of Claim. The First Defendant arranged for the pipe to be repaired within a few hours of the occurrence of the burst.

3.   Paragraphs 4 and 5 of the Particulars of Claim are denied. The pipe was at all material times properly insulated. Further, under their Lease with Mrs Margaret Pike dated the 17th October 2002 the Defendants had no obligation to repair or maintain the pipe. A true copy of the Lease is served with this Defence.

4.   For the reasons set out in paragraph 3 above it is denied that the Defendants, their employees or agents were negligent as alleged in paragraph 6 of the Particulars of Claim or at all. It is further denied that the flood was caused by the alleged or any negligence on the part of the Defendants, their employees or agents.

5.   Further or alternatively, the flood was caused by the negligence of Margaret Pike.

PARTICULARS OF NEGLIGENCE

(a)   Failing to insulate or otherwise protect the pipe against the elements whether by lagging or otherwise adequately or at all.

(b)   Failing to inspect, maintain or repair the pipe whether adequately or at all.

(c)   Failing to identify that the pipe was a source of danger to the building.

(d)   Failing to eliminate the danger to the building presented by the pipe by relaying it inside the building.

(e)   The Defendants will further rely upon the doctrine of res ipsa loquitur.

6.   The Claimant is required to prove the loss and damage particularised in paragraph 7 of the Particulars of Claim, and the Claimant is required to prove the amounts claimed. Damage sustained by the Defendants as a result of the flood was to a value of about £1,600, and it is estimated that the Claimant's loss would have been at about the same level.

7.   The First Defendant's date of birth is 7th June 1952 and the Second Defendent's date of birth is 18th May 1953.

BRIAN BARRISTER

Statement of Truth
The Defendants believe that the facts stated in this Defence are true. I am duly authorised by the Defendants to sign this statement.

SIGNED *F Godfrey*

Defendants' Solicitor
DATED the 21st day of November 2007.
Messrs Godfrey & Co, of 27 Cressey Street, Wakefield, West Yorkshire, WF5 3SL, Solicitors for the Defendants.

IN THE WAKEFIELD COUNTY COURT   Claim No. WF07 048972

BETWEEN:-

Mr. ANTHONY MALCOLM LOWE   Claimant

-and-

(1) Mr. HENRY GEORGE MAINWARING

(2) Mrs. ELSA ANN MAINWARING   Defendants

DEFENDANTS' REQUEST FOR FURTHER INFORMATION AGAINST
THE CLAIMANT PURSUANT TO THE CPR, 1998, PART 18
DATED 21 NOVEMBER 2007

Note: This request must be answered by 4 pm on 12 December 2007.

Paragraph references in this Request for Further Information are references to paragraphs in the Particulars of Claim.

Under paragraph 3.

Of: ' . . . the Ground Floor sustained severe flood damage . . . '

REQUEST

1.   Please give full information on all the damage alleged to have been sustained to the Ground Floor by reason of the alleged flooding.

Under paragraph 4.

Of: ' . . . the Defendants were responsible for maintaining and repairing the pipe'

REQUEST

2.   Please state whether it is alleged the Defendants were responsible for maintaining and repairing the pipe by reason of contract or otherwise.

3.   If by contract, state the contract relied upon, the parties to the contract, its date and the clauses relied upon.

4.   If otherwise than by contract, state the basis of the Claimant's contention that the Defendants were responsible for the repair and maintenance of the pipe.

Under paragraph 5.

Of: ' . . . the Defendants knew or ought to have known that the pipe carried mains water at mains pressure . . . '

REQUEST

5.   State every fact and matter relied upon by the Claimant in support of the contention that the Defendants knew, alternatively ought to have known, that the pipe:

   (a) carried mains water; and

   (b) carried water at mains pressure.

Under paragraph 7.

Of: '(a) Flooding damage to the Ground Floor £19,503.40'

REQUEST

6.   Please specify how the alleged loss of £19,503.40 is made up.

Of: ' . . . the Claimant's snooker hall business that he ran from the Ground Floor was worth £145,000 . . . '

REQUEST

7.   Specify each and every fact and matter relied upon in support of the contention that the business was worth £145,000.

Of: 'Before the flood the Claimant's snooker hall business generated profits of £32,000 per annum.'

REQUEST

8.   Specify how the figure of £32,000 is made up.

9.   State the period used in calculating the figure of £32,000.

10. State whether the figure of £32,000 is:

    (a) before or after trade expenses;

    (b) net of tax.

BRIAN BARRISTER

DATED the 21st day of November 2007.

Messrs Godfrey & Co, of 27 Cressey Street, Wakefield, West Yorkshire, WF5 3SL, Solicitors for the Defendants.

To: The Claimant

and to the Court Manager.

IN THE WAKEFIELD COUNTY COURT   Claim No. WF07 048972

BETWEEN:-

Mr. ANTHONY MALCOLM LOWE   <u>Claimant</u>

-and-

(1) Mr. HENRY GEORGE MAINWARING

(2) Mrs. ELSA ANN MAINWARING   <u>Defendants</u>

CLAIMANT'S RESPONSE TO THE REQUEST FOR FURTHER
INFORMATION OF THE PARTICULARS OF CLAIM
DATED 21 NOVEMBER 2007

<u>Under paragraph 3.</u>

Of: ' . . . the Ground Floor sustained severe flood damage . . . '

<u>REQUEST</u>

1.   Please give full information on all the damage alleged to have been sustained to the Ground Floor by reason of the alleged flooding.

<u>ANSWER</u>

1.   The matter requested has already been sufficiently set out. Full particulars will be given in a surveyor's report which will be mutually exchanged in accordance with directions.

<u>Under paragraph 4.</u>

Of: ' . . . the Defendants were responsible for maintaining and repairing the pipe'

<u>REQUEST</u>

2.   Please state whether it is alleged the Defendants were responsible for maintaining and repairing the pipe by reason of contract or otherwise.

3.   If by contract, the contract relied upon, the parties to the contract, its date and the clauses relied upon.

4.   If otherwise than by contract, the basis of the Claimant's contention that the Defendants were responsible for the repair and maintenance of the pipe.

<u>ANSWER</u>

2.   Contract.

3.   Lease between the Defendants and Mrs Margaret Pike dated the 17th October 2002. The Claimant cannot identify the requested provision thereof until after disclosure of documents.

4.   Not applicable.

<u>Under paragraph 5.</u>

Of: ' . . . the Defendants knew or ought to have known that the pipe carried mains water at mains pressure, was not insulated . . . '

REQUEST

5.   State every fact and matter relied upon by the Claimant in support of the contention that the Defendants knew, alternatively ought to have known, that the pipe:

  (a) carried mains water; and

  (b) carried water at mains pressure.

ANSWER

5.   The pipe is and was at all material times located on the outside of the building and is and was open to view. Access to and viewing of the pipe can and could be achieved by way of a nearby emergency escape staircase on the outside of the building and from a flat roof over the rear of the Ground Floor. The Defendants or their employees or agents viewed the pipe and thereby its condition and the fact that it was a mains pipe, or should have viewed the pipe and ought to have known of its condition and that it was a mains pipe carrying water at mains pressure.

Under paragraph 7.

Of: '(a) Flooding damage to the Ground Floor £19,503.40'

REQUEST

6.   Please specify how the alleged loss of £9,503.40 is made up.

ANSWER

6.   The loss of £19,503.40 comprises the following:

Repairs and refelting of snooker tables	£4,400.00	
VAT at 17.5%	£770.00	
Sub-total		£5,170.00
Replastering ceilings	£3,735.00	
Repairs to floors	£3,900.00	
Repairs to electrics	£1,863.63	
Redecoration	£2,700.00	
VAT at 17.5%	£2,134.77	
Sub-total		£14,333.40
Total		£19,503.40

Of: ' . . . the Claimant's snooker hall business that he ran from the Ground Floor was worth £145,000 . . . '

REQUEST

7.   Specify each and every fact and matter relied upon in support of the contention that the business was worth £145,000.

ANSWER

7.   The matter requested has already been sufficiently stated. Full particulars will be given in an accountant's report which will be mutually exchanged in accordance with directions.

Of: 'Before the flood the Claimant's snooker hall business generated profits of £32,000 per annum.

REQUEST

8. Specify how the figure of £32,000 is made up.

9. State the period used in calculating the figure of £32,000.

10. State whether the figure of £32,000 is:

    (a) before or after trade expenses;

    (b) net of tax.

ANSWER

8. Full particulars will be provided in the accounts disclosed on disclosure of documents.

9. 1st August 2005 to 31st July 2006.

10. (a) After trade expenses

    (b) Yes

ALISON COUNSEL

Statement of Truth

The Claimant believes that the facts stated in this response to the request for further information dated the 21st November 2007 are true.

Full name: Graham Harding

Name of Claimant's solicitor's firm: Fraser & Co

Signed: *G Harding*

Claimant's Solicitor

DATED the 3rd day of March 2008.

Messrs Fraser & Co, of Bank Chambers, Ripon Road, Wakefield, WF1 9GR, Solicitors for the Claimant.

To: The Defendants

and to the Court Manager.

Notice of Allocation
to the Multi-track

To [Claimant's] [Defendants'] Solicitor
Godfrey & Co,
27 Cressey Street
Wakefield
West Yorkshire
WF5 3SL

<u>IN THE WAKEFIELD COUNTY COURT</u>
Claim No. WF07 048972
Claimant ANTHONY MALCOM LOWE
(including ref) TBC/DH/07.0247
Defendants HENRY GEORGE MAINWARING
(including ref) ELSA ANN MAINWARING
JTG/AP

Date 10th January 2008

Seal

District Judge Jones has considered the statements of case and allocation questionnaires filed and allocated the claim to the multi-track.

The District Judge has ordered that:—

1.   Any request for further information based on another party's statement of case shall be served no later than 4.00 pm on Friday 2nd February 2008.
Any such request shall be dealt with no later than 4.00 pm on Friday 7th March 2008.

2.   Each party shall give to every other party standard disclosure of documents by list. The latest date for delivery of the lists is 4.00 pm on Friday 21st March 2008.
The latest date for service of any request to inspect or for a copy of a document is 4.00 pm on Friday 28th March 2008.

3.   Each party shall serve on every other party the witness statements of all witnesses of fact on whom he intends to rely.
There shall be simultaneous exchange of such statements no later than 4.00 pm on Friday 25th April 2008.

4.   A case management conference shall be held at 2.00 pm on Tuesday 6th May 2008.

5.   Costs in the claim.

The claim is being transferred to the [Civil Trial Centre at   County Court]

[Division of the Royal Courts of Justice] where all future applications, correspondence and so on will be dealt with.

[The reasons the judge has given for allocation to this track [is] [are] that the value of the claim exceeds £15,000 and the multi-track is the normal track for the claim.]

Notes:

You and the other party, or parties, may agree to extend the time periods given in the directions above provided this does not affect the date given for any case management conference, for returning the pre-trial checklist, for any pre-trial review or the date of the trial or trial period.

If you do not comply with these directions, any other party to the claim will be entitled to apply to the court for an order that your statement of case (claim or defence) be struck out.

Leaflets explaining more about what happens when your case is allocated to the multi-track are available from the court office.

The court office at The Crown House, 127 Kirkgate, Wakefield, W. Yorkshire WF1 1JW is open between 10 am and 4 pm Monday to Friday. Address all communications to the Court Manager quoting the claim number.

CHRIS HODGES FRICS
CHARTERED SURVEYOR
43 High Street, Wakefield WF1 6YM
Facsimile: 01926 412020 Telephone 01924 412019

Solicitor's Ref: TBC/DH/07.0247

13th March 2008

Our Ref: GH/AMT

Court's Ref: WF07 048972

Wakefield County Court
The Crown House
127 Kirkgate
Wakefield
WF1 1JW

Dear Sirs,

83–87 Leeds Road, Wakefield: Mr T Lowe

I have been instructed on behalf of Fraser & Co, the solicitors for Mr Lowe, to inspect the above premises and to report on their condition and the damage which is alleged to have occurred as a result of a flood caused by a burst water pipe at the end of December 2006. I carried out all inspections personally.

SITUATION AND DESCRIPTION:

The premises form part of continuous shopping parades built 80 years ago or there-abouts. It comprises the whole of the ground floor of a three-storey terrace unit generally of substantial stock brick construction under a pitched slated main roof with iron guttering.

In respect of the shop front and return display, these are of old timber with large windows mainly sheeted over. Decorations are fair and condition of woodwork is generally reasonable for its age. There is a dwarf tiled stall riser. There is a lead flashing above the fascia box projection probably replaced and an illuminated fascia board to the front corner and side. Immediately to the rear is a door and entrance and iron staircase leading to workrooms on the upper floors.

INTERNALLY:

GROUND FLOOR:

Front lobby (carpeted). Main snooker hall 9.94 m wide by 12.12 m long rear bay, false ceiling, parquet floor.

Bar area to side (number 87) leading to store rooms (both with linoleum flooring) and office. Office 4.57m by 4.36m and carpeted.

Small back addition Rear lobby 2 WCs & washbasins.

REAR:

The rear external staircase presumably part of Landlord's liability is somewhat poor with various rusted sections. The rear main wall is of solid stock brickwork with a metal casement window to the ground floor of the subject property and modern concrete lintel over. Directly above is part of the old iron fire escape landing which has a bearing into the wall. Rust expansion of the steelwork going into the brickwork has caused flaking to pointing and slight gaps underneath the steel landing.

Gerald Walker MA FRICS (Consultant)   VAT Reg No. 405 189622

I enclose copy sketch of the rear showing the staircase and landing and the external half- inch mains water pipe with a brass compression fitting which I understand was replaced as this was the source of the burst. The upper section of the pipe has been partly lagged but not to a good standard and the section below the iron staircase still remains unlagged to this day! Below the joint are streaks to the paintwork where water has washed down. A certain amount of water does drip from the staircase but not directly against the wall. It appears to me that the source of water damage was indeed this defective pipe as I could see no other water pipes to the ground floor and clearly there was a considerable amount of water in the ground floor causing sporadic lifting and damage to the parquet flooring.

There is a flush backdoor to the subject property which appears to be in fair order.

INTERNALLY:

GROUND FLOOR:

Lobby Section

Ceiling	— false plaster ceiling with a few holes where fitments have been removed and otherwise satisfactory.
Floor	— carpet—generally satisfactory.
Walls	— wallpapered and generally in satisfactory condition. 9-light glazed double doors leading to:

Main Area

Ceiling	— plasterboard painted black—from limited view appears generally satisfactory. More recent false ceiling under with sive water streaking with many panels bowed and expanded by water.
	Above the false ceiling towards the rear near the source of dampness there are a few cracks and small holes in the ceiling where water has percolated through. Behind the bar area are beer pumps and cooling apparatus with mains water supply for glass washing.
Walls	— Papered and painted—condition generally good.
Floor	— whole area parquet flooring about a quarter of an inch thick probably on sheet material. Clearly this was affected by a considerable volume of water as there are various sections dotted all over which are lifting and parquet material has become loose or is missing.
	Decorations to the main area are generally reasonable but in reinstating the floor, checking electrics etc, a certain amount of disturbance would need to be made good.

Store rooms

Ceiling	— generally satisfactory
Walls	— plastered but patches of blown plaster from inherent dampness to the front and partly to side adjacent to number 89.
Floor	— old linoleum probably on sheet material, lifting in places as a result of old dampness. This area is used mainly for storage. No apparent damage from the burst water pipe.

Office

Ceiling	— plaster painted white—condition generally satisfactory.

Walls	— wallpapered. Condition generally satisfactory and no apparent water damage.
Floor	— carpet on concrete floor. Worn in places.
Decorations	— fair only with some evidence of wear and tear.

Small Back Addition

Rear lobby

| Ceiling | — plasterboard—some of this is missing as a result of water damage, also damaged plaster above the flush door and frame leading to the middle section and this area will need to be hacked off, rendered and set. Allow for renewing ceiling to this area and treating timbers above. Right-hand party wall covered with wall boarding. Bottom section rotted away clearly from recent water damage and the boards are noticeably warped from water damage and will need to be renewed. |
| Floor | — blue tiles on sheet material—water damaged in places, therefore allow to take up and renew. |

Ladies' lobby/wash basin and WC

Ceiling	— plastered—surface lifting in places—allow for repair and redecoration.
Walls	— stained by water and need redecorating
Floor	— water damage in places to PVC tiles on concrete—strip and relay.

Gents' lobby/wash basin and WCs

| Ceiling | — plaster on concrete—make good where cracked and damaged by water ingress and redecorate. |
| Walls | — the WC areas are fully tiled and various sections are lifting as a result of water damage. Wall plastering at low level has blown as a result of dampness and the plaster between the WC doors has partly washed away as a result of dampness also extending between the lobby door and WC door—therefore allow 100% strip, render, set and fully tile WCs together with new splashback to wash basin and renew enclosure to wash basin which is water damaged. |

Redecorate the whole of this area.

| Floor | — quarry tiles on concrete—appears satisfactory. |
| Electrics | — there is some damage and disturbance to electrical wiring to the lobby and gents' WCs which will need to be renewed and to the ladies' lavatory where there was extensive water damage—it is likely that electrics may be affected and would need to be checked and properly reinstated where necessary. |

I understand my duty to the court and have complied with that duty in compiling this report.

I confirm that insofar as the facts stated in my report are within my own knowledge I have made clear which they are and I believe them to be true, and that the opinions I have expressed represent my true and complete professional opinion.

Should you require any further information or advice, please do not hesitate to let me know.

| Signed: | CHRIS HODGES F.R.I.C.S. |

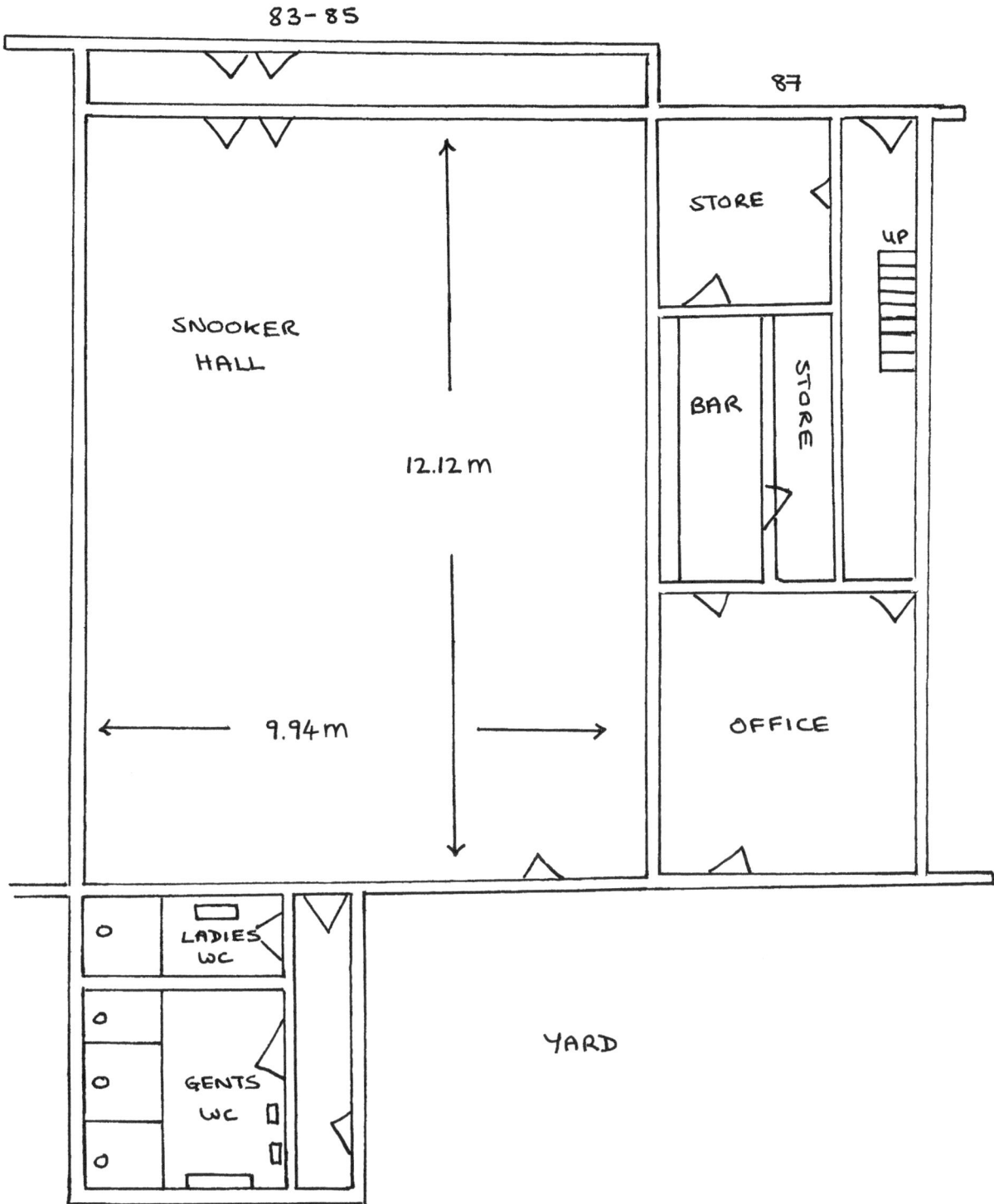

83-85

87

STORE

UP

SNOOKER
HALL

BAR

STORE

12.12 m

9.94 m

OFFICE

LADIES
WC

GENTS
WC

YARD

GROUND FLOOR

GROUND FLOOR

83-87 LEEDS ROAD, WAKEFIELD

NOT TO SCALE

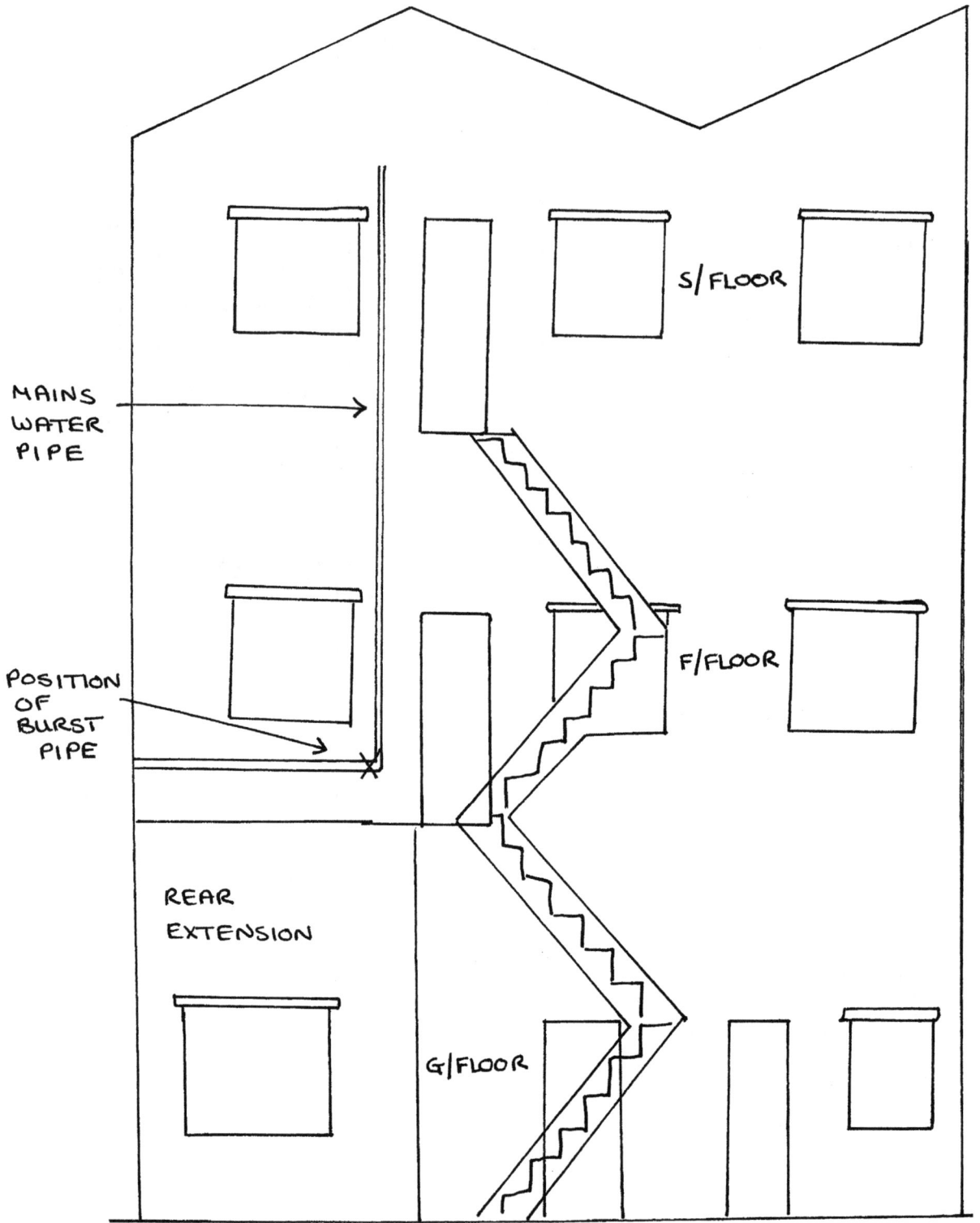

MAINS WATER PIPE

POSITION OF BURST PIPE

S/FLOOR

F/FLOOR

REAR EXTENSION

G/FLOOR

SKETCH OF REAR ELEVATION
83-87 LEEDS ROAD, WAKEFIELD

NOT TO SCALE

EXTRACT

LEGAL SERVICES COMMISSION

COMMUNITY LEGAL SERVICE CERTIFICATE

Assisted person:	Mr Henry George Mainwaring
Level of service:	Full representation
Description:	To defend a claim in negligence brought by Anthony Malcolm Lowe seeking damages arising from an alleged flood at 83–87 Leeds Road, Wakefield, West Yorkshire, WF4 1AP between 26th December 2006 and 1st January 2007.
Conditions:	It is a condition that the solicitor shall report to the area office if profit costs disbursements and counsel's fees exceed £2,500.
Limitations:	Limited to all steps to track allocation, disclosure and asking Part 35 questions to experts, and to obtaining written advice from an independent advocate with higher rights of audience on merits.

12.12.07

13.2.1   C.A.P. in action

Notes for advice on merits
STAGE 1 THE CONTEXT OF THE CASE

(1) THE STAGE OF THE PROCEEDINGS
  (a) What steps have been taken?
    Particulars of Claim, Defence, Request for Further Information served.
    Copy Surveyor's Report prepared for Claimant.
    Limited Community Legal Service Certificate granted to Defendants on 12.12.07.
  (b) Your Instructions
    To advise on merits and quantum in order to:

- Advise on prospects of success.

- Identify further information necessary.

- Remove limitation from Community Legal Service certificate.

- Fulfil Bar Council's Guidelines. (See Code of Conduct: Annexe E, Guidelines on Opinions under the Funding Code.)

(2) UNDERSTANDING THE PROBLEM
  Defendants' business now closed down. Main remaining asset is their home. They are anxious that if they cannot defend claim at trial, any award of damages may be enforced against their home. Certificate limited to steps to disclosure and exchange of witness statements.

(3) COLLECTING THE FACTS
  Only new sources of information are the Response to the Request for Further Information and the report of the Claimant's Surveyor. See below at 2(b)(1).

STAGE 2 ANALYSIS OF ISSUES AND EVIDENCE

(a) THE ISSUES

(1) THE LEGAL AND FACTUAL ISSUES
  See Particulars of Claim, paragraphs 3, 4, 5, 6 and 7 and Response to the Request for Further Information, and Defence, paragraphs 2, 3, 4, 5 and 6. See also **13.1.1** above and (b)(1) below.

(b) THE EVIDENCE

(1) THE STRENGTH OF THE CASE ON EACH ISSUE
Note: Claimant bears burden of proof on each issue.
  (a) Issue (i) Responsibility for maintaining pipes: Depends on construction of lease: Claimant will rely on fact that no express covenant to repair on part of landlord. However, case law favours construction in support of Defendants (implied covenants to repair, *contra proferentem*). Terms of lease ambiguous (clause 2(6) of the tenants' covenants, paragraph 4 of preamble, Schedule Part I and Part III).

  (b) Issue (ii) Insulation of the pipes: Dispute between C. Hodges' report and statement of Mr Mainwaring reported by wife. Report of expert not contemporaneous and difficult to interpret. *Need to get further statement from Mr Mainwaring and plumber called to repair pipe on 1.1.2007. Need to refer expert's report to Mr Mainwaring to confirm location of burst pipe or identify it.*

(c) Issue (iii) Knowledge of Defendants: Claimant's allegations in Response to the Request for Further Information need answering by Defendants, further information needed from Defendants as to knowledge of state of pipes, access to pipes, etc.

(d) Issue (iv) Causation of pipe bursting: Claimant will need to establish why pipe burst, i.e., because of failure to insulate?

(e) Issue (v) Effect of flood on Claimant's premises: Report of C. Hodges shows water damage on ground floor but inconclusive on causation of this. Several potential weaknesses, e.g., entry point of water, alternative reasons for damage. Defendants will need to instruct own surveyor to report.

(f) Issue (vi) Heads of damage: No evidence/detail of losses given. Possible alternative reason for closure of business—financial difficulty. In any event Claimant cannot claim both lost profits and lost value (double recovery).

(g) Issue (vii) The amounts of each head: Need to await disclosure for Claimant's accounts. Will also need inspection of Claimant's financial books and records, and to consider instructing an expert accountant to form an opinion on the value of the Claimant's business. Alternatively, could wait for the Claimant's accountant's report to see if it can be agreed without incurring the expense of a report on behalf of the Defendants. A further alternative would be to apply for an order that the Claimant answer Request No. 8. Details of the £19,503.40 damage to property claim need to be sought on disclosure, or should be given in exchange of witness's statements or expert reports. *Need to consider seeking permission or an order for an expert (builder or surveyor) to inspect the ground floor for the purpose of giving evidence on the damage, cause and cost of repairs.*

(2) GAPS AND AMBIGUITIES

Defendants should be asked to confirm position of burst pipe identified by C. Hodges. Further Information identified at 2(b)(1) above needed from Defendants, also witness statement from Plumber and report from Surveyor on behalf of Defendants. Unclear whether Paula, who helped dry out Defendants' premises, can assist on any of these issues, so a witness statement should be taken from her to find out what she knows.

Details of Claimant's losses etc should be received on disclosure, if not may need to consider alternative options to secure information.

STAGE 3 PRESENTATION

(1) THE CHOSEN THEORY

Claimant overstating events, hoping to solve present financial crisis by blaming Defendants. Defendants not to blame and Claimant will not be able to establish either fault or loss. See **13.1.1**, Stage 2(3) above.

(2) SUPPORTING THE LEGAL FRAMEWORK

List of Authorities.

Construction of Lease: *Cockburn v Smith* [1924] 2 KB 119

Construction of Lease: *Hope Brothers v Cowan* [1913] 2 Ch 312

Quantum: *C. R. Taylor (Wholesale) Ltd v Hepworth Ltd* [1977] 1 WLR 659

(3) CARRYING OUT INSTRUCTIONS

Plan opinion. See *Opinion Writing* manual.

(See **13.3** for completed Opinion.)

13.3 Brief for application

IN THE WAKEFIELD COUNTY COURT   Claim No. WF07 048972
BETWEEN:-

Mr ANTHONY MALCOLM LOWE   <u>Claimant</u>

-and-

(1) Mr HENRY GEORGE MAINWARING
(2) Mrs ELSA ANN MAINWARING   <u>Defendants</u>

BRIEF TO COUNSEL TO APPEAR ON CASE MANAGEMENT
CONFERENCE, 2.00 PM, TUESDAY 6TH MAY 2008

Counsel has herewith the papers previously before Counsel [not reproduced] together with:

9. Counsel's Opinion dated 9th April 2008;

10. Claimant's List of Documents;

11. Defendants' List of Documents [not reproduced];

12. Documents disclosed by Claimant on Disclosure;

13. Application Notice;

14. Witness Statement and exhibits in support.

Instructing Solicitors have settled the Application for Specific Disclosure and for an Order granting access to the Claimant's premises for the Defendants' surveyor. The Claimant has been very uncooperative on the questions of disclosure and obtaining access, and Counsel is asked to press not only for the Orders sought but also for suitable Costs Orders against the Claimant.

This application has been listed to be heard at the same time as a case management conference.

If counsel has any questions prior to the hearing, please do not hesitate to contact Miss Pemberton of Instructing Solicitors.

Lowe v Mainwaring

OPINION

---

1.   I have been asked to advise Mr and Mrs Mainwaring, who are tenants of the first and second floors of 83–87 Leeds Road, Wakefield, on their prospects of successfully defending the claim brought against them by Mr Anthony Lowe (the Claimant), a tenant of the ground floor of the same building. Mr and Mrs Mainwaring have been granted public funding by the Legal Services Commission to continue to defend this claim. However, at present, the grant of public funding is limited to proceedings up to asking Part 35 questions to experts, and to obtaining my advice on merits.

2.   The claim arose as a result of a burst water pipe situated on the outside of the building on the first-floor level and which it is alleged caused water to flood in and onto the ground floor premises in December 2006 or 1 January 2007, thereby allegedly causing considerable damage. The Claimant is alleging that Mr and Mrs Mainwaring are responsible for the upkeep of the pipe and that the pipe burst as a result of their negligence and that they are therefore responsible for the damage. I have not as yet seen Mr or Mrs Mainwaring in conference due to the ill-health of Mr Mainwaring, but I have read a letter from Mrs Mainwaring explaining the relevant circumstances and the report of Mr Chris Hodges, the Claimant's surveyor.

Summary of Advice

3.   In my opinion Mr and Mrs Mainwaring have good prospects of successfully defending this claim. However, an initial question is to identify precisely where the burst pipe was located. Mr Mainwaring discovered the burst, so he should be asked to confirm that the location of the burst as identified by Mr Hodges in his report is correct. For the purpose of this opinion I have assumed this is so. The Claimant has provided very little evidence on quantum, so I am only able to give limited advice on the damages aspect of the case at this stage.

The Duty to Repair

4.   Responsibility for the condition of the external water pipe in this case depends on the terms of the lease between the Mainwarings and their landlord, Margaret Pike dated 17 October 2002. I am however unable to give definite advice on whether the Mainwarings are responsible for the pipe, because the terms of the lease concerning who is responsible for the condition of the external water pipes are ambiguous.

5.   By clause 2(6) of the lease the Mainwarings, as tenants of the first and second floors, covenanted 'to keep the whole of the demised premises and the conduits . . . in good and substantial repair and condition'. Conduits are themselves defined in paragraph (4) of the preamble as including supply pipes 'under or upon the demised premises'. The definition of the demised premises in Part 1 of the Schedule refers to 'all that first and second floors of the Building'.

6.   On this wording it is unclear whether:

(a) Paragraph (4) of the preamble includes pipes upon the outside of building as well as those within the premises.

(b) The demised premises as defined in the Schedule includes pipes fixed to the exterior of those premises.

(c) The landlord has retained the exterior of the Building and/or the pipes and other installations upon it.

7.   In my opinion, a court is likely to construe clause 2(6) in favour of the Mainwarings and limit their obligation to repair and maintain to those conduits which are within the

demised premises and for the benefit of the tenant. Being an external pipe, the Mainwarings will have no liability for its condition. There are two reasons:

(a) First, terms in a lease are usually interpreted against the grantor and for the benefit of the tenant.

(b) Secondly the courts have long held that where the lease contains no express provision as to parts of a building, particularly where those parts are for the common benefit of a number of tenants, those parts will generally not be considered to be included in the demise. They will consequently remain in the control of the landlord who will therefore be under an obligation to take reasonable care of the parts of the premises retained (*Cockburn v Smith* [1924] 2 KB 119).

8.   However, a demise of a floor in a building has in the past been held to include the exterior of a wall *(Hope Brothers v Cowan* [1913] 2 Ch 312). A favourable construction of the lease is therefore far from certain, although each lease must be construed on its own wording and case law is of limited value.

9.   If the terms of the lease are construed in Mr and Mrs Mainwaring's favour the responsibility for the repair and maintenance of the pipe would be upon the landlord, and the Mainwarings as tenants would not be responsible for any damage that occurred when the pipe burst.

Breach of Duty

10.   If it were established that the Mainwarings had any responsibility to insulate or repair the pipe, the Claimant would need to adduce convincing evidence to establish that they had in fact been negligent and that it was their negligence which caused the pipe to burst.

11.   The allegation that the pipe was not insulated adequately or at all is disputed by the Mainwarings. However, the surveyor's report prepared by Mr Hodges for the Claimant states that on the date of his visit, the upper section of the water pipe at the rear of the property was only partly lagged and not to a good standard, and that 'below the iron staircase' there was no lagging at all. The report refers both to an iron staircase at the rear and an old iron fire escape. However, the only staircase on the attached plan seems to extend over the whole height of the building, so I have found it difficult to identify the area 'below the iron staircase' from the plan.

12.   As requested above, could my Instructing Solicitors ask the Mainwarings to clarify the position of the pipe which burst and also the position of the staircase or staircases at the rear of the building? Obviously it is of the utmost importance to be absolutely clear where the burst pipe was located.

13.   Mr Mainwaring's witness statement will need to describe in detail the insulation on the pipes at the rear of the building on 1 January 2007. He had apparently told his wife that all the pipes were insulated. This should also be covered in the witness statement from the plumber who repaired the pipe. Mr and Mrs Mainwaring should also be asked to comment on the ease of access to the pipe. A witness statement should also be taken from Paula (I have not been given her full name), who I see assisted in drying out the Mainwarings' premises.

14.   If satisfactory answers are given to the points above I think it will be possible to refute the allegations of any negligence on the part of the Mainwarings in the event that they are held to have responsibility for the condition of the pipe.

Causation

15.   To date it has not been possible to obtain further details of the claim for loss and damage from the Claimant, but it seems very unlikely that he will be able to prove that the losses claimed arose as a result of flood damage from the burst pipe.

16.   The plumber who was called to fix the pipe on 1 January 2007 told the Mainwarings that he considered that the water may not have been escaping for more than a few hours. Further, Mrs Mainwaring was of the view that their premises took the brunt of the flood.

17.   The extensive claim made by the Claimant seems strangely in contrast with the Mainwarings' statement that the total loss they suffered from the flood was some £1,100 (taking into account the £500 salvaged). It is also difficult to reconcile the surveyor's plan with the presence of water inside the Mainwarings' premises.

18.   Mr Hodges' report, on the other hand, does describe considerable water damage to the ceiling and to the floor of the snooker hall. There appears from the report to be no water damage to the walls even at the point water from the burst pipe would be expected to have entered the hall, i.e. from the flat roof of the extension. The rear addition which includes a rear lobby and ladies' and gents' WCs appears to be badly affected by water damage. Mr Hodges has given his opinion that the water damage must have been caused by the defective pipe as he could see no other water pipes to the ground floor. There must, however, be a water supply for the WCs in the back addition. A survey of the ground floor on behalf of the Defendants will be necessary to try to discover accurately the condition of the Claimant's premises and whether the condition of the premises is consistent with any cause other than water penetration from the burst pipe.

19.   It will in due course be necessary for a detailed statement to be obtained from the Mainwarings and the plumber about these matters. As yet, not having seen Mr and Mrs Mainwaring in conference, I am unable to comment on the reliability of their evidence, but the only issues on which this may be relevant are on whether the pipe in question was lagged, whether Mr Hodges has identified the correct pipe and certain aspects on the Claimant's damages claim (see below). The report of Mr Hodges, however, leaves a number of matters uncertain. It is my opinion that the Claimant has a number of difficulties in establishing that the various alleged losses were caused by negligence on the part of the Defendants.

Loss and Damage

20.   The Claimant's claim for loss and damage is in the sum of about £190,000 and includes a claim for continuing loss. Of this sum only some £19,503.40 is for damage to the premises themselves. The remainder is alleged to arise from loss of profits and the lost value of the business. It is alleged that the Claimant has ceased trading as a result of the damage from the flood.

21.   The Mainwarings assert, contrary to the Claimant's pleaded case, that the snooker hall on the Claimant's premises has been in operation since the pipe burst. This would suggest that the 'flood' was not as extensive as the Claimant alleges and indeed that the reason the business ceased trading was not because of water damage from the flood. In support of this, Mrs Mainwaring has reported that a bailiff called to serve a distress warrant for arrears of rent which does suggest at the least that other factors may have been operating which affected the financial viability of the business.

22.   The lost value claim would include the profit-making potential of the business, and there is therefore a measure of double recovery in the Claimant's claim. The Claimant

will not succeed in recovering all the heads of claim and will instead have to choose between the cost of cure together with the loss of profits while the property is being repaired, or the diminution in value of the business.

23.   The court will in general choose the measure of damages which provides fair compensation for the Claimant for any loss suffered but which results in the least damages being payable (*C.R. Taylor (Wholesale) Ltd v Hepworth Ltd* [1977] 1 WLR 659). At the present time it is uncertain whether, by the time of trial, the claim for lost profits would exceed that of lost value, but it is likely that the lost value claim of £85,000 would be taken as the maximum amount of the potential claim.

Public Funding

24.   I consider that the prospects of the Defendants in successfully defending themselves from all liability to the Claimant are Good (Category B). Even if the issue of liability were to be found against them I consider that on the limited information now before me there are serious issues as to quantum. The claim as formulated in the Particulars of Claim has a present value of £190,000 odd (including one year's alleged continuing loss of profits). That is considerably more than double the estimated costs of defending (see below). The cost-benefit criteria for public funding therefore appear to be satisfied, and I recommend the continuation of Legal Services Commission assistance for both Mr and Mrs Mainwaring.

25.   Once witness statements have been exchanged and disclosure has taken place, it will be necessary to reassess whether the Claimant will be able to adduce evidence in support of his sizeable claim for loss. In my view the limitation on the certificates should be altered to cover the exchange of witness statements and filing of pre-trial checklists, and it would be sensible to increase the financial condition to (say) £15,000.

9th April 2008   BRIAN BARRISTER

Temple Court

IN THE WAKEFIELD COUNTY COURT   Claim No. WF07 048972

BETWEEN:-

Mr ANTHONY MALCOLM LOWE   <u>Claimant</u>

-and-

(1) Mr HENRY GEORGE MAINWARING

(2) Mrs ELSA ANN MAINWARING   <u>Defendants</u>

List of Documents

Standard Disclosure

Notes:

The rules relating to standard disclosure are contained in Part 31 of the Civil Procedure Rules. Documents to be included under standard disclosure are contained in Rule 31.6. A document has or will have been under your control if you have or have had possession, or a right of possession, of it or a right to inspect or take copies of it.

Disclosure Statement

I, the above named Claimant state that I have carried out a reasonable and proportionate search to locate all the documents which I am required to disclose under the order made by the court on 10th January 2008.

(I did not search for documents—

1.   Pre-dating 2002

2.   Located elsewhere than my office and that of my solicitors

3.   In categories other than the lease of the premises, repairs arising out of the flood, and papers relating to the conduct of this claim.)

I carried out a search for electronic documents contained on or created by the following: Mail files and document files on PCs; laptops; notebooks; mobile phones.

- I did not search for the following:
- documents created before January 2002
- documents contained on or created by the Claimant on databases; back-up tapes; PDA devices; portable storage media; servers; off-site storage; handheld devices
- documents contained on or created by the Claimant as calender files; web-based applications or graphic and presentation files
- documents other than by reference to the following keywords/concepts (not applicable).

I certify that I understand the duty of disclosure and to the best of my knowledge I have carried out that duty. I further certify that the list of documents set out in or attached to this form, is a complete list of all documents which are or have been in my control and which I am obliged under the court order to disclose.

I understand that I must inform the court and the other parties immediately if any further document required to be disclosed by Rule 31.6 comes into my control at any time before the conclusion of the case.

(I have not permitted inspection of documents within the category or class of documents (as set out below) required to be disclosed under Rule 31.6(b) or (c) on the grounds that to do so would be disproportionate to the issues in the case.)

Signed: Date: 5th March 2008

Claimant _____

I have control of the documents numbered and listed here. I do not object to you inspecting them/producing copies.

1.	Lease Claimant and Margaret Pike [not reproduced]	17.10.2002
2.	Estimate Snooker Restorers Ltd	3.1.2007
3.	Letter Claimant to WY Property Management Ltd	17.1.2007
4.	Copy letter WY Property Management to Belsize Loss Adjusters	14.2.2007
5.	Copy letter Belsize Loss Adjusters to WY Property Management	28.2.2007
6.	Copy letter Claimant's solicitors to WY Property Management	7.3.2007
7.	Letter WY Property Management to Claimant's Solicitors	21.3.2007
8.	Copy Letter Belsize Loss Adjusters to WY Property Management	23.3.2007
9.	Letter WY Property Management to Claimant's solicitors	4.4.2007
10.	Correspondence common to both parties [not reproduced]	Various
11.	Statements of case, orders [not reproduced]	Various

I have control of the documents numbered and listed here but I object to you inspecting them:

Communications between the Claimant and his solicitors for the purpose of obtaining or giving legal advice, communications between the Claimant's solicitors and third parties in relation to this claim, instructions to, opinions of, and statements of case settled by Counsel.

I object to you inspecting these documents because they are protected by legal professional privilege.

I have had the documents numbered and listed below, but they are no longer in my control.

Originals of copy documents listed as items 1 to 11 above which were last in my control before being posted to their respective addressees.

SNOOKER RESTORERS LIMITED

48 Shaftsbury Road, Leeds, LS3 9IW

Tel: 0113 2879872

ESTIMATE

To:

Repairs and refelting Table 1	£1,650.00
Repairs and refelting Table 2	£1,850.00
Refelting Table 3	£900.00
Sub-total	£4,400.00
VAT at 17.5%	£770.00
Total	£5,170.00

Date: 3rd January 2007.

Mr Lowe
83–87 Leeds Road
Wakefield
West Yorkshire
WF4 1AP

Topspin Snooker Hall
83–87 Leeds Road
Wakefield
WF4 1AP

Mrs Bainbridge
WY Property Management Limited   17th January 2007

29 Commerce Street
Wakefield
WF1 8FJ

FOR THE ATTENTION OF MRS BAINBRIDGE

Dear Madam,

TOPSPIN SNOOKER HALL, 83–87 LEEDS ROAD, WAKEFIELD

I enclose my insurance claim form together with the two builders' estimates you asked for. I also enclose an estimate from a specialist snooker table repairer with the estimated cost of repairing the felts on the three tables damaged in the flood.

Please pass the claims form and estimates on to the insurance company as quickly as possible. The snooker hall is in a shambles, and I cannot open for business with the place in this state. Could you please impress on the insurance company that this claim is urgent.

Yours sincerely,

Tony Lowe

W Y Property Management Ltd
29 Commerce Street, Wakefield, WF1 8FJ
Tel: 01924 433692

Our ref:	DB/4327
Your ref:	9328721
Date:	14th Feb. 2007

Mr D Beddoes
Belsize Loss Adjusters Ltd
8 Grovelands Road
London
EC4M 6YL

Dear Sirs,

83–87 Leeds Road, Wakefield

I refer to our telephone conversation this morning.

As I mentioned to you on the telephone, there are two matters arising out of that letter which I find quite extraordinary. The first is that there is a suggestion that if a pipe bursts outside then it is not covered by insurance, and the second is the suggestion that 'the escape of water has served only to bring to light the maintenance problem with the premises'. These suggestions are quite extraordinary and I wonder whether your surveyor has addressed his mind to this claim in any meaningful way.

A great deal of money has been spent in the last 3 years on maintenance of the exterior of the property, and whilst I would not suggest that problems might have arisen, I really cannot accept the proposition that the property had not been adequately maintained.

This is a valid claim, having resulted from an insured risk. Damage caused by a burst pipe is an insured risk. Also covered under the policy is loss of rent and in that connection we are chasing the tenant for the quarter's rent due 25th December and the tenant is saying, probably quite rightly, that the rent should be paid by the Insurers until reinstatement of the property has taken place. He is also saying that in the event that the Insurers do not meet the claim, then he will be looking to the landlord to meet the claim as she should have had the property adequately maintained and insured.

It seems to me that my Client did have the property adequately maintained and insured, but if the Insurers wish to maintain their present stance and the tenant takes action against my client, then she will be making a claim to the Insurers under the Property Owner's Liability section of the policy. One way or the other therefore the Insurer will have to meet this claim and it seems to me that the claim can best be mitigated if dealt with quickly.

In the circumstances, therefore, can I ask you to take this matter up direct with the Insurer so that a satisfactory conclusion can be arrived at without further delay.

Yours faithfully,

Donna Bainbridge (Mrs) FRICS

Belsize Loss Adjusters Ltd

8 Grovelands Road

London EC4M 6YL

Telephone: 0207 631 2971 Facsimile: 0207 631 3111

Date: 28th February 2007

Our ref: 9328721   Your Ref: DB/4327

Mrs Bainbridge

WY Property Management Ltd

29 Commerce Street

Wakefield WF1 8FJ

Dear Madam

83–87 Leeds Road, Wakefield

We acknowledge receipt of your letter of 14th February 2007 and comment on its contents as follows. We have in fact given serious thought to this claim. We confirm that a burst pipe is an insured peril covered by the policy and have never suggested otherwise. For a valid claim to arise, it must be shown that an insured peril had operated to bring about the damage for which the Insured is claiming. This gives rise to two points.

The first is that the Insured must take reasonable care to maintain his property and to prevent loss. From the information provided regarding this incident, it would appear that the pipe located externally to the premises had burst due to lack of insulation and protection against the elements and the Insured was thus in possible breach of her policy in failing to take reasonable care in the maintenance of her property by failing to insulate the two external mains pipes which led to the escape of the water.

Secondly, the policy does not cover damage caused by wear and tear, general weathering or gradual deterioration. Much of what we were shown by way of 'damage' did not appear consistent with having been damaged by water escaping from a burst pipe. In point of fact, there were several areas shown to our representative by Mr Lowe that were clearly no more than wear and tear.

We would only be too happy to make available a selection of photographs taken by our representative of the premises which in our view shows clear signs that the premises occupied by Mr Lowe are suffering from lack of maintenance. By this we are not suggesting in any way that the Landlord is not performing her repairing obligations or not adequately maintaining her premises but by way of illustrating the problem as we saw it at the time of our visit.

As regards the claim for loss of rent, it is our understanding from Mr Lowe that the reason why he has been unable to trade from the premises is not solely due to the water ingress and in any event, the policy will only respond to indemnify the Insured for loss of rent if the Insured had taken all reasonable steps to mitigate her loss.

To date we have yet to receive the Insurer's instructions as to how to proceed with this claim and until then we are unable on behalf of Insurers to accept or deny liability and trust this letter has addressed fully your concerns.

Yours faithfully

Belsize Loss Adjusters

FRASER & COMPANY
SOLICITORS

Bank Chambers
Ripon Road
Wakefield
WF1 9GR
Tele: 01924 782364
Fax: 01924 807243
Ref: TBC/DH/07.0247
Date: 7th March 2007

Dear Sir,

TOPSPIN SNOOKER HALL, 83–87 LEEDS ROAD, WAKEFIELD

Our Client: Mr A. LOWE

We have been instructed on behalf of Mr Lowe.

What progress has been made concerning our client's insurance claim in respect of the flooding on the 26th December 2006 to 1st January 2007? Pending receipt of funds in respect of the claim our client is unable to reinstate the premises which are not fit for use at the present time.

Yours faithfully,

Fraser & Co

Mrs Bainbridge
WY Property Management Limited
29 Commerce Street
Wakefield
WF1 8FJ

W Y Property Management Ltd
29 Commerce Street, Wakefield, WF1 8FJ
Tel: 01924 433692

Our ref:	DB/4327
Your ref:	TBC/DH/07.0247
Date:	21st March 2007

WITHOUT PREJUDICE

Messrs Fraser & Co
Bank Chambers
Ripon Road
Wakefield
WF1 9GR

Dear Sirs,

83–87 Leeds Road, Wakefield

We thank you for your letter of the 7th March 2007.

We have heard further from the Loss Adjusters regarding the matter and, without going into too much detail at this stage, it does appear that what they are in fact saying is that the items of damage which your Client is claiming are the result of the lack of his maintenance rather than having been damaged by any water penetration.

However, we are arranging a meeting on site with the Loss Adjusters in an endeavour to get to the bottom of the situation and we hope therefore to be able to write to you more comprehensively following that meeting.

Yours faithfully,

Donna Bainbridge (Mrs) FRICS

Belsize Loss Adjusters Ltd
8 Grovelands Road
London EC4M 6YL
Telephone: 0207 631 2971   Facsimile: 0207 631 3111

Date: 23rd March 2007

Our Ref: 9328721   Your Ref: DB/4327

Mrs Bainbridge
WY Property Management Ltd
29 Commerce Street
Wakefield
WF1 8FJ

Dear Mrs Bainbridge,

83–87 Leeds Road, Wakefield

I refer to the above matter and our meeting on 14th March at 2.30 pm.

I have to advise regretfully, as per my conversation with you, that I was unable to see for myself from my external examination that there has been any real damage to this property.

I have seen both pipes which are alleged to have been the cause of the damage and from my examination cannot see that there is evidence of a burst nor can I see that there has been a recent repair.

I noticed that above the window where the suspended ceiling is alleged to have been damaged by water ingress there has been a recent fitting of a concrete lintel. There is also evidence of recent re-pointing above the lintel.

It does appear to me from the photographic evidence I have in my possession that a lot of the reinstatement works being claimed for by Mr Lowe are of a maintenance nature.

The Lease agreement is clear inasmuch as it places the responsibility upon the tenant to maintain the property and I fear that this has not been done properly.

Yours sincerely,

Belsize Loss Adjusters

W Y Property Management Ltd
29 Commerce Street, Wakefield, WF1 8FJ
Tel: 01924 433692

Our ref:	DB/4327
Your ref:	TBC/DH/07.0247
Date:	4th April 2007

Messrs Fraser & Co
Bank Chambers
Ripon Road
Wakefield
WF1 9GR

Dear Sirs,

83–87 Leeds Road, Wakefield

I refer to my letter dated 21st March and enclose a copy of correspondence received from Insurers' Loss Adjusters dated 23rd March 2007.

The contents are not very promising, but whilst at the moment they are not prepared to agree to a compromise settlement, we are entering into further discussions in an effort to try and obtain some form of payment here.

As soon as there is any better news to report, I will contact you.

Yours faithfully,

Donna Bainbridge (Mrs) FRICS

Application Notice	IN THE WAKEFIELD COUNTRY COURT	
You must complete Parts A	Claim No.	WF07 048972
and B and C if applicable	Claimant	ANTHONY MALCOM LOWE
Send any relevant fee and the	(including ref)	TBC/DH/07.0247
completed application to the	Defendants	HENRY GEORGE MAINWARING
court with any draft order,	(including ref)	ELSA ANN MAINWARING
witness statement or other		JTG/A
evidence; and sufficient copies	Date	5th April 2008
of these for service on each		
respondent		

You should provide this information for listing the application

1. Do you wish to have your application dealt with at a hearing?

Yes   No   If yes, please complete 2

2. Time estimate   0 hours   30 mins

Is this agreed by all parties?   Yes   No

Level of Judge   District Judge

3. Parties to be served   Claimant

Part A

We, Godfrey & Co, on behalf of the Defendants intend to apply for an order that:

(1) The Claimant do within 14 days of the date of service of such Order file and serve evidence stating whether the documents specified in the Schedule to this Application are or have at any time been in the Claimant's possession, custody or power, and if not now in his possession, custody or power, when he parted with the same and what has become of them.

(2) Unless the Claimant gives access to the Defendants' surveyor to the Claimant's property at the Ground Floor, 83–87 Leeds Road, Wakefield by 4 pm on the 14th day after the hearing of this application, the Claimant's claim be struck out and judgment entered for the Defendants with costs.

(3) The costs of this application may be provided for.

SCHEDULE

1. Accounts for the years ending 31.7.05; 31.7.06 and 31.7.07

2. Tax returns since 1.1.2005

3. VAT returns since 1.1.2005

4. All accounts books and financial documentation and invoices since 1.1.2005

5. All bank statements since 1.1.2005

6. Insurance claim form about January 2007

7. Builders' estimates (two) about January 2007

because the Claimant has not given full standard disclosure of documents, and has failed to allow the Defendants' surveyor access to the Claimant's premises for the purpose of reporting on the alleged damage to those premises.

Part B

We wish to rely on: tick one box

the attached (witness statement) (affidavit)   my statement of case

evidence in Part C overleaf in support of my application

Signed:

Applicant's Solicitor

Address to which documents about this claim should be sent (including reference if appropriate)

Godfrey & Co, 27 Cressey Street, Wakefield, West Yorkshire, WF5 3SL

Ref. JTG/AP

The court office at The Crown House, 127 Kirkgate, Wakefield, W. Yorkshire WF1 1JW is open between 10 am and 4 pm Monday to Friday. Address all communications to the Court Manager and quote the claim number.

Made on behalf of the Defendants
Witness: H.K. Jones
1st Statement of witness
Exhibits: HJK 1
Signed: 5.4.2008

IN THE WAKEFIELD COUNTY COURT   Claim No. WF07 048972
BETWEEN:—

Mr. ANTHONY MALCOLM LOWE   <u>Claimant</u>

-and-

(1) Mr. HENRY GEORGE MAINWARING
(2) Mrs. ELSA ANN MAINWARING   <u>Defendants</u>

1.   My name is Helen Katherine Jones. I am a Solicitor of the Supreme Court and employed as an Assistant Solicitor by the firm of Godfrey & Co of 27 Cressey Street, Wakefield, West Yorkshire, WF5 3SL. I have conduct of this claim on behalf of the Defendants. I am duly authorised to make this statement in support of the Defendants' application for specific disclosure.

2.   I have read a copy of the List of Documents served in this claim on behalf of the Claimant dated the 5 March 2008. It is my belief that this List does not disclose all the documents that are or have been in the Claimant's custody relating to the matters in question in this claim.

3.   In my belief the Claimant has or at some time has had in his custody the various documents and classes of documents specified or described in the Schedule to the present Application Notice (referred to below as 'the Schedule').

4.   My belief is based on the following matters. It is common ground that the Claimant was running a business at his premises, and the Claimant alleges this business has been damaged by the alleged flood. Anyone running a business will keep accounts (item 1 in the Schedule) and will keep books, invoices and other documentation (item 4 in the Schedule). He will be required to file tax returns and in all probability VAT returns (items 2 and 3 in the Schedule). Unless the business is very small (and the Claimant alleges that it generated profits, not turnover, of £32,000 per annum) it will need to operate a bank account, not least for paying in cheques. Therefore item 5 in the Schedule is likely to apply. The insurance claim form and estimates (items 6 and 7 in the Schedule) are expressly referred to in the letter dated 17 January 2007 referred to in the List of Documents at item 3. I refer to the bundle of correspondence marked '**HKJ 1**' and a true copy of that letter appears at page 1 of the exhibit.

5.   The documents and classes of documents sought in this application all relate to matters in question in this claim. Items 1 to 5 of the Schedule relate to the Claimant's claim for lost profits and the loss of the value of his business, item 6 relates to the issue of liability and is also relevant to the claim on quantum, and item 7 relates to the claim for the cost of putting right the alleged damage.

6.   At pages [2] to [4] of my exhibit are letters to the Claimant's solicitors requesting the disclosure sought in this application and access for the Defendant's surveyor, and the Claimant's solicitor's response.

7.   I ask the Court to grant the orders sought in this application.

Statement of truth

I believe that the facts stated in this witness statement are true.

Signed: *Helen Katherine Jones*

Date: 5th April 2008

Exhibit HKJ 1
Topspin Snooker Hall
83–87 Leeds Road
Wakefield
WF4 1AP

Mrs Bainbridge
WY Property Management Limited

17th January 2007

29 Commerce Street
Wakefield
WF1 8FJ

<u>FOR THE ATTENTION OF MRS BAINBRIDGE</u>

Dear Madam,

<u>TOPSPIN SNOOKER HALL, 83–87 LEEDS ROAD, WAKEFIELD</u>

I enclose my insurance claim form together with the two builders' estimates you asked for. I also enclose an estimate from a specialist snooker table repairer with the estimated cost of repairing the felts on the three tables damaged in the flood.

Please pass the claims form and estimates on to the insurance company as quickly as possible. The snooker hall is in a shambles, and I cannot open for business with the place in this state. Could you please impress on the insurance company that this claim is urgent.

Yours sincerely,

Tony Lowe

[1]

GODFREY & Co,
27 Cressey Street, Wakefield, West Yorkshire, WF5 3SL
Tel: 01924 985579   Fax: 01924 985877

Our Ref: JTG/AP
Your Ref: TBC/DH/07.0247
Date: 18th February 2008

Messrs Fraser & Co
Bank Chambers
Ripon Road
Wakefield WF1 9GR

Dear Sir,

TOPSPIN SNOOKER HALL, 83–87 LEEDS ROAD, WAKEFIELD

When compiling your List of Documents we would be grateful if you could provide full documentation in support of your client's claims for loss of profits and loss of the value of your client's business. These should include tax and VAT returns, bank statements and accounts.

Our expert surveyor needs to inspect the interior of your client's premises for the purposes of preparing his report, and we should be grateful if you could provide us with dates when this would be convenient to your client.

Yours faithfully,

[2]

FRASER & COMPANY
SOLICITORS

Bank Chambers
Ripon Road
Wakefield
WF19GR
Tel: 01926 782364
Fax: 01924 807243

Ref: TBC/DH/07.0247
Your ref: JTG/AP
Date: 21st February 2008

Dear Sir,

TOPSPIN SNOOKER HALL, 83–87 LEEDS ROAD, WAKEFIELD

Further to your letter of the 18th February 2008, we are taking our client's instructions on the second paragraph of your letter. Our List of Documents is currently being prepared, and we hope to be able to serve this in the near future.

Yours faithfully,

Fraser & Co

[3]

GODFREY & Co,

27 Cressey Street, Wakefield, West Yorkshire, WF5 3SL
Tel: 01924 985579   Fax: 01924 985877

Our Ref: JTG/AP
Your Ref: TBC/DH/07.0247
Date: 12th March 2008

Messrs Fraser & Co
Bank Chambers
Ripon Road
Wakefield WF1 9GR

Dear Sir,

TOPSPIN SNOOKER HALL, 83–87 LEEDS ROAD, WAKEFIELD

We acknowledge receipt of the copy documents from your List. We consider your List to be defective in that it does not include the accounts, returns and bank statements that we referred to in our letter of the 18th February 2008. It also does not include the insurance claim form nor the two builders' invoices that your client submitted to the landlord's insurer in about January 2007. Kindly provide us with these documents within the next 7 days, failing which we will be making an application to the Court for an order for specific disclosure.

We still have not heard from you regarding access for our surveyor. Please may we hear from you on this also within 7 days, failing which we will be making an application to the Court.

Yours faithfully,

[4]

13.3.1 C.A.P. in action

Notes on brief for application

STAGE 1 THE CONTEXT OF THE CASE

CHECKLIST

(1) The stage of the proceedings

A. What steps have been taken:

- Statement of case served/filed including request for further information. C's Expert Report served.
- Exchange of lists. Copies of documents exchanged.
- Directions re exchange of expert reports?

APPLICATION FOR HEARING ON 8.5.2008

B. Your Instructions:

- Appear at case management conference and obtain:

    Order for specific disclosure: of specific documents relating to C's loss.
    Order for inspection (for purposes of Ds' expert report).

(2) Understanding the problem

A. Cause of the problem:

- Why not get documents? C failed to disclose in list.
- Why not get access? C failed to allow.

B. Client's objective

- Purpose of Disclosure: to enable proper preparation, encourage settlement and full argument on all issues, e.g., here on what losses actually suffered.
- Purpose of access: to enable Ds' expert to do survey and prepare report to ascertain damage done by flood and ensure C does not have an unfair advantage by depriving Ds of their own expert evidence.

(3) Collecting the facts

A. Application for disclosure

- Chronology:

10.1.08	Direction requiring disclosure
18.2.08	Letter D to C—requesting full disclosure of documents in support of financial claim
21.2.08	Letter C to D—consider List served by D
5.3.08	C's list of documents
12.3.08	Letter D to C—asks for additional documents
5.4.08	Application Notice

- Documents sought:

    Financial Info from 1.1.05: accounts, tax returns, VAT returns, accounts, books, documents, invoices, bank statements (to show loss of profit/value)

    Insurance Claim Jan 07: see letter 17.1.07 in List

    Two estimates: see letter 17.1.07 in List

B. Application for inspection

- Chronology:

  18.2.08   First request on behalf of D for access for surveyor C's survey done

  13.3.08   C's surveyor's report

  5.4.08   Application Notice

(4) The legal framework

A. Disclosure: CPR, Part 31

- Procedure: application on notice supported by evidence
- Grounds: party not disclosed document(s) which leads applicant to conclude that documents exist, are disclosable, and within control of C.

B. Inspection: CPR, Part 25.

- Procedure: application on notice

  'Unless order' (attached to application for inspection): empowers court to strike out unless order obeyed
- Grounds: party has been prevented from inspecting property:
  — which is subject matter of the claim or to which any question may arise AND
  — is in possession of a party to the claim

STAGE 2 ANALYSIS OF LEGAL AND FACTUAL ISSUES AND EVIDENCE

A. Grounds fulfilled—Disclosure:

Application:
  — sets out documents sought (schedule)
  — Evidence—Witness Statement:
  — states belief list not complete (para 2)
  — states belief C has had in possession, custody or power (para 3)
  — states grounds for belief (para 4)
  — states relate to matters in question; relate to issues (para 5)
  — exhibits relevant evidence/requests (para 4, 6)

B. Grounds fulfilled—Inspection:

Application:
  — correct address
  — seeks access by surveyor
  — to inspect to do report
  — Evidence—Witness Statement:
  — exhibits letters requesting access (para 6)

STAGE 3 PRESENTATION OF THE CASE

A. ORDERS SOUGHT

1. Disclosure: Seek Order: C file/serve written evidence stating whether has docs in schedule in control, if not when parted & what became of them.

2. Inspection: Seek Order: C give access to D's surveyor by 4 pm, 14 days of hearing date to do inspection for survey report. If not strike out.

B. ARGUMENTS

(i) Disclosure: In C's possession etc
   — Docs 1, 4, 5: normal business requirement
   — Docs 2 and 3: required by HM Revenue and Customs
   — Docs 1–5: all recent, see para 4 wit statement
   — Doc 6, 7: C's own documents refer to these: see HKJ1 and C's list
   Relate to Issues
   — Doc 1–5: C claim loss of profit/value; these docs give information by which can be calculated
   — Doc 6: insurance claim form; relevant to liability and quantum
   — Doc 7: estimates of repair cost; relevant to quantum
   Failed to disclose see list, correspondence—Exhibit

(ii) Inspection
   Arguments: C controls the premises, so has obtained an expert's report which has been disclosed
   D requested access: see exhibits
   C refused
   D no access/no report—inequality of arms; denial of access by C is a serious issue so court should impose a serious penalty if C fails to comply

The criminal brief

14.1 Bail application

IN THE COLCHESTER MAGISTRATES' COURT

THE QUEEN

V

COSTAS GEORGIOU

INSTRUCTIONS TO COUNSEL
TO MAKE A BAIL APPLICATION

Public Funding

Counsel: Ms Nicola Grey

Brown Dingle & Slattery
New Buildings,
Chelmsford, Essex

100/NG/15/6/08

<u>IN THE COLCHESTER MAGISTRATES' COURT</u>

THE QUEEN

Vs

COSTAS GEORGIOU

INSTRUCTIONS TO COUNSEL
TO MAKE BAIL APPLICATION
ON 11TH JUNE 2008

Those Instructing apologise for the lateness of the Instructions to Counsel.

The above-named defendant was remanded into custody on 3rd June 2008, charged with an offence of Section 18 wounding with intent, following a full bail application having been made by our Mr Johnson. The CPS's objection to bail was on the basis that the client may fail to surrender as he had only recently arrived in this country from Greece and he was charged with a serious offence. We have since then managed to take our client's instructions through the services of an interpreter on matters which might be pertinent to the making of a second bail application—please see proof of evidence enclosed. Furthermore, our client's uncle, Mr Demetri Ionides, who will be at court that morning, has also, since the application made last week, offered to stand surety up to the sum of £1000. Mr Georgiou's girlfriend will also be attending court.

Counsel is instructed to use his best endeavours to obtain bail for the client. Public funding was obtained at the hearing last week and a copy of the Representation Order is enclosed with these instructions.

Brown Dingle & Slattery COSTAS GEORGIOU

COSTAS GEORGIOU

PROOF OF EVIDENCE

I am Costas Georgiou and I live at 27 White Hart Lane Tottenham, N15 OHE. I arrived in this country from Greece at Easter of this year. I am currently studying English at a language school and I hope to go on and study engineering at London Metropolitan University when my English is proficient enough. In order to make ends meet, I help out at my relatives' kebab vans in Colchester on most weekends.

I share the above address with my girlfriend, Anna Constantinou, who holds both a British and a Cypriot passport and who has been living in this country on and off for the past 5 years.

I strongly deny committing this offence. My cousin Alexis Ionides has already told the police that he did it. Given the way that Mr Canning and his friend behaved, it is, in my opinion, hardly surprising that Alexis behaved in the manner that he did.

I have no previous convictions either in this country or in Greece and I have found the past few days in prison to be an awful shock.

Signed: Costas Georgiou   6th June 2008

Colchester Magistrates' Court (Code 12343)

Representation Order No.2656–6088–02

In accordance with the provisions of Section 14 and schedule 3 Access to Justices Act 1999, a right to representation
is granted as follows

DATE OF GRANT	8.6.08	DATE OF FIRST HEARING AFTER GRANT (M.C.)	9.6 at 10am
NAME	COSTAS GEORGIOU		
ADDRESS WHERE IN CUSTODY	COLCHESTER POLICE STATION		
NAME AND ADDRESS OF SOLICITOR IF APPOINTED	BROWN, DINGLE & SLATTERY 27, NEW BUILDINGS CHELMSFORD, ESSEX		

TERMS OF REPRESENTATION delete as necessary	MAGISTRATES' COURTS PROCEEDINGS (1) ~~SOLICITOR~~ (2) SOLICITOR AND JUNIOR COUNSEL	CROWN COURT PROCEEDINGS (1) SOLICITOR & JUNIOR COUNSEL
PURPOSE OF ORDER	(1) ~~Proceedings before Magistrates court in connection with (state nature of proceedings)~~ (2) ~~Appealing to the Crown Court against a decision of the said Magistrates' Court~~ (3) ~~Resisting an Appeal to the Crown Court against a decision of the said Magistrates' Court on~~ (4) Proceedings before (both a Magistrates' Court and*) the Crown Court in connection with (state nature of proceedings) including in the event of a person to whom this order being convicted or sentenced in those proceedings, advice and assistance in regard to the making of an appeal to the criminal division of the Court of Appeal. (5) ~~Other (state nature of proceedings)~~	

Distribution **Legal Services** **Commission Copy** **Crown Court** **Solicitor's File** **Court File**	

CRIMINAL DEFENCE SERVICE Representation order	**Justices' Clerk** **Officer Designated to Act on Behalf of Justices' Clerk**

14.1.1   C.A.P. in action

Notes for the bail application

STAGE 1 THE CONTEXT OF THE CASE

(1) THE STAGE OF THE PROCEEDINGS

  (a) What steps have been taken?

   Defendant arrested. Police bail refused.

   Defendant remanded in Custody on 3.6.08.

   Representation Order granted on 6.6.08.

   Application for bail made by IS refused by magistrates on 6.6.08.

   (Objection to Bail—likely to fail to surrender to custody, only recently arrived in this country from Greece, charged with serious offence.)

  (b) Instructions: to see Defendant and make Bail Application on his behalf at Colchester Magistrates' Court on 11.6.08 at 10.00 am.

NOTE: Interpreter will be at Court. Query client's understanding of/use of English.

  (c) Objective: to secure release of Defendant on Bail.

   Will need to show that either prosecution objection without foundation or can be overcome.

(2) UNDERSTANDING THE PROBLEM

   Defendant in custody since 3.6.08. Last chance for defence to apply for bail as it is second fully argued application before magistrates.

(3) LEGAL FRAMEWORK

  (i) Offences against the Person Act 1861, s 18. (See **Table 11.5**).

  (ii) Bail Act 1976.

Refusal of bail—if court satisfied that there are substantial grounds for believing that the defendant, if released on bail (whether subject to conditions or not) would . . . fail to surrender to custody etc (Sch 1, Pt I, para 2).

Matters to be considered by court in deciding whether grounds applicable (Sch 1, Pt I, para 9):

  (a) nature and seriousness of offence,

  (b) character, antecedents . . . community ties of defendant,

  (c) . . .

  (d) strength of evidence of his having committed offence.

Conditional bail—imposition of such requirements as necessary to secure that defendant surrenders to custody etc. (s 3), e.g., residence at particular address, reporting to police, curfew, surrender of passport, provision of surety, security for surrender to custody. Unless material change in circumstances, only two fully argued Bail Applications can be made before magistrates. Thereafter Application must be made to Crown Court (Sch 1, Pt IIA).

STAGE 2 ANALYSIS OF ISSUES AND EVIDENCE

(a)   The Issues

  (1) LEGAL AND FACTUAL ISSUES

Validity of prosecution objection on basis that Defendant has only just arrived in UK and therefore has limited community ties (and there is therefore a greater incentive to abscond to avoid custodial sentence which is the likely outcome if convicted of such a serious offence). See **Figure 11.3**—Mind-map.

  (2) POTENTIAL THEORY

Law abiding, strong community ties, unlikely to abscond, strong incentive to clear name, intention to strengthen links in UK.

  (3) GAPS AND AMBIGUITIES

   (a) Points to clarify with Client

When did he arrive in UK? Where is he presently studying? Has he enrolled at University? How many relations does he have in UK? How many close relations in Greece? Details of arrest.

How long has Anna Constantinou lived in Tottenham? Is she likely to return to Cyprus in near future? How long has relationship lasted?

   (b) Points to clarify with Mr Ionides

Can he show that he has necessary funds to pay amount promised if defendant absconds, e.g., building society passbook?

His suitability to act as surety, e.g., his influence over his nephew, whether he has any previous convictions.

(b)   The Evidence

  (1) THE STRENGTHS AND WEAKNESSES OF THE CASE

Defendant Greek national, short period of residence in UK, speaks little or no English: inference of risk of return to Greece. Custodial sentence almost certain if convicted.

Has number of close relatives in England, long-term plans to study in England, lives with girlfriend, Anna Constantinou (holder of British passport), in Tottenham: inference that Defendant has strong incentives to remain in UK, stand trial and clear his name—no previous convictions. Probably undesirable to reveal nature of defence to prosecution at this stage.

Likely outcome—Conditional bail. Possible conditions—surrender of passport, condition of residence, Mr D. Ionides to stand as surety.

STAGE 3 PREPARATION OF CASE

(1) CHOSEN THEORY

See above at Stage 2(**a**)(2).

(2) CARRYING OUT INSTRUCTIONS

  (a) Prepare for Conference

See *Conference Skills* manual, Chapter 5.

  (b) Prepare to interview Mr Ionides if Solicitor not present.

  (c) Prepare for Hearing

See Advocacy manual, Part III.

Mr Ionides will need to give evidence if acting as surety.

14.2 Advice on evidence

IN THE CROWN COURT, CHELMSFORD No. T 08/0656

THE QUEEN

V

COSTAS GEORGIOU

INSTRUCTIONS TO COUNSEL
TO ADVISE

1. Counsel will please find enclosed the following:

    (a) Papers previously before Counsel [only back sheet reproduced]

    (b) Indictment

    (c) Prosecution witness statements

    (d) Prosecution Exhibits

    (e) Unused material disclosed by Prosecution on 10 September 2008

    (f) Defendant's proof of evidence.

2. Those Instructing act on behalf of the Defendant, Mr Costas Georgiou, who was committed to the Crown Court from the Colchester Magistrates' Court on 5th September 2008 under the provisions of Section 6(2) Magistrates' Courts Act 1980. The Defendant is currently on conditional bail, the one condition being to reside with his uncle Mr D. Ionides at 51 Piggott Close, Colchester.

3. The Prosecution, in view of the statements of their witnesses, have taken the decision to proceed against Mr Georgiou despite the admission of Mr A. Ionides, which they consider unreliable.

4. Mr Georgiou is the cousin of Mr Ionides. Mr Georgiou has only recently come to live in the United Kingdom and speaks little English. However, both his interview and the statement he has given to those Instructing have been properly translated.

5. Counsel is instructed to draft Defence Statement and advise those Instructing on what further steps should be taken in preparation for the forthcoming hearing.

Brown, Dingle & Slattery
27 New Buildings
Chelmsford
Essex

IN THE COLCHESTER MAGISTRATES' COURT

THE QUEEN

V

COSTAS GEORGIOU

INSTRUCTIONS TO COUNSEL
TO MAKE A BAIL APPLICATION

Public Funding

Coram: Lay JJ
Ms Smith for CPS
Client attends in custody
Full bail app. made
c/bail granted
Conditions: Residence with
D. Ionides at 51 Piggott
Close, Colchester
R on c/bail to 28·7·08
Crown Court

N. Grey 13/6/08

Brown, Dingle & Slattery
27 New Buildings
Chelmsford
Essex

100/NG/11/6/08

INDICTMENT   No. T 08/0656

IN THE CROWN COURT AT CHELMSFORD

THE QUEEN v COSTAS GEORGIOU

COSTAS GEORGIOU IS CHARGED AS FOLLOWS:
STATEMENT OF OFFENCE

Wounding with intent contrary to section 18 of the Offences against the Person Act 1861.

PARTICULARS OF OFFENCE

Costas Georgiou on the 24th day of May 2008 unlawfully wounded Andrew David Canning with intent to do him grievous bodily harm.

Officer of the Court

Statement of Witness

(CJ Act 1967 s 9; MC Act 1980 ss 5A(3)(a) and 5B; MC Rules 1981 r 70)

STATEMENT OF   ANDREW DAVID CANNING

Age of Witness (date of birth)   Over 18

Occupation of Witness   Casual Labourer

This statement (consisting of 2 pages each signed by me), is true to the best of my knowledge and belief and I make it knowing that, if it is tendered in evidence, I shall be liable to prosecution if I have wilfully stated in it anything which I know to be false or do not believe to be true.

Dated the 28th day of May 2008   Signed: Andrew David Canning
                                        Signature Witnessed by: Richard Jones

1.   I am Andrew Canning and I live at the address overleaf. I have never been in any very serious trouble with the police before.

2.   At about 7.45 pm on Friday 23rd May 2008, I arrived at the Nine Bells Public House in the Oakridge Centre, Colchester, having walked from my home address. I was met there 20 minutes later by my girlfriend Jackie Perry. We stayed in the pub until 9 pm where I had drunk 1/2 bottles of Budweiser. I think that Jackie had a mineral water or an orange juice because she was driving.

3.   At 9 pm we got into Jackie's car, which is a white Nissan Micra, Y36 YYT, and we drove to the Haven Public House at Thorpe to celebrate the landlord's (Mr Patrick du Pont) birthday. We had met a friend of mine at the Nine Bells and he travelled to Thorpe with us. His name is John Archer.

4.   We stayed at the Haven until about 10.30 pm and I had drunk about 3 or 4 bottles of Budweiser whilst there. John was drinking pints of lager. Jackie still drank non-alcoholic drinks. We then drove to the Rabbit Public House at Kirby, arriving at about 10.45 pm where I chatted to Lee, the landlord's son. John was chatting to the landlord. We stayed there until just gone midnight where I drank another 2 bottles of Budweiser and a large vodka. John had another pint of lager and a large whisky.

5.   We then drove back towards Colchester. I felt fine, John seemed fine and we decided to get something to eat. I was sat in the back of the Nissan and I fell asleep. I had already given my food order and I knew that we were going to the Shetland Road kebab van in Colchester for a chicken kebab.

6.   The next thing I remember is being woken up by Jackie. We were parked right next to the van. Jackie looked panicky and said, 'The geezer's threatening John with a knife'. I got out of the passenger side, got onto the grass and walked up to the kebab van.

Signed: Andrew David Canning   Signature witnessed by: Richard Jones

CONTINUATION OF STATEMENT OF ANDREW DAVID CANNING

7.   I saw John stood at the right-hand front of the van, backing away. Inside the van I saw 3 people. Directly in the front of the van was a male who I'd seen working there before. I would describe him as a Greek male, about 5'10" to 5'11", with a muscular build, about 16 years looking. He was wearing a shirt with his arms showing. He was waving an orange-handled knife with about a 12" blade. He appeared to be threatening John with the knife. Both he and John were shouting abuse at each other. It was a slanging match but I could not understand what it was all about. The Greek kept saying 'I'm going to cut you'.

8.   Also in the van was a Greek female who was positioned just to the side of the young male. She appeared to be hysterical, and was grabbing the young male by the arms and by the neck. She appeared to be trying to pull him away from the front of the van. The young man kept trying to throw her off.

9.   There was a second Greek male in the van, and he was stood at the back, to the left of centre. He was about 25 years old, about 5'9", and with a wiry build. He had stubble on his face, and eyes that made him look older. His face was drawn. He wasn't involved at this point and I didn't take much notice of him.

10. I went to the front of the van just left of centre, and started remonstrating with the younger Greek. I rested my left arm on the front of the counter, and waved my right arm towards the young Greek, and was saying, 'Look there's no fucking need for this, put the knife down', and I looked towards the older Greek saying, 'Look, fucking sort him out'. This carried on for less than 30 seconds, and I was concentrating mostly on the young bloke with the knife.

11. I then saw the older Greek move. He was carrying a large knife in his right hand, the one they use for cutting the meat, with a blade about 16" long. He moved around to my left, and I felt a pressure on my left arm just above my elbow. I didn't see the blow, and I thought he had hit me with the handle or the back of the knife. I moved to try and grab him with my left hand, but he pulled back.

12. I was then pulled back from the front of the van by one of my friends. At this point I was very angry, and I punched the perspex at the front of the van 4 or 5 times with the right fist, causing a graze to my knuckle. The three in the van were standing back by this point, and the girl was screaming.

13. I realised I was bleeding from my left arm at this point, but I didn't realise how bad it was. I asked for the car keys off Jackie, and I stormed to the back of the Nissan to fetch the wheelbrace to hit the perspex with. Once at the back of the car I was approached by John and Jackie, and I could see how bad the cut was. I was then taken in the car up to the North Essex Hospital at Colchester. In Accident and Emergency I realised that my jeans and shirt were soaked in blood. I was treated in casualty and then moved up to the ward. I underwent emergency surgery to stitch up the arteries and was later informed that the cut was to the bone. I was discharged on Monday 26th May in the evening. I can't remember any of the doctors' names. My arm is now in a sling and I have no feeling in my lower arm. I am on painkillers and I am likely to be off work for about two months.

14. On the Friday I was dressed in blue jeans, a cream and red T-shirt and red shoes. John was dressed in blue jeans, a shooting jumper with two dogs on it and a denim jacket. Jackie had boots, ski pants and a beige waistcoat.

Signed: Andrew David Canning   Signature witnessed by: Richard Jones

Statement of Witness

(CJ Act 1967 s 9; MC Act 1980 ss 5A(3)(a) and 5B; MC Rules 1981 r 70)

STATEMENT OF	JOHN FREDERICK ARCHER
Age of Witness (date of birth)	Over 18
Occupation of Witness	Self-employed Roofer

This statement (consisting of 2 pages each signed by me), is true to the best of my knowledge and belief and I make it knowing that, if it is tendered in evidence, I shall be liable to prosecution if I have wilfully stated in it anything which I know to be false or do not believe to be true.

Dated the 29th day of May 2008	Signed: John Archer
Signature Witnessed by:	Richard Jones

1. I am John Archer and I live at the address overleaf. I have been in trouble with the police before but that was some time ago.

2. At 8.10 pm on Friday 23rd May 2008 I went to the Nine Bells Public House in the Oakridge Centre, Colchester. Inside I met Andrew Canning, a friend from the pub. After 10 or 20 minutes, Andrew's girlfriend Jackie arrived. I had a pint of light and Kronenburg and Andrew had a bottle of Budweiser. I'm not sure what Jackie was having.

3. The pub was quiet, and the three of us decided to travel to the Haven Public House at Thorpe. We travelled in Jackie's car and arrived there between 9 and a quarter past. Andy knows the landlord and it was his birthday. We stayed there until about 10 or 10.30 pm. I drank 3 pints of Stella lager, Andy had 3 bottles of Budweiser. Jackie was on soft drinks and she also had a meal.

4. We left and went to the Rabbit Public House at Kirby. I know the landlord, Roger Mates. He used to be a gamekeeper. We stayed there until about half past midnight, talking to the landlord and friends. I drank 2 pints of Lowenbrau and a large whisky and coke. Andy had another couple of bottles of Bud, and a couple of large whiskies. Jackie stayed on soft drinks.

5. We left and got into Jackie's car and we decided to go and get a kebab. I sat in the front passenger seat and Andy was sat in the back. We drove to the kebab van in Shetland Road, Colchester, which is the one that we usually use. We parked up next to the kebab van and myself and Jackie got out. I think Andy was asleep in the back at this stage.

6. I went to the front of the kebab van, and I could see that there were 3 people inside. There was a male, about 18 or 19 years old, smooth skin, standing just right of centre, from whom I was to order. I've seen him working there before. Behind him was a girl, sat on the bar at the back, young looking, wearing an orange T-shirt and jeans. I've seen her working there before as well. The third person was standing to the left, next to the kebab on the spit. He looked about 25ish, with stubble on his face, about the same height as the younger one, and the same build. He was carrying a large knife and was cutting meat.

Signed: John Archer   Signature witnessed by: Richard Jones

CONTINUATION OF STATEMENT OF JOHN ARCHER

7. I stepped up and said, 'I'll have a small chicken kebab'. Jackie asked for a large mixed. I spoke to the younger Greek, who then spoke to his mate by the meat, who then started cutting up the chicken. The younger Greek was carrying what looked like a steak knife, with an orange handle and a twelve-inch blade. The older Greek had a wooden-handled knife with a two-foot blade.

8. After I'd ordered, the younger Greek turned to the girl and spoke to her in a foreign language. I thought that they were talking about me and I said, 'If you've got anything to say about me, say it in English'. With that he said, 'I wasn't fucking talking to you, I was talking to the girl'. He turned to me and brandished his knife in his right hand. He waved it around in front of my face, and I stepped back. He was shouting and abusive and I was abusive back.

9. During the slanging match I noticed Andrew had arrived. By this time the young girl was trying to hold the young Greek back, and she was hysterical. Andrew leant on the van with his left arm, and started pointing at the young Greek who was arguing with me. He said, 'Put the knife down, you're not going to use it, so you might as well put it down'.

10. All of a sudden, I saw the older Greek move forward from the left-hand side, and chop down on to Andrew's left arm with the large knife. I saw it strike just before his elbow, and I saw the flesh open up. It started bleeding almost immediately. I saw Andy punch the van twice with his right fist as I went across to pull him away. We tied some clothing around his arm, and got him in the car, and took him straight up to hospital.

11. That night I was wearing a pair of black jeans, Doc Marten shoes and a blue woollen jumper with two dogs and a man embroidered on the front. I am of stocky build and at the time was sporting a day's growth of stubble.

Signed: John Archer   Signature witnessed by: Richard Jones

Statement of Witness

(CJ Act 1967 s 9; MC Act 1980 ss 5A(3)(a) and 5B; MC Rules 1981 r 70)

STATEMENT OF	JACQUELINE ELIZABETH PERRY
Age of Witness (date of birth)	Over 18
Occupation of Witness	Trainee Hairdresser

This statement, (consisting of 2 pages each signed by me), is true to the best of my knowledge and belief and I make it knowing that, if it is tendered in evidence, I shall be liable to prosecution if I have wilfully stated anything which I know to be false or do not believe to be true.

Dated the 29th day of June 2008   Signed: Jacqueline Perry

Signature Witnessed by: Richard Jones

1. I am Jackie Perry, and I live at the address overleaf. I am the girlfriend of Andrew Canning, and we have a two and half month old son. I have no previous convictions.

2. At 1945 hrs on Friday 23rd May 2008 I drove to the Nine Bells public house, Oakridge, Colchester, where I met Andrew and a friend called John Archer was also there. I was driving a white Nissan Micra, index number Y36 YYT, and I was wearing black ski pants and a cream waistcoat. I had an orange juice. Andrew drank one or two bottles of Budweiser. John had one Kronenberg top whilst I was there.

3. We left at about 8.45 pm and I drove to the Haven public house at Thorpe. We were going to have a meal there, and it was Patrick, the landlord's birthday. I had something to eat, but Andrew and John didn't. Andrew had one or two bottles of lager, I think, and John about the same.

4. We left the Haven about 10 or half 10, and I drove us to the Rabbit public house at Kirby. John said that it was a good pub and he knew the landlord. I played on the fruit machine while Andrew and John spoke to the landlord. I think both had a pint of lager each, followed by a short each. We finally left the Rabbit shortly after midnight and got back into the car. Andrew got into the back. As we travelled back we decided to go for a kebab at the van in Shetland Road, Colchester. I drove into the road and pulled up next to the van.

5. Andy didn't want anything to eat, and he offered me his shirt to put on because it was cold. It was a denim shirt which was mine anyway. He then tried to go to sleep, while myself and John got out. There were 3 people just getting their kebabs in front of us before they walked off. I think there were 2 girls and a boy.

6. There were 3 people in the caravan. The first was about 5'11", clean shaven, about 18 to 20 years old, wearing a T-shirt and jeans. I've seen him working there before. The second male was shorter, about 5'8", about 24 years old. He had stubble, and was wearing a pastel vest. The third was a female, wearing a yellow T-shirt.

7. John ordered a large kebab from the younger man, who then turned to me, and I asked for a large mixed kebab. I was standing on the grass waiting. The younger man then turned to the girl and started talking in a foreign language. They were laughing and looking at John.

John said, 'What was that mate?'

Signed: Jacqueline Perry   Signature witnessed by: Richard Jones

CONTINUATION OF STATEMENT OF JOHN ARCHER

> The younger man replied, 'Private conversation'
>
> John said, 'What are you talking about?
>
> He replied, 'It's none of your business'
>
> The argument then escalated, and both began swearing at each other, and then I saw the man pick up an orange-handled knife with a 14" blade, which he held high in his right hand, and said, 'Just fuck off mate, just leave'.

8. John laughed when he picked the knife up, and I could see that the girl was now crying, seated in the corner. The older man was still stood over by the meat and looked upset. I got scared and went to get Andrew. I banged on the window and he got out. Andrew walked across to the left-hand side of the van, and I stood about six feet behind him, just to the left. John and the younger man were still arguing with each other to the right-hand side of the van. By this time the young girl had got up, and was trying to pull the young man back from behind, and I think he pushed her off. She became more hysterical.

9. Andrew tends to use his arms to talk, and they were on the ledge as he talked to the older man. The older man was now holding a large knife in his hand. It was the long one that they use for cutting the kebab. Andy said, 'You're not going to use that, just put it down'. I don't know who he was talking to. The next thing I could see was blood coming from Andrew's left arm. The older man was just in front of him. I could see a deep gash across Andrew's arm. I grabbed hold of John and pulled him towards Andrew. John grabbed Andrew, and as he pulled away, he punched the van.

10. I took off my shirt, and it was wrapped around Andy's arm. He then went to the back of the car, where I persuaded him to get into the car, and drove him to Colchester Hospital.

Signed: Jacqueline Perry   Signature witnessed by: Richard Jones

Statement of Witness

(CJ Act 1967 s 9; MC Act 1980 ss 5A(3)(a) and 5B; MC Rules 1981 r 70)

STATEMENT OF	P.C. 250 RICHARD JONES
Age of Witness (date of birth)	Over 18
Occupation of Witness	Police Constable

This statement, (consisting of 1 page signed by me), is true to the best of my knowledge and belief and I make it knowing that, if it is tendered in evidence, I shall be liable to prosecution if I have wilfully stated in it anything which I know to be false or do not believe to be true.

Dated the 28th day of May 2008   Signed: Richard Jones

Signature Witnessed by: Thomas Bright

1.   At 1.25 am on Saturday 24th May 2008 I was on uniformed duty in a marked police car with PC 807 Smith, when we responded to an assault allegation, the location being given as the kebab van at Popley Way, Colchester. At 1.32 am we arrived at the kebab van which was in fact in Shetland Road. The shutters on the kebab van were up, and the occupant of the van could be clearly seen in the street lighting and interior lighting of the van.

2.   I went to the front of the van and spoke to one of the occupants, a man I now know to be Alexis Ionides. Also in the kebab van were a female crying, Sophia Ionides, and a second male, Costas Georgiou. The female, who was standing on the right-hand side of the van as I looked at it, by the door, was very upset. Alexis Ionides stood next to her, but nearer to the front counter and he spoke to both myself and PC Smith. The male Costas Georgiou stood on the left side of the van next to the kebab meat. I did not speak to this male, as Alexis Ionides told me that he could not speak English.

3.   Alexis Ionides was very excitable and told me that he had an argument with a customer some 15 minutes earlier. He stated that 3 to 4 males approached the kebab van, and a fat male, quite tall, about 30 years old, with a beard, who was drunk, began telling him not to talk with Sophia Ionides in their own language. Mr Ionides refused to serve the fat male, and as a result says that the fat male punched him on the nose, but did not cause him any injury. He then said that the fat male tried to climb into the kebab van through the serving hatch area.

4.   He then showed a long kebab knife, with which he stated that he cut the fat male's arm. I seized the knife as an exhibit, which I now produce as Exhibit RJ/1. Alexis Ionides stated that he warned the fat male that he would cut him if he didn't withdraw, but he claims that the fat male carried on trying to climb into the van, and ended up cutting his arm with the knife. I saw that there was fresh blood on the top of the counter on the left hand side of the counter, directly in front of where the kebab spit was situated, and where Costas Georgiou stood.

5.   As a result of enquiries that I made, Alexis Ionides and 2 juvenile female witnesses agreed to accompany us back to the Police Station, at Colchester. At the Police Station PC Smith arrested Alexis Ionides on suspicion of s.18 grievous bodily harm at 2 am. Alexis Ionides was booked into the custody area, but continued to behave in an excitable manner, making comments to the effect that he meant to take the fat male's head off with the knife.

Signed: Richard Jones   Signature witnessed by: Thomas Bright

Statement of Witness

(CJ Act 1967 s 9; MC Act 1980 ss 5A(3)(a) and 5B; MC Rules 1981 r 70)

STATEMENT OF	JOHN GOLDSTEIN
Age of Witness (date of birth)	Over 18
Occupation of Witness	General Surgeon, Fellow of the Royal College of Surgeons

This statement, (consisting of 1 page signed by me), is true to the best of my knowledge and belief and I make it knowing that, if it is tendered in evidence, I shall be liable to prosecution if I have wilfully stated anything which I know to be false or do not believe to be true.

Dated the 30th day of May 2008	Signed: John Goldstein
	Signature Witnessed by: Richard Jones

1. At 2 am on Saturday 24th May 2008, Mr Andrew David Canning was admitted to the Casualty Department of the Colchester Hospital. I had to be called out because of the seriousness of the injuries that he had suffered.

2. On examination at 3 am I noticed that he had a deep cut to his left arm just above the elbow. The wound required some 21 stitches to close. A small piece of bone had actually got knocked off the distal humerus and this was replaced back with some periosteal sutures and the wound closed. He was placed in a plaster at this stage to help splint the muscles whilst they healed. He was discharged on the following Monday, 26th May, to be seen in clinic some 4 weeks later.

Signed: John Goldstein   Signature witnessed by: Richard Jones

Statement of Witness

(CJ Act 1967 s 9; MC Act 1980 ss 5A(3)(a) and 5B; MC Rules 1981 r 70)

STATEMENT OF   SCOTT LESLIE

Age of Witness (date of birth)   Over 18

Occupation of Witness   Police Photographer

This statement, (consisting of 1 page signed by me), is true to the best of my knowledge and belief and I make it knowing that, if it is tendered in evidence, I shall be liable to prosecution if I have wilfully stated in it anything which I know to be false or do not believe to be true.

Dated the 26th day of May 2008   Signed: Scott Leslie

                                         Signature Witnessed by: Richard Jones

1. I am a civilian photographer employed by the Essex Constabulary, stationed at Colchester Police Station.

2. At 4 p.m. on Saturday 24th May 2008, I attended Ramsey Close, Colchester where I photographed a kebab trailer. In total I took 2 photographs which I produce as Exhibit SL/1.

Signed: Scott Leslie   Signature witnessed by: Richard Jones

Statement of Witness

(CJ Act 1967 s 9; MC Act 1980 ss 5A(3)(a) and 5B; MC Rules 1981 r 70)

STATEMENT OF   STEPHEN JOHN CAREY

Age of Witness (date of birth)   Over 18

Occupation of Witness   Detective Constable

This statement, (consisting of 1 page signed by me) is true to the best of my knowledge and belief and I make it knowing that, if it is tendered in evidence, I shall be liable to prosecution if I have wilfully stated in it anything which I know to be false or do not believe to be true.

Dated the 6th day of June 2008   Signed: Stephen J. Carey
                                        Signature Witnessed by: Thomas Bright

1. At 12.16 pm on Saturday 24th May 2008, together with DC Dingwall, I interviewed Alexis Ionides at Colchester Police Station in the presence of his solicitor Mr Melville-Walker. The interview was tape recorded and a copy of the tape is produced as Exhibit SJC/1. A summary of the interview is produced as Exhibit SJC/1A. The interview concluded at 1 pm.

2. On Monday 2nd June 2008, Mr Costas Georgiou attended Colchester Police Station by pre-arranged appointment at 12.30 pm. At 12.33 pm. I attended the front desk and arrested and cautioned Mr Georgiou on suspicion of unlawfully wounding Andrew David Canning on 24th May 2008. He made no reply to the caution.

3. At 1.42 pm on 2nd June 2008, together with DC Johnson, I interviewed Costas Georgiou, in the presence of an interpreter, Mrs Dorothy Hove. The interview was tape recorded and I produce a copy of the tape as Exhibit SJC/2 and a summary of that interview as Exhibit SJC/2A. The interview concluded at 2.26 pm.

4. I was present the same day (2nd June 2008) when at 7.49 pm Georgiou was charged with wounding with intent contrary to section 18 Offences Against the Person Act 1861.

Signed: Stephen J. Carey   Signature witnessed by: Thomas Bright

THE QUEEN

Vs

COSTAS GEORGIOU

EXHIBITS

(1) Exhibit SL/1 (photographs)

(2) Exhibit SJC/2A (summary of interview)

(3) Exhibit SJC/2 (interview tape) is available if required

(4) Exhibit RJ/1 (knife) can be viewed by arrangement.

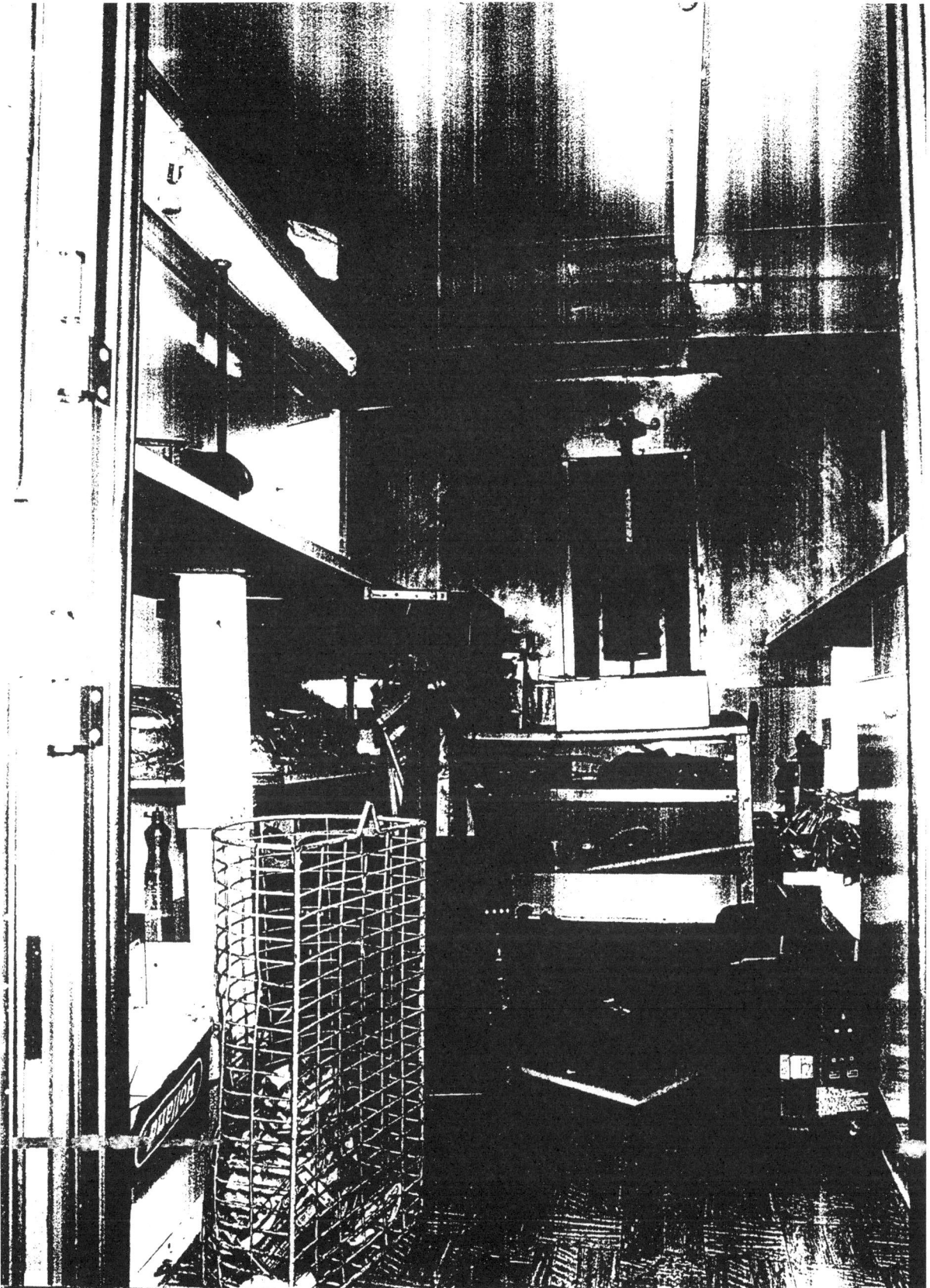

<u>RECORD OF TAPE-RECORDED INTERVIEW</u>

Person Interviewed:	Costas Georgiou
Place of Interview:	Colchester Police Station
Date of Interview:	2/6/08 Time commenced: 1.42 pm Time concluded: 2.26 pm
Interviewing Officers	DC Carey DC Johnson
Other Persons Present	Mrs Dorothy Hove (Translator)

PERSON SPEAKING	TEXT
	Introduction and caution. Rights explained.
	Mr Georgiou explained that on the night in question he was working in the kebab van in Shetland Road, Colchester. They had opened up for business at approximately 8 pm. He was cutting the kebabs and cooking chickens and was assisted by Alexis Ionides' sister-in-law, Mrs Sophia Ionides. As he speaks no English, he was not able to take orders from the customers and this was done by Alexis. He explained that there were 3 knives in the kebab van on the night in question, namely a salad knife, a knife with which to cut the chickens and the kebab knife.
DC Carey	Right, at about 1 o'clock in the morning, a large man who's been described as having a beard but in fact has got stubble came to the kebab van and ordered two kebabs. Does he remember that?
Translator	He remembers being asked by Alexis to prepare 2 kebabs and then an argument developing between Alexis and this man who was enormous over Alexis speaking to Sophia in Greek. He remembers this man punching Alexis on the nose and then Alexis picking up the salad knife and threatening the man with it.
DC Carey	And then what happened?
Translator	The girl that the fat man was with ran and got another man from the car. That man came up to the van and he was angry. During that time he was holding the knife that he uses to cut the chickens and the man thumped the back window of the van and he thumped the glass and he tried to take the knife away from him.
DC Carey	And what did Alexis do at this point?
Translator	Alexis picked up the kebab knife which was by the spit and then he didn't actually see the cutting taking place, but he knew that the man had been cut. The man continued to be violent and aggressive even after he was cut.
DC Carey	How did Ionides manage to get past you in the small confines of the kebab van to pick up the kebab knife?
Translator	He doesn't know how he managed it but he just did. The man had been holding on to his arm in which he was holding the chicken knife and he had just broken free of the man's grip when Alexis picked up the kebab knife.
	The interview concluded at 2.26 pm.

CROWN PROSECUTION SERVICE

UNUSED MATERIAL DISCLOSED UNDER

Section 3 Criminal Procedure and Investigations Act 1996

THE QUEEN

V

COSTAS GEORGIOU

(1)   Statement Tracey Collins

(2)   Exhibit SJC/1A—Interview with Alexis Ionides

(3)   Exhibit SJC/1 (interview tape) is available if required

Statement of Witness

(CJ Act 1967 s 9; MC Act 1980 ss 5A(3)(a) and 5B; MC Rules 1981 r 70)

STATEMENT OF	TRACEY COLLINS
Age of Witness (date of birth)	25th January 1991
Occupation of Witness	Schoolgirl

This statement, (consisting of 1 page signed by me) is true to the best of my knowledge and belief and I make it knowing that, if it is tendered in evidence, I shall be liable to prosecution if I have wilfully stated in it anything which I know to be false or do not believe to be true.

Dated the 30th day of May 2008   Signed: Tracey Collins
                                        Signature Witnessed by: Richard Jones

1. I am the above named person. At approximately 1 am on Saturday 24th May 2008 I was with my friends Kelly Longyear and Aaron Constantine at the kebab van in Shetland Road, Colchester.

2. I noticed behind me in the queue for kebabs a white male, approximately mid to late thirties. He was of very big build and at least 6′ tall. He had a beard and dark hair. My friend Kelly spoke to this man briefly and offered him a piece of her kebab, but the male refused.

3. Inside the kebab van was a man I know as 'Smiles' who is of Greek appearance. Smiles was putting the meat into the kebabs and taking orders from the customers. There was also another Greek male inside the kebab van who is known as 'Rambo', and a Greek woman.

4. We were served our kebabs and left the van and walked up Popley Way towards the local infants' school. Aaron and I were together but my friend Kelly had to run back to the van as she had left her purse on the serving counter.

5. I heard shouting and looked around to see a man punching and kicking the screen of the kebab van and trying to get inside. I had not seen this man before. He was probably in his early 20s, blond hair, wearing a white top with jeans. He was shouting, 'C'mon then, I'll give you a fight, I'll have you'. Kelly was already within the vicinity of the van as myself and Aaron started walking back towards it. The large man who was originally behind me in the queue was trying to rock the van.

6. I then saw 'Smiles' come out from the back of the kebab van carrying a long knife with about a 2″ blade. The knife looked to be the same one that they use to slice the meat for the doner kebabs.

7. I saw the white man with the blond hair, who had been banging on the van, holding his right arm to his body and he was bent over. He was being helped by the man who was originally behind us in the queue and a woman who was with them. At the time we were queuing for our kebabs, this woman was sat in a car near the van.

Signed: Tracey Collins   Signature witnessed by: Richard Jones

<u>RECORD OF TAPE-RECORDED INTERVIEW</u>

Person Interviewed:	Alexis Ionides
Place of Interview:	Colchester Police Station
Date of Interview:	24/5/08 Time commenced: 12.16 pm Time concluded: 1 pm
Interviewing Officers	DC Carey
Other Persons Present:	David Melville-Walker (Solicitor)
	DC Dingwall

PERSON SPEAKING	TEXT
	Mr Ionides recounted how they had just served two regular customers (2 teenage girls) when an enormous man came up to the van together with a female and placed an order. He described how the argument started and how the female went and got another male with blond hair who came and remonstrated with him. He described how violent and aggressive they were and how scared they all were inside the van, in particular his sister in-law, Sophia Ionides. He arrived at the point where the blond-haired male was holding on to Georgiou's arm with his left arm and Georgiou in turn was holding on to the knife that they use to cut the chickens.
DC Carey	Where were you at this point and what knife did you have in your hand?
Ionides	I was on the left-hand side of the van facing out and I had the salad knife in my hand.
DC Carey	Then what did you do?
Ionides	I rushed over to where the kebab spit is and picked up the big kebab knife. I told the blond man to let go but he would not. I then rested the knife on his left arm and he continued to pull at my friend's arm and therefore was cut. He only let go of Costas's arm when his friends told him that he was bleeding.
DC Carey	So you cut him with the big kebab knife?
Ionides	Yes, but it was in self-defence.
	General discussion then ensued with regard to reasonableness and self-defence and the interview concluded at 1 pm.

COSTAS GEORGIOU

PROOF OF EVIDENCE

1. I, Costas Georgiou (date of birth 12th August 1983) of 27 White Hart Lane, Tottenham, London N15, deny the charge of wounding with intent which has been laid against me.

2. The incident in question took place in the early hours of the morning of Saturday 24th May 2008. That evening, I had been assisting my cousin Alexis Ionides in his kebab van in Colchester.

3. At approximately 1 am, we had just finished serving 2 young girls and a boy when an enormous man with a beard came up to the van and placed an order. He was accompanied by a young woman.

4. He started an argument with Alexis because (so I was later told) he objected to Alexis speaking to Sophia (his sister-in-law) in Greek. The argument escalated with the man raising his voice and banging and thumping the kebab van. After he'd punched Alexis on the nose, Alexis picked up the salad knife and threatened the fat man with it saying, 'Go away or else I will cut you'.

5. At this stage, the woman who the fat man was with went to their car and fetched a blond-haired man who came out and leant on my side of the van (the right-hand side of the van looking out). He was being just as aggressive as the fat man, and fearing for my safety, I picked up the chicken knife in my right hand and gestured to the blond man to go away.

6. The blond man then grabbed hold of my arm with his left hand, and seeing this, Alexis came behind me and picked up the big kebab knife that was to my right. I'd managed to free myself from this man's grip by the time that Alexis had picked up the kebab knife. I did not actually see the man being cut but I did see him holding his arm afterwards.

7. I have no previous convictions either in this country or in Greece.

8. I am very concerned to avoid a conviction as I have recently become engaged to a Greek girl from a very respectable family who might not consider me a suitable fiancé if I were convicted.

Signed: Costas Georgiou

Date 11th September 2008

14.2.1   C.A.P. in action

Notes for advice on evidence

STAGE 1   THE CONTEXT OF THE CASE

(1)   THE STAGE OF THE PROCEEDINGS

    (a)   What steps have been taken?

        Bail application 11.6.08

        Defendant on conditional bail—residence with D. Ionides

        28.7.08: 1st appearance—Chelmsford Crown Court

        Charge—Offences against the Person Act 1861, s 18

        Primary Prosecution disclosure 10.9.08

    (b)   Your Instructions: to draft defence statement and to advise on further steps before trial.

    (c)   Objectives: Meet defence disclosure obligations, evaluate strength of defence case and identify any further evidence necessary.

(2)   COLLECTING THE FACTS

    (a)   Dramatis personae

Costas Georgious (CG)	The Defendant, inside the kebab van on 24.5.08
Alexis Ionides (AI)	Cousin of Defendant, inside van on 24.5.08, arrested on 24.5.08
Sophia Ionides (SI)	Sister-in-law of AI, inside van on 24.5.08
Andrew Canning (AC)	Injured in incident
John Archer (JA)	Friend of AC and with him when AC injured
Jackie Perry (JP)	Girlfriend of AC and mother of his child. Drove AC and JA to van
Tracy Collins (TC)	Schoolgirl, gave witness statement to police
Kelly Longyear (KL)	Friend of TC, with her at kebab van on 24.5.08
Aaron Constantine (AaC)	Friend of TC, with her at kebab van
John Goldstein (JG)	Doctor who treated AC on 24.5.08
Richard Jones (RJ)	PC attended incident on 24.5.08 and arrested AI
Scott Leslie (SL)	Police photographer
Stephen Carey (SC)	DC who interviewed AI, and arrested and interviewed CG

(3)   AGREED AND DISPUTED FACTS

Prosecution Version	Witness	Defendant's Version	Witness	Notes/Queries
AC, JP, JA visited 3 pubs on evening of 23.5.08. Left Rabbit public house by car approx 12.00 midnight and JP drove them to Shetland Rd to get kebabs	AC			Witnesses vary re times and amount drunk.
AC asleep in back of car.	AC			
JP parked car next to kebab van. JP and JA got out.	JA JP			TC says JP did not get out of car with JA.
3 people getting kebabs in front of JP and JA. 2 girls 1 boy.	JP	TC, KL and AaC in front of big man in queue for kebab. Served two teenage girls.	TC AI	Why no statement from KL or AaC?

Prosecution Version	Witness	Defendant's Version	Witness	Notes/Queries
JA went to front of van 3 people in van. Male, 18, to right of centre, girl at back, male on left next to kebab spit about 25, stubble, cutting meat with large knife.	JA	CG was working in the kebab van on 24.5.08, cutting kebabs and cooking chickens, assisted by AI and SI. AI took orders as CG speaks no English.	CG	JA only one to describe two men as of same height and build.
		Smiles was taking the orders, there was another Greek male in the van known as Rambo and a Greek woman.	TC	It seems that Smiles is AI, CG is Rambo?
		3 knives in van—salad knife, chicken knife and kebab knife.	CG	Size of each knife?
JA ordered a chicken kebab from the younger male, older male started to cut up the chicken.	JA	Enormous man with girl came up to van and placed order.	AI	
		CG asked to prepare two kebabs.	CG	
The younger male was holding an orange-handled knife. The older Greek had a wooden-handled knife with a two-foot blade.	JA			Salad/ chicken/ kebab
Young Greek spoke to girl in Greek. An argument ensued between the younger male and JA.	JA JP	Argument between enormous man and AI about speaking Greek. Fat male told AI not to speak in Greek to girlfriend. AI refused to serve him.	CG RJ	
		The argument escalated with the man raising his voice and banging and thumping on the van.	CG	Any damage to van?
		Enormous man punched AI on nose.	CG RJ	
Younger man brandished knife in right hand at JA.	JA JP	AI picked up salad knife and threatened man with it, saying, 'Go away or else I will cut you'.	CG CG	
JP went to get AC	JP	Fat male tried to climb into van through serving hatch.	RJ	
		AI warned fat man that he would cut him if he didn't withdraw. Fat man continued to try to climb into van.	RJ	
AC woken by JP. She said, 'The geezer's threatening John with a knife'. AC walked up to van.	AC	Girl with fat man ran and got other man from the car. He came up to van, he was angry.	CG	
During slanging match AC arrived.	JA			
Male 5' 10", muscular build, 16, waving orange-handled 12" bladed knife shouting at JA saying, 'I'm going to cut you'	AC			
Greek girl trying to pull young male from front of van by arms.	AC FA			Why no statement from SI?
Older Greek, 25, to left of centre about 5' 9" wiry, stubble.	AC	CG holding chicken knife.	CG	

Prosecution Version	Witness	Defendant's Version	Witness	Notes/Queries
AC went to front of van, left of centre.	AC	Blond-haired man came and leant on my side of the van (right side looking out). CG picked up chicken knife and gestured to man to go away.	CG	
AC leant his left arm on the van counter and spoke to the young man to get him to put down the knife.	AC JA	Man was very angry and thumped on back window and on glass.	CG	
The older man was holding a large knife in his hand, it was the long one that they use for cutting the kebab.	JP			
		Heard shouting, looked around and saw man punching and kicking the screen of the van and trying to get inside. He had blond hair. He shouted 'C'mon then, I'll give you a fight' etc.	TC	
		The large man who had originally been behind me in the queue was trying to rock the van.	TC	
The older man moved forward carrying knife with 16" blade used for cutting the meat to AC's left	AC	Man tried to get chicken knife away from CG and held on to his arm. CG managed to break away from man's grip.	CG AI CG	Dispute between CG & AI as to when CG freed.
AC felt pressure on arm above elbow.		AI picked up kebab knife from near spit.		
		Told man to let go. Smiles came out from the back of the van carrying a knife with a 22"-blade like the ones they use to slice the kebabs.	CG AI TC	How did AI get behind CG to pick up kebab knife?
		AI rested knife on man's left arm. Man continued to pull on CG's arm and was cut. Man did not let go until he was told he was bleeding	AI	
Older Greek chopped down on to AC's left arm with large knife. Flesh opened up. Started to bleed.	JA	AI cut fat man's arm with long kebab knife. Ex RJ/1.	RJ	
AC tried to grab him with left hand but he pulled back.	AC			
The older man was just in front of AC.	JP			
AC pulled away from the van.	AC JA			
AC punched the van with his right fist as he was pulled away by JA.	AC	Man continued to be aggressive even after cut.	SJCA	Dispute about how often van punched?
AC taken to hospital.	AC			
AC treated in hospital. Piece of bone which had been knocked off distal humerus replaced, 21 stitches required to close deep cut to left arm just above elbow, arm put in plaster.				How hard a blow necessary to chip bone?

Prosecution Version	Witness	Defendant's Version	Witness	Notes/Queries
Police called to van, arrived about 1.32 a.m.	RJ			
Kebab knife seized as Ex RJ/1.	RJ			Any fingerprints?
Fresh blood on top of counter on left in front of kebab spit	RJ			
RJ spoke to AI.	RJ			
AI interviewed by police on 24.5.08	SJC			
Photographs taken of kebab trailer.	SL			
CG interviewed by police on 2.6.08.	SJC			

(4)   LEGAL FRAMEWORK

(i)   The Offence (See **Table 11.5.**)

(ii)   Criminal Procedure and Investigations Act 1996 (as amended by Criminal Justice Act 2003)

Section 3	Primary prosecution disclosure of previously undisclosed material which might undermine the case for the prosecution or support the accused's defence.
Section 5	Defence disclosure within 14 days of primary prosecution disclosure by service of written defence statement setting out nature of defence and indicating the matters on which Defendant takes issue with the prosecution and the reasons why.
Section 7 A	Continuing duty of prosecutor to disclose.
Section 8	Defence can apply to court for disclosure of undisclosed material which ought to have seen disclosed.

STAGE 2 ANALYSIS OF ISSUES AND EVIDENCE

(a)   The Issues

(1)   THE LEGAL AND FACTUAL ISSUES

(i)   Identification—Whether it was the Defendant who cut AC?

(ii)   Self-defence—Whether, if it was the Defendant who cut AC, he acted in self-defence?

The witnesses describe a very confused situation—there are a number of discrepancies, e.g., JP's whereabouts before and during the incident. Which knife was held by whom? See above at Stage 1(3). The fact that there are discrepancies in the prosecution evidence is of positive benefit to the Defence.

(2)   THE POTENTIAL THEORY

It was Alexis Ionides, acting in self-defence, not the Defendant who cut Andrew Canning who had been acting in a violent and threatening manner towards those in the kebab van in what was a very confusing situation.

(3)   GAPS AND AMBIGUITIES

See table at Stage 1(3) above.

No statement from Sophia Ionides, Kelly Longyear, Aaron Constantine. Only prosecution statements from Alexis Ionides and Tracey Collins. No forensic statement on condition of van or examination of knife Exhibit RJ/1.

(b)   The Evidence

(1)   STRENGTHS AND WEAKNESSES OF CASE

(i)   Strength of identification evidence depends on credibility of prosecution witnesses—obvious weaknesses in discrepancies, amount of alcohol consumed, previous convictions. (Check on previous convictions of defence witnesses.) Defence version might be strengthened by statements from other eye witnesses, from site visit to van to view width of van, from viewing knives. Do police have any further evidence pointing to identification, e.g., comments of Alexis Ionides/Defendant recorded on custody records?

(ii)   Strong evidence of self-defence—weakness appears to be seriousness of injury and original behaviour of Alexis Ionides. Opinion of Doctor might be sought and proof of evidence from Alexis and Sophia Ionides.

STAGE 3 PRESENTATION

(1)   CHOSEN THEORY
See above at Stage 2(a)(2).

(2)   CARRYING OUT INSTRUCTIONS

(i)   Draft the Defence Statement
(See General Council of the Bar: The Preparation of Defence Case Statements: Guidance on the duties of Counsel.)
Identify nature of defence, indicate matters on which defence take issue with reasons, provide name, address and d.o.b. of each witness.

(ii)   Plan and Write the Advice on Evidence
Identify and explain what further evidence required.
(See **14.3** for completed Advice on Evidence and Defence Statement.)

14.3 Brief for hearing

IN THE CROWN COURT, CHELMSFORD   T08/0656

THE QUEEN

V

COSTAS GEORGIOU

FURTHER INSTRUCTIONS TO COUNSEL

Further to Counsel's written advice, a copy of which is enclosed, together with the Defence Statement, Counsel will also please find enclosed the following documents namely:

(a) Proof of evidence from Sophia Ionides.

(b) Proof of evidence from Alexis Ionides.

(c) Proof of evidence from Aaron Constantine

(d) Previous convictions of Andrew Canning, John Archer, and Tracey Collins. [Reproduced on one page for convenience.]

With regard to the other items requested by Counsel those Instructing can state the following:

(a) Full statement from Tracey Collins. She was contacted by those Instructing but she has nothing further to add to her original statement. Counsel will no doubt take note of her hitherto undisclosed previous conviction.

(b) Statement from Kelly Longyear. Despite exhaustive efforts by those Instructing it has not been possible to trace this witness. It would appear that she left her last address several months ago to travel around Australia and is not contactable in that country.

(c) Viewing of knives. Counsel will no doubt recall the recent viewing of these items. The knives were much as the witnesses have described, the lengths of the salad, chicken and kebab knives being 12", 16" and 24" respectively. The salad knife has an orange handle and both the chicken and kebab knives have wooden handles.

(d) Scientific report on knife. This confirmed that it was in fact the kebab knife which cut Mr Canning on the night in question. The prosecution have informed those Instructing that the report will be included in the prosecution continuing disclosure.

(e) Forensic report on van. Unfortunately, no such report was carried out by Essex Police, although Counsel will no doubt take note of the fact that fresh blood was seen on the kebab van counter by PC Jones.

(f) Expert medical evidence of force needed for injury. Those Instructing discussed this matter with Mr Goldstein and he felt unable to give a conclusive opinion on the subject.

(g) Interview tapes. Those Instructing have requested the tapes and these will be forwarded to Counsel as soon as they are received. We would be grateful if Counsel could inform those Instructing when she has listened to them as to whether the transcript is a fair and accurate summary of same.

(h) Following the recent site visit, the sketch plan is not yet completed. However, the inside of the van is 3′ in width and 10′ in length. The width of the work surfaces inside the van is 18″.

Counsel is now instructed to attend the Plea and Directions Hearing on 17th October 2008, prepare this matter for trial and use her best endeavours to secure an Acquittal at the forthcoming Hearing due to start on 18th November next.

Brown Dingle & Slattery
27 New Buildings
Chelmsford, Essex.

10th October 2008

IN THE CROWN COURT, CHELMSFORD   T08/0656

THE QUEEN

V

COSTAS GEORGIOU

ADVICE ON EVIDENCE

---

1. Mr Georgiou currently stands indicted for an offence that he on the 24th May 2008 unlawfully wounded a Mr Andrew David Canning with intent to do him grievous bodily harm. I would advise that the following steps are taken in readiness for the forthcoming trial on the basis that Mr Georgiou is intending to plead Not Guilty.

2. Mr Georgiou maintains that he was not the person who wounded Mr Canning on the night in question. Indeed, this version of events is supported by his cousin, Mr Alexis Ionides, who has already confessed to the Police that he was the person who carried out the wounding. Although we have the transcript of interview to hand, it would appear that no proof of evidence has been taken from this person and I would therefore advise that this be done as soon as possible.

3. Also in the kebab van on the evening in question was Mr Ionides' sister-in-law, Sophia. It is hoped that she would support our client's version of events and therefore a proof of evidence should be obtained from her. I note that Tracey Collins's statement has been disclosed by the prosecution as Unused Material. Although she does not see exactly what happened, her evidence, in my opinion, is useful in demonstrating the unacceptable manner in which Mr Canning and Mr Archer behaved, which might in turn assist any suggestion of self-defence that we make at the trial. She should therefore be contacted, asked if she wishes to add anything further to the statement that she made to the Police, and then requested to attend court and give evidence at the trial.

4. Miss Collins was with two friends on the evening in question, namely Kelly Longyear and Aaron Constantine. I am particularly interested in any evidence that Kelly Longyear might be able to give as it would appear that she was much closer to the kebab van than her friends when the wounding actually took place. Having said that, I feel that both of them should be contacted and proofs of evidence obtained.

5. I note that only one of the prosecution witnesses, namely John Archer, allegedly saw our client wounding Mr Canning. Even if the witnesses from whom I have requested proofs of evidence do not support either the defence or the prosecution version of events, they can be used to depict what I am sure was a fairly chaotic situation. The obvious question for Mr Archer would then be, 'How can you be sure that it was Mr Georgiou who wielded the knife on Mr Canning?'

6. I am sure that it would be of assistance in re-constructing the events of 24th May last, if a site view of the kebab van could be arranged. At the same time we could also take exact measurements of the inside of the van and draw up a floor plan. I am particularly concerned with regard to the question as to how Mr Ionides managed to squeeze past Mr Georgiou in order to pick up the kebab knife. I would therefore be grateful if those Instructing could liaise with my Clerk to arrange a mutually convenient date and time for the visit.

7.   The Police currently have in their possession Exhibit RJ/1, the kebab knife. If possible, I would like to have sight of this prior to the trial. There were also apparently two other knives in use on the evening in question, namely the chicken knife and the salad knife. As these were not seized as exhibits, I presume that they are still in the possession of the Ionides family. Perhaps these could be shown to me at the same time as the site view.

8.   I note that PC Jones observed fresh blood on the counter of the kebab van when he was called to the scene. Can enquiries be made of the Police as to whether a forensic examination was carried out on the van? At the same time they can perhaps be asked whether a similar examination was carried out on the knife.

9.   There can be little doubt that the injury inflicted on Mr Canning was a serious one, it requiring some 21 stitches. Alexis Ionides states that the wound was inflicted by him resting the kebab knife on Mr Canning's left arm. Mr Archer states that the injury was inflicted by a chopping movement. The surgeon, Mr Goldstein, might be able to shed some light on whether or not the wound is consistent with either or both of the above versions.

10.   It would appear from their statements that both Andrew Canning and John Archer have previous convictions. Exact details of these should be requested from the Police. Furthermore, all the witnesses from whom I have requested statements should be asked whether or not they have previous convictions.

11.   Could those Instructing ask formally for the interview tapes of Mr Georgiou and Mr Ionides to be forwarded to the Defence. We shall also require the custody records of Mr Georgiou and the Computer Aided Dispatch message (CAD) and Crime Report (CRIS) dealing with the incident and I have included a request for these in the Defence Statement. If Prosecution do not serve these under their continuing duty I shall make a formal request for same at the forthcoming Plea and Directions Hearing under s 7A of the Criminal Procedure and Investigations Act 1996.

12.   Whilst I have not taken specific instructions from Mr Georgiou with regard to the contents of his Defence Statement, which as those Instructing are no doubt aware, needs to be served on the Prosecution no later than 24th September 2008, I feel that as I have had conduct of this case throughout, I am well acquainted with the nature of our client's defence. I have therefore prepared a draft Defence Statement pursuant to s 5 of the Criminal Procedure and Investigations Act 1996, which should be shown to the client for his approval prior to its service on the Crown Prosecution Service.

13.   In summary, therefore, the following steps need to be taken in preparation for the forthcoming trial namely:

(a) Proofs of evidence to be obtained from:

(i)   Alexis Ionides,

(ii) Sophia Ionides,

(iii) Tracey Collins,

(iv) Kelly Longyear,

(v)   Aaron Constantine.

(b) Site view of kebab van to be arranged.

(c) Floor plan of kebab van, showing exact measurements, to be drawn.

(d) Viewing of exhibit RJ/1 and other 2 knives in use on evening in question to be arranged.

(e) Enquiries to be made as to whether a forensic report was prepared on the kebab van and also Exhibit RJ/1.

(f) If possible, expert medical evidence on the force required to inflict the injury, to be obtained. Note that under s 6D CPIA 1996 (as amended) we must provide name and address of any expert witness we instruct, whether or not we call them.

(g) Defence statement to be served on Prosecution.

14. Please do not hesitate to contact me if you have any queries on this matter.

Nicola Grey   19th September 2008

IN THE CROWN COURT, CHELMSFORD   T08/0656

THE QUEEN

V

COSTAS GEORGIOU

DEFENCE STATEMENT

PURSUANT TO s 5 CPIA 1996

---

1. The Defendant admits that he was working at a kebab van in Shetland Road, Colchester during the early hours of the morning of 24th May 2008.

2. The Defendant denies inflicting any injury on the alleged victim, Andrew David Canning. He asserts that any injuries caused to the victim were as a result of actions taken in self-defence by his cousin, Alexis Ionides.

3. It is submitted that the above case disclosed by the Defendant might reasonably be assisted by the following documents and a formal request is made for same:

    (a) Incident Report Book of PC 250 Richard Jones.

    (b) Custody record relating to the Defendant.

    (c) CAD message.

    (d) CRIS report.

4. The Defendant intends to call the following witnesses to give evidence at trial:
    Sophia Ionides; 51, Piggott Close, Colchester CO10 0AU; 10/02/1987.
    Alexis Ionides: 51, Piggott Close, Colchester, CO10 0AU; 26/03/1987.
    Aaron Constantine: 63, Hillside Drive, Colchester CO6 2YP; 16/10/1987.
    Tracey Collins: 17, Starling Walk, Colchester CO4 3NX; 25/01/1991.

5. This statement has been prepared on the basis of evidence supplied by the Prosecution to date and the Defendant reserves the right to add to or amend his Defence at trial, in the light of any further evidence that might be served by the Crown.

Dated 24th September 2008

Brown Dingle & Slattery,
27 New Buildings,
Chelmsford, Essex.

SOPHIA IONIDES

PROOF OF EVIDENCE

I am Sophia Ionides (date of birth 10th February 1987) and I live at 51 Piggott Close, Colchester CO10 OAU. I have no previous convictions.

On Friday 24th May 2008 I was assisting my husband's brother Alexis Ionides serve customers at our kebab van which was that evening parked at Shetland Road, Colchester. Also present in the van that evening was my husband's cousin, Costas Georgiou.

We opened up for business at approximately 8 pm and everything went smoothly until about 1 am when the van was approached by a big fat man in his late twenties, early thirties, who appeared to be growing a beard. He was accompanied by a girl who I would say was in her early twenties.

After they had placed their order, Alexis turned round to me and said in Greek words to the effect that the gentleman who had just ordered was a bit of a drunken slob. The fat gentleman appeared to take offence at this although I am almost certain that he did not understand what Alexis had said. An argument then developed between Alexis and the fat man. The girl who was with the fat man then went and got a third man who also joined in the argument in support of the big fat man.

I became quite hysterical whilst all this was occurring and for a lot of the time I had my face buried in my hands. I therefore cannot say who cut the arm of the man who joined the argument later on. I saw both Costas and Alexis holding knives whilst the fight was in progress. I can state that the fat man and his friend were both swearing, rocking the van and banging the perspex window whilst the argument was in progress.

Signed: Sophia Ionides

Date: 9th October 2008

ALEXIS IONIDES

PROOF OF EVIDENCE

I am Alexis Ionides (date of birth 26th March 1987) and I live at 51 Piggott Close, Colchester CO10 0AU. I have no previous convictions.

I confirm that all that I said in my interview of 24th May 2008 was true and accurate to the best of my knowledge and belief. In particular, I was the person who cut Mr Canning by means of the kebab knife. I did this by resting it on Mr Canning's left arm when he would not let go of my cousin Costas's right arm. I only did this in self-defence. At the time I felt that I had no other option given the behaviour of Mr Canning and his friend Mr Archer.

I would further add that Mr Archer punched me in the nose fairly soon after he started to argue with me.

Signed: Alexis Ionides

Date: 9th October 2008

AARON CONSTANTINE

PROOF OF EVIDENCE

I am Aaron Constantine (date of birth 16th October 1987) and I live at 63 Hillside Drive, Colchester CO6 2YP. I have no previous convictions.

On Friday 23rd May 2008 I, together with my friends Tracey Collins and Kelly Longyear, had been to the Green Man public house and then on to a nightclub. We decided to buy a kebab on the way home. The time must have been approximately 1 a.m. when we ordered our food. I remember that there was a fat man and a woman behind us in the queue although I didn't take much notice of them at the time.

When we were about 50 yards away from the van, I remember hearing a lot of screaming, shouting and banging. I turned around to see the fat man who had been behind us in the queue rocking the van backwards and forwards. I also saw another man whom I'd not seen before banging the perspex windows on the kebab van with his fists. I don't remember seeing any of the Greek occupants of the van holding knives. This might have been due to the fact that my attention was primarily focused on the men outside the van.

On seeing what was happening, we started walking back towards the van. However, by the time that we got there, the people who had caused the disturbance had driven off.

Signed: Aaron Constantine

Date: 10th October 2008

CRO 08/633421

PREVIOUS CONVICTIONS OF
ANDREW DAVID CANNING

DATE	COURT	OFFENCE	SENTENCE
9th June 2007	Colchester Magistrates	Drunk and Disorderly	Bound Over to Keep the Peace—£100 for 12 months
29th February 2008	Colchester Magistrates	Section 5 POA 1986	Fine: £100 Costs: £50

CRO 02/492178

PREVIOUS CONVICTIONS
OF JOHN FREDERICK ARCHER

DATE	COURT	OFFENCE	SENTENCE
1st February 2002	Winchester Crown Court	S.2 POA 1986	CSO 240 hours

CRO 07/305125

PREVIOUS CONVICTIONS OF
TRACEY BERNADETTE COLLINS

DATE	COURT	OFFENCE	SENTENCE
15th November 2007	Colchester Magistrates	Theft (shoplifting)	Fine: £50 Costs: £25

14.3.1   C.A.P. in action

Notes for plea and directions hearing and for trial

STAGE 1   THE CONTEXT OF THE CASE

(1)   STAGE OF PROCEEDINGS

(a)   What steps have been taken?

Case sent to Crown Court.

Defence disclosure made. Prosecution disclosure made.

Defence Witness statements taken from SI and AaC and AI.

(b)   Your Instructions

(i)   To appear at the PDH on 17.10.08.

(ii)   To prepare for trial on 18.11.08.

(c)   Objectives

(i)   Of the Plea and Directions Hearing

Agree and settle plea, issues in case, prosecution witnesses required, number of Defence witnesses, length of trial, further information required, to be inserted on standard form. *(Practice Direction (Criminal Proceedings: Consolidation)* [2002] 1 WLR 2870, Para 41)

(ii)   Of trial

Represent Defendant on Not Guilty Plea, examine and cross-examine witnesses.

(2)   COLLECTING THE FACTS

Further information obtained by Instructing Solicitors does not alter significantly the previous position. However, note previous conviction of Tracey Collins, difference in size of chicken and kebab knives (although both have wooden handles) and narrowness of van.

(3)   AGREED/DISPUTED FACTS

Table in **14.2.1** shows witnesses who can give evidence on issues of identity and self-defence.

The new information in statements of SI, AI and AaC, obtained by Instructing Solicitors, needs to be included in that analysis but although useful it is not decisive in any way.

(4)   LEGAL FRAMEWORK

Elements of offence. Prosecution must prove that:

Andrew Canning was wounded.

It was Costas Georgiou who wounded him.

CG intended when he wounded him to inflict really serious harm.

The wounding was unlawful, e.g., not inflicted in self-defence.

Burden of proof. On Prosecution throughout but note Prosecution do not have to prove absence of self-defence unless the possibility of self-defence has been raised; but note Defence Statement.

Standard of proof. Beyond reasonable doubt.

(See **14.3** for completed Advice on Evidence and Defence Statement.)

Before trial serve updated defence statement (or written statement that no changes) (CPIA s 6B).

STAGE 2   ANALYSIS OF ISSUES AND EVIDENCE
(a) The Issues

(1)   LEGAL AND FACTUAL ISSUES
See Defence Statement.

(a) Identity of the person who cut AC. Was it CG or AI?

(b) There is evidence of violence in support of self-defence. Also the Defence might want to raise sufficient possibility of this to necessitate the Judge leaving the matter to the jury but note CPIA 1996, s 11.

(c) *Mens rea* not in issue as such. Defendant denies wounding. If issue of identity decided in Prosecution's favour, i.e., on JA's evidence, his statement of nature of blow, i.e., a chop, sufficient for jury to infer intent.

(d) No dispute that AC wounded in incident.

(2)   GAPS AND AMBIGUITIES

Further information required—forensic report, interview tapes, custody record, computer aided dispatch (CAD) message/crime report.

(b)   The Evidence

(1)   STRENGTHS AND WEAKNESSES OF CASE

A.   Weaknesses of Prosecution case

The Prosecution case relies on the evidence of AC, JA and JP. Their evidence can be undermined by cross-examination of:

(a)   AC, JA, and JP on how much AC and JA drank between 8.00 and midnight, to show that JA and AC's evidence on detail is not reliable.

(b)   AC and JA on previous convictions to show lack of credibility.

(c)   JP on accuracy of statement—delay in joining JA in queue, left to get AC, 6 feet behind AC at time of wounding, and on credibility, relationship with AC (and mother of his child) has motive to withhold full story.

(d)   AC as to behaviour—trying to get into van, punching, kicking van before wounding to show clear vision of what happened unlikely.

(e)   JA about rocking van—how could he have seen what was happening clearly?

(f)   JA about possible confusion between two Greeks, both same build and height.

(g)   AC, JA and JC about knives to show possible confusion—AC sees CG holding 16" knife—chicken not kebab?

(h)   Establish violence and confusion of incident from all witnesses.

B.   Strength of Defence case

Independent witnesses support Defence story of attack on van. TC supports D's version that it was AI who was holding the kebab knife.

C.   Weaknesses of Defence case

(a)   AI's initial story that it was fat man he cut (ie, JA not AC).

(b)   TC was not close to van (50 yards away according to AaC). Statement does not give description of 'Smiles' or 'Rambo' identifying AI clearly as person holding the kebab knife.

(c)   TC has previous conviction for offence of dishonesty.

(d)   Van very narrow. (But if CG pulled forward by AC, might not be difficult for AI to get behind, when CG breaks away and AI comes forward. AC who has not seen AI's movement thinks it is CG.)

(e)   SI's statement that AI made derogatory remark might, in minds of jury, justify to some extent behaviour of AC and JA.

(f)   Need for interpreter might affect jury's perception of CG as witness.

STAGE 3   PRESENTATION OF THE CASE

(1)   CHOSEN THEORY

CG and young relatives in van in early hours of 24.5.08. Argument developed between large male customer (JA) and AI. CG not involved (English poor). AI tried to get JA to leave. JA became violent. Tried to climb into van, rocked van.

AC joined JA in attack on van. He was angry and aggressive, he thumped on the back window and on the glass and tried to climb in while JA continued to rock the van.

It was very frightening and SI became hysterical.

Costas gestured to AC to go away. AC grabbed his hand in which he was holding the chicken knife. CG tried to pull away. AI moved behind CG, picked up the kebab knife, rested it on AC's arm. AC tried to recapture CG and arm cut in confusion.

(2)   CHOSEN THEMES

Occupants of van in very vulnerable position.

Attack by two angry, violent, drunken lager louts.

Scene of confusion.

(3)   CONSIDER YOUR AUDIENCE

Tactics: Consider how to deal with Tracey Collins's previous conviction.

Best approach to this case in terms of its theory? Self-defence is inconsistent with client's denial of blow and presenting alternative theories reduces persuasiveness and gives rise to inferences under CPIA 1996, s 11.

(4)   CARRYING OUT INSTRUCTIONS

(i) The Plea and Directions Hearing

Plea: not guilty.
Issues: identity, self-defence.
Prosecution witnesses required: all except Dr and photographer.
Defence witnesses: defendant plus 4 (AI, SI, TC, AaC).
Length of trial: 3–4 days.
Make s 8 application if secondary prosecution disclosure not made.

Note: Check with Instructing Solicitor if interpreter needed at Trial.
(ii) Trial
Prepare for Trial (see *Advocacy* manual).
Desirable to make opening speech in this case?
Prepare to cross-examine Prosecution Witnesses.
Prepare to examine Defendant and Defence Witnesses.

15

Dealing with figures

15.1 Introduction

Dealing with figures is part of dealing with the facts of a case. This chapter introduces the role of figures in the work of the barrister, and the contexts in which work with figures may be required.

Some people are quite confident in dealing with numbers, others are rather less confident, but in professional terms, no barrister can tell a client or solicitor, 'I never was much good at arithmetic!' A client will want to know exactly what will be recovered under each head of damages, and many tax and accounts issues may need to be dealt with by the barrister in a case where the fees of an accountant cannot be justified in terms of costs.

15.2 Importance of numeracy

It is a common misconception that law is about words, not figures. Law is based on written statutes and precendents.

Unfortunately, any suggestion that a barrister can get by without a facility with numbers is not true in practice. Although a contract textbook may have few figures in it, it will include substantial coverage of the legal principles for dealing with figures in awarding damages for a breach of contract. At the end of the day, it is the figures that count—the client will care less about a Court of Appeal precedent than about the figure for a head of damage, bearing in mind mitigation and interest, or whatever else is relevant. The client may need you to assist with quite a bit of arithmetic so that he or she can weigh up the potential financial benefits, and the risks, of bringing a case.

There are many circumstances in which a barrister will have to progress a case without the help of an accountant. In reading and understanding a brief, and in understanding witness statements and expert reports, a barrister may well need to deal with quite complex accounts—not just so as to understand them, but also to be able to see if there is anything unusual, making calculations to check points.

In the simplest terms, as a barrister, you must as a minimum be able to tell the client in detail and using firgures what he or she might hope to get in damages; you need to be able to deal with figures given to you; you need to be able to identify what further figures you need; and you need to be able to talk intelligently about figures to a solicitor or an accountant. Building the ability to do this is part of developing the practical approach of a real barrister in practice.

15.3   Relevance of figures in a barrister's practice

15.3.1   Areas requiring numerical skill

15.3.1.1   Accounts

It is very important to be familiar with the basic terminology of accounting, the elements of a set of accounts, and the principles and interpretation of a set of accounts. You don't need to be able to draw up a set of accounts (unless you are doing your own accounts as a barrister), but you need enough knowledge to be able to read and understand a set of accounts that may come with a brief in almost any sort of case, including tort, contract, family, and crime. A set of accounts can be a useful source of information on many things beyond basic income and expenditure. What is the business worth? How profitable was it at the time the premises were damaged? What parts of the business does a man own, and to what extent might a business fund part of a divorce settlement?

15.3.1.2   Tax law

It is also important to know the basic principles of income and capital taxation. Many earnings, business profits, and assets are subject to tax, and the difference between figures before and after tax may be substantial. In assessing damages, you will need to decide which figures should be taken as more accurately representing the loss. Damages often include a figure for loss of earnings—but should the figure before or after tax be taken? In a divorce settlement, what effect will tax have on the former husband and the former wife?

15.3.1.3   Damages

Principles for assessing damages in the major types of contract and tort action are outlined in the *Remedies* manual. You should know the principles for assessing damages in the core subject areas. Once you have drawn up a list of heads of damage from the facts of the case, you will have to find a way of providing a figure for each one. This can sometimes be quite complex or even theoretical; for example, to decide what profit a business might have made if its premises had not been damaged you may have to base a calculation on what the business made during a similar period, or on the profits of a similar company.

15.3.1.4   Percentages

Deciding on the level of contributory negligence is a matter of fact, but also of looking at facts through arithmetical concepts. The lawyer needs to decide which facts make which party liable, and then turn that into a percentage for contributory negligence.

15.3.1.5   Interest

In a contract case, a figure that is claimed might carry interest under the contract itself. In many types of case, the court may award interest on damages to compensate for the fact that the claimant has been kept out of money. There are a variety of rules on what rates of interest the court may award in what circumstances, and different rates may apply to different heads of loss.

15.3.1.6   Costs

Even if a client wins, the client may not recover from the other side all costs. Costs will be taxed to ensure that sums spent on litigation are reasonable. If the client does not win, the client is likely to bear his or her own costs, and the costs for the other side. The client needs to know likely costs as part of making a sensible and informed decision whether to sue, and as part of deciding how to conduct the case. The recovery of costs is dealt with in the *Civil Litigation* manual.

15.3.2 Typical practical issues involving numbers

Dealing with figures requires an agile mind. Figures may reveal interesting aspects of a case. A few practical points to watch out for are summarised here:

(a) *What numerical issues are there in a case?* Never be happy with just the obvious possibility of damages, or dealing simply with the figures you are given. Are there other arithmetical or financial issues?

(b) *What financial needs are there?* You will only get damages if you identify and quantify a loss. If your client has been injured, identify everything he or she had before but no longer has.

(c) *What financial resources are there?* If your client is seeking maintenance, you need to know in detail what your client needs, and also how much the other side may have to meet your claim. If you are suing for damages, you may need to consider what a potential defendant might be able to pay.

(d) *Where has the money gone to?* A question you may well wish to ask if your client's money, or property, has passed into the hands of someone else and you wish to reclaim it.

(e) *What is the relevance of an individual figure?* It may be necessary to identify and characterise a particular figure to be able to deal with it properly. Is it capital or income? Does it include tax? Does it include VAT?

(f) *Is a particular figure reliable?* Don't accept any figure without question. A figure may not be accurate. How good is the source of the figure? Has it been reached taking all relevant matters into account? Be suspicious if a figure looks too big or too small—and remember that accounts can hide as well as reveal things.

(g) *What does a figure really mean?* Don't be mesmerised by big figures or long lists of figures. Find out what each of the figures mean and which figures are most important.

(h) *Be specific about figures.* Even if the figures given to you are vague, this is no excuse for you to be vague.

(i) *Deal with figures comprehensively.* Make sure you have dealt with every aspect of the figures as fully as every aspect of the case. Deal with all relevant aspects of the figure, the interest, and the tax.

(j) *Be realistic and practical.* It is no use settling for a figure for maintenance for a client if you are not sure it will really cover the client's needs. It is no good offering a figure to settle a claim if you are not sure that your client can raise it.

15.3.3 Types of practice

Numeracy is going to be important to a barrister in any area of practice, from the solely civil to the wholly criminal, albeit in slightly different ways. To provide some examples:

(a) *Commercial practice.* The relevance of figures is obvious in dealing with companies or partnerships, especially as regards a detailed knowledge of accountancy and tax. You are also likely to need to know about commercial finance.

(b) *Chancery practice.* To deal with breach of trust, or for the administration of an estate, you are likely to need to have a thorough knowledge of relevant tax provisions and how to read a set of accounts.

(c) *General common law practice.* This has many elements, but to give some basic examples:

   (i) *Tort.* An accident case may turn on facts, but the assessment of damages can be very complex in cases of severe injury or fatal accident.

   (ii) *Employment law.* Many questions relating to pay may arise, and in some cases there will be a need to deal with statistics.

   (iii) *Family law practice.* Both income and capital provision may require complex calculations. There is not simply the question of how much to pay, but also of how much is really available, how much a person needs to live on, the tax consequences, and so on.

   (iv) *Criminal practice.* The importance of numeracy here ranges from the complex fraud trial to the small-scale fiddling of the books. Complete understanding is essential for clear presentation to the judge and the jury. There are also other possibilities, from being able to deal with tracing the monetary proceeds from the sale of illegal drugs to finding out what fine a defendant may be able to afford.

15.3.4 Working with an accountant

When dealing with a case that has a substantial financial factor it is possible that assistance will be available from an accountant. An accountant may be called in as an expert witness in a case, in which case you may have a role in retaining and briefing the expert witness. You might advise the client to employ an accountant to assist in dealing with particular aspects of a case, and you will be able to get a written report or see the accountant in conference. If the client employs an accountant you may direct questions to the client's accountant through the client.

An accountant can be of great assistance, but it is not an answer in itself.. You will still have to talk to the accountant, to know what to ask about, to know exactly what questions to ask to get the answers you need, to be able to understand the answers, and to be able to present relevant information from the answers in court. If an accountant is to be involved in a case, you need to prepare thoroughly, and keep in mind the potential costs of employing the accountant.

In the vast majority of cases, there will be no accountant to help, for the very simple reason that having an accountant costs money and the client either may not be able to afford this, or the financial issues may not be substantial or vital enough to justify the expense of an accountant.

Whenever there is no accountant you will have to deal with all the figures and financial issues personally, finding the figures, analysing them, and coming to conclusions that can be communicated to the client and be presented in court. You will personally have to deal with any relevant accounts and tax issues.

15.3.5 Personal relevance

There is a personal relevance for the barrister in practice having a reasonable arithmetical ability and a knowledge of the principles of accounting and taxation. The point is simply that as a self-employed person, each barrister will be responsible for drawing up a set of accounts each year and will be personally liable for paying his or her own tax.

The reaction of those starting to train for the Bar tends to be that this point is in fact not very important—you employ an accountant to do your accounts and you get a good accountant so that you pay as little tax as possible, so why does a barrister need to be personally concerned? Such a reaction again shows a lack of practical appreciation of how things really work. Even if you are going to have an accountant to draw up your annual accounts, you need to keep all the records on which those accounts are to be based. Indeed, with self-assessment there is a legal duty to keep such records. You need to know what is taxable and should be entered and what is not. It is also in your interests to know what is tax-deductible so that you know what to keep receipts for. Tax rules mean that there is sometimes a choice of doing things in a tax-effective or a non-tax-effective way, and it is in your interests to know which is which. In addition to income tax, the barrister with sufficient income will be liable for value added tax, with the need to make quarterly returns. It is easy to obtain software to assist.

15.4 Risk assessment

Although there is respect for legal principle as being strong and long lasting, in fact much litigation involves significant risk assessment. Once you have investigated facts and legal principle, you generally find some points in your favour and some against you—it is necessary to weight up the actual chance of success by balancing these. Some lawyers hedge their bets and say something like 'There is a good case,' but that is very vague. Is that a 60 per cent chance of success? An 80 per cent chance? If the client is to risk money in paying his/her own costs, and potentially also the other side's costs, then the client needs to the best assessment of the percentage chance of success that you can give. The client needs to be able to weigh up the likely costs against the chance of success to make an informed decision.

This may be difficult until you have enough evidence but it is important to be as accurate as you can. At an early stage in a case, you need to give a rough figure for the chance of success for your client to decide whether to pay to get more evidence. As the case develops and you have more evidence, you need to re-evaluate and refine the figure for the chance of success.

15.5 Stages in a claim when you may need to deal with figures

15.5.1 In a conference

When planning for or carrying out a conference, dealing with relevant facts must include all the relevant figures. The lawyer should identify the figures that will be required to pursue the case and ask the client about them. Any figures that the client provides should be noted. Often the client will not be able to provide the figures personally, in which case you will have to consider with the solicitor how the figure might be obtained. You will also need to collect evidence for each figure.

15.5.2   In preparing a case

Fact management principles cover figures as well as facts. In dealing with the facts of a case, the barrister will need to identify:

- all the areas of the case for which figures will be needed;
- precisely what figures will be needed;
- what figures are already known;
- what figures need to be ascertained;
- how each figure will be ascertained;
- how each figure can be used and proved.

15.5.3   In writing an opinion

A good solicitor will send you most of the figures that you need, but even a good solicitor is unlikely to send all the figures you need in the initial brief. At that stage, the main issue is whether there is a case and the strength of the case. But figures will still need to be dealt with—even at an early stage, the client will want to know not only whether he or she might win but also at least in general terms what damages might be awarded.

In analysing a brief, you must consider in what areas figures are relevant. In writing the opinion, you should deal with figures as far as possible. The figures that are provided in the brief should be dealt with and other areas where figures are relevant should be dealt with in outline. You also need to decide on a suitable way to present the figures in the opinion, whether as part of the text or in a tabulated form.

In writing an initial opinion, it is easy to underestimate the numerical and arithmetical side of a case simply because detailed figures may well not be available. Figures must never be underestimated—the barrister is not there to accept what is provided, it is for the barrister to indicate what information is needed for the case to progress. Areas where more detailed figures are required should be clearly identified in an opinion. Also, remember to deal with the figures comprehensively in writing.

If you advise your client that he or she can expect £40,000 in damages, it is verging on the negligent not to advise that the money will be liable to 40 per cent tax, if that is the case.

15.5.4   In drafting

A draft is a summary of the facts that are the foundation of a case. You should always consider carefully how far figures are facts that need to be included. Detailed figures or facts relevant to the calculation of damages may need to be included in the body of a draft or added as a schedule. You may need to cover a number of areas, including all heads of damage resulting from an accident, personal injury, and financial loss. You may also need to include facts and figures relevant to interest. A summary of damages and interest may also need to be included in the prayer. Examples are provided in the **Drafting** manual.

An affidavit or witness statement in a case may require figures to be included in great detail. A draft order will of course need to have any relevant figures specifically included. If the figures are complex they should be presented in a schedule.

15.5.5   In advocacy

When presenting a case to a judge or jury, it goes without saying that it is vital for the barrister to have total command of any figures in the case, be they sums of money, measurements or anything else. Only if the barrister has personally gathered all the relevant figures and mastered them will he or she have any chance of explaining them clearly, let alone convincing someone of their relevance. Even someone who is confident in dealing with figures in writing may find it more challenging to deal with them orally.

There are various ways in which a barrister may have to deal with figures in the course of presenting a case in court. First and most simply, figures may need to be dealt with in opening and closing speeches. Second, figures will need to be dealt with in offering evidence, whether through documents or witnesses. Clearly, the barrister must be capable of examining or cross-examining a witness on figures. At every stage, you need to be able to present any numerical information in a way which really communicates your meaning to the jury and the judge. Even if you understand the figures, helping someone else to understand them can be very difficult.

If you have complex figures, you may need to plan very carefully how to present them in court. Paper may well be enough, but clear presentation can help comprehension. Flip charts and overhead projectors may be useful. Computers and video display units are increasingly used if appropriate.

At an interim hearing, you may need to provide and orally present a summary of the costs to date.

15.5.6   In negotiating a settlement

Before attempting to negotiate a settlement, you must have all the relevant figures to evaluate the case and identify the most and the least that the client might expect to win or pay. Sometimes a settlement is seen as a quick and easy way of avoiding a legal claim, but of course no settlement should be contemplated until one has a full grasp of all the relevant figures. It would be potentially negligent to negotiate a final settlement without a full understanding of the facts of a case.

15.6   Collecting evidence of figures

Figures need to be ascertained just like other matters of fact, and admissible evidence will need to be found to prove each figure just as much as any other fact in the case. Having identified an area where figures are relevant, you need to sort out precisely what evidence you need and exactly where it may be obtained. Some figures the client will be able to provide, but you will still need to find evidence to support the figure in most cases For others, it is for the barrister to indicate to the solicitor what figures are required and for the solicitor to endeavour to find the amount and the proof.

The sources of evidence of figures are wide ranging, from a full set of accounts, to cash books, invoices, and receipts. There may also be less direct ways of proving figures. Even if the client has not kept bank statements, it is possible to get copies. Every figure needs to be proved but at the end of the day, it is especially important to be able to prove the larger figures that are most important to the damages.

You also need to be aware of the procedural ways of getting evidence of figures that your client does not have. An obvious possibility is disclosure, but there are many others that are covered in the civil litigation and evidence parts of the course.

You need to be aware of the problems that can arise in presenting such evidence. If you need to take an accountant through his or her evidence, you will have to be familiar with all the appropriate terminology. You need to be able to present evidence in a form in which it can be understood. Most important of all, you will sooner or later need to be able to cross-examine on the figures presented by the other side, which requires a most thorough understanding.

Having stressed the importance of figures, it is equally important for the barrister to be able to deal with the lack of figures—you will often come across a case where you need certain figures to advise in detail and they are simply not obtainable. You can only do your best. Try to think of all the sources from which figures might be obtained. If there are no sources, or if the figures are in any event theoretical, you will have to do your best to argue what the figure should be, from common sense, analogy or some other source. There can, for example, be a problem in arguing for loss of future profit in a breach of contract case. If there is a claim for future loss of profits, students tend to think that the claim is weak if it is difficult to assess what the potential profits might have been. This is of course a problem, but it is by no means fatal. The fact that a figure is difficult to assess simply means that you need to set about constructing a good argument for how it might be assessed. Refer to profits over recent years, or profits of similar businesses to construct an argument.

15.7 Statistics and graphs

15.7.1 When may the use of statistics be helpful to you?

Statistical methods and statistical terms are used in reporting the mass data of social and economic trends, business conditions, opinion polls, and the census. You should get used to reading statistics and utilise them whenever you seek to prove by inference that in your submission a state of affairs exists. Such information is particularly useful when seeking to establish racial or sexual discrimination, risk factors in such areas as sentencing, parole release from mental hospital, danger from chemicals and other environmental pollutants, risk factors in giving informed consent to medical treatment, future profit forecasts, blood test evidence, genetic fingerprinting evidence, etc.

15.7.2 The language of statistics: averages

There are three different kinds of average: the mean, the median, and the mode.

The mean is the arithmetic average arrived at by totalling the number of each of whatever it is you want to average and then dividing that by the total number in the sample. For example, you want to know the average (mean) number of cigarettes that Bar students who smoked, smoke on a particular Monday. If 400 of you smoke, and the total smoked by all 400 on the Monday in question was 8,120, the mean would be 8,120/400 = 20.3.

The median, using the same example, is the number of cigarettes which half the smokers smoke more than, and half smoke less than. In this example, the figure could be less than the mean, and might be about 19.

The mode, again using the same example, is the number of cigarettes which the largest number of people in the sample smoke, so that if the greatest number of people in the group actually smoked 16 cigarettes on Monday, then 16 is the modal number.

If presenting an average to the court, always know what kind of average you are using; and if you are confronted with statistical information by your opponent, always ask what kind of average is being used.

15.7.3 The reliability of statistical information

The major difficulty with all statistics is that they may be biased or based on too small a sample to give anything like a reasonable or believable result. Statistical data are generally developed from information collected in questionnaires. It is important to know: how many were sent out, how the respondents were selected, how many were returned, who did not return them, and whether the respondents were likely to respond truthfully to the questions posed or whether there may have been a desire to give a pleasing answer. To be valid, the sample must be representative and randomly selected.

15.7.4 Sources of statistics

The government's statistics department provides monthly and annual figures which may be of use to you. Such publications as *Social Trends*, *Home Office Statistical Bulletin*, *Annual Abstract of Statistics*, *Regional Trends*, *Key Data*, *United Kingdom National Accounts*, *Economic Trends*, and *Monthly Digest of Statistics* may all be of use to you. The *Guide to Official Statistics* will enable you to decide which of the published statistics may be particularly relevant to a case you are pursuing.

Communication and information technology use in case preparation and presentation

16.1 Introduction

Most barristers in independent practice use communication and information technology (C&IT) to prepare and present their cases in court. Solicitors require written opinions prior to the case going to court, judges frequently demand skeleton arguments when legal arguments are presented to them, and it is often necessary or preferable to carry out legal research when at home, at court, or on the move, rather than in chambers.

Although barristers are members of chambers, there tends not to be a uniform use of technology, even between members of the same set. Some well-organised sets have IT committees, but in most sets of chambers barristers develop their C&IT use in an *ad hoc* way, depending on the needs of their practice and their own financial resources. A barrister will have to devote time to learning new skills throughout his or her practice, as technology changes and new developments occur.

As prospective pupils, now is the time to ensure that your use of C&IT is up to date and that you are proficient in the most important and essential skills. You will be extremely busy during pupillage and will not have time to learn new C&IT skills then. Those pupils who are able to use C&IT well, will have a distinct advantage.

16.2 Modern practice

Practice varies from barrister to barrister and from chambers to chambers. The way a barrister works depends largely on the type of work he or she does and the type of solicitor or agency who sends the work.

16.2.1 Receiving the brief

If work comes from small high street firms, the usual form of contact will be by sending hard-copy briefs by post or DX (Document Exchange, which is a kind of postal method frequently used between members of the legal profession), faxed documents, and telephone contact.

Commercial work, large Very High Cost Cases (VHCC), Customs or Serious Fraud Office (SFO) criminal cases or work from other government agencies will require much more C&IT use. Documents are often sent in scanned pdf format or on disc instead of or as well as by hard copy.

16.2.2   Preparing the brief

In every case, on receipt of the papers it will be necessary to read them and liaise with the solicitor or agency involved. This is increasingly done by email as well as by phone. Solicitors will receive advices, statements of case, requests for further information, and other correspondence from counsel and will send further information and attachments direct by email. Often both solicitor and counsel will send scanned pdf documents to each other instead of original ones.

It is wise, however, to send a signed hard copy of any final advice or statement of case, in addition to any emailed copy.

16.2.3   Contact with the court

Experience of C&IT use with the courts is variable. Much will depend on the willingness and/or ability of the judge or his clerk to liaise directly with counsel by email. Contact with judges, when made, is usually concerned with the service of skeleton arguments, draft orders, or corrections to judgments. Where it is necessary to sign Grounds of Appeal, such documents should be sent as hard-copy documents.

Clerks are increasingly liaising with the list offices of courts by email, particularly in relation to long-term case management and date fixing. Daily contact is still maintained by phone, but the increasing preference of the courts is to send any requests about listing in writing by email.

16.3   Essential skills

It is essential that every prospective pupil is able to use C&IT. Proficient word processing and document formatting are now necessary tools of the barrister's trade. Email and online legal research are also essential and will make practice at the Bar more efficient and up to date. The ability to scan documents into pdf format is also increasingly important.

16.3.1   Word

It is absolutely essential that every prospective pupil is able to use Word (whether Microsoft or its Apple counterpart) and is able to type and format documents quickly and in the correct form. Opinions, skeleton arguments, statements of case, and other documents are written daily by barristers in practice and it is often necessary to draft them quickly. Every prospective pupil must be proficient at typing and word processing to ensure an efficient use of time. Touch-typing is a distinct advantage.

16.3.2   Excel

Many cases benefit from data being set out clearly in spreadsheet format, e.g. chronologies, financial ancillary relief schedules, damages schedules, and other data-handling documents. Excel software is by far the best software for producing such spreadsheets in this context. Proficiency in advance of pupillage will enable any pupil to be able to deal with such working documents competently and efficiently and in a way which is immediately useful to their pupil supervisor.

16.3.3   Outlook

Email is now an important part of contact between many of the parties in litigation. When sending email at a professional level, it is preferable to use Outlook (or an equivalent) rather than a typical web-based email like, for example, Yahoo! or Hotmail.

16.3.4   Online legal research

An ability to conduct thorough, precise, and efficient legal research is one of the most important skills any barrister can have. It is the basis for the understanding and presentation of any case, whether written or oral. Increasingly, barristers work not only in chambers, but also at home, and whilst on the way to court or at court. They require access to up-to-date law at all times. Online legal research tools are therefore increasingly important to them.

The skill in using such tools requires practice and a thorough understanding of the way the particular service functions. Any such service is only as good as the person using it and the search term chosen by that person. **Chapters 2** to **8** of this manual will assist you as a starting point in developing these skills. However, such a skill can only ever improve with training and frequent use.

Useful and frequently used services include *Westlaw*, *LexisNexis Butterworths*, *Lawtel*, *Casetrack*, *Justis* and *Jordans*, *Bailii*, and *CrimeLine*.

The extent of use of online subscription services, however, is hampered by two practical considerations. First, the courts do not have any system to allow barristers access to the Internet whilst at court, and so access to the Internet at court or whilst travelling to court requires an individual barrister to set up an Internet link, usually via a mobile phone. Second, subscription to many of these online services is often too expensive for an individual barrister or set of chambers to afford. There are many providers and some are more affordable than others. Of course, the quality of service offered may be reflected in this difference.

16.3.5   Use of CD-ROMS

Many texts are now also available on CD-ROM. This makes it easier for a barrister to transport effectively a library of material on his or her computer, making access at court or at home much easier. Some CD-ROMS are more user-friendly than others. Again, it is practice and frequent usage that makes these tools easier and more efficient to use.

Some useful and frequently used CD-ROMS include *Archbold*, *Blackstone's Criminal and Civil Practice*, *The White Book*, *Kemp & Kemp*, *The Planning Encyclopaedia*, *Crime Desktop*, *and Family Law Practitioner*.

16.3.6 Navigation of the Web

When preparing a case, it may often be necessary to expand your general area of knowledge. Such knowledge broadens your understanding of the factual background of a case and gives you a wider insight into the problem you are dealing with. You may need to research a geographical location, an industrial process, a medical term, or other topic. Make use of the web. Do not assume that you know everything. You should be interested in the factual background of the case you are preparing. A broader knowledge will not only be useful to your own understanding, but will also reassure your solicitor and lay client.

Many government agencies have useful websites. These often contain policy documents or notes for guidance which will assist you in your research and analysis of a problem.

There are also websites which help you navigate rules of etiquette and conduct, the court structure and hierarchy, barristers' names and chambers, and the logistical arrangements which are integral to practice at the Bar.

<u>Some useful websites</u>

<http://www.barcouncil.org.uk/guidance/>
<http://www.barstandardsboard.org.uk/standardsandguidance/codeofconduct/>
<http://www.hmcourts-service.gov.uk/>
<http://www.courtserve2.net/court-lists.htm>
<http://www.justice.gov.uk>
<http://www.opsi.gov.uk>
<http://www.dca.gov.uk/>
<http://www.jsboard.co.uk/>
<http://www.publications.parliament.uk/pa/ld/ldjudgmt.htm>
<http://www.legislation.gov.uk/acts.htm>
<http://www.hrothgar.co.uk/YAWS/>
<http://www.officialsolicitor.gov.uk/os/icacu.htm>
<http://www.incadat.com>
<http://www.eur-lex.europa.eu/en/index.htm>
<http://www.curia.europa.eu/>
<http://www.echr.coe.int/ECHR/EN/Header/Case-Law/HUDOC/HUDOC+database/>
<http://www.informationtribunal.gov.uk/>
<http://www.employmentappeals.gov.uk/>
<http://www.cps.gov.uk/legal/index.html>
<http://www.sentencing-guidelines.gov.uk/>
<http://www.hmprisonservice.gov.uk/>
<http://www.homeoffice.gov.uk/>
<http://www.criminalbar.com/>
<http://www.piba.org.uk/>
<http://www.flba.co.uk/>
<http://www.combar.com/>
<http://www.propertybar.org.uk>
<http://www.landregisteronline.gov.uk/>
<http://www.environment-agency.gov.uk/>
<http://www.hse.gov.uk>
<http://www.tradingstandards.gov.uk/>
<http://www.communities.gov.uk/corporate/>

<http://www.companieshouse.gov.uk>
<http://www.corporateaccountability.org/>
<http://www.fsa.gov.uk/>
<http://www.graysinn.info/>
<http://www.innertemple.org.uk/>
<http://www.lincolnsinn.org.uk/>
<http://www.middletemple.org.uk/>
<http://www.legalhub.org.uk/>
<http://www.timeanddate.org.uk/>
<http://www.nationalrail.org.uk/>

16.4 Data protection

Every organisation that processes personal information must notify the Information Commissioner's Office (ICO), unless they are exempt. Failure to notify is a criminal offence. It follows that every barrister must now register with the Information Commissioner. Guidance is offered by the ICO on data retention and other responsibilities in connection with the processing and storing of data. It goes without saying that opinions and other legal documents contain confidential and privileged personal material and need protecting. Password protection and email security should be observed at all times when dealing with such material.

17

Self-assessment exercises

17.1 Finding a legal framework

Your client is the mother of a nine-year-old child. She took the child on a picnic in the countryside. They ate their picnic at the side of a cultivated field near a stream. After eating their picnic, your client fell asleep and was woken by her child crying out as he had fallen into the stream and cut his arm quite badly. It appears that the child had tripped on some rusty wire at the edge of the stream, but it is not clear how he cut himself. The client is worried that the water in the stream did not seem to be very clean. She took the child to hospital but had to wait some time to get attention for him. The child was not well for several weeks after the incident.

Deal with the following:

- list the gaps and ambiguities that you would wish to pursue before trying to identify the possible legal framework;

- make a key list of as many potentially legally relevant factors as you can that might be involved in finding a legal framework.

17.2 Identifying potential theories

A man and a woman who are in the living room of the man's house are heard arguing by a neighbour. Shortly afterwards, two shots are heard. The man shouts for help, and the neighbour rushes in to find the man nursing the woman, who has a severe head wound. A doctor is called and the woman is taken to hospital but she later dies.

You have evidence that a handgun was found in the man's pocket shortly after the incident by a policeman investigating what happened. The man admits that he has owned the gun for several years. You also have evidence that the man and woman had been living together for several years, but their relationship had not been happy recently.

You are acting for the defence of the man on a charge of murder.

Deal with the following:

- list the factual aspects of the case that will require investigation on behalf of the defence;

- construct as many potential theories of the case as possible which may show the man's innocence.

17.3   Lateral thinking

Consider the following:

(a) There are three witnesses who saw a woman running away from the scene of an armed robbery shortly after the robbery occurred. How many different factual reasons might there be for her conduct? How many different legal hypotheses can these factual possibilities lead to?

(b) You are representing Cinderella's stepmother, who has been charged with ill-treating her stepdaughter. Tell the story from the point of view of the stepmother, offering possible lines of defence.

(c) A man believes that he has developed a way of predicting how an individual's career may progress by looking at specific factors. He charges a fee for his service, which is popular with young people. He accepts that he is not infallible, and it is a term of paying for his service that if his prediction is wrong, he will return double the original fee. He makes a lot of money. He has just been arrested. What might he have been arrested for?

17.4   Analysing the evidence

THE CASE OF *R v PETER PENNY*

Facts:

Report by PC Giles: dated 2 January 2008. In response to a call from a neighbour I visited 26 Acacia Court at 5 pm this afternoon. I spoke initially to John Thorp, the neighbour who called the police. I found the front door ajar. On entering the flat I discovered a body in the living room. I called for assistance and made a thorough search of the flat. There was no one else present. While in the flat I ascertained that there was no rear entry.

PC David Giles, 8.30 pm, 2.1.08

Summary of police report on the body discovered by PC Giles on 2 January 2008. The body has been identified as that of David Star, of 26 Acacia Court, London SE11. Medical evidence suggests that he was strangled between 4 and 5 pm, on 2.1.08.

John Thorp will say: I was in my lounge on the afternoon of 2nd January 2008, watching out of the window. From here I have a good view of the flats opposite. At around 4.30 pm I saw a tall dark-haired man with a moustache run from the flat opposite: 26 Acacia Court. He appeared to be in a great hurry and this made me suspicious, so I telephoned the police. A constable arrived at around 5 o'clock. I told him what I had seen and he entered the flat and found poor David Star dead. I had been watching from my window for most of the time between 4 and 5 pm, and I am sure that no one entered or left the flat apart from the man I have described.

Paula Lyle will say: I am a neighbour of Peter Penny, who lives at 32 Tamarisk Court, London SE11. I was returning to my own flat on 2nd January 2008, when, at 4.05 pm, I saw Peter Penny enter the Flat at 26 Acacia Court. I know Peter and am confident that it was him I saw.

Alice Lion will say: I was at a party to see the New Year in, where I saw two friends of mine, Peter Penny and David Star. They were engaged in a heated argument, but I do not know what it was about as I did not want to get involved.

Police report on Peter Penny: Mr Penny is 6 ft 2in tall, has dark hair and a moustache, and walks with a pronounced limp. He lives at 32 Tamarisk Court SE11, a block of flats on the same estate as Acacia Court. He is known to have been an acquaintance of the deceased.

Acknowledgment

The facts here are based on materials prepared by Professor Twining, which may be seen used in a different way in Terence Anderson and William Twining, *Analysis of Evidence* (London, 1991), and in Neil Gold, Karl Mackie, and William Twining (eds), *Learning Lawyers' Skills* (London, 1989), at p. 253. (These materials are used with the permission of Professor Twining.)

Assignment

Draw a chart which analyses the evidence in respect of the identification element only of the potential murder charge. The chart should show the facts and inferences leading to the conclusion that it was Peter Penny who killed David Star. It should also show the facts and inferences which weaken that conclusion.

An example of a completed chart in this case is shown in **Appendix 4**.

17.5 Preparing a criminal case

Your pupillage supervisor has asked you to write notes on the case of *R v Juliet Stevens*, which:

- set out the legal framework of the case;
- identify the issues in the case;
- identify what evidence there is on each issue;
- identify any points to clarify with the client in conference.

You may find it useful to review **Chapters 10** and **11** before beginning any detailed preparation of this exercise. Further examples of analytical techniques can be found in **Chapter 14** in the preparation of the criminal brief.

<u>IN THE SOUTH LONDON MAGISTRATES' COURT</u>

THE QUEEN

v

JULIET STEVENS

BRIEF TO COUNSEL FOR THE DEFENCE

Public Funding

Starling & Co
11 West Square
London WC1R 1AB

<u>IN THE SOUTH LONDON MAGISTRATES' COURT</u>

THE QUEEN

v

JULIET STEVENS

INSTRUCTIONS TO COUNSEL TO
ADVISE IN CONFERENCE

Counsel has herewith:

1. Copy of the charge.
2. Witness statements served under the Advance Disclosure rules.
3. Miss Stevens' proof of evidence.

Miss Stevens is charged with causing criminal damage to a motor car. The cost of repair is in excess of £5,000.

The facts appear from the statements of the prosecution witnesses and her proof of evidence.

Miss Stevens is a lady of good character, with no experience of the courts.

Miss Stevens will need advice as to her plea and she is very anxious to know whether it is better to elect trial in the Crown Court or to get the case over with quickly in the Magistrates' Court.

Counsel is instructed to advise Miss Stevens in conference.

CHARGE

Damaging property, contrary to section 1(1) of the Criminal Damage Act 1971

PARTICULARS

Juliet Stevens on the 1st day of August 2008, without lawful excuse damaged a car belonging to James Kirby, intending to damage such property or being reckless as to whether such property would be damaged.

STATEMENT OF WITNESS

(CJ Act 1967 s 9; MC Act 1980 ss 5A(3)(a) and 5B; MC Rules 1981 r 70)

STATEMENT OF	JAMES KIRBY
Age of Witness (date of birth)	Over 18
Occupation of Witness	Stockbroker

This statement consisting of 1 page, signed by me, is true to the best of my knowledge and belief and I make it knowing that, if it is tendered in evidence, I shall be liable to prosecution if I have wilfully stated in it anything which I know to be false or do not believe to be true.

Dated the 4th day of August 2008   Signed: James Kirby

Signature witnessed by: Jane Smart

I live at 23 Arcadia Mansions, Battersea SW11, with my girlfriend Paula Vernon. Until May of this year I had been living with Juliet Stevens. This relationship had lasted several years.

During the course of that relationship I had bought a BMW 323i motor car, index number WT02 RGT. We both used to drive it, but it was my car.

Juliet was very bitter when the relationship came to an end. She said I ought to compensate her for the fact that she had to move out and had nowhere to live.

She kept asking me if she could have the car, and I kept saying no. She seemed to be determined to have it.

Feelings between us remained very bad and there were many disputes over various items of property in the flat which we had acquired during the relationship.

In the early hours of Friday 1st August I was woken by a very loud banging in the street outside. My flat is on the ground floor. I looked outside and saw Juliet attacking the car with a sledgehammer.

I went outside to try to stop her, but she seemed to have gone berserk.

She had smashed all the windows and lights. All the body panels were dented.

She was really furious and kept saying, 'You said I could have the car, but all I ever see is the two of you in it. Well, it's mine and no one will drive it again.'

Shortly afterwards the police arrived. As far as I am concerned I had not given Juliet Stevens the car and it was not hers to damage.

I am willing to attend court and give evidence.

Signed: James Kirby   Signature witnessed by: Jane Smart

STATEMENT OF WITNESS

(CJ Act 1967 s 9; MC Act 1980 ss 5A(3)(a) and 5B; MC Rules 1981 r 70)

STATEMENT OF	JAMES KIRBY
Age of Witness	Over 18
Occupation of Witness	Stockbroker

This statement consisting of 1 page, signed by me, is true to the best of my knowledge and belief and I make it knowing that, if it is tendered in evidence, I shall be liable to prosecution if I have wilfully stated in it anything which I know to be false or do not believe to be true.

Dated the 20th day of August 2008

Signed: James Kirby

Signature witnessed by: Jane Smart

Further to my previous statement, I have now obtained an estimate for repairs to the car. It will need new windows and lights, new body panels and a complete respray. The estimate is £7,500.

Signed: James Kirby   Signature witnessed by: Jane Smart

STATEMENT OF WITNESS

(CJ Act 1967 s 9; MC Act 1980 ss 5A(3)(a) and 5B; MC Rules 1981 r 70)

STATEMENT OF	JANE SMART
Age of Witness	Over 18
Occupation of Witness	Police Officer

This statement consisting of 1 page, signed by me, is true to the best of my knowledge and belief and I make it knowing that, if it is tendered in evidence, I shall be liable to prosecution if I have wilfully stated in it anything I know to be false or do not believe to be true.

Dated 4th day of August 2008   Signed: Jane Smart

Signature witnessed by: Paul Dunn

At 0200 on Friday 1st August 2008 I attended the scene of a disturbance at Arcadia Mansions SW11. On arrival I saw a person I now know to be Juliet Stevens repeatedly hitting a BMW motor car with a sledgehammer. The car appeared to be severely damaged. A man who I now know to be James Kirby was yelling at her and trying to stop her.

She appeared to calm down when she saw me, and I took her to one side to speak to her.

I asked her whose car it was and she replied, 'mine'. I asked her why she was smashing it up and she said, 'When I broke up with James, he said I could have the car since I'd been living with him for years and had lost out on the chance of getting my own place. I kept asking him for it, and he kept putting it off, saying I could have it soon. This evening I saw James and Paula driving around in it—my car—and I just saw red. It's my car'. Miss Stevens was very distressed.

I spoke to Mr Kirby who told me it was his car. He showed me the Vehicle Registration Document which was in his name. A check on the PNC also revealed him to be the registered keeper.

I went back to Miss Stevens and said, 'It appears that it is not your car. I am arresting you for causing criminal damage to that car.' I then cautioned her and she said, 'It's my car'.

She was taken to Battersea police station.

I was present at 7 am when she was charged and further cautioned, to which she made no reply.

Signed: Jane Smart   Signature witnessed by: Paul Dunn

PROOF OF EVIDENCE

Juliet Stevens will say:

I am 25 years old. I am single and I live at 32 Malpas Road SW11. This is rented accommodation. I am a PR consultant.

I had been living with James Kirby in his flat for six years until May 2007 when we split up, because he met someone else.

During this time we both bought lots of things for the flat, and it was our home. We occasionally discussed what would happen if we broke up, since I had put a lot of money and time into making the flat our home, rather than buying somewhere of my own. He said we wouldn't break up, but if we ever did he would make sure I was all right financially by giving me the car. He bought the car, but we both drove it.

We always referred to it as my car, as a sort of private joke.

When we broke up I expected him to honour his promise to give me the car. I had taken the promise seriously. At first he said he would, but he kept putting it off. He never said I couldn't have it, but said I'd have to wait until he got another one.

I accept I was very bitter about the way he treated me.

In the evening of 31st July I was walking to a friend's house when I saw James and Paula drive past in the car. James hooted and waved. I was furious. By the time I got home I was even more furious. There is building work going on in the house where I am living, and when I saw a sledgehammer I decided I was going to wreck the car—my car.

By now I had decided he was not going to hand it over to me, so I decided if I couldn't have it, they certainly would not drive it.

I walked around to Arcadia Mansions, which is not far, and attacked the car.

I honestly believed it was my car and that I was entitled to do what I wanted with it.

I am worried about my employers finding out about this court case and want it dealt with as quickly as possible.

17.6 Preparing a civil case

Your pupillage supervisor has asked you to write notes on the case of *Norman v Finings Engineering Ltd,* which:

- set out the legal framework of the case;
- identify the issues in the case;
- identify what evidence there is on each issue.

You may find it useful to review **Chapters 9** and **11** before beginning any detailed preparation of this exercise. Worked examples of some analytical techniques can also be found in **Chapter 13**, in the preparation of civil briefs.

IN THE CANTERBURY COUNTY COURT   Claim No. CT7/01306
BETWEEN:

MELVYN NORMAN   <u>Claimant</u>

v

FININGS ENGINEERING LIMITED   <u>Defendants</u>

BRIEF TO COUNSEL ON BEHALF OF THE CLAIMANT

Agreed Brief Fee £600

Blister & Co
Ryder House
Park Lane
Sevenoaks
Kent

<u>IN THE CANTERBURY COUNTY COURT</u>   Claim No. CT7/01306
BETWEEN:

MELVYN NORMAN   <u>Claimant</u>

v

FININGS ENGINEERING LIMITED   <u>Defendants</u>

_____

INSTRUCTIONS TO COUNSEL
_____

Counsel has herewith:

1. Statements of case.

2. The agreed trial bundle (paginated [1]–[6]).

Instructing Solicitors act on behalf of the Claimant Melvyn Norman who was injured in an accident at his place of work on 2nd July 2007. The facts of the accident are straightforward. Mr Norman was walking across the press shop floor of the Defendants' premises when he slipped on a patch of oil and fell.

Counsel is asked to appear on behalf of the Claimant at the trial of this claim. Special damages have been agreed in the sum of £1,110. Unfortunately it has not been possible to agree general damages. However, the Claimant's medical report is agreed. The trial bundle contains the only two relevant extracts from the Accident Report Book, ie, the Claimant's accident and one other similar accident in 2006.

It is also agreed that the oil can is to be an exhibit.

IN THE CANTERBURY COUNTY COURT   Claim No. CT7/01306

BETWEEN:

MELVYN NORMAN   <u>Claimant</u>

v

FININGS ENGINEERING LIMITED   <u>Defendants</u>

PARTICULARS OF CLAIM

---

1.   At the time of the accident described below the Claimant was employed by the Defendants as a service hand at their works at Eagle Road, Canterbury, Kent, which was at all material times a workplace to which the Workplace (Health, Safety and Welfare) Regulations 1992 ('the Regulations') applied.

2.   At about 3.45 pm on 2nd July 2007 the Claimant, in the course of his employment, was walking across the floor of the 'press shop' at these premises when he slipped on a patch of oil and fell.

3.   The accident was caused by a breach of statutory duty under the Regulations and/or negligence on the part of the Defendants, their servants or agents.

PARTICULARS OF BREACH OF STATUTORY DUTY

(a) Failing to maintain the press shop floor in an efficient state, contrary to regulation 5(1) of the Regulations;

(b) Failing to keep the floor free from a substance which may cause a person to slip, namely oil, contrary to regulation 12(3) of the Regulations.

PARTICULARS OF NEGLIGENCE

(c) The Claimant repeats the allegations of breach of statutory duty above;

(d) Causing or permitting the patch of oil to be and/or to remain upon the press shop floor;

(e) Failing to carry out any or any adequate cleaning and/or failing to remove the oil from the press shop floor;

(f) Failing to warn the Claimant of the dangers of the oil;

(g) Failing to heed an oral complaint about the danger of oil on the floor made by the Claimant on 25th June 2007 to the Defendants' responsible servant one Andrew Jackson, the works foreman;

(h) Failing to provide a safe system of work;

(i) In the premises, failing to take any or any adequate care for the Claimant's safety and exposing him to the unnecessary risk of injury.

4.   By reason of the matters described above the Claimant suffered personal injuries and was put to loss and expense.

PARTICULARS OF INJURIES

The Claimant who was born on 18th March 1976 suffered bruising to and a ligamentous strain of his right knee. He was away from work for 3 weeks during which time he underwent a course of intensive physiotherapy. Pain, swelling and tenderness remained. The Claimant had a further 2-week course of physiotherapy in August 2007. During this 2-week period he was again absent from work. There is still some restriction of movement of the knee joint but this should fully resolve within 18 months from the date of the accident. There is no evidence of osteoarthritis. Full details of the Claimant's injuries are set out in the medical report of Mr Westside of St Hugh's Hospital in Sevenoaks, Kent, dated 30th March 2006 a copy of which is served pursuant to Civil Procedure Rules, PD 16, para 4.3.

PARTICULARS OF SPECIAL DAMAGE

Particulars of the Claimant's loss and damage appear in the statement of special damages served herewith.

5.   Further the Claimant claims interest pursuant to section 69 of the County Courts Act 1984 on such sum as may be found to be due to the Claimant at such rate and for such period as the Court shall think fit.

AND the Claimant claims:

1.   Damages.

2.   The aforesaid interest pursuant to statute to be assessed.

Statement of Truth

I believe that the facts stated in these particulars of claim are true.

Dated the 22nd day of April 2008   *M. Norm*

SAINT HUGH'S HOSPITAL, SEVENOAKS, KENT
MEDICAL REPORT ON MELVYN NORMAN

Melvyn Norman aged 32

34 Copping Rise, Sevenoaks, Kent

Occupation: Service Hand at Finings Engineering Limited

Date of accident: 2.7.07

Date of Examination for this Report 22.7.07

Mr Norman tells me that whilst at work on 2/7/07 he slipped on a patch of oil and injured his right knee. He was taken to hospital where X-rays revealed no bony injury. There was severe bruising over the lateral aspect of the knee joint. A ligamentous strain was diagnosed, a supportive bandage provided and analgesics prescribed.

Mr Norman was off work initially for three weeks. During this period he had a course of intensive physiotherapy at Sevenoaks Hospital. At home he was restricted in his activities. He could not play with his two young children. He had difficulty negotiating stairs, his sleep was interrupted and he could not perform his normal household jobs. Mrs Norman therefore had to do more by way of jobs around the house and looking after the children in this period. Mr Norman says that when he returned to work he was still in pain. He worked for a week and then had a further two weeks off. In this period he had another course of physiotherapy. I have had the benefit of reading notes supplied by Mr Norman's GP, Mr Strange, and also from Mr Irwin the physiotherapist. There was an initial reduction in flexion of 40% in the joint, but this has steadily improved. Mr Norman still experiences pain when kneeling at work but this is a dull ache and not severe. He has needed pain-killing tablets intermittently since the accident but the instances of need have become less frequent.

Examination

General health: good

Height: 6 ft 1. Weight: 12 stone

Mr Norman presented as a pleasant if somewhat absent minded man. On examination his gait was normal. There was a 10% reduction in flexion of the right knee joint. Kneeling is still painful. There is no current bruising but there is a little residual tenderness over the lateral aspect of the joint.

Conclusion

There is a clear evidence of an initially severe ligamentous injury of the right knee joint. There is no evidence of osteoarthritis. I foresee no long-term effects and would anticipate full resolution of the injury within 18 months from the date of the accident.

TIM WESTSIDE

Consultant

28th March 2008

<u>IN THE CANTERBURY COUNTY COURT</u>   Claim No. CT7/01306
BETWEEN:

MELVYN NORMAN   <u>Claimant</u>

v

FININGS ENGINEERING LIMITED   <u>Defendants</u>

SCHEDULE OF LOSS AND EXPENSE PURSUANT
TO CPR PD 16, PARA 4.2

5 weeks' loss of earnings	£1,500
Taxi fares to and from hospital	£ 75
Damaged clothing	£ 35
TOTAL	£1,610

Dated the 22nd day of April 2008 M. Norman

Blister & Co
Ryder House
Park Lane
Sevenoaks, Kent

<u>Solicitors for the Claimant</u>

To the Defendants:
Finings Engineering Limited
Eagle Road
Canterbury, Kent

And to the Court Manager

IN THE CANTERBURY COUNTY COURT   Claim No. CT7/01306
BETWEEN:

MELVYN NORMAN   Claimant

v

FININGS ENGINEERING LIMITED   Defendants

DEFENCE

---

1. Paragraphs 1 and 2 of the Particulars of Claim are admitted.

2. It is denied that the Defendants were negligent or in breach of statutory duty as alleged in the Particulars of Claim or at all.

3. The Defendants aver that they maintained the press shop floor in an efficient state and did all that was reasonably practicable to keep the floor free from oil or any other substance which may cause a person to slip or fall. The Defendants' servant one James Stonehouse was charged with cleaning the floor twice each day and had cleaned the floor approximately 2 hours before the accident.

4. The accident referred to in the Particulars of Claim was caused solely or alternatively contributed to by the negligence of the Claimant.

PARTICULARS OF NEGLIGENCE

(a) Carrying an oil can with him across the floor in such a manner that oil was dripped on to the floor;

(b) Causing or permitting oil to fall onto the floor;

(c) Failing to look where he was going and slipping on the oil he had dropped;

(d) In the premises failing to take any or any adequate care for his own safety and exposing himself to the unnecessary risk of injury.

5. Further or alternatively, if, which is denied, the oil upon which the Claimant slipped was not dropped by him immediately prior to the accident, the Defendants will rely upon the failure of the Claimant to look where he was going and thereby avoid the patch of oil upon which he slipped.

6. The Defendants make no admissions as to the alleged or any injury, loss or damage, or as to the amount thereof.

7. Save in so far as has been expressly admitted the Defendants deny each and every allegation in the Particulars of Claim as if the same were set out in turn and specifically denied.

Statement of Truth

I believe that the facts stated in this defence are true.

Dated the 23rd day of May 2008

J Temple, Director

for Finings Engineering Ltd

<u>TRIAL BUNDLE</u>
<u>INDEX</u>

[1]

Claimant
M. Norman
1st
1.9.2008
Claim No. CT7/01306

<u>IN THE CANTERBURY COUNTY COURT</u>

MELVYN NORMAN   <u>Claimant</u>

v

FININGS ENGINEERING LIMITED   <u>Defendants</u>

<u>WITNESS STATEMENT OF MELVYN NORMAN</u>

I, Melvyn Norman of, 34 Copping Rise, Sevenoaks, Kent, service hand, will say as follows:

1.   I am the Claimant in this action. I make this statement concerning the accident that occurred at work on 2nd July 2007.

2.   I am married with two daughters aged 5 and 7. I have worked for the Defendants for two years as a service hand at their Eagle Road works. My job involves me in looking after and adjusting the press machines on the press shop floor. At about 3.40 pm on the day of the accident I was adjusting a B/44 press machine in the press shop when I realised that I needed an adjustable spanner. I decided to go to the tool shop to get the spanner. I had just oiled a B/44 machine and had the oil can in my hand. As far as I can recall I was holding the oil can in an upright position. The can has a long, thin spout that points upwards. I believe that it was pointing upwards at the time of the accident. It is possible that a few drops of oil were dripping from the can as I made my way to the tool shop. If this was the case then they would most likely have dripped on to my overalls rather than the floor as I always carry the oil can very close to me.

3.   I had reached the middle of the press shop floor when I slipped and fell. I had been chatting to workmates as I passed them. Simon Packer was working on a press near to where I fell and saw the whole thing.

4.   James Stonehouse the press shop apprentice had been standing at the door of the press shop, some 20 feet away from the place where the accident occurred. After the accident I remember him coming over and helping me to the sickroom. I remember Simon Packer saying something about there having been a large patch of oil on the floor for some time.

5.   Oil has always been a problem in the press shop. Lately the problem has got worse. On 25.6.07 I actually spoke to the works foreman, Mr Jackson, about it. It was a sort of general chat but I told him I thought the floor was dangerous.

6.   I was in great pain when I fell. My knee was badly bruised. At hospital they said it was ligaments. I had the bandage on for three weeks. I was off work and couldn't play with the kids. Also I had difficulty getting up and down stairs and doing jobs around the house. The wife had to do it all. I went to physiotherapy for 3 weeks then I went back to work. The pain was still bad and after a week I had to have 2 more weeks off work and more physiotherapy.

7.   I like a game of football now and again but I haven't played since the accident. I don't trust the leg. The same applies to the gardening which was one of my favourite hobbies. I was a very keen gardener and kept our front and rear gardens immaculately.

[2]

I was particularly keen on the bedded plants and shrubs and very proud of the way I'd arranged and groomed the flower beds. Since the accident I have had difficulty bending down to do the gardening. My wife has done most of the gardening but she isn't so much of a perfectionist as I am and the garden looks pretty untidy as a result.

STATEMENT OF TRUTH

I believe that the facts stated in this witness statement are true.

M. Norm
....

Dated the 1st day of September 2008

[3]

Claimant
S. Packer
1st
1.9.2008
Claim No. CT7/01306

IN THE CANTERBURY COUNTY COURT

MELVYN NORMAN   Claimant

v

FININGS ENGINEERING LIMITED   Defendants

WITNESS STATEMENT OF SIMON PACKER

I, Simon Packer, of 4 Blood Lane, Sevenoaks, Kent will say as follows:

1.   I am employed as a press operator at Finings Engineering's Eagle Road works. I know Melvyn Norman as a fellow employee but we are not friends. On the day of his accident I was in the press shop working on my press. When I returned from lunch at about 2.15 pm I noticed that there was a patch of oil by the side of my machine. The floor of the press shop is often oily. The apprentice is supposed to keep the floor clean but he often forgets. I do not remember him cleaning the floor on the day of the accident.

2.   It is difficult to keep the floor clear of oil. The machines shed some oil and the adjusting and maintenance work involves the use of oil. Really the floors should be inspected and, if necessary, cleaned every couple of hours just to be on the safe side. Even that might not solve the problem.

3.   I remember that Melvyn was carrying a can of oil as he approached my press. I can't say if it was leaking or not. He seemed to be walking in a line that would have taken him wide of the oil but he must have altered his course. When he fell the oil can went flying and Melvyn clutched his right knee in agony.

4.   James Stonehouse helped me to take him to the sickroom. I do remember that there were some oil stains down the front of Melvyn's overalls and on the top of his boots when we picked him up.

STATEMENT OF TRUTH

I believe that the facts stated in this witness statement are true.

S Packer
....

Dated the 1st day of September 2008

[4]

Defendant
J. Stonehouse
1st
1.9.2008
Claim No. CT7/01306

IN THE CANTERBURY COUNTY COURT

MELVYN NORMAN   <u>Claimant</u>

v

FININGS ENGINEERING LIMITED   <u>Defendants</u>

WITNESS STATEMENT OF JAMES STONEHOUSE

I, James Stonehouse of 39 Snargate Road, Sevenoaks, Kent, will say as follows:

1.   I am 17 years old and work as an apprentice at Finings Engineering in the press shop. The foreman, Mr Jackson, asked me to keep the floor of the shop clean. I give it a clean twice a day. The problem is that oil gets all over the place and there isn't much you can do. Some of the lads are careless with their oil cans, and the presses spurt out a bit as well.

2.   At about 3.40 pm on 2.7.07 I was standing by the door of the press shop. I saw Melvyn Norman walking across the shop towards the door. I particularly noticed him because he was carrying an oil can in one of his hands, I can't remember which. The spout was facing downwards and oil was leaking out. Melvyn didn't seem to realise. I was about to shout out when he slipped and fell. When we picked him up there was some oil on the front of his shoes. I was surprised that there wasn't more oil on his clothes and shoes. I usually clean the floor at about 1.30 pm at the end of the morning shift, and again at about 4 pm in the afternoon. A few days earlier Mr Jackson, the works foreman, had asked me to clean the floor carefully, that's why I'm pretty sure that I had cleaned the floor at 1.30 pm on 2.7.07.

<u>STATEMENT OF TRUTH</u>

I believe that the facts stated in this witness statement are true.

J. Stonehouse
....
Dated the 1st day of September 2008

[5]

Defendant
A. Jackson
1st
1.9.2008
Claim No. CT7/01306

IN THE CANTERBURY COUNTY COURT

MELVYN NORMAN   Claimant

v

FININGS ENGINEERING LIMITED   Defendants

WITNESS STATEMENT OF ANDREW JACKSON

I, Andrew Jackson, of 5 Rosebush Lane, Canterbury, Kent, will say as follows:

1.   I am the works foreman at the Defendants' premises at Eagle Road, Canterbury, Kent. I have worked at those premises for the Defendants since that particular factory opened in 1977. I started as an apprentice press operator and have been works foreman for the last five years.

2.   The press shop floor contains 10 presses in all. The maintenance of the presses involves them being regularly oiled to ensure that the moving parts move freely and do not grind causing wear. Any oil spillage from routine maintenance should be minimal.

3.   When the presses are operating there is some minimal release of oil. This is the oil used for maintenance which will sometimes escape from the moving parts when a press is working at full capacity. Most of the moving parts are boxed in, but occasionally oil escapes. The amount of oil is small, more in the nature of a few droplets than a pool or puddle.

4.   Melvyn Norman is a service hand at the Defendants' Eagle Road works. He is responsible for maintaining the presses on the press shop floor. This involves him regularly oiling the moving parts of the machine.

5.   On 25.6.07 he spoke to me about a number of maintenance matters. He mentioned in a general way that he thought that there might have been more oil on the press shop floor in the last few days. He did not say that he thought that this oil was causing a greater hazard than usual. The floor is cleaned twice a day by one of our apprentices, James Stonehouse. Even though Mr Norman had made no mention of a greater hazard being caused by the oil, following my discussion with him on 25.6.07 I told James Stonehouse to clean the floor particularly carefully.

STATEMENT OF TRUTH

I believe that the facts stated in this witness statement are true.

A.Jackson
....

Dated the 1st day of September 2008

[6]

<u>ACCIDENT REPORT BOOK</u>

<u>Date/Time</u>	<u>Location</u>	<u>Details</u>
10/2/06	Press shop	F. Collins. Slipped on oil, Injured elbow and shoulder.
. . .		
1/7/07	Press shop	M. Norman. Slipped on oil, injured knee.

[7]

17.7 Dealing with figures

Problem 1

Examine the following facts in detail, and identify as many areas as you can where information about numbers must be sought and dealt with.

In each case, identify where information about relevant figures might be sought by yourself or by instructing solicitors.

Mr Duff, aged 59, was injured in April 2008 when he was driving his car and it was hit by another vehicle. His father was a passenger in his car at the time and was killed in the accident. The accident was caused by the driver of the other car, Mr Young, who has since been convicted of dangerous driving with regard to the incident. Mr Duff is suing Mr Young for negligence. As a result of the accident, which broke both his legs and caused serious internal injuries, Mr Duff could not work for six months. In order to be able to return to work as quickly as possible, Mr Duff used a substantial amount from his savings to pay for private medical treatment.

Mr Duff has had particular difficulties in that he is the manager of an interior design business. The business was incorporated in 2001 as Duff Decor Ltd, with Mr Duff as a 60 per cent shareholder and his brother as a 40 per cent shareholder. Business has suffered while Mr Duff has not been able to work. His brother is not good at business, so a manager had to be employed while Mr Duff was not there. In addition, a few months before the accident, £100,000 was borrowed to fund expansion of the business, and there have been problems keeping up with repayments on this loan.

Mr Duff's father left a will appointing Mr Duff and his brother as his executors. The main provisions of the father's will was to leave the residue of his estate in trust for his grandchildren.

Mr Duff left his wife and two children three years ago, and he has since lived in a flat. The wife and children are still in the former matrimonial home, and Mr Duff had been voluntarily paying maintenance to them. However, following his accident he has been unable to make such payments, and his wife is currently in receipt of social security benefits. Mr Duff has heard rumours that his wife has formed a relationship with another man who has done substantial work on the home.

Problem 2

A wife tells you that she needs maintenance from her husband. Both parties have made full disclosure of their financial situation and below you will find each party's schedule of income and expenditure. Is she right?

Wife	£
Gross income	15, 708.00 p.a.
Net income, approximately	927.50 per month
National insurance	50.36 per month
Monthly expenditure:	
Gas	25.00
Electricity	15.00
Television licence	8.00
Contents insurance	13.00
Car tax and insurance	24.00
Car maintenance	34.00

Wife	£
Petrol	50.00
Dental treatment	10.00
House repairs, etc.	40.00
Investments: life assurance, etc.	154.25
Increase in national insurance contribution	68.00
Council tax, water rates, buildings insurance, etc.	136.50
Food	200.00
Clothes	100.00

Husband	£
Gross income	34,000.00 pa
Net income, approximately	1,845.00 per month
Monthly expenditure:	
Expenses of former matrimonial home, council tax, etc.	136.30
Mortgage	719.00
Endowment policy	198.00
Gas	50.00
Electricity	20.00
Telephone	20.00
Contents insurance	10.00
Ground rent and maintenance charge	12.00
Television licence	8.00
Council tax and water rates	58.00
Hire purchase: car, furniture	135.82
Savings	152.00
Food	200.00
Clothes	20.00
Holidays	150.00

Problem 3

The XYZ Building Society is unwilling to advance money for the purchase of terraced houses without front gardens in an area where members of ethnic minority groups live. Your instructing solicitors have presented you with a copy of a report compiled by the Commission for Racial Equality which states that 86 per cent of ethnic minority families living in that area live in terraced houses without front gardens, and that 46 per cent of white families living there live in terraced houses without front gardens.

Your instructing solicitors believe that their client (a member of an ethnic minority group) can successfully claim that she has been indirectly discriminated against on racial grounds by the Building Society, which has refused to advance her a mortgage to purchase a terraced house without a front garden in the area. Explain how you can use the figures supplied to help to prove discrimination.

Problem 4

The defendant is charged with fraud. The prosecution wishes to prove that in May of a particular year her level of income and expenditure rose significantly, and has obtained copies of her bank statements. Do they bear this out?

BARTLETT'S BANK PLC
27 Old Street   Account: J Park
London EC8Y 2HR   14278693

Date	Details		Withdrawals	Deposits	Balance
					3,018.88
27 Mar		000621	50.00		2,968.88
28 Mar	CHEQUES			321.67	3,290.55
30 Mar		000620	98.27		
	PAYROLL			948.25	
		AC	30.00		4,110.53
3 Apr	HOLT FINANCE	SO	59.28		
	BROADWAY RENTALS	SO	22.90		4,028.35
5 Apr		000622	31.84		3,996.51
6 Apr		AC	75.00		3,921.51
7 Apr	W LONDON CTY CT	SO	100.00		3,821.51
10 Apr		000623	1,260.55		2,560.96
11 Apr		CC		13.60	
		000624	80.00		2,494.56
14 Apr		AC	50.00		
		000627	142.88		2,301.68
17 Apr	WESTLAND B/SOC	SO	392.27		
		000628	50.00		1,859.41
18 Apr		000625	27.00		1,832.41
19 Apr		AC	75.00		
	L. B. LAMBETH	SO	76.82		
		CC		500.00	2,180.59
20 Apr		000626	60.48		2,120.11
21 Apr		000629	100.00		2,020.11
25 Apr	S/ELEC	SO	43.00		1,977.11
26 Apr		000630	5,000.00		3,022.89 OD
27 Apr		CC		142.80	2,880.09 OD
28 Apr	PAYROLL			948.25	
		AC	75.00		2,006.84 OD
2 May	HOLT FINANCE	SO	59.28		
		000632	50.00		2,116.12 OD
3 May	BROADWAY RENTALS	SO	22.90		
	CHEQUES			347.80	1,791.22 OD
5 May		000633	50.00		1,841.22 OD
8 May		AC	25.00		
	W LONDON CTY CT	SO	100.00		1,966.22 OD
9 May		CC		87.30	1,878.92 OD
10 May		000636	32.99		1,911.91 OD
11 May		000635	50.00		1,961.91 OD
12 May	BANK CHARGES		36.80		
		AC	75.00		
		CC		7.21	2,066.50 OD
16 May	WESTLAND B/SOC	SO	392.27		
	P. LANGTON			2, 500.00	41.23

Date	Details		Withdrawals	Deposits	Balance
17 May	INTEREST		36.67		
		000634	186.21		181.65 OD
18 May	STAR CLUB	DD	32.00		
		AC	75.00		
		CC		500.00	211.35
19 May	L. B. LAMBETH	SO	76.82		134.53
22 May		000637	75.00		59.53
25 May		AC	75.00		
	S/ELEC	SO	43.00		58.47 OD
26 May		000638	21.95		
		CC		142.80	62.38
30 May	PAYROLL			948.25	
		000639	50.00		
		000640	17.90		
		000641	100.00		
	CHEQUES			338.92	1,181.65
1Jun		AC	50.00		1,131.65
2Jun	INTEREST		2.86		1,128.79
5 Jun	HOLT FINANCE	SO	59.28		
	BROADWAY RENTALS	SO	22.90		
		000642	50.00		996.61
7 Jun		000644	250.00		
	P. LANGTON			2, 500.00	
	W LONDON CTY CT	SO	100.00		3,146.61
8 Jun		000643	44.99		3,101.62
9 Jun		AC	75.00		3,026.62
12 Jun		AC	50.00		2,976.62
13 Jun		CC		28.50	3,005.12
16 Jun	WESTLAND B/SOC	SO	392.27		
		000645	50.00		2,562.85
19 Jun	L. B. LAMBETH	SO	76.82		
		CC		500.00	2,986.03
20 Jun		000646	60.00		2,926.03
23 Jun		000647	23.90		2,902.13
23 Jun		AC	75.00		2,827.13

Key: SO STANDING ORDER AC AUTOMATED CASH OD OVERDRAWN CC CASH AND/
OR CHEQUES DD DIRECT DEBIT

APPENDIX 1
LEGAL SOURCES FOR THE PRACTITIONER:
A BIBLIOGRAPHY

The list of books, law reports, journals, and electronic sources that follows offers a subject guide to some of the leading sources within each field of law. It is by no means a comprehensive list and there are many excellent practical legal works that are not listed here.

Works usually updated by one or more supplements before the publication of a new edition are indicated in the text. Most of the loose-leaf works referred to are available on CD-ROM or by subscription via an online subscription service—more details can be obtained direct from the publisher. The main commercial legal databases are described in more detail in **Chapter 5** at **5.3**; a guide to free legal resources on the Internet is at **5.4.3**.

1.1 Legal encyclopaedias

Atkin's Encyclopaedia of Court Forms in Civil Procedure, 2nd edn (LexisNexis). Updated by reissued volumes and loose-leaf noter-up.

Current Law Cases and *Current Law Statutes* (Sweet & Maxwell). Includes *Yearbooks* and *Citator*. Updated by *Current Law Monthly Digest*. Available online via *Westlaw*.

The Digest: Annotated British, Commonwealth and European Cases, 3rd edn (LexisNexis). Updated by regular reissued volumes, annual *Cumulative Supplement* and quarterly *Survey*.

The Encyclopaedia of Forms and Precedents, 5th edn (LexisNexis). Updated by reissued volumes and loose-leaf noter-up. Available online via *LexisNexis*.

Halsbury's Laws of England, 4th edn reissue (LexisNexis). Updated by regular reissued volumes, annual *Cumulative Supplement*, and monthly *Current Service Noter-up*. Available online via *LexisNexis*.

Halsbury's Statutes of England and Wales, 4th edn (LexisNexis). Updated by regular reissued volumes, annual *Cumulative Supplement* and monthly *Current Service Noter-up*.

1.2 Legal dictionaries

Stroud's Judicial Dictionary of Words and Phrases, 7th edn (Sweet & Maxwell, 2006). Updated by supplement.

Words and Phrases Legally Defined, 4th edn (LexisNexis). Updated by supplement.

1.3   Law reports

The principal series of 'general' law reports are listed below. For a more detailed analysis of the key series of law reports, refer to **Chapter 4** at **4.11.2**. Other law reports are listed by subject matter at **App 1.5**.

All England Law Reports, 1936– (LexisNexis).
The Law Reports (The Incorporated Council of Law Reporting for England and Wales), also known as *The Official Series*. For details of individual series, see the table below.

The Law Reports	*Citation*	*The Law Reports*	*Citation*
Admiralty & Ecclesiastical	LRA & E	Exchequer Division	Ex D
Appeal Cases	AC	Family Division	Fam
Chancery Appeals	Ch App	King's Bench	KB
Chancery Division	Ch D	Privy Council	LR PC
Common Pleas	CP	Probate & Divorce	LR P&D
Common Pleas Division	CPD	Probate Division	PD
Crown Cases Reserved	LR CCR	Probate Division	P
English & Irish Appeals	LR HL	Queen's Bench	QB
Equity	LR Eq	Queen's Bench Division	QBD
Exchequer	LR Ex	Scotch & Divorce Appeals	Sc & D

Weekly Law Reports, 1953– (The Incorporated Council of Law Reporting for England and Wales).

1.4   Journals

Key journals of a general legal nature are listed below. These will keep the reader up to date with legal news and current legal issues. Other journals are listed by subject matter at **App 1.5** below.

Counsel: Incorporating Bar Council and Bar Standards Board News. (Bar Council).
The Law Society's Gazette. (Law Society). Available online at <http://www.lawgazette. co.uk>.
The Lawyer. Available online at <http://www.thelawyer.com>.
Legal Week (Legal Week). Available online at <http://www.legalweek.com>.
New Law Journal (LexisNexis). Available online via *LexisNexis* (2001).
Solicitors' Journal (Sweet & Maxwell). Available online at <http://www.solicitors-journal.com>.

1.5   Legal sources—by subject area

Administrative Law
See also: **Civil Litigation**
See also: **Criminal Litigation**

Administrative Court Digest, law reports (Sweet & Maxwell).

Fordham, *Judicial Review Handbook*, 4th edn (Hart Publishing, 2004).

Lewis, *Judicial Remedies in Public Law*, 4th edn (Sweet & Maxwell, 2008). Updated by supplement.

Supperstone & Goudie, *Judicial Review*, 3rd edn (LexisNexis, 2005).

Wade & Forsyth, *Administrative Law*, 9th edn (Oxford University Press, 2004).

Woolf, Jowell & Le Sueur, *De Smith's Judicial Review*, 6th edn (Sweet & Maxwell, 2007). Updated by supplement.

Agency

Bowstead & Reynolds, *Law of Agency*, 18th edn (Sweet & Maxwell, 2006). Updated by supplement.

Arbitration

Arbitration Law Monthly, journal (Informa Publishing).

Lloyd's Arbitration Reports, law reports (Lloyd's).

Mustill & Boyd, *The Law and Practice of Commercial Arbitration in England*, 2nd edn (Butterworths, 1989). Updated by companion volume (2001).

Redfern & Hunter, *The Law and Practice of International Commercial Arbitration*, 4th edn (Sweet & Maxwell, 2004). Available online via *Westlaw*.

Banking

Elliott, *Byles on Bills of Exchange and Cheques*, 28th edn (Sweet & Maxwell, 2007).

Encyclopaedia of Banking Law, loose-leaf (LexisNexis). Available online via *LexisNexis*.

Guest, *Chalmers & Guest on Bills of Exchange*, 16th edn (Sweet & Maxwell, 2005).

Hapgood, *Paget's Law of Banking*, 13th edn (LexisNexis, 2006). Available online via *LexisNexis*.

Bankruptcy and Personal Insolvency

Bankruptcy and Personal Insolvency Reports, law reports (Jordans).

Dennis, *The New Law of Insolvency* (Law Society, 2003).

Muir Hunter on Personal Insolvency, loose-leaf (Sweet & Maxwell).

Totty & Moss, *Insolvency,* loose-leaf (Sweet & Maxwell). Available online via *Westlaw*.

Building

Construction Law Journal, journal (Sweet & Maxwell).

Construction Law Reports, law reports (LexisNexis).

Emden's Construction Law, loose-leaf (LexisNexis).

Furst, *Keating on Construction Contracts*, 8th edn (Sweet & Maxwell, 2006).

Charities

Tudor, *Tudor on Charities*, 9th edn (Sweet & Maxwell, 2003). Updated by supplement.

Children

See also: **Family Law**

Child & Family Law Quarterly, journal (Jordans).

Childright, journal (University of Essex).

Clarke, Hall & Morrison on Children, loose-leaf (LexisNexis). Available online via *LexisNexis*.

Hershman & McFarlane, *Children Law and Practice*, loose-leaf (Jordans). Available online via *Jordans*.

Civil Litigation

See also: **Administrative Law**

See also: **Costs**

Blackstone's Civil Practice, annual (Oxford University Press).

Blake, *A Practical Approach to Effective Litigation*, 6th edn (Oxford University Press, 2005).

Bullen & Leake & Jacob's Precedents of Pleadings, 16th edn (Sweet & Maxwell, 2007). Available online via *Westlaw*.

Butterworths Civil Court Precedents, loose-leaf (LexisNexis).

The Civil Court Practice ('The Green Book'), annual (LexisNexis). Updated by supplements and regular reissues. Available online via *LexisNexis*.

Civil Procedure ('The White Book'), annual (Sweet & Maxwell). Updated by supplements and regular reissues. Available online via *Westlaw*.

Lawtel Civil Procedure, online service (Lawtel/Sweet & Maxwell).

Practical Civil Court Precedents, loose-leaf (Sweet & Maxwell).

Rose, *Pleadings without Tears: A Guide to Legal Drafting under the Civil Procedure Rules*, 7th edn (Oxford University Press, 2007).

Westlaw UK Civil Procedure, online service (Sweet & Maxwell).

Company and Commercial Law

See also: **Sale of Goods and Consumer Law**

All England Law Reports: Commercial Cases, 1996– (LexisNexis).

British Company Law and Practice, loose-leaf (CCH).

British Company Cases, law reports (CCH).

Butterworths Company Law Cases, law reports (LexisNexis).

Butterworths Company Law Service, loose-leaf (LexisNexis).

Butterworths Corporate Law Service, loose-leaf (LexisNexis). Available online via *LexisNexis*.

Company Lawyer, journal (Sweet & Maxwell).

Gore-Browne on Companies, 44th edn, loose-leaf (Jordans). Available online via *Jordans*.

Journal of Business Law, journal (Sweet & Maxwell).

Palmer's Company Law, loose-leaf (Sweet & Maxwell). Available online via *Westlaw*.

PLC Competition, Corporate, Property, database services (Practical Law for Companies).

PLC Magazine, journal (Practical Law for Companies).

Roberts, *Law Relating to Financial Services*, 4th edn (Financial World Publishing, 2004).

Westlaw UK Corporate Business, online service (Sweet & Maxwell).

Competition Law

Bellamy & Child, *European Community Law of Competition*, 6th edn (Oxford University Press, 2008).

Butterworths Competition Law, loose-leaf (LexisNexis).

European Competition Law Review, journal (ESC Publishing).

Korah, *An Introductory Guide to EC Competition Law and Practice*, 9th edn (Hart Publishing, 2007).

Sweet & Maxwell's Encyclopedia of Competition Law, loose-leaf (Sweet & Maxwell).

Whish, *Competition Law*, 6th edn (2008).

Conflict of Laws

Cheshire, North, & Fawcett, *Private International Law*, 14th edn (LexisNexis, 2008).

Dicey & Morris, *Conflict of Laws*, 14th edn (Sweet & Maxwell, 2006). Updated by supplement.

Contract

Chitty & Beale, *Chitty on Contracts*, 29th edn (Sweet & Maxwell, 2004). Updated by supplement.

Goff & Jones, *Law of Restitution*, 7th edn (Sweet & Maxwell, 2006). Updated by supplement.

Conveyancing

See also: **Real Property**

Emmet & Farrand, *Emmet on Title*, loose-leaf (Sweet & Maxwell).

Encyclopedia of Compulsory Purchase, loose-leaf & CD-ROM (Sweet & Maxwell).

Fisher, *Fisher & Lightwood's Law of Mortgage*, 12th edn (LexisNexis, 2006). Updated by supplement.

Ruoff & Roper, *Law and Practice of Registered Conveyancing*, loose-leaf & CD-ROM (Sweet & Maxwell).

Silverman, *The Law Society's Conveyancing Handbook*, annual (Law Society).

Sweet & Maxwell's Conveyancing Practice, loose-leaf (Sweet & Maxwell).

Coroners

Burton & Mathews, *Jervis on the Office and Duties of Coroners: with forms and precedents*, 12th edn (Sweet & Maxwell, 2002). Updated by supplement.

Costs

See also: **Civil Litigation**

See also: **Criminal Litigation**

Butterworths Costs Service, loose-leaf (LexisNexis).

Cook on Costs, annual (LexisNexis).

Criminal Litigation

See also: **Administrative Law**

See also: **Costs**

See also: **Sentencing**

Anthony & Berryman, *Magistrates' Court Guide*, annual (LexisNexis).

Archbold, *Criminal Pleading, Evidence and Practice*, annual (Sweet & Maxwell). Updated by supplement. Available online via *Westlaw*.

Blackstone's Criminal Practice, annual (Oxford University Press). Available online via *LexisNexis*. Updated by *Bulletin* and online companion website.

Criminal Appeal Reports, law reports (Sweet & Maxwell).

Criminal Law Review, journal (Sweet & Maxwell).

Stone's Justices' manual, annual (LexisNexis). Available online via *LexisNexis*.

Westlaw UK Crime, online service (Sweet & Maxwell).

Wilkinson's Road Traffic Offences, annual (Sweet & Maxwell). Updated by *Bulletin*.

Damages

See also: **Personal Injury**

Allen, *APIL Guide to Damages* (Jordans, 2004).

Bell, *Guidelines for the Assessment of Damages in Personal Injury Cases*, annual (Judicial Studies Board/Oxford University Press). Available online via *Lawtel*.

Kemp & Kemp: The Quantum of Damages in Personal Injury and Fatal Accident Claims, loose-leaf & CD-ROM (Sweet & Maxwell).

Lawtel Personal Injury, online service (Lawtel/Sweet & Maxwell).

McGregor, *Damages*, 17th edn (Sweet & Maxwell, 2003). Updated by supplement.

Personal Injury and Quantum Reports, law reports (Sweet & Maxwell).

Wilde, *Facts and Figures: Tables for the Calculation of Damages*, annual (Professional Negligence Bar Association/Sweet & Maxwell).

Data Protection
Carey, *Data Protection Handbook*, 2nd edn (Law Society, 2004).
Encyclopedia of Data Protection, loose-leaf (Sweet & Maxwell).

E-Commerce
See: **Information Technology**

Ecclesiastical Law
Hill, *Ecclesiastical Law*, 3rd edn (Oxford University Press, 2007).

Education
Hyams, The *Law of Education*, 2nd edn (Jordans, 2004).
The Law of Education, loose-leaf (LexisNexis). Available online via *LexisNexis*.

Employment Law
See also: **Health and Safety**
Encyclopedia of Employment Law and Practice, loose-leaf (Sweet & Maxwell).
Employment Law Journal, journal (Legalease).
Harvey on Industrial Relations and Employment Law, loose-leaf (LexisNexis). Available online via *LexisNexis*.
Industrial Cases Reports, law reports (Incorporated Council of Law Reporting).
Industrial Relations Law Reports, law reports (LexisNexis).

Environmental Law
Encyclopedia of Environmental Health Law and Practice, loose-leaf (Sweet & Maxwell).
Encyclopedia of Environmental Law and Practice, 2nd edn, loose-leaf (Sweet & Maxwell).
Environmental Law Reports, law reports (Sweet & Maxwell).
Garner's Environmental Law, loose-leaf (LexisNexis). Available online via *LexisNexis*.

Equity and Trusts
McGhee, *Snell's Equity*, 31st edn (Sweet & Maxwell, 2004). Updated by supplement.
Underhill & Hayton, *Law Relating to Trustees*, 17th edn (LexisNexis, 2006).

European Union Law
See also: **Competition Law**
All England Law Reports: European Cases, 1983– (LexisNexis).
Common Market Law Reports, law reports (Sweet & Maxwell).
Common Market Law Review, journal (Kluwer).
Encyclopedia of European Community Law, loose-leaf (Sweet & Maxwell).
European Court Reports, law reports (European Court of Justice). Available online via Eur-Lex <http://eur-lex.europa.eu/en/index.htm>.
European Law Review, journal (Sweet & Maxwell).
Official Journal of the European Union, journal (Office for Official Publications of the European Union). Available online via Europa <http://eur-lex.europa.eu/>.
Vaughan, *Law of the European Communities*, loose-leaf (LexisNexis).

Evidence
Cross & Tapper, *Evidence*, 11th edn (LexisNexis, 2007).
Dennis, *The Law of Evidence*, 3rd edn (Sweet & Maxwell, 2007).
Keane, *The Modern Law of Evidence*, 7th edn (Oxford University Press, 2008).

May, *Criminal Evidence*, 5th edn (Sweet & Maxwell, 2004).

Phipson, *On Evidence*, 16th edn (Sweet & Maxwell, 2005). Updated by supplement.

Family Law

See also: **Children**

Bird, *Ancillary Relief Handbook*, 6th edn (Jordans, 2007).

Butterworths Family Law Service, loose-leaf (LexisNexis). Available online via *LexisNexis*.

Family Court Reports, law reports (LexisNexis).

Family Law, journal (Jordans). Available online via *Jordans*.

Family Law Reports, law reports (Jordans). Available online via *Jordans*.

Jackson, *Matrimonial Finance and Taxation*, 8th edn (LexisNexis, 2008). Available online via *LexisNexis*.

Practical Matrimonial Precedents, loose-leaf & CD-ROM. (Sweet & Maxwell).

Rayden & Jackson's Divorce and Family Matters, 18th edn, loose-leaf (LexisNexis, 2005). Available online via *LexisNexis*.

Forms and Precedents

See also: **Civil Litigation**

See also: **Criminal Litigation**

See also: Individual subject areas

Atkin's Encyclopaedia of Court Forms in Civil Procedure, 2nd edn (LexisNexis). Updated by reissued volumes and loose-leaf noter-up. Available online via *LexisNexis*.

The Court Service, online service at <http://www.hmcourts-service.gov.uk> (Court Service).

The Encyclopaedia of Forms and Precedents, 5th edn (LexisNexis). Updated by reissued volumes and loose-leaf noter-up. Available online via *LexisNexis*.

EveryForm, online service at <http://www.everyform.co.uk>.

Kelly, *Kelly's Draftsman*, 19th edn (LexisNexis, 2006).

Health and Safety

See also: **Employment**

Encyclopedia of Health and Safety at Work Law and Practice, loose-leaf (Sweet & Maxwell).

Ford, *Redgrave's Health and Safety*, 5th edn (LexisNexis, 2007). Updated by supplement. Available online via *LexisNexis*.

Housing Law

Arden & Partington, *Housing Law*, 2nd edn, loose-leaf (Sweet & Maxwell).

Dowding, *Dilapidations: The Modern Law and Practice*, 3rd edn (Sweet & Maxwell, 2006).

Encyclopedia of Housing Law and Practice, loose-leaf (Sweet & Maxwell).

Housing Law Reports, law reports (Sweet & Maxwell).

Human Rights

Emmerson, *Human Rights and Criminal Justice*, 2nd edn (Sweet & Maxwell, 2007).

European Human Rights Reports, law reports (Sweet & Maxwell).

Human Rights Practice, loose-leaf (Sweet & Maxwell). Available online via *Westlaw*.

Lester & Pannick, *Human Rights Law and Practice*, 2nd edn (LexisNexis, 2004). Available online via *LexisNexis*.

Immigration Law

Butterworths Immigration Law Service, loose-leaf (LexisNexis). Available online via *LexisNexis*.

MacDonald, *Immigration Law and Practice*, 6th edn (LexisNexis, 2005). Available online via *LexisNexis*. Updated by supplement.

Information Technology

Computers and Law, journal (Society for Computers and Law).

Encyclopaedia of Information Technology Law, loose-leaf (Sweet & Maxwell).

Journal of Information Law and Technology, journal (University of Warwick). Available online at <http://www2.warwick.ac.uk/fac/soc/law/elj/jilt>.

Rowland & MacDonald, *Information Technology Law*, 3rd edn (Routledge Cavendish, 2005).

Insolvency
See: **Bankruptcy and Personal Insolvency**

Insurance

Birds, *Birds' Modern Insurance Law*, 7th edn (Sweet & Maxwell, 2007).

Encyclopedia of Insurance Law, loose-leaf (Sweet & Maxwell).

Leigh-Jones, *MacGillivray on Insurance Law*, 10th edn (Sweet & Maxwell, 2005). Updated by supplement.

Lloyd's Law Reports: Insurance and Reinsurance, law report (Informa).

Intellectual Property

Copinger & Skone Jones on Copyright, 15th edn (Sweet & Maxwell, 2007). Updated by supplement. Available online via *Westlaw*.

Cornish, *Intellectual Property Patents, Copyright, Trademarks and Allied Rights*, 6th edn (Sweet & Maxwell, 2007).

Encyclopedia of United Kingdom and European Patent Law, loose-leaf (Sweet & Maxwell).

Fleet Street Reports, law reports (Sweet & Maxwell).

Kerly's Law of Trade Marks and Trade Names, 14th edn (Sweet & Maxwell, 2005). Available online via *Westlaw*.

Laddie, *Modern Law of Copyright and Designs*, 3rd edn (Butterworths, 2000). Available online via *LexisNexis*.

Merkin & Black, *Copyright and Designs Law*, loose-leaf (Sweet & Maxwell).

Terrell on the Law of Patents, 16th edn (Sweet & Maxwell, 2005). Available online via *Westlaw*.

Landlord and Tenant
See also: **Housing**

Hill and Redman's Law of Landlord and Tenant, loose-leaf (LexisNexis). Available online via *LexisNexis*.

The Landlord and Tenant Factbook, loose-leaf (Sweet & Maxwell).

Landlord and Tenant Reports, law reports (Sweet & Maxwell).

Smith, *The Law of Landlord and Tenant*, 6th edn (Butterworths, 2002).

Woodfall's Law of Landlord and Tenant, loose-leaf (Sweet & Maxwell). Available online via *Westlaw*.

Legal Profession

Bird & Weir, *The Law, Practice and Conduct of Solicitors* (Waterlow, 1989).

The Bar Handbook, annual (LexisNexis)

Boon & Levin, *The Ethics and Conduct of Lawyers in England and Wales* (Hart, 1999).

Cordery on Solicitors, loose-leaf (LexisNexis).

The Guide to the Professional Conduct of Solicitors, 8th edn (Law Society, 1999).

Paterson & Ritchie, *The Law Practice and Conduct of Solicitors* (Sweet & Maxwell, 2006).

Solicitors' Accounts Manual, 10th edn (Law Society, 2008).

Legal Research

De Bono, *Six Thinking Hats* (Penguin, 2000).

Holborn, *Butterworths Legal Research Guide*, 2nd edn (Butterworths, 2001).

Hutchinson, *Researching and Writing in Law*, 2nd edn (Law Book Co. of Australasia, 2001).

Legal Skills

Beardsmore, *Opinion Writing and Drafting in Tort* (Cavendish, 1996).

Bennion, *Statutory Interpretation: A Code*, 5th edn (LexisNexis, 2008). Updated by supplement.

Blake, *A Practical Approach to Effective Litigation*, 6th edn (Oxford University Press, 2005).

Fridd, *Basic Practice in Courts, Tribunals and Enquiries*, 3rd edn (Sweet & Maxwell, 2000).

Hyam, *Advocacy Skills*, 4th edn (Blackstone, 1999).

Munkman, *The Technique of Advocacy* (Universal Law Publishing Co. Ltd, 2003).

Libel

Carter-Ruck, *Libel and Slander*, 5th edn (Butterworths, 1997).

Gatley, *Libel and Slander*, 10th edn (Sweet & Maxwell, 2007). Updated by supplement.

Licensing

Entertainment and Media Law Reports, law reports (Sweet & Maxwell).

Hyde, *Licensing Procedures and Precedents*, loose-leaf (Sweet & Maxwell).

Pain, *Licensing Practice and Procedure*, 9th edn (Callow, 2008).

Paterson, *Paterson's Licensing Acts*, annual (LexisNexis).

Local Government

Bailey, *Cross on Principles of Local Government Law*, 3rd edn (Sweet & Maxwell, 2004).

Cross on Local Government Law, 8th edn, loose-leaf (Sweet & Maxwell).

Encyclopedia of Local Government Law, loose-leaf (Sweet & Maxwell).

Encyclopedia of Rating and Local Taxation, loose-leaf (Sweet & Maxwell).

Lawtel Local Government, online service (Sweet & Maxwell).

Ryde on Rating and the Council Tax, loose-leaf (LexisNexis). Available online via *LexisNexis*.

Maritime Law

Baughen, *Shipping Law*, 3rd edn (Cavendish, 2004).

Benedict on Admiralty, 7th edn, loose-leaf (Bender).

Carver on Bills of Lading, 2nd edn (Sweet & Maxwell, 2005).

Hill, *Maritime Law*, 6th edn (LLP, 2003).

Lloyd's Law Reports, law report (Lloyd's).

Lloyd's Maritime and Commercial Law Quarterly, journal (Informa).

Lorenzon, *CIF and FOB Contracts*, 5th edn (Sweet & Maxwell, 2006).

Scrutton on Charterparties and Bills of Lading, 20th edn (Sweet & Maxwell, 1996).

Thomas, *Modern Law of Marine Insurance* (LLP, 2002).

Medical Law

Grubb, *Principles of Medical Law*, 2nd edn (Oxford University Press, 2004).

LS Law Medical, Law Report (Informa).

Malsher, *Medical Records for Lawyers* (EMIS, 2002).

Montgomery, *Health Care Law*, 2nd edn (Oxford University Press, 2002).

Palmer, *Medicine for Lawyers* (Royal Society of Medicine, 2005).

Mental Health

Gostin on Mental Health Law, loose-leaf (Shaw & Sons).

Heywood & Massey, *Court of Protection Practice*, loose-leaf, 13th edn (Sweet & Maxwell).

Journal of Mental Health Law, journal (Northumbria Law Press).

Cretney, *Cretney & Lush: Lasting and Enduring Powers of Attorney*, 6th edn (Jordans, 2008).

Negligence
See: **Torts**

Partnership

Encyclopaedia of Professional Partnerships, loose-leaf (Sweet & Maxwell).

Lindley & Banks, *Lindley & Banks on Partnership*, 18th rev. edn (Sweet & Maxwell, 2005). Updated by supplement.

Personal Injury
See also: **Damages and Road Traffic Law**

Barrie, *Personal Injury Law: Liability, Compensation, and Procedure*, 2nd edn (Oxford University Press, 2005).

Bingham and Berrymans' Personal Injury and Motor Claims Cases, 12th edn (LexisNexis, 2006). Updated by supplement.

Buchan, *Personal Injury Practice: The Guide to Litigation in the County Court and High Court*, 4th edn (LexisNexis, 2003).

Butterworths Personal Injury Litigation Service, loose-leaf (LexisNexis). Available online via *LexisNexis*.

Curran, *Personal Injury Pleadings*, 3rd edn (Sweet & Maxwell, 2005).

Journal of Personal Injury Law, journal (Sweet & Maxwell).

Lawtel Personal Injury, online service (Lawtel/Sweet & Maxwell).

Personal Injury and Quantum Reports, law reports (Sweet & Maxwell).

Solomon, *Personal Injury Practice and Procedure*, 11th edn (Sweet & Maxwell, 2004).

Planning Law

Butterworths Planning Law Service, loose-leaf (LexisNexis). Available online via *LexisNexis*.

Encyclopedia of Planning Law and Practice, loose-leaf (Sweet & Maxwell).

Estates Gazette Law Reports, law reports (Estates Gazette).

Estates Gazette Planning Law Reports, law reports (Estates Gazette).

Journal of Planning and Environmental Law, journal (Sweet & Maxwell).

Property, Planning and Compensation Reports, law reports (Sweet & Maxwell).

Rating
See: **Local Government**

Real Property
See also: **Conveyancing**

Butterworths Property Law Service, loose-leaf (LexisNexis).

Encyclopedia of Compulsory Purchase, loose-leaf (Sweet & Maxwell).

Estates Gazette Law Reports, law reports (Estates Gazette).

Megarry & Wade, *The Law of Real Property*, 7th edn (Sweet & Maxwell, 2008).

Property Planning and Compensation Reports, law reports (Sweet & Maxwell).

Sara, *Boundaries and Easements*, 4th edn (Sweet & Maxwell, 2007). Updated by supplement.

Road Traffic Law
See also: **Personal Injury**

Bingham & Berryman's Personal Injury and Motor Claims Cases, 12th edn (LexisNexis, 2006). Updated by supplement.

Butterworths Road Traffic Service, loose-leaf (LexisNexis).

Encyclopedia of Highway Law and Practice, loose-leaf (Sweet & Maxwell).

Encyclopedia of Road Traffic Law and Practice, loose-leaf (Sweet & Maxwell).

Road Traffic Reports, law reports (Sweet & Maxwell).

Wilkinson's Road Traffic Offences, annual (Sweet & Maxwell). Updated by supplement.

Sale of Goods and Consumer Law
Atiyah, *Sale of Goods*, 11th edn (Pearson/Longman, 2005).

Benjamin, *Sale of Goods*, 7th edn (Sweet & Maxwell, 2006). Updated by supplement.

Butterworths Law of Food and Drugs, loose-leaf (LexisNexis). Available online via *LexisNexis*.

Butterworths Trading and Consumer Law, loose-leaf (LexisNexis). Available online via *LexisNexis*.

Encyclopedia of Consumer Credit Law, loose-leaf (Sweet & Maxwell).

Encyclopedia of Consumer Law, loose-leaf (Sweet & Maxwell).

Goode, *Consumer Credit Law & Practice*, loose-leaf (LexisNexis).

Miller, *Product Liability and Safety Encyclopaedia*, loose-leaf (LexisNexis). Available online via *LexisNexis*.

O'Keefe, *Law of Weights and Measures*, loose-leaf (LexisNexis). Available online via *LexisNexis*.

Sentencing
See also: **Crime**

Criminal Appeal Reports (Sentencing), law reports (Sweet & Maxwell).

Magistrates Bench Handbook: A Manual for Lay Magistrates, loose-leaf (Waterside).

Thomas, *Current Sentencing Practice*, loose-leaf (Sweet & Maxwell). Available online via *Westlaw*.

Thomas, *Sentencing Referencer*, annual (Sweet & Maxwell). Available online via *Westlaw*.

Wasik, *Emmins on Sentencing*, 4th edn (Blackstone Press, 2001).

Shipping
See: **Maritime Law**

Social Security and Welfare Law
Encyclopedia of Social Services and Child Care Law, loose-leaf (Sweet & Maxwell).

Journal of Social Welfare and Family Law, journal (Routledge).

Tolley's Social Security and State Benefits Handbook, annual (LexisNexis).

Wikeley & Ogus, *Law of Social Security*, 5th edn (Butterworths, 2002).

Taxation
See also: **Local Government**

Bramwell, *Taxation of Companies and Company Reconstructions*, loose-leaf, 8th edn (Sweet & Maxwell).

British Tax Review, journal (Sweet & Maxwell).

De Voil's Indirect Tax Service, loose-leaf (LexisNexis). Available online via *LexisNexis*.

Foster's Inheritance Tax, loose-leaf (LexisNexis). Available online via *LexisNexis*.

Simon's Direct Tax Service, loose-leaf (LexisNexis). Available online via *LexisNexis*.

Sumption, *Taxation Capital Gains*, loose-leaf (LexisNexis).

Taxation, journal (LexisNexis).

Tolley's Orange Tax Handbook, annual (LexisNexis).

Tolley's Yellow Tax Handbook, annual (LexisNexis).

Whiteman, *On Capital Gains Tax*, 4th edn (Sweet & Maxwell, 2007). Updated by supplement.

Whiteman, *On Income Tax*, 4th edn (Sweet & Maxwell, 2008). Updated by supplement.

Torts

Charlesworth & Percy on Negligence, 11th edn (Sweet & Maxwell, 2006). Updated by supplement. Available online via *Westlaw*.

Clerk & Lindsell on Torts, 19th edn (Sweet & Maxwell, 2005). Updated by supplement.

Jackson & Powell on Professional Liability, 6th edn (Sweet & Maxwell, 2007). Updated by supplement.

Lloyd's Law Reports: Professional Negligence, law reports (LLP/Informa).

Maddison, *Bingham's Negligence Cases*, 5th edn (Sweet & Maxwell, 2002).

Pittaway, *Professional Negligence Cases* (Butterworths, 1998).

Powers and Harris, *Clinical Negligence*, 3rd edn (Butterworths, 1999).

Wills, Probate, and Succession

Butterworths Wills, Probate and Administration Service, loose-leaf (LexisNexis). Available online via *LexisNexis*.

Griffin & Walker, *Administration of Estates*, 2nd rev. edn (Financial World Publishing, 2004).

Sherrin, *Williams on Wills*, 9th edn (LexisNexis, 2008). Updated by supplement.

Sherrin & Bonehill, *Law and Practice of Intestate Succession*, 3rd edn (Sweet & Maxwell, 2004). Updated by supplement.

Theobald on Wills, 16th edn (Sweet & Maxwell, 2001). Updated by supplement.

Tristram & Coote, *Probate Practice*, 30th edn (LexisNexis, 2006). Updated by supplement.

Williams, Mortimer, and Sunnucks, *Executors, Administrators & Probate*, 19th edn (Sweet & Maxwell, 2007). Updated by supplement.

APPENDIX 2
GLOSSARY OF MEDICAL TERMS

This glossary contains the meaning of certain technical terms commonly found in medical reports.

Abduction: movement away from the mid-line

Adduction: movement towards the mid-line

Amnesia: absence of memory

Analgesic: pain-relieving medication

Ankylosis: obliteration of a joint by fusion, either bony or fibrous

Aphasia: loss of power of speech

Arthrodesis: fusion of a joint by operation

Arthroplasty: production of movement in a joint by operation

Arthroscopy: direct vision inside a joint using a fibre-optic scope

Aspiration: sucking out fluid (e.g., from a joint or a cavity) through a hollow needle

Ataxia: unsteadiness of gait

Atrophy: wasting of a body part from lack of vascular or nerve supply

Avascular necrosis: death of tissue through deprivation of blood supply; refers particularly to bones—e.g., head of femur following fracture of neck of femur

Avulsion: wrenching away of a part, e.g. avulsion fracture, the wrenching away of a fragment of bone by force applied by an attached tendon

Axonotmesis: interruption of conductivity in a nerve by 'physiological' (i.e., not physical) division of the axons, resulting in paralysis and anaesthesia in the distribution of the nerve; spontaneous recovery can be expected but will take some months (cf. neurapraxia and neurotmesis)

Biopsy: microscopic examination of tissue taken from the living body

Bi-valve: removal of a plaster cast by cutting along each side of its length, permitting replacement if required

Brachial: pertaining to the arm

Brachioradialis: muscle of the forearm

B.S.R. (or E.S.R.): blood (or erythrocyte) rate—a laboratory test upon the blood to detect the presence of an inflammatory process somewhere in the body

Bursa: a cyst-like sac between a bony prominence and the skin—e.g., prepatellar bursa, inflammation in which constitutes 'housemaid's knee'

Calcaneal: pertaining to the calcaneus

Calcaneus: the heel bone, or os calcis

Callus: the cement-like new bone formation which produces union of the fragments of a fracture

Cardiac: pertaining to the heart

Cephalic: pertaining to the head

Cervical: pertaining to the neck

Chondral: pertaining to cartilage

Chronic: long-lasting, the reverse of acute

Claudication: lameness; applied particularly to pain in the calf muscles resulting from defective blood supply owing to arterial disease

Comminuted: a type of fracture of a bone in which there are more than two fragments

Concussion of the brain: to establish the diagnosis, the loss of consciousness must be immediate and complete, though it may be of very short duration

Condyle: a rounded articular eminence

Cortex: the outer layer of a structure—e.g., the 'shell' of a bone; the surface of the brain

Costal: pertaining to the ribs

Crepitus: a creaking or grating, found in osteoarthritic joints; also in recent fractures and with inflammation of tendons and their sheaths (tenosynovitis)

C.S.F.: cerebro-spinal fluid, which lies on the surface of the brain and spinal cord and inside the ventricles of the brain

Cuboid: a small bone of the foot

Cyanosis: blueness from deficient oxygenation of the blood

Deltoid region: the outer region of the upper third of the arm

Diplopia: double vision

Disarticulation: amputation through a joint

Disc, intervertebral: fibro-cartilaginous 'cushion' between two vertebrae

Distal: farthest point from the centre (opposite to proximal)

Dorsal spine: that part of the spine from which the ribs spring; known also as the 'thoracic' spine

Dorsiflexion: movement of a joint in a backward direction (syn. extension)

Dorsum: back or top—e.g., back of hand, top of foot

Dupuytren's contracture: thickened fibrous tissue in the palm of the hand causing contracture of the fingers

Dys-: prefix meaning difficult, defective, painful—e.g., dyspnoea, meaning shortness of breath

-ectomy: suffix meaning surgical excision—e.g., patellectomy, removal of the patella

E.E.G.: electro-encephalogram (graph of electric impulses in the brain)

Effusion: extravasation of fluid in a joint (or any cavity—e.g., 'water on the knee' (i.e., synovitis)

Embolism: blockage of blood vessel by a clot which has migrated

Emphysema, surgical: collection of air in the tissues through puncture of the lung by a fractured rib

E.N.T.: ear, nose, and throat

Epiphyseal line: the cartilaginous plate near the end of a bone at which the bone grows in length

Epiphysis: the end of a bone during the period of growth

Erythema: superficial blush or redness of the skin—e.g., as from a very slight burn or scald

Erythrocyte: red blood corpuscle

Eschar: crust of dead skin

Extension: moving a joint into the straight position (opposite to flexion)

External: outer side, syn. lateral (opposite to medial)

Fascia: a fibrous membrane

Femoral: pertaining to the femur

Femur: the thigh bone

Flexion: moving a joint into the bent position (opposite to extension)

Flexor: a muscle that bends or flexes a part

Fossa: anatomical term for a depression or furrow

Gangrene: total death of a structure through deprivation of blood supply

Genu: the knee joint

Gluteal: pertaining to the buttock

Haemarthrosis: effusion of blood in a joint

Haematoma: localised collection of blood

Hallux: the great toe

Humerus: the bone of the upper arm

Hyper-: prefix meaning increase above the normal

Hypo-: prefix meaning decrease below the normal; anatomical term for below

Ileum: the lower half of the small intestine

Ilium: the main bone of the pelvis

Induration: hardening of a tissue

Infarct: a wedge-shaped haemorrhagic or necrotic area produced by obstruction of a terminal artery

Inguinal: pertaining to the groin

Intercostal: between the ribs

Interosseous: between bones

Intracranial: within the skull

Intubation: insertion of a breathing tube through the vocal cords

Ischaemia: reduction of local blood supply to a structure

-itis: suffix meaning inflammation—e.g., osteitis, inflammation of a bone

Keloid: a scar which is thickened and deep pink in colour

Kyphosis: posterior convexity of the spine

Laceration: physical tearing of a structure, e.g., lacerated skin

Lateral: outer side, or external (opposite to medial)

Leg: that part of the lower limb between the knee and ankle

Lesion: a structural change in a tissue caused by disease or injury

Leucocyte: white blood corpuscle

Ligamentous: pertaining to a ligament

Lipping: ridge of adventitious bone at joint edges in arthritis (syn. osteophytic formation)

Lordosis: anterior convexity of the spine

Lumbar: the 'small' of the back—i.e., situated between the dorsal (thoracic) and sacral levels

Lumen: the cavity of a tubular structure

Macro-: prefix meaning abnormally large size

Malar: pertaining to cheek

Mallet finger: inability actively to straighten the terminal joint of a finger

Mandible: the lower jaw

Maxilla: the upper jaw

Medial: inner side, or internal (opposite to lateral)

Medullary cavity: the soft interior of a bone

Meniscus: the semilunar cartilage of the knee

Metacarp-phalangeal: pertaining to the joint between the fingers and the bones of the palm of the hand

Micro-: prefix meaning abnormally small size

Motor: pertaining to movement (applied particularly to peripheral nerve function)

Myelo-: prefix meaning pertaining to the spinal cord

Myo-: prefix meaning pertaining to muscle

Necrosis: death of tissue

Neurapraxia: interruption of conductivity in a nerve owing to pressure thereon, resulting in temporary paralysis and anaesthesia in the distribution of the nerve; full recovery will take place spontaneously in a matter of days or very few weeks (cf. axonotmesis and neurotmesis)

Neurotmesis: interruption of conductivity in a nerve by anatomical division causing permanent paralysis and anaesthesia in the distribution of the nerve; recovery cannot take place unless the nerve is surgically repaired (cf. axonotmesis and neurapraxia)

Nystagmus: oscillatory movement of the eyes

Oedema: accumulation of fluid in the tissues

Oesophagus: the gullet, the muscular tube connecting the back of the mouth and the stomach

Olfactory: pertaining to the sense of smell

Oligo-: prefix meaning lack of

Optic fundi: optic disc, where the optic nerve enters the retina

Orthopaedic: pertaining to bony deformity

Os calcis: see calcaneus

Osteitis: inflammation of bone

Osteoarthritis: degeneration of a joint from wear and tear

Osteophyte: ridge of adventitious bone at joint edges in arthritis (syn. 'lipping')

Osteoporosis: loss of mineral salts from bones, the result of lack of use owing to injury or disease and causing softening of the bone

Palmarflexion: moving the wrist in the direction that the palm faces (syn. flexion)

Para-: prefix meaning by the side of, near, through, abnormality

Paramedian: pertaining to a vertical line parallel with the midline, i.e. a line drawn down through the xiphoid process and umbilicus

Paresis: incomplete paralysis

Patella: the knee bone

Periarthritis: inflammation round a joint, due to infection or injury, causing pain and restricted movement

Phalanx: a finger

Phlebo-: prefix meaning pertaining to a vein

Plantarflexion: flexing the foot—i.e., 'pointing the toes'

-plegia: suffix meaning paralysis

Plexus: a network of nerves or veins

Pneumothorax: air in the pleural cavity—e.g., from the puncture of the lung by a fractured rib—and causing collapse of the lung

Poly-: prefix meaning much or many

Prolapse: falling down, or extrusion or protrusion, of a structure

Pronation: twisting the forearm, the elbow being fixed, to bring the palm of the hand facing downwards (opposite to supination)

Proximal: nearest the centre (opposite to distal)

Pulmonary: pertaining to the lung

Quadriceps: the main muscle of the front of the thigh

Recurvatum deformity: bent backwards

Reduction: restoration to a normal position—e.g., of a fractured bone or a dislocated joint

Renal: pertaining to the kidney

Retro-: prefix meaning behind or backward

Rhomberg's Test: a test of balance—the patient stands erect with toes and heels touching and eyes closed; unsteadiness occurs if test positive

Sclerosis: increased density, e.g., of a bone, owing to disease or injury

Scoliosis: lateral (i.e., sideways) curvature of the spine

Sensory: pertaining to sensation (applied particularly to peripheral nerve function)

Sequestrum: a fragment of dead bone

Sinus: a track leading from an infected focus—e.g., in a bone—to an opening on the surface of the skin

Slough: tissue, usually skin, dead from infection

Spondylosis: degenerative changes in the spine

Sternum: the breastbone

Subscapular: beneath the shoulder blade

Subtalar: beneath the talar bone

Supination: twisting the forearm, the elbow being fixed, to bring the palm of hand facing upwards (opposite to pronation)

Supraclavicular: above the clavicle

Suture: stitch

Synovitis: inflammation of the lining membrane of a joint

Tachycardia: increased pulse rate

Talar: bone of the foot

Therapeutic: pertaining to treatment, the application of a remedy

Thorax, thoracic: the chest, pertaining to the chest

Thrombosis: clotting (thrombus) in a blood vessel or in the heart

Tissue: anatomically a complex of similar cells and fibres forming a structure

Tracheotomy: operative opening into the trachea (windpipe) to assist breathing in certain chest injuries

Traction: method by which fractures, particularly of the femur, are treated—the lower limb is suspended by weights and pulleys and a continously pulling force is applied by means of further weights and pulleys attached to a metal pin (Steinmann pin) passed through the upper end of the tibia

Trauma: an injury, e.g., physical, emotional

Ulcer: localised destruction, by injury or disease, of a surface tissue (i.e., skin, mucous membrane)

Umbilicus: the navel

Valgus: outward deviation—e.g., genu valgum knock knee (the tibia deviates outwards from the knee)

Varicosity: dilation and pouching of the veins

Varus: inward deviation—e.g., genu valugum bow leg (the tibia deviates inwards from the knee)

Ventilation: the movement of oxygen in and carbon dioxide out of the lungs, mechanical ventilation is ventilation by means of a machine

Vertebra: one of the backbones

Whiplash injury: strain of cervical structure from the head moving violently in one direction and then bounding back in the reverse direction

Xanth-: prefix meaning yellow

Xiphoid process: the lowermost bony part of the sternum

APPENDIX 3
WIGMORE ANALYSIS CHARTS

For an introduction to Wigmorean analysis, see **11.5.5** to **11.5.9**.

The aim of producing a Wigmore chart is to identify the chain of proof, including inferences which stengthen or weaken the main proposition to be proved. The chart is developed according to the purpose for which it is required and the standpoint of the person producing it. While there is often not time to produce this level of sophisticated analysis, for those who persevere, it is well worth the effort. To produce a Wigmorean analysis chart:

(a) Identify the ultimate probandum—the proposition ultimately required to be proved.

(b) Identify the penultimate probanda—the matters leading directly to what must be proved.

(c) List the facts in a key list which can include the whole case, or only certain elements in a case. Each proposition is then charted with a specific symbol. A square indicates evidence that can be directly perceived, e.g. the detective's statement in the example below. A circle indicates an inference from another source.

(d) Draw the chart from top to bottom and from right to left. One item stands for one proposition and no more.

In the case example in **11.5.8**, the 'ultimate probandum'—the proposition that must be proved—is that Cassie Charnel stole a bottle of whisky from Super Stores plc. **Figure App 3.1** shows how this would look on a Wigmorean analysis. Note that items 1–4 represent the 'penultimate probanda', i.e. matters leading to the main proposition to be proved. Concentrating on the line of proof for the first item—(item 1 on the key list) that she appropriated a bottle of whisky—items 5, 7, 9, and 11 are only inferences from, respectively, 6, 8, 10, and 12. These last are facts to which you have direct access—the detective's statement—on the assumption that you either have the original statement, or a copy of it. The special nature of these facts is shown by the square, rather than the circle.

Figure App 3.1   Wigmorean analysis

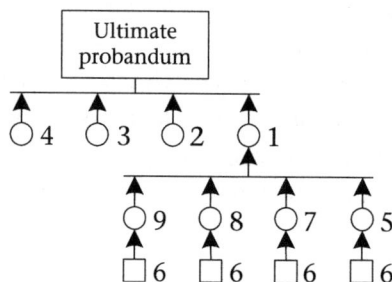

Key list:

1. CC appropriated a bottle of whisky.
2. The whisky belonged to Super Stores.
3. CC appropriated the whisky dishonestly.
4. At the time, she intended to deprive Super Stores of the whisky permanently.
5. CC took the whisky from the display.
6. Store detective's statement to this effect.
7. CC put it in her coat instead of the basket.
8. CC failed to produce or pay for the whisky at checkout.
9. CC left store with whisky.

Strictly speaking, there is another stage of thought which the chart might have shown. The move from the store detective's statement to the inference that what she stated was in fact the case involves a generalisation and could be charted as in **Figure App 3.2**.

Figure App 3.2   Wigmorean analysis

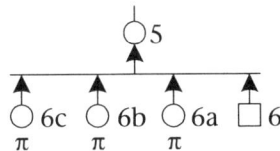

Key list:

5. CC took the whisky from the display.
6. Store detective's statement to this effect.
6a. In the absence of a motive to lie or opportunity for erroneous observation, a person's account of what he has seen is likely to be true.
6b. The store detective had no known motive to lie.
6c. He had no known opportunity for erroneous observation.

The symbol π is used to designate a fact noticed as a matter of general knowledge or inference without evidence being introduced specifically on the point. Here, 6a takes the form of a generalisation about the trustworthiness of a particular type of evidence, whilst 6b and 6c may be inferred from the absence of evidence to the contrary.

The objective of the chart is to clarify, and since clarity is likely to be obscured by density of items it may be thought unnecessary to chart all the generalisations on which inferences depend. But care should be taken because some generalisations which are necessary to support an inference are a good deal more questionable than might at first appear. With or without explicit generalisations, the chart should always show the fact that a witness states something to be the case and the inference that that is indeed the case as two distinct items. One of the dangers of the Wigmorean exercise is that it can lead to the production of a rigid pattern of unnaturally solid 'facts', whereas reality is altogether more fragile and elusive.

Strengthening and weakening inferences

Suppose the evidence of the store detective's observation is not so clear-cut. There are difficulties because he admits in his statement that the store was crowded and so he did not have the defendant in view for the whole time at the spirits display. But an assistant manager who had been alerted was also observing the defendant and he confirms the detective's account that the bottle of whisky was taken. The appropriate section of the chart will look something like **Figure App 3.3**.

Figure App 3.3 Wigmorean analysis

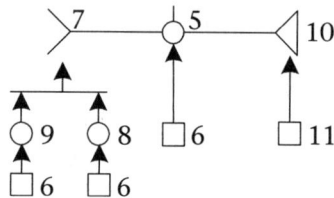

Key list:

5. CC took whisky from display.

6. Detective's statement to this effect.

7. His observation may have been mistaken.

8. Store was crowded.

9. Detective could not have defendant in view all the time at the spirits display.

10. Assistant manager confirms 5.

11. His statement to this effect.

(The numbers of the items shown in **Figures App 3.1** and **3.2** will have to be adjusted.) The symbol ≻— shows something which weakens the effect of another piece of charted information. It appears on the left of the symbol which represents the weakened information. The symbol —◁ shows something which strengthens the effect of another piece of charted information. It appears on the right of the symbol which represents the strengthened information.

The most basic features of Wigmore's system have been shown. It should now be possible to construct a chart and key list, either for a whole case or for part of one.

With the task completed, you will have a better idea of how your information hangs together. The chart cannot, of course, tell you which propositions are likely to be accepted by the court but your own judgment will be greatly assisted in dealing with that problem by the construction of the chart. Wigmore observed that the use of this method came more readily to some than to others. Experience has shown, however, that initial difficulties disappear if the student persists in trying to make the method work. The best way to learn this technique is to use it.

Wigmore's ideas have since been elaborated by Terence Anderson, William Twining, and David Schum in *Analysis of Evidence*, 2nd edn (Cambridge University Press, 2005).

APPENDIX 4
COMPLETED CHART FOR *R V PENNY*
(SEE PP. 339–340)

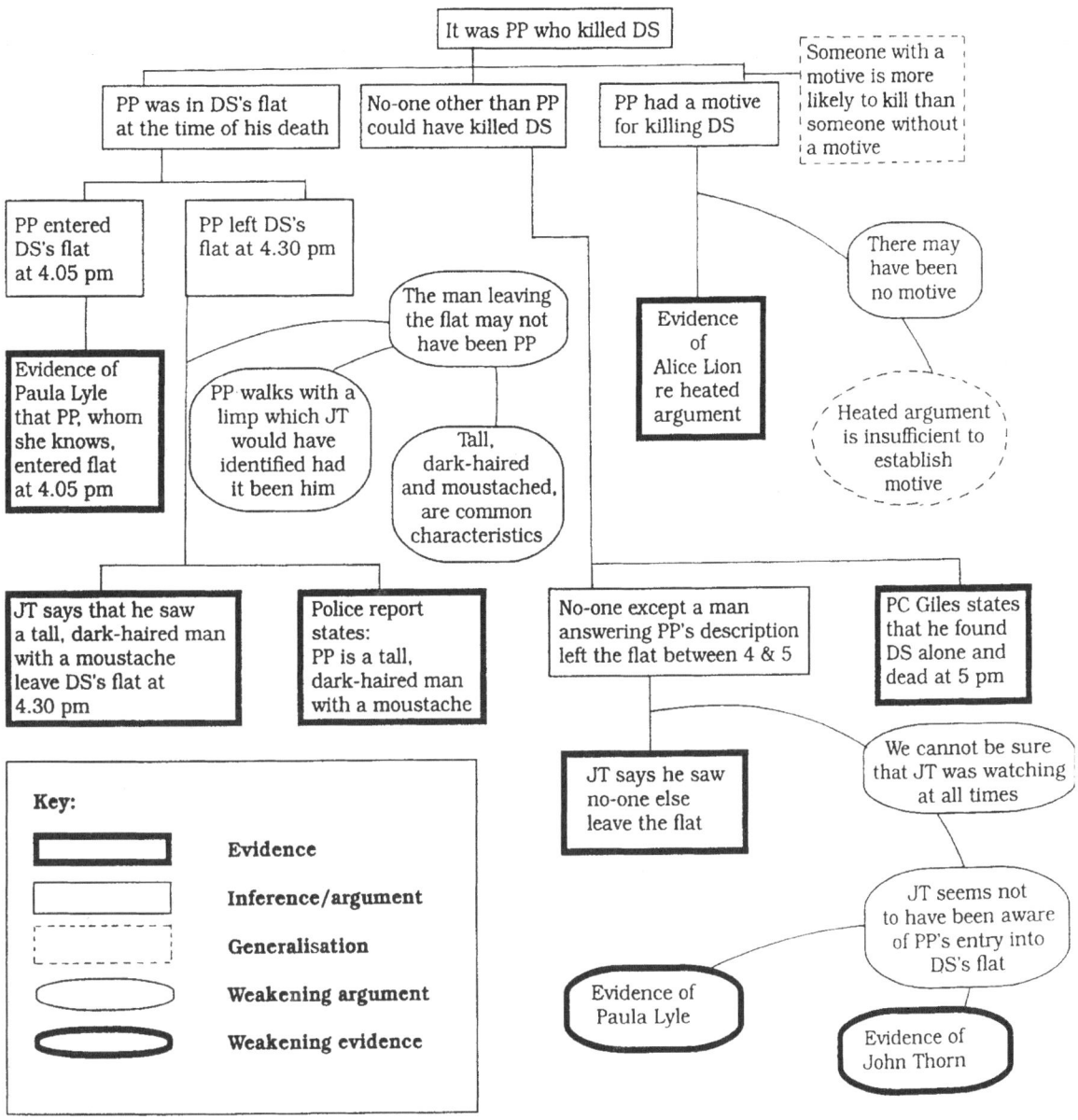

It was PP who killed DS

PP was in DS's flat at the time of his death

No-one other than PP could have killed DS

PP had a motive for killing DS

Someone with a motive is more likely to kill than someone without a motive

PP entered DS's flat at 4.05 pm

PP left DS's flat at 4.30 pm

The man leaving the flat may not have been PP

There may have been no motive

Evidence of Paula Lyle that PP, whom she knows, entered flat at 4.05 pm

PP walks with a limp which JT would have identified had it been him

Tall, dark-haired and moustached, are common characteristics

Evidence of Alice Lion re heated argument

Heated argument is insufficient to establish motive

JT says that he saw a tall, dark-haired man with a moustache leave DS's flat at 4.30 pm

Police report states: PP is a tall, dark-haired man with a moustache

No-one except a man answering PP's description left the flat between 4 & 5

PC Giles states that he found DS alone and dead at 5 pm

JT says he saw no-one else leave the flat

We cannot be sure that JT was watching at all times

JT seems not to have been aware of PP's entry into DS's flat

Evidence of Paula Lyle

Evidence of John Thorn

Key:

▭	**Evidence**
▭	**Inference/argument**
⊏⊐	**Generalisation**
⬭	**Weakening argument**
⬭	**Weakening evidence**

APPENDIX 5
FURTHER READING

Anderson, T., Schum, D., and Twining, W., *Analysis of Evidence*, 2nd edn, Cambridge, 2005.

Binder, D. A. and Bergman, P., *Fact Investigation: From Hypothesis to Proof*, West Publishing Co., 1984.

Bono, E. De, *Lateral Thinking*, Penguin, 1990.

Bono, E. De, *New Thinking for the Millennium*, Penguin, 2000.

Bono, E. De, *Six Thinking Hats*, Penguin, 2000.

Bono, E. De, *Teach Yourself to Think*, Penguin, 1996.

Buzan, T., *Use Your Head*, BBC Books, 1995.

Constanzo, M., *Problem Solving*, Cavendish Publishing, 1995.

Gold, N., Mackie, K., and Twining, W., *Learning Lawyers' Skills*, Butterworths, 1989.

Moore, A. J., Bergman, D., and Binder, D. A., *Trial Advocacy: Inferences, Arguments and Techniques*, American Case Book Series, West Publishing Co., 1996.

Nathanson, S., *What Lawyers Do: A Problem-Solving Approach to Legal Practice*, Sweet & Maxwell, 1997.

Purver, J. M., et al., *The Trial Lawyer's Book: Preparing and Winning Cases*, Lawyer's Cooperative Publishing, New York, 1990.

Sonsteng, J., Haydock, R., and Boyd, J., *The Trial Book: A Total System for the Preparation & Presentation of a Case*, West Publishing Co., 1984.

Twining, W., *Theories of Evidence: Bentham and Wigmore*, Butterworths, 1985.

Twining, W. and Miers, D., *How to Do Things with Rules*, 4th edn, Cambridge, 1999.

Wigmore, J. H., 'The problem of proof', *University of Illinois Law Review*, 1913, vol. 8, p. 7.

Wigmore, J. H., *The Science of Judicial Proof*, 3rd edn, Little, Brown & Co., 1937.

INDEX